RESEARCH in ORGANIZATIONS

A Publication in the Berrett-Koehler Organizational Performance Series
Richard A. Swanson & Barbara L. Swanson, *Series Editors*

Sponsored by the Academy of Human Resource Development

RESEARCH in ORGANIZATIONS
Foundations and Methods of Inquiry

Richard A. Swanson
Elwood F. Holton III
Editors

BK

BERRETT-KOEHLER PUBLISHERS, INC.
San Francisco

Berrett-Koehler Publishers, Inc.
235 Montgomery Street, Suite 650
San Francisco, CA 94104-2916
Tel: (415) 288-0260   Fax: (415) 362-2512   www.bkconnection.com

Ordering Information

Quantity sales. Special discounts are available on quantity purchases by corporations, associations, and others. For details, contact the "Special Sales Department" at the Berrett-Koehler address above.

Individual sales. Berrett-Koehler publications are available through most bookstores. They can also be ordered directly from Berrett-Koehler: Tel: (800) 929-2929; Fax: (802) 864-7626; www.bkconnection.com

Orders for college textbook/course adoption use. Please contact Berrett-Koehler: Tel: (800) 929-2929; Fax: (802) 864-7626.

Orders by U.S. trade bookstores and wholesalers. Please contact Publishers Group West, 1700 Fourth Street, Berkeley, CA 94710. Tel: (510) 528-1444; Fax (510) 528-3444.

Production Management: Michael Bass Associates

Berrett-Koehler and the BK logo are registered trademarks of Berrett-Koehler Publishers, Inc.

Printed in the United States of America

Berrett-Koehler books are printed on long-lasting acid-free paper. When it is available, we choose paper that has been manufactured by environmentally responsible processes. These may include using trees grown in sustainable forests, incorporating recycled paper, minimizing chlorine in bleaching, or recycling the energy produced at the paper mill.

Library of Congress Cataloging-in-Publication Data

Research in organizations: foundations and methods of inquiry / by Richard A. Swanson and
    Elwood F. Holton III, editors.
        p.   cm.
    Includes bibliographical references and index.
    ISBN: 978-1-57675-314-9
    1. Organization—Research—Methodology. 2. Organizational sociology. I. Swanson,
Richard A., 1942– II. Holton, Ed, 1957–
HD30.4.R468.2005
302.3′5′072—dc22

                                                                        2004066341

First Edition
10 09 08 07 06 05   10 9 8 7 6 5 4 3 2 1

Contents

List of Figures

List of Tables

Foreword

Advancing Research in Organizations through Learning Communities

Andrew H. Van de Ven, *University of Minnesota*

The primary purpose of this book is to advance research in organizations. As discussed throughout its chapters, research in organizations presents a milieu of challenges and opportunities that are unique. The challenge that this book confronts is to introduce organizational scholars to the vast landscape of methods of inquiry and research that can be utilized to advance research in organizations. Two overarching themes of this book are (1) that conducting research in organizational contexts demands that traditional research methods be adapted and adjusted to fit organizational realities, and (2) that researchers' toolkits must include the entire array of quantitative and qualitative methods. In doing so, I suggest that it lays the foundation for inquiry that can build what I (Van de Ven, 2002) and Herbert Simon (1976) have advocated as learning communities to significantly advance organizational research and practice.

THE UNIQUE CHALLENGE OF ORGANIZATIONAL RESEARCH

Scholarship is the creation and dissemination of knowledge about research, teaching, and practice. In his 1996 Academy of Management Presidential Address, Rick Mowday (1997) called for us to reaffirm our scholarly values by adopting Ernest Boyer's (1997) engaged view of "scholarship" as the scholarship of discovery, teaching, practice, and integration. Just as the development and testing of new research knowledge are central to informing our teaching and practice, so also the discovery of new questions and ideas from teaching and practice should nourish and guide our research.

It is vain to think that researchers have a monopoly on knowledge creation. Practitioners and consultants discover anomalies and insights from their practices, as teachers do with their students and scientists do with their research. The knowledge that researchers, teachers, consultants, and practitioners learn by themselves is different and partial. If it could be coproduced and combined in some novel ways, the results could produce a dazzling synthesis that might profoundly advance theory, teaching, and practice.

Rynes, Bartunek, and Dalt (2001), along with many others, claim that academic research has become less useful for solving the practical problems in organizations. The gulf between science and practice in organizations is widening. There is growing criticism that findings from academic and consulting studies are not useful for practitioners and do not get implemented (Beer, 2001). There is also growing debate between advocates of normal science and action science methods (Beer & Nohria, 2000). In short, academic researchers are being criticized for not adequately putting their organizational knowledge into practice. But this criticism goes both ways. Managers and consultants are not doing enough to put their practice into theory. As a result, organizations are not learning fast enough to keep up with the changing times.

I do not believe this gulf is due to a lack of interest or commitment. On the contrary, in our interactions with students and managers, we struggle each day with the challenges of developing and applying management principles in practice. This is no longer a luxury of time—it is a necessity. In this knowledge-intensive economy, it is incumbent on managers, consultants, and academics to develop valid knowledge.

BUILDING LEARNING COMMUNITIES FOR RESEARCH AND PRACTICE

The gap between research and practice of organizational knowledge is a complex and controversial subject. As he did on so many topics, Herbert Simon (1976) provided a useful way to frame this problem. He proposed that a basic challenge for scholars in professional schools is to contribute to both organizational science and practice—not either/or. The information and skills relevant to accomplishing this came from the social system of practitioners and the social system of scientists in the relevant disciplines. These social systems have elaborate institutions and procedures for storing, transmitting, developing, and applying knowledge. Each represents a different community of practice, and the main way to understand each community is to participate in it.

Simon (1976) points out that a social system, if left to itself, gravitates toward an equilibrium position of maximum entropy. One segment gets absorbed in the applied culture of managers and organizations. It is dependent on the world of practice as its sole source of knowledge inputs. Instead of creating new knowledge that can advance the profession, this segment becomes a slightly out-of-date purveyor of almost current organizational practices.

The other segment, often trained intensively in a basic discipline, gets absorbed in the culture of that discipline and is largely dependent on it for goals, values, and approval. For the most part sealed off from the practitioner's community, these disciplinary scientists begin to view organizational practice as an irrelevant source for generating, developing, or applying new knowledge. If left unchecked, this evolutionary drift breeds intolerance and polarized conflicts.

Simon cautions that building a culture that respects and tolerates diversity among researchers and practitioners is very much like mixing oil with water. It is easy to describe the intended product but less easy to produce it. And the task is not finished when the goal has been achieved. Left to themselves, the oil and water will separate again. This natural separation occurs not only between practitioner-oriented and discipline-oriented members but also between scholars from different disciplines.

I may be dreaming, but wouldn't it be nice if professional learning communities could be created that nurtured the coproduction of organizational knowledge? These learning communities could be gathering places and forums where academics, consultants, and practitioners would view each other as equals and complements. Through frequent interactions, these individuals could come to know and respect each other and could share their common interests and different perspectives about problems and topics. They could push one another to appreciate issues in ways that are richer and more penetrating than we understood before.

As you know, all kinds of basic and applied scholarship go on, and you might think that I am advocating that more applied and less basic research should be conducted. That is clearly not my intention. On the contrary, following Simon, I am arguing that the quality and impact of fundamental research can improve substantially when scholars do three things: (1) confront questions and anomalies arising in organizational practice, (2) conduct research that is designed in appropriate and rigorous ways to examine these questions, and (3) analyze and translate research findings not only to contribute knowledge to a scientific discipline but also to advance organizational practices (Van de Ven, 2005).

Simon points out that significant invention stems from two different kinds of knowledge: (1) applied knowledge about practical issues or needs of a profession and (2) scientific knowledge about new ideas and processes that are potentially possible. Invention is easiest and likely to be incremental, when it operates in one extreme of the continuum. For example, applied researchers tend to immerse themselves in information about problems of the end users, and they then apply known knowledge and technology to provide solutions to their clients. Such transfer and application of knowledge to solve practical business problems often does not result in creating new knowledge that advances the discipline and the profession.

At the other end of the range, pure scientists immerse themselves in their disciplines to discover what questions have not been answered, and they then apply research techniques to answer these questions. If scientists cannot answer their initial questions, they modify and simplify them until they can be answered. If this process repeats itself, as is customary, the research questions and answers become increasingly trivial contributions to science and even more irrelevant to practice.

But if scholars are equally exposed to the social systems of practice and science, they are likely to be confronted with the real-life questions at the forefront of knowledge creation—a setting that increases the chance of significant invention and research. As Louis Pasteur stated, "Chance favors the prepared mind." Research in this context is also more demanding because scholars do not have the option of substituting more simple questions if they cannot solve the real-life problems. But if research becomes more challenging when it is undertaken to answer questions posed from outside science, it also acquires the potential to become more significant and fruitful.

The history of science and technology demonstrates that many of the extraordinary developments in the pure sciences have been initiated by problems or questions posed from outside. Necessity is indeed the mother of important inventions. Thus, a professional learning community, as proposed here, can be an exceedingly productive and challenging environment for making significant advances to organizational disciplines and practices.

REFERENCES

Beer, M. (2001). Why management research findings are unimplementable: An action science perspective. *Reflections*, *2*(3), 58–65.

Beer, M., & Nohria, N. (Eds.). (2000). *Breaking the code of change*. Boston: Harvard Business School Press.

Mowday, R. T. (1997). 1996 presidential address: Reaffirming our scholarly values. *Academy of Management Review*, *22*, 335–345.

Rynes, S. L., Bartunek, J. M., & Daft, R. L. (2001). Across the great divide: Knowledge creation and transfer among practitioners and academics. *Academy of Management Journal*, *44*, 340–355.

Simon, H. A. (1976). *Administrative behavior* (3rd ed.). New York: Free Press.

Van de Ven, A. H. (2002). 2001 presidential address: Strategic directions for the Academy of Management—This academy is for you! *Academy of Management Review*, *27*, 171–184.

Van de Ven, A. H. (2005). *Engaged scholarship: Creating knowledge for science and practice.* Unpublished manuscript, University of Minnesota, Minneapolis.

Preface

Researchers from many disciplines are interested in conducting research in organizations. The context of organizations dominates most societies and serves to mediate the majority of human activity. The complexity of organizations and the people who create them and function in them are fodder for important questions posed by researchers and practitioners.

PURPOSE OF THIS BOOK

The purpose of this book is to help beginning and expanding scholars learn about research in organizations. It is a textbook to learn about the foundations and methods of inquiry from multiple perspectives. There is no one-approach-fits-all when it comes to research in organizations. This book embraces multiple approaches to research and includes perspectives from distinguished scholars who are grounded in a wide variety of disciplines—human resource development, management, anthropology, psychology, organizational behavior, education, leadership, history, and more.

   The origin of this book is rooted in an earlier complementary book that we edited, *Human Resource Development Research Handbook: Linking Research and Practice*. The purpose of that book was to speak to both practitioners and scholars about research, whereas this book strives to speak to scholars across multiple disciplines.

   We asked the authors to do two things in their chapters. First, we asked them to provide a conceptual overview and introduction to each research method appropriate for beginning researchers. The chapters are not designed to be a complete guide to all the technical issues involved in using each method. Thus, the second thing we asked each author to do was to provide references to the key sources to which researchers should turn if they plan to use a particular methodology. As a result, this book provides a broad introduction to the full array of research methods an organizational researcher needs and connections to critical resources for the method(s) he or she plans to utilize.

OVERVIEW OF THE CONTENTS

Research in Organizations: Foundations and Methods of Inquiry is organized into four major parts. The two chapters in Part I, Research in Organizations, set the stage for organizational research and the important process of the framing research. The ten chapters in Part II, Quantitative Research Methods, provide an orientation to quantitative research and specific methods. The five chapters in Part III, Qualitative Research Methods, discuss qualitative research and specific methods. The four chapters in Part IV, Mixed Methods Research, describe mixed methods research and specific methods. The concluding two chapters in Part V, Research Resources, highlight the use of contemporary information sources and the management of research projects.

ACKNOWLEDGMENTS

The uniqueness of this book could not have been achieved without the generous contributions of the chapter authors. We take our hats off to each—thank you. We also want to acknowledge the sponsorship of this book by the Academy of Human Resource Development. This book advances the Academy's vision of leading the profession through research.

There is an emotional journey in creating a book—from the original concept to holding the finished product. The reality is that book authors are generally the only ones to experience the full process, the highs and the lows. If you are fortunate (and we have been), you have a publisher that is with you all the way. Once again, we gratefully acknowledge Berrett-Koehler Publishers for contributing to efforts in advancing inquiry and understanding.

Richard A. Swanson
St. Paul, Minnesota, USA

Elwood F. Holton III
Baton Rouge, Louisiana, USA

P A R T   O N E

Research in Organizations

CHAPTERS

1. **The Challenge of Research in Organizations**

   RICHARD A. SWANSON, *University of Minnesota*

2. **The Process of Framing Research in Organizations**

   RICHARD A. SWANSON, *Univeristy of Minnesota*

The Challenge of Research in Organizations

Richard A. Swanson, *University of Minnesota*

The title of this book, *Research in Organizations*, was purposeful. It is not simply about research *on* organizations. The context of the organization is fundamentally interesting to most people. Without any obvious initiation, organizational questions arise about leaders, purposes, strategies, processes, effectiveness, trends, workers, customers, and more.

Organizations are human-made entities. There are for-profit and nonprofit organizations, global and small locally held organizations, organizations having multiple purposes, and organizations producing a mind-boggling range of goods or services. As human-made entities, organizations engage all kinds of human beings. No wonder organizations and the functioning of human beings in relation to organizations are of such great interest to so many fields of applied endeavor.

Applied disciplines, by their very nature, require that theory and practice come together (Dubin, 1978; Lynham, 2002; Van de Ven, 2002). When they do not come together, there is angst. This angst of not knowing is a signal to both practitioners and scholars that there is work to be done. Clearly, scholars from disciplines such as human resources, business, organizational behavior, education, sociology, and economics see organizations as meaningful contexts for their inquiry.

DEFINITION OF RESEARCH

Research is often thought of in terms of a job or a task. Actually, research is a process having a specific type of outcome. *Research is an orderly investigative process for the purpose of creating new knowledge.* Furthermore, the simple dictionary definition portrays research as "1. Scholarly or scientific investigation or inquiry; 2. Close and careful study" (*American Heritage College Dictionary*, 2002, p. 1182).

Each of you reading this chapter has most likely done research and may even do research on a regular basis in certain arenas of your work and personal lives. You may not call it research. Even so, the psychological barriers to officially doing research remain and are typified by (1) the pressures of time limitations and/or (2) the concern over being criticized as to the significance, method, or conclusions. They are part of the human side of the research process.

In balancing the two barriers, researchers talk about the importance of humility and skepticism as attributes of a scholar. Certainly the press of time and the potential of criticism help keep the researcher humble. Internal skepticism keeps the researcher motivated. Researchers are skeptics extraordinaire. When somebody says, "I know everything will turn out well," the researcher will retort, "Not necessarily." When somebody says, "I know everything will go badly," the researcher will similarly retort, "Not necessarily." Unverified generalizations do not satisfy the researcher. They are the beginnings of research, not the conclusions.

THE RESEARCH PROCESS

While the general research process typically starts with a problem and ends with a conclusion, research is not just a problem-solving method. Problem solving is situational and is judged by the results, with or without a theoretical explanation. If through trial and error you learn to kick the lawn mower engine that will not start, and then it starts, the problem of getting the mower engine running is solved without any theoretical understanding. Yet, there is a point when problem solving and the generation of new knowledge touch or overlap. Very thorough and systematic problem solving that purposefully retains and reports data can move into the realm of research. Many people involved with research in organizations talk about *action research*. For example, action research is not considered research by some scholars. They would classify action research as a formalized method of problem solving relevant to a particular organization or setting.

As scholars in applied disciplines, the theory–practice dilemma is of particular importance. Most scholars in applied disciplines recognize *practice-to-theory* to be as true as *theory-to-practice*. Scholars are respectful of the fact that theory often has to catch up to sound practice in that practitioners can be ahead of researchers. Thoughtful practitioners often do things that work, and scholars learn how to explain the successes at a later time. For applied research in functioning organizations, the concept of the practitioner being a research partner is legitimate and crucial to the maturity of related applied disciplines.

From my experience in the profession, it is clear that thoughtful and expert practitioners do indeed apply research findings in their day-to-day work decisions. Whether they are *advancing* theory and practice is another matter. It is critical to the profession that numerous thoughtful practitioners recognize that they are in a perfect position to help advance the scholarship related to organizations (Swanson & Holton, 1997).

RATIONALE FOR CONDUCTING RESEARCH IN ORGANIZATIONS

Organizations are messy entities. Just studying people within organizations is challenging. Studying the information flow in organizations is challenging as well as studying power in organizations. Studying the external economic forces and their impact on an organization adds another challenge. The list goes on.

Although scholars from many applied disciplines are drawn to the organization as the ultimate context of their scholarly focus, it is not always easy to conduct research in organizations. Organizations are worth studying, yet it is important to recognize that they are

- complex systems
- open systems
- dynamic systems

These system realities are the source of many scholarly and practitioner questions and the need for research-based answers. Such inquiry is for the sake of understanding of the organization itself, a phenomenon operating within a host organization, or the behavior of the phenomenon in the context of the organizational and its external environment.

While scholars from many applied disciplines are drawn to the organization as the ultimate context of their scholarly focus, it is not always easy to conduct research in organizations. It is the very attractiveness and complexity of organizations that stimulate this book focused on the principles and methods of inquiry for conducting research in organizations.

GENERAL STRATEGIES FOR CONDUCTING RESEARCH IN ORGANIZATIONS

Specific disciplines and individual scholars tend to rely on favored research methods. This condition will not likely change, and if there is change, it will likely be evolutionary. An important message of this book is that there are alternative inquiry methods that allow scholars to investigate a wider range of phenomena and to ask a wider range of important questions that exceeds any single research method.

This book is not intended to fuel epistemological discord among philosophers of research. Our position is that to bombard beginning scholars with this issue is counterproductive to the advancement of sound research in most applied disciplines. Most professions are complex enough that they deserve scholarship from all corners. Our role is to be rational and inclusive. Our simple overarching paradigm for research in organizations is to classify research into

- quantitative methods of research
- qualitative methods of research
- mixed methods of research

Quantitative research relies on methods based on "cause and effect thinking, reduction to specific variables and hypotheses and questions, use of measurement and observation, and the test of theories" (Creswell, 2003, p. 18). Qualitative research relies on methods based on "multiple meanings of individual experiences, meanings socially and historically constructed, and with the intent of developing a theory or pattern" (Creswell, 2003, p. 18). Mixed methods research relies on both quantitative and qualitative methods that are "consequence-oriented, problem-centered, and pluralistic" (Creswell, 2003, p. 18).

Readers wanting greater familiarity with these three approaches to research at this time may want to jump ahead and read the introductory chapters in each of these sections of the book (i.e., chapters 3, 13, and 18).

THE THEORY-RESEARCH-DEVELOPMENT-PRACTICE CYCLE

Theory, research, development, and practice together compose a vital cycle that allows ideas to be progressively refined as they evolve from concepts to practices and from practices to concepts. The theory-research-development-practice cycle illustrates the systematic application of inquiry methods working to advance the knowledge used by both organizational researchers and practitioners (see Swanson, 1997).

Although we find no historical evidence in the philosophy of science that an a priori linkage among theory, research, development, and practice was ever established, a relationship among these elements has emerged within and across professional disciplines. The call to inform practice with theory, research, and development has come relatively recently in such fields as human resource development and management (Passmore, 1990; Torraco, 1994; Swanson, 1997; Van de Ven, 2002; Wilson, 1998). Other fields of study, such as medicine, have had a longer tradition of pursuing research, development, practice, and theory in ways that are mutually beneficial to each element.

However, there are those who caution us in constructing the relationships among research, development, practice, and theory. In offering the notion of a scientific *paradigm*, Kuhn (1970) compelled philosophers and researchers to rethink the assumptions underlying the scientific method and paved the way for alternative, postpositivistic approaches to research in the behavioral sciences. Ethnography and naturalistic inquiry allow theory to *emerge from data derived from practice and experience*; theory does not necessarily precede research, as theory can be generated through it. The model of theory, research, development, and practice for applied disciplines embraces these cautions (see Figure 1.1).

The cyclical model brings theory, research, development, and practice together in the same forum for research in organizations. The union of these domains is itself an important purpose of the model. Two other purposes also exist. First, each of the four domains makes a necessary contribution to effective practices in organizations. There is no presumption about the importance to the profession of contributions from practice versus theory. The model demonstrates the need for *all* domains to inform each other in order to enrich the profession as a whole. Second, exchange among the domains is multidirectional. Any of the domains can serve as an appropriate starting point for proceeding through the cycle. Improvements in the profession can occur whether one begins with theory, research, development, or practice. The multidirectional flow of the model is examined next.

The process of working through the theory-research-development-practice cycle demonstrates how any of the four domains can be used as a starting point for knowledge generation. As one starting point of the cycle, *research* is under-

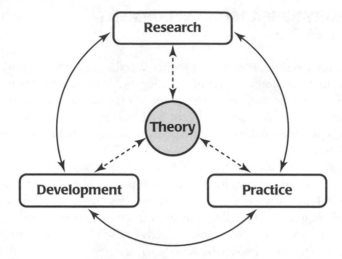

Figure 1.1   Theory-Research-Development-Practice Cycle
Source: R. A. Swanson (1997), "HRD Research: Don't Go to Work without It," in R. A. Swanson & E. F. Holton III
(Eds.), *Human Resource Development Research Handbook* (San Francisco: Berrett-Koehler), pp. 3–20.

taken to expand our professional knowledge base and frequently yields recommendations for the development of new systems or the improvement of practice.
This link from research to *practice* is illustrated by influential research that has
yielded innovative models of job design, work motivation, performance analysis,
organizational change, and other products of research that have led directly to
improvements in the profession.

Research can also proceed along the cycle to produce *theory*. Theory building
is an important function of research that will be addressed in later chapters. Although applied disciplines focused on organizations have benefited from a rich
foundation of theories, many have originated in related fields of study. Additional
theories are needed for greater understanding of a wide range of human and organizational phenomena. Thus, research serves a dual role in advancing organizational knowledge. Research provides knowledge that can be directly applied to
the improvement of practice, and it is used to develop core theories.

Organizational *development* efforts offer a unique opportunity to enter the
cycle. The demands of practice and the need for fundamental change establish
the conditions for the creation of fundamentally new organizational models and
methods. An organization intervention is viewed as a subsystem within a larger
system. The subsystem and system influence one another to the point that innovative and practical new developments often become bold starting points of activity and inquiry.

Illustrations of development efforts that have stimulated advances in the
profession (theory, research, and practice) have come from large-scale change ef-

forts, military training challenges, global economy issues facing multinational corporations, and the introduction of new information technologies. In this realm of research, a rigorous development process that embraces the organization's quality requirements is as important, or more important, than the evaluation of the effectiveness of the end product. For example, Sayre's (1990) research on the development and evaluation of a computer-based system for managing the design and pilot testing of interactive videos necessarily invested much more effort in development than in summative evaluation.

When starting with practice, there is no shortage of problems and challenges facing functioning organizations. These challenges provide an inexhaustible source of researchable problems. Proceeding from practice to research or practice to development along the cycle traces the familiar path between the problems that continuously arise in organizations and the research and development efforts they stimulate. For example, research is often stimulated by the need for organizations to improve core processes and their effectiveness. New methods, new process techniques, and alternative providers of services are just some of the recurring practice options. Other problems occur when new technical systems are acquired before personnel have the expertise to use them. Research continues to identify effective ways of developing the expertise to take advantage of emerging technologies. Scores of other practical research projects are undertaken to address pressing problems of practice.

Each of the domains of the theory-research-development-practice cycle serves to advance research in organizations. Each can be a catalyst to inquiry and a source of verification.

The cycle frequently starts with theory when it is used to guide and inform the processes of research, development, or practice. The variables and relationships to be considered are identified by reviewing the literature, which includes relevant theory. For example, if we wish to examine the influence of recent changes in work design on work motivation, we might start with existing theories of work motivation and identify variables from these theories that are relevant to our question. In the realm of work analysis, Torraco (1994) challenged this large area of professional activity as being highly researched but essentially atheoretical given the contemporary conditions under which organizations may function.

In summary, the process of knowledge generation can begin at any point along the theory-research-development-practice cycle, and flow along the cycle is multidirectional. The researcher or practitioner can start at any point and proceed in any direction. Thus, each of the cycle's domains both *informs* and *is informed by* each of the other domains.

This continuum provides a context for theory that helps explain why theory has so many important roles. Whether one is an organizational researcher or practitioner, theory serves several roles that can greatly enhance the effectiveness of our work.

CONCLUSION

As human-made entities, organizations engage all kinds of phenomena. No wonder organizations and the functioning of human beings in relation to organizations are of such great interest to so many fields of applied endeavor. All forms of research and all forms of researchers are needed to take on the challenge. The purpose of this book is to provide the basic principles and methods needed to take up this challenge.

REFERENCES

The American Heritage college dictionary. (2002). 4th ed. Boston: Houghton Mifflin.

Creswell, J. W. (2003). *Research design: Qualitative, quantitative, and mixed-methods approaches* (2nd ed.). Thousand Oaks, CA: Sage.

Dubin, R. (1978). *Theory building* (rev. ed.). New York: Free Press.

Kuhn, T. S. (1970). *The structure of the scientific revolutions.* Chicago: University of Chicago Press.

Lynham, S. A. (Ed.). (2002). Theory building in applied disciplines. *Advances in Developing Human Resources, 4*(3).

Passmore, D. L. (1990). Pick a paradigm, any paradigm. *Human Resource Development Quarterly, 1*(1), 25–34.

Sayre, S. (1990). *The development and evaluation of a computer-based system for managing the design and pilot testing of interactive videodisks program.* Unpublished doctoral dissertation, University of Minnesota, St. Paul.

Swanson, R. A. (1997). HRD research: Don't go to work without it. In R. A. Swanson & E. F. Holton III (Eds.), *Human resource development research handbook* (pp. 3–20). San Francisco: Berrett-Koehler.

Swanson, R. A., & Holton, E. F., III. (Eds.). (1997). *Human resource development research handbook.* San Francisco: Berrett-Koehler.

Torraco, R. J. (1994). *The development and validation of a theory of work analysis.* St. Paul: Human Resource Development Research Center, University of Minnesota.

Van de Ven, A. (2002). *Professional science.* Thousand Oaks, CA: Sage.

Wilson, E. O. (1998). *Consilience: The unity of knowledge.* New York: Knopf.

Wilson, W. O. (1998). Back from chaos. *Atlantic Monthly, 281*(3), 41.

The Process of Framing Research in Organizations

Richard A. Swanson, *University of Minnesota*

This chapter focuses on the task of identifying important research problems and connecting them to appropriate research questions, paradigms, and methods. This is viewed as the process of framing research in organizations (see Figure 2.1). To accomplish this, the chapter aims to move from valuing the idea that research and the generation of new knowledge is important (chapter 1) to learning about specific research approaches and methodologies (remainder of the book). Although this transition sounds easy enough, it is indeed a thorny patch. Three hurdles are standing in the way:

- Identifying important problems from the milieu of existing knowledge
- Understanding the philosophy of research
- Choosing the most appropriate research question and method

The process of framing research in organizations begins with an initial problem area and ends up with specific research-planning decisions. The three hurdles in this process serve as organizers for the remainder of the chapter.

IDENTIFYING IMPORTANT PROBLEMS

Almost everyone reading this book on research in organizations has an applied orientation. Applied disciplines, and the organizational contexts that they purport to focus on, are almost always messy—messy in the sense that research-based theories and practices must ultimately be verified in practice. A problem can be thought of as "a situation, matter, or person that presents perplexity or difficulty" (*American Heritage Dictionary*, 2002, p. 1110). Problems generally lead researchers to questions that search for solutions, meaning, or for both meaning *and* solutions.

In chapter 1, the case was made for the synergy among research, development, practice, and theory. Scholars focused on research in organizations are clear about the prerequisite need to have studied or experienced organizations in order to be able to identify important problems. Research provides two kinds of knowledge: *outcome knowledge*, usually in the form of explanatory and predictive knowledge, and *process knowledge*, in the form of understanding how something works and what it means (Dubin, 1978; Lynham, 2002). To these ends, Van de Ven (2002) carefully instructs those conducting research in organizations to "ground the research problem and question in reality." He goes on to prod the researcher to observe the problem or issue by talking to people who know the problem, giving examples from experience, presenting evidence for the problem's existence, and reviewing the literature on the problem (p. 20). This advice is consistent with my methodology (Swanson, 1996) for analyzing knowledge tasks in organizations, which involves conducting direct observation and interviews, reviewing the relevant literature on the phenomenon, as well as providing eight knowledge synthesis methods for gaining understanding.

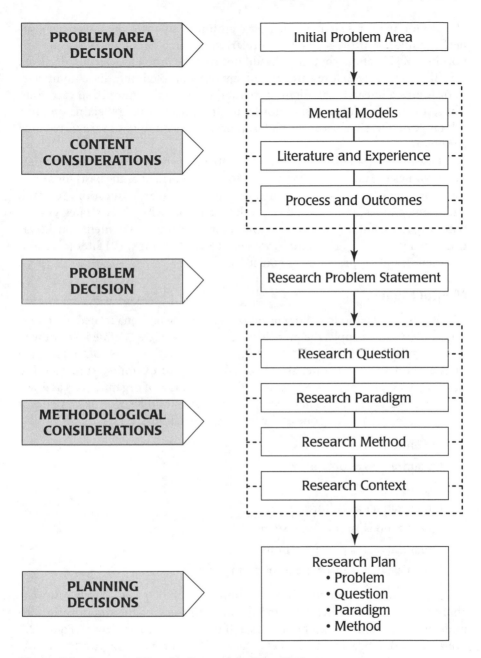

Figure 2.1   Process of Framing Research in Organizations

Far too many research problems are grounded solely in the researcher's superficial interest or the researcher's preferred research paradigm. These are important considerations, but they should not rule the problem selection decision. It is highly unlikely that researchers will choose a problem they have no interest in or follow a research paradigm or method they feel ill equipped to carry out. Thus, it is not fruitful to spend inordinate amounts of time reflecting on one's full range of interest areas or the philosophical underpinnings of various research paradigms.

Researchers searching for a research problem are better advised to gain additional knowledge and experience related to a problem area as the basis for selecting a problem to study. Once done, the specific research question, research paradigm, and research method will follow. The following three strategies contributing to identifying research problems are portrayed as content considerations in Figure 2.1: (1) mental models of organizations, (2) literature and experience, and (3) processes and outcomes.

Mental Models

We all have mental models of organizations and of phenomena related to organizations. For some people, the models are conscious and well defined. For others, they are subconscious and ill defined. Along the consciousness continuum, the mental models can be either simple or complex. For example, Rummler and Brache (1998) present a *complex and well-defined* model of organizations as a system (Figure 2.2), and Morgan (1996) presents a *simple and well-defined* model of organizations as matching one of the following metaphors:

Organizations as machines

Organizations as organisms

Organizations as brains

Organizations as cultures

Organizations as political systems

Organizations as psychic prisons

Organizations as instruments of domination

Making our own model of organizations explicit helps us identify researchable problems. It also helps us understand our view of the organization, to understand the limitations of our view, and to expand on our view(s). Figure 2.3 presents a worldview mental model focused on performance improvement that organizational researchers could find useful in thinking about research problems.

This presentation is an open systems model that situates the organization as the focal point. The overall features of the organization (mission and strategy, organization structure, technology, and human resources) are presented. The systemic

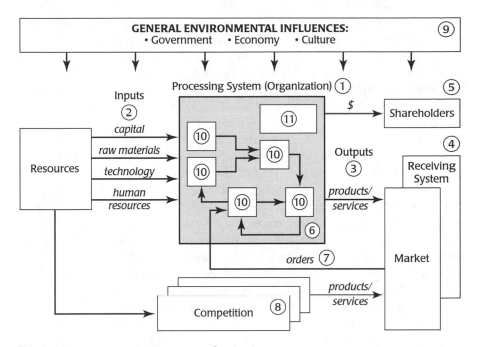

Figure 2.2 An Organization as an Adaptive System

Source: G. A. Rummler & A. P. Brache (1995), *Improving Performance: How to Manage the White Space on the Organizational Chart* (San Francisco: Jossey-Bass), p. 10. Reprinted with permission.

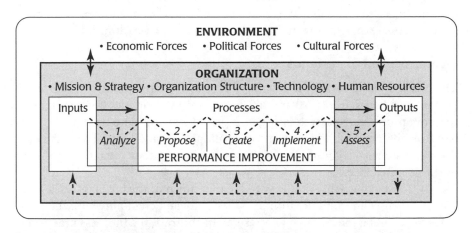

Figure 2.3 Systems Model of Performance Improvement in Organizations

Source: R. A. Swanson (1996), *Analysis for Improving Performance: Tools for Diagnosing Organizations and Documenting Workplace Expertise* (San Francisco: Berrett-Koehler), p. 20.

perspective of the organization itself (inputs, processes, outputs, and their connections) are also portrayed. In addition, the external environment in which the
organization functions is specified (economic, political, and cultural forces). Also
portrayed in Figure 2.3 is one selected organizational subsystem (subprocess):
performance improvement and its interactions. Numerous other parallel
processes are working to achieve the goals of the organization that can be in-
serted in the model.

This model, and similar mental models of organizations, can help researchers think about and locate research problems. One way a model like this
helps is in its ability to reveal the complexities surrounding the problem. Having an
organizational worldview mental model can also help in refining or redefining problems from the milieu of existing knowledge. In addition, an organizational mental
model can help to identify important and relevant problems more accurately.
One vivid example has been the long-suffering topic of improving learning
transfer in organizations. So much of this research has been tightly focused
through a mental model of the learner and the content to be learned. The larger
transfer problem was actually investigated years ago by organizational practitioners
who demonstrated the need to first focus on the system and its required outcomes
(Dooley, 1944). Yet, the psychology–learning worldview has focused on the internal processes of the learner. Recent work by Holton and Baldwin (2003) attempts
to modify that narrow transfer mental model by taking an organization view.

The criticism of having defined mental models is that they can become so
technical and rigid that they can blind the researcher to important problems. The
original premise was that we have these models at either the conscious or unconscious levels. Thus, I argue that mental models should be conscious, with the caution that having mental models that are either too simplistic or too complex can
be limiting. I also contend that having a mental model of phenomena with no related personal experience with that phenomena can be very limiting.

Literature and Experience

The case was made earlier for the importance of collecting information from literature and experience (firsthand or observation) to help identifying important
research problems. Research in organizations by people who have no firsthand
work or observational experience comes off lacking credibility. The naive questions and simplistic "connection of the organizational dots" often reveals the lack
of direct experience.

In terms of literature, it is easy to see that much of the business research literature opens with examples from experience to gain credibility with the reader
before presenting the research and results. In contrast, the business practitioner
literature often claims results, with or without actual evidence beyond self-report
perceptions and a text of homilies.

Those wanting to conduct research in organizations should rigorously follow
both the literature and experience tracks as important steps in verifying an im-

portant research problem area and in fine-tuning the focus of the research problem. And, these efforts, combined with mental models, will enhance the quality of the research focus.

Processes and Outcomes

Those interested in conducting research in organizations need to be keenly aware of the perspectives of processes and outcomes. People who feel responsibility for organizations have a pragmatic view of outcomes. They ask big performance outcome questions (Swanson, 1996):

- Will the organization perform better?
- Will the process perform better?
- Will the individuals perform better?

And, they ask questions about results from multiple perspectives (Swanson & Holton, 1999):

- Has performance increased (system level and financial performance)?
- Have people learned (knowledge and expertise learning)?
- Are people satisfied (participant and stakeholder satisfaction)?

This does not mean that they do not ask questions about specific subprocesses or the state of a narrow element in the organization. Scholars and organizational decision makers may value a specific factor (e.g., employee satisfaction) and value gains in that factor (e.g., significant gains in employee satisfaction), but at some point the question of costs and benefits to the organization will arise. It is best to think about the direct and extended connections between processes and outcomes when identifying a research problem. One example here is when a researcher started with a need to improve leadership development as the initial problem, which then led to a need to better define leadership, and then finally the realization that the important problem was a need to fill the void of research-based leadership theory having any direct connection to performance (Lynham, 2002). The assumption that leadership was connected to enduring results was missing from reports of practice and theory.

In summary, the three strategies for identifying research problems include (1) mental models, (2) literature and experience, and (3) processes and outcomes. These three strategies assist in leading the scholar to a defensible research problem.

PHILOSOPHY OF RESEARCH

Sometimes it feels like too much has been written and said about the ideology and philosophy of research by those who have done very little research. Passmore's

(1990) sage advice is to choose a paradigm, any paradigm. In the end, researchers need to conduct rigorous research and let time test the ultimate integrity of the inquiry. Ultimately, research rigor and impact, not philosophical debate as to worthiness of various research paradigms, comprise the true grist of active scholars (unless you are in the discipline of philosophy).

Even though I have taken the stance described here, it is important to understand the philosophical discord that does exist among some scholars (Geddes, 2003; Ghoshal, 2005; Wilson, 1998a, 1998b). The position taken here is that understanding the rival philosophical views can allow for expansion, tolerance, and inclusion in research thinking and methodology instead of rivalry and exclusivity. It is deemed shallow and immature to justify one's research question and methodology by discounting an alternative research paradigm. The arguments supporting a chosen research question and methodology should stand on their own two legs.

The rival philosophical views around research are focused on overarching philosophical research paradigms. A *paradigm*, according to Kuhn (1970), is the dominant understanding of a particular class of phenomena at a particular time. This book is structured around the apolitical research paradigm of

- quantitative research,
- qualitative research, and
- mixed methods research.

Alternative Paradigms and Research Methods

Gephart (1999) has discussed succinctly the rivalry among research paradigms; the essence of his essay is presented here. He discusses the alternative philosophical paradigm of positivistic, interpretative, and critical science research.

Recently there has been interest in the role of philosophical assumptions and paradigms in conducting research. During the late 1900s, concerns about the dominant positivistic research paradigm and the limits of quantitative data and methods connected with positivism have been raised. Positivism assumes that an objective world exists and that scientific methods can mirror and measure while seeking to predict and explain causal relations among variables. Conversely, critics take the position that positivistic methods remove meaning from contexts in the pursuit of quantifying phenomena (Guba & Lincoln, 1994, p. 106). The exclusion of meanings and interpretations from quantitative data is seen as a fundamental shortcoming in that contrived quantitative methods are believed to impose meanings and ultimately their interpretation. "And they require statistical samples that often do not represent specific intact groups and which do not allow generalization to or understanding of individual cases. Finally, quantitative and positivistic methods tend to exclude discovery from the domain of scientific inquiry" (Gephart, 1999, 1).

It is fair to say that positivism dominates research in organizations. Even so, scholars regularly challenge this dominance from two alternative interpretive and critical science approaches (Hatch, 1997). Both raise philosophical challenges for positivism and offer alternative methodological approaches to research in organizations. These philosophical perspectives are believed by advocates to address issues that positivistic or quantitative researchers have tended to overlook.

Interpretive scholars have challenged the positivistic approach to uncover truths and facts using quantitative methods. They contend that these methods impose a view of the world rather than grasping and describing these world-views. Critical scientists go further in saying that these imposed views implicitly support forms of positivistic knowledge and advance capitalist organizations and inequality.

This brief discussion summarizes the three *philosophical* views—positivism, interpretivism, and critical science (postmodernism)—presented by some organizational researchers. Interpretivism and critical science are present in organizational scholarship, though they are still outliers compared to quantitative research. The core features, such as assumptions and goals, for of each of the three paradigms are summarized in Figure 2.4 (based on Gephart, 1999).

The abbreviated comparisons are intended to highlight different ways of thinking and researching so that the various philosophical perspectives can be understood and potentially combined for the advancement of new and important understandings.

Positivism

Positivism assumes that the world is objective. Therefore, positivist researchers generally seek out facts in terms of relationships among variables. They focus on quantitative methods used to test and verify hypotheses. Logically, then there is also a focus on falsification rather than verification given the complexity of organizational phenomena. The challenge is to assess all essential variables to verify that a relationship is consistent in like conditions. Effort is made to establish the generalizability of findings based on careful sampling.

Interpretivism

Interpretive research is concerned with meaning; it seeks to understand organizational members' meaning of a situation (Schwandt, 1994, p. 118). Interpretive researchers assume that knowledge and meaning are individual interpretations. Thus, there is no objective knowledge apart from individual interpretations by reasoning humans. Although there are numerous interpretivist perspectives, they all are focused on subjective meanings as to how individuals or members apprehend, understand, and make sense of events and settings and how this sense making produces features of the very settings to which sense making is responsive.

One form of interpretive research is *social constructionism*, which seeks to understand the social construction dialectic, involving objective, intersubjective,

	Positivism	Interpretivism	Critical Science
Assumptions	Objective world that science can "mirror" with privileged knowledge	Intersubjective world that science can represent with concepts of actors; social construction of reality	Material world of structured contra-dictions and/or exploitation that can be objectively known only by removing tacit ideological biases
Key Focus or Ideas	Search for contextual and organizational variables that cause organizational actions	Search for patterns of meaning	Search for disguised contradictions hidden by ideology; open spaces for pre-viously silenced voices
Goal of Paradigm	Uncover truth and facts as quantitatively specified relations among variables	Describe meanings, understand members' definitions of the situation, examine how objective realities are produced	Uncover hidden interests; expose con-tractions; enable more informed consciousness; displace ideology with scientific insights; change
Nature of Knowledge or Form of Theory	Verified hypotheses involving valid, reliable, and precisely measured variables	Abstract descriptions of meanings and members—definitions of situations produced in natural contexts	Structural or historical insights revealing contradictions
Criteria for Assessing Research	Prediction-explanation	Trustworthiness	Theoretical consistency
	Rigor; internal and external validity, reliability	Authenticity	Historical insights
			Transcendent interpretations
			Basis for action; change potential and mobilization
Unit of Analysis	The variable	Meaning; symbolic act	Contradictions; incidents of exploitation
Research Methods and Type(s) of Analysis	Experiments; questionnaires; secondary data analysis; quantitatively coded documents	Ethnography; participant observation; interviews; conversational analysis; grounded theory development	Field research; historical analysis; dialectical analysis; deconstruction; textual analysis
	Quantitative: regression; Likert scaling; structural equation modeling	Case studies; conver-sational and textual analysis; expansion analysis	
	Qualitative: grounded theory testing		

Figure 2.4   Alternative Paradigms for Research in Organizations (adapted from Gephart, 1999)

and subjective knowledge (Berger & Luckmann, 1967; Knorr-Cetina, 1981; Gephart, 1978). This philosophical view investigates how the objective features of society (e.g., organizations, social classes, technology, and scientific facts) emerge from, depend on, and are constituted by subjective meanings of individuals and intersubjective processes such as discourses or discussions in groups (Gephart, 1993, 1999).

Critical Science

The third philosophical paradigm, *critical science*, is a combination of critical theory and postmodernism. Critical theory was developed by the Frankfurt School (Germany) and is based on the politics and philosophy from Marx, Kant, Hegel, and Weber (Kincheloe & McLaren, 1994, p. 138). Critical theorists separate from Marxism on numerous points, but they retain a focus on challenging capitalism along with the domination, injustice, and subjugation that they believe capitalism produces.

Critical science can take various forms, including historical essays, field research, and case studies (Boje, Gephart, & Thatchenkery, 1996). Philosophically, critical postmodern research is consistent with Marxist, critical, and postmodern concepts (e.g., commodification, alienation, and contradictions). Critical science also seeks to provide historical understandings through the reexamination of important events to surface unacknowledged forms of exploitation and domination.

Alternative Paradigms Conclusions

Positivism continues to dominate research in organizations and those specific disciplines doing organizationally related research. However, challenges to the limits of positivism and the rise of alternatives to positivism challenge the landscape of research (Ghoshal, 2005). Interpretive research offers ways to understand members' own meanings and theories of the world, a fundamental challenge for any scholarly inquiry seeking to have practical relevance. Critical science challenges the value-neutral nature of positivism and interpretive research.

CHOOSING THE MOST APPROPRIATE QUESTION, PARADIGM, AND METHOD

There are two intense focal points in the process getting to the point of specifying the planning decisions (research question, paradigm, and method). These points are the *content considerations* and the *methodological considerations*.

Content Considerations Revisited

Mental models, literature and observations, and processes and outcomes are the *content considerations* leading to the identification of a research problem. While the content considerations (as presented earlier) serve in making the *problem decision*, they are also helpful in dealing with the *methodological considerations* and making the *planning decisions* (choosing the most appropriate question, paradigm, and method).

The content considerations provide a lens for the researcher when entertaining the research questions, paradigms, and methods considerations. In other words, content consideration information moves forward and is added to the methodological consideration information, and both ultimately help shape the planning decisions.

Methodological Considerations

The process of framing research in organizations (see Figure 2.1) is the primary focal point of this chapter. It is worth repeating that this process is different than the processes commonly followed by many beginning scholars. They will often follow inappropriate or inadequate processes such as the following:

Research Paradigm → Research Question → Research Plan

Research Method → Research Question → Research Plan

Research Question → Research Method → Research Plan

By engaging in all three of the content consideration strategies, the research problem can be identified, and there then will be a focus on a limited range of rational research question, paradigm, method, and contextual options. (Note that the research problem is missing from all three of the inadequate processes cited above.)

It is important to note that when it comes to methodological considerations, phenomena that are not well understood will likely give rise to specific research questions of meaning or contradictions. These questions would more naturally move into qualitative methods. In contrast, well-understood phenomena will likely give rise to specific research questions of action and verification. These questions would more naturally move into quantitative methods.

It is important for the researcher not to have the specific research question, paradigm, methodology, or context firmly established before identifying the research problem. Not following this advice will find the researcher arguing about the significance of the question (which should have been clearly established) and the philosophy of research (usually deriding alternative research paradigms and methods).

Research Questions

Once you have identified a research problem in the form of a knowledge void, numerous valid research questions can be asked, not just one. This is a simple and critical point often misunderstood. Research questions develop out of the research problem previously framed by content considerations, including a deep knowledge of the literature and experience with the phenomenon, and consideration of the mental models, processes, and outcomes operating within the initial problem area (see Figure 2.1).

A common mistake is to focus on the formulation of research questions before gaining a deep understanding the phenomenon through experience and the literature. The research questions develop and evolve from a deeper understanding of the phenomenon through an iterative process of formulating a question that drives one back to experience and the literature, which then brings one back to refine the question, and so forth. This iterative process between developing research questions and the other steps in framing research continues forward into the planning decisions.

Research questions have an interactive relationship with the other methodological considerations—the research paradigm, the research method, and the research context. Typical research methodology tells us that the research method and context are derived from the research question. However, the method and context also shape the question making the entire process more coherent. It is critical first to identify the initial problem area, then to consider the content of the problem area and decide on the frame of the research problem before refining research questions.

Developing research questions is an ongoing activity throughout the entire process of framing the research. For example, Boeker (1992) identified a problem of not knowing who controls the process of chief executive succession. Depending on how much is known about chief executive succession, the research questions could range from how succession is handled in a particular organization to surveying the top 500 corporations in the United States to determine which of the preestablished methods they use and why. Clearly, the research question being entertained should first be judged as appropriate through the lens of the content considerations that justified the research problem. The key is to determine whether there is anything illogical about the proposed research question based on the substance of the content considerations.

Research Paradigms

The apolitical research paradigm of quantitative, qualitative, and mixed methods research has been adopted for this book. Although ideological differences undergird many research paradigms, the intent here is to be aware of those differences and to be intellectually agile enough to move across paradigms logically, not ideologically.

An example of this logical agility would be Danielson's (2004) work related to organizational socialization. Her theory development research recognized that there was extensive empirical research related to organizational socialization and that it focused on the individual being socialized into a static organization. Her research problem was that contemporary organizations keep changing and that the present theory is of minimal use. She went on to pose the research question "Can an alternative theory of organizational socialization be developed to facilitate continuous organizational renewal and agility?" (p. 357). Her research question was justified by the content considerations and was aligned to her mixed methods research paradigm of theory-building research.

Research Methods

The bulk of this text covers numerous research methods within the paradigms of quantitative, qualitative, and mixed-methods research. Choosing a research method requires logic and judgment.

For example, a researcher drawn toward qualitative research methods and, more specifically, phenomenology needs to reach back logically to the research problem decision and the tentative research question. Although the problem area is of high interest to the researcher, if the researcher does not bring forward the *content considerations,* he or she may naively choose a favored methodology (e.g., phenomenology) when a great deal is already known related to the research question by the way of self-report and storytelling data. An extreme case could be the availability of extensive quantitative research on the topic as to justify a meta-analysis.

Research Context

The most pragmatic and powerful methodological consideration for doing research in organizations has to do with the research context. The context of research in organizations almost always offers opportunities and constraints. Opportunities entice and constraints redirect efforts. Organizations collect data, address questions and problems, experience processes and events within established time frames, and have people and resources with particular characteristics and varying accessibility.

For example, one time I was consulting with a VP of a Fortune 50 firm in the realm of plant startups. He began to agonize about the fact that he believed that spending money on training associated with organizational performance requirements had a great return on investment but that his organization had no research or substantiated rules of thumb about such investments. The agonizing turned into a funded experimental research study (Swanson & Sawzin, 1976). The opportunity caused me to reprioritize my research agenda (new problem), and the constraints caused the firm to accept an off-site experimental research study with high-fidelity organizational simulation so as to honor the ability to answer the causal research questions they wanted answered.

In the end, there must be harmony or logical trade-offs among the chosen research question, research paradigm, research method, and research context. These considerations are not linear, and tentative decisions in one realm will influence the other three realms. For example, the pragmatic impact of using a survey method with a particular population and sample may modify the research questions as it becomes apparent that particular data will or will not be available.

CONCLUSION

The process of framing research in organizations (Figure 2.1) focuses on the task of identifying important research problems and connecting them to appropriate research questions, paradigms, and methods. In order to do this work well, researchers need to be knowledgeable of a variety of specific research methods within research paradigms. The next 19 chapters of this book cover specific research methods that are categorized into the three sections: "Quantitative Research Methods," "Qualitative Research Methods," and "Mixed Methods Research."

REFERENCES

The American Heritage collegiate dictionary. (2002). 4th ed. Boston: Houghton Mifflin.

Berger, P., & Luckmann, T. J. (1966). *The social construction of reality.* New York: Doubleday.

Boeker, W. (1992). Power and managerial dismal: Scapegoating at the top. *Administrative Science Quarterly, 37,* 400–421.

Boje, D., Gephart, R., & Thatchenkery, T. (1996). *Postmodern management and organization theory.* Newbury Park, CA: Sage.

Daniclson, M. M. (2004). A theory of continuous socialization for organizational renewal. *Human Resource Development Review, 3*(4) 354–384.

Dooley, C. R. (1944). *The training within industry report, 1910–1945.* Washington, DC: War Manpower Commission Bureau of Training, Training within Industry Service.

Dubin, R. (1978). *Theory building* (rev. ed). New York: Free Press.

Geddes, B. (2003). *Paradigms and sand castles: Theory building research design in comparative politics.* Ann Arbor: University of Michigan Press.

Gephart, R. P. (1978). Status degradation and organizational succession: An ethnomethodological approach. *Administrative Science Quarterly, 23*(4), 553–581.

Gephart, R. P. (1993). The textual approach: Risk and blame in disaster sensemaking. *Academy of Management Journal, 36*(6), 1465–1514.

Gephart, R. P. (1999). Paradigms and research methods. *Academy of Management Research Methods Forum, 4,* 1–12.

Ghoshal, S. (2005). Bad management theories are destroying good management practices. *Academy of Management Learning & Education, 4*(1), 75–91.

Guba, E. G., & Lincoln, Y. S. (1994). Competing paradigms in qualitative research. In N. K. Denzin & Y. S. Lincoln (Eds.), *Handbook of qualitative research* (pp. 105–117). Newbury Park, CA: Sage.

Hatch, M. J. (1997). *Organization theory: Modern symbolic and postmodern perspectives.* Oxford: Oxford University Press.

Holton, E. F., & Baldwin, T. T. (Eds.). (2003). *Improving learning transfer in organizations.* San Francisco: Jossey-Bass.

Kincheloe, J. L., & McLaren, P. L. (1994). Rethinking critical theory and qualitative research. In N. K. Denzin & Y. S. Lincoln (Eds.), *Handbook of qualitative research* (pp. 138–157). Newbury Park, CA: Sage.

Knorr-Cetina, K. D. (1981). *The manufacture of knowledge: An essay on the constructivist and contextual nature of science.* Oxford: Pergamon.

Kuhn, T. (1970). *The structure of scientific revolutions* (2nd ed.). Chicago: University of Chicago Press.

Lynham, S. A. (2002). The general method of theory building research in applied disciplines. *Advances in Developing Human Resources, 5*(4), 221–241.

Morgan, G. (1996). *Images of organizations* (2nd ed.). Thousand Oaks, CA: Sage.

Passmore, D. L. (1990). Pick a paradigm, any paradigm. *Human Resource Development Quarterly, 1*(1), 25–27.

Rummler, G., & Brache, A. P. (1995). *Improving performance: Managing the white space in organizations.* San Francisco: Jossey-Bass.

Schwandt, T. A. (1994). Constructivist, interpretivist approaches to human inquiry. In N. K. Denzin & Y. S. Lincoln (Eds.), *Handbook of qualitative research* (pp. 118–137). Newbury Park, CA: Sage.

Swanson, R. A. (1996). *Analysis for improving performance: Tools for diagnosing organizations and documenting workplace expertise.* San Francisco: Berrett-Koehler.

Swanson, R. A. (1997). HRD research: Don't go to work without it. In R. A. Swanson & E. F. Holton III (Eds.), *Human resource development research handbook: Linking research and practice* (pp. 3–20). San Francisco: Berrett-Koehler.

Swanson, R. A., & Holton, E. F., III. (1999). *Results: How to assess performance, learning, and satisfaction in organizations.* San Francisco: Berrett-Koehler.

Swanson, R. A., & Sawzin, S. A. (1975). *Industrial training research project.* Bowling Green, OH: Bowling Green State University.

Wilson, E. O. (1998a). Back from chaos. *Atlantic Monthly, 281*(3), 41.

Wilson, E. O. (1998b). *Consilience: The unity of knowledge.* New York: Knopf.

Van de Ven, A. H. (2002). *Professional science.* Thousand Oaks, CA: Sage.

Quantitative Research Methods

The Basics of Quantitative Research

Elwood F. Holton III, *Louisiana State University*
Michael F. Burnett, *Louisiana State University*

CHAPTER OUTLINE

Quantitative methods and the scientific method are the foundation of modern science. This approach to research usually starts with a specific theory, either proposed or previously developed, which leads to specific hypotheses that are then measured quantitatively and rigorously analyzed and evaluated according to established research procedures. This approach has a rich tradition and has contributed a substantial portion of the knowledge in human resource development (HRD).

This chapter attempts to demystify the quantitative research process and tools that HRD researchers use. It is not a statistics chapter, though we will discuss statistical tools. The purpose of this chapter is to give you a basic overview of quantitative research so you can do two things: (1) *read research reports* more easily and (2) *understand choices made by researchers*. It is not complete in describing every statistical tool or in explaining all the nuances of the various methods. The chapters that follow in this section will explain each of the concepts in more detail. Rather, this chapter should provide a frame of reference to feel comfortable in the world of quantitative research.

WHY USE QUANTITATIVE RESEARCH?

HRD researchers use both quantitative and qualitative methods (see Part III, "Qualitative Research Methods"). This book's basic premise is that both research methods are valuable; in fact, they are often quite powerful when used together. Researchers collect data for two basic reasons: to better understand phenomena in a specific group being studied, and to make inferences about broader groups beyond those being studied. We'll say more about these two concepts later. Quantitative techniques are particularly strong at studying large groups of people and making generalizations from the sample being studied to broader groups beyond that sample. Qualitative methods are particularly strong at attaining deep and detailed understandings about a specific group or sample, but at the expense of generalizability. Each approach has unique strengths and weaknesses; each is valuable depending on the purpose of the research.

QUALITY CONSIDERATIONS

The area of greatest misunderstanding between researchers and practitioners about quantitative methods probably lies in issues of quality. It is quite common for researchers to want to use procedures that seem like excessive work to practitioners. Researchers and their methods then may be labeled as "unrealistic" or as working in an "ivory tower." As discussed earlier in the book, research has a different purpose than practice. Whereas "seat of the pants" methods might be quite acceptable for certain organizational decisions, research has a higher quality standard that is quite necessary.

How Much Quality Is Needed?

Most research is not conducted solely for the purpose of understanding a single event occurring for a single group of people. Research is almost always used to draw some conclusions beyond the group being studied. For example, if evaluation research is conducted on the first two training programs offered in a new supervisory training program, it will likely be used to make decisions about how well it will work for other groups of supervisors who will complete the program. Researchers call this *generalization*. Depending on the level of generalization, the research procedures may need to be quite complex or quite simple. If all we care about is understanding the results for these two groups of supervisors—and nothing more—the procedures will be much simpler than if we want to know whether the results will likely be the same for any group of supervisors from any of the organization's facilities in the United States. The procedures will be even more complex if we want to know whether it will work at any of the company's facilities in the world. They will grow even more complex if the organization conducting the research is a consulting firm that wants to know whether the program will work not only anywhere in the world but with any type of company.

The other parameter that affects the complexity of the procedures is the *degree of certainty* required from the research. If the stakes are very high (e.g., a huge amount of money is being invested in the intervention, lives depend on the outcomes, etc.), then the researcher needs to have a very high degree of certainty that there is no error in the research results. This will require very strict and complex research procedures. On the other hand, if the stakes are much lower, then a lower degree of certainty may be acceptable.

Researchers are concerned about breadth of generalization and the degree of certainty they have in the findings because the implications of the research cannot exceed the scope of what was studied and how it was studied. However, practitioners under pressure to make quick business decisions often want only narrow generalization and will accept lower degrees of certainty. This usually presents a challenge when researchers and practitioners create partnerships because their goals may differ. What is most important in partnerships is that both parties negotiate and agree to the goal of the research. If the goal is simply to provide one organization with data it needs to make appropriate decisions, then the organization should make that clear; and the researchers, if they choose to accept the project, must design the research procedures accordingly. However, if the organization also wants to contribute to the growth of the HRD profession through research, then they should be prepared to accept more complex research procedures than necessary for their own short-term needs.

OVERVIEW OF QUANTITATIVE RESEARCH PROCESS

The quantitative research process can be viewed as a five-step process as outlined here and detailed in the follow-up sections:

1. Determining basic questions to be answered by study
2. Determining participants in the study (population and sample)
3. Selecting the methods needed to answer questions
   a. Variables
   b. Measures of the variables
   c. Overall design
4. Selecting analysis tools
5. Understanding and interpreting the results

Step 1: Determining Basic Questions to Be Answered by Study

Formulating the research question is perhaps the most important step in any research effort (see chapter 2). Without a clear understanding of the outcomes expected from the study and the questions to be answered, there is a high likelihood of error.

Quantitative research is generally experimental, quasi-experimental, correlational, or descriptive. In experimental research, researchers deliberately set out to create specific conditions to test a theory or proposition. Specific hypotheses are created from theory that are then tested by the experiment. For example, you might randomly select and assign trainees to two different types of training methods to see whether it affects their performance because you believe training method will affect the outcomes. In experimental research, the researcher has control over many of the factors that influence the phenomenon of interest to isolate relationship between conditions or behaviors we can change and the outcomes they seek.

Nonexperimental research, on the other hand, uses existing situations in the field to study phenomena. It is used when it is impractical to conduct a true experiment or to study more variables than can be controlled in an experiment, or when there is a need for descriptive quantitative data. However, the researcher does not take control of variables as in experimental research. For example, through quasi-experimental research, you could also test the proposition that training method affects performance, but you would be using existing training classes and methods, rather than deliberately creating the training and training situation. Quasi-experimental research to test theory is a very common type of quantitative research in HRD because of the difficulties in creating true experiments in organizational settings.

The other forms of nonexperimental research can be thought of as causal-comparative, correlational, and descriptive (survey) research (Ary, Jacobs, & Razavieh, 1996). *Causal-comparative research* is similar to an experiment except that the researcher does not manipulate the variable(s) being studied. Researchers attempt to find subjects who differ on some variable of interest and then attempt to discover other variables that explain the difference in order to infer causality. *Correlational research* seeks to determine relationships among two or more variables without necessarily inferring causality. Both causal-comparative and correlational research generally begin with hypotheses generated from theory. *Descriptive research* uses surveys to gather information about people, groups, organizations, and so forth. Its purpose is simply to describe characteristics of the domain.

An overlooked role for quantitative methods is their role in discovering theory (McCall & Bobko, 1990). Quantitative research can also be exploratory—that is, used to discover relationships, interpretations, and characteristics of subjects that suggest new theory and define new problems. When used for this purpose, research questions are used instead of specific hypotheses. Thus, a "loose-tight" approach to the application of quantitative methods is advocated, depending on the overriding goal of the research. If the purpose is to test theory for broad generalization to many audiences, then rigorous application of quantitative methodology is needed. If the purpose is to discover theoretical propositions or define problems in need of theory, then looser application of these techniques is perfectly acceptable. It is in the later arena that quantitative and qualitative techniques are most similar.

Step 2: Determining Participants in the Study

One of the real advantages of quantitative methods is their ability to use smaller groups of people to make inferences about larger groups that would be prohibitively expensive to study. For example, can you imagine the cost of establishing the effectiveness of a particular supervisory development tool if researchers had to study every supervisor in the company throughout the country!

The research term for all the supervisors in this example is the *population*. In any study there is usually a population—the larger group to which the results from the research being conducted are believed to be applicable. It is very important to define the degree to which the results will need to be generalized beyond the study because that is one of the factors that determines the rigor of the study. Statistical tools let us use smaller groups, called *samples*, in our studies. However, in order to make generalizations from the study, researchers prefer to choose that sample randomly. By doing so, they can have much greater confidence that their findings are not due to some special characteristic of the sample but, rather, are truly representative of the whole population.

Obtaining random samples is often a difficult issue in HRD research because much research is conducted inside organizations. Sometimes organizational conditions, such as production schedules or the requirement to work with intact groups simply won't accommodate it. Other times ethical issues preclude it, such as giving one group of employees tools that enable them to perform better than their peers. Sometimes the nature of the intervention itself precludes it, such as when developing teams. Other times economics limit it because it simply is not good business. Despite these limitations, HRD researchers need sites willing to accommodate strict sampling procedures to advance the field. Chapter 4 will discuss sampling strategies in more detail.

Step 3: Selecting the Methods
Needed to Answer Questions

Once the researcher has identified the research questions and the participants in the study, the specific methods to be used in the study can be determined. These include identifying the variables, measures, and research design.

Variables

Variables are the phenomena that varies depending on the conditions affecting it. Researchers talk about two types of variables: dependent and independent. A *dependent* variable is the variable that is the object of the study or the studied outcome. Examples might include learning, job performance, or company market share. An *independent* variable is a measure that is believed to be related in some way to the dependent variable. For example, supervisor support for training (independent variable) is widely believed to influence the use of training on the job (dependent variable). A further extension here would be that the use of training (independent variable) is widely believed to influence the quantity and quality of work (dependent variable).

Measures

Both independent and dependent variables can be measured by categorical, continuous, or ordinal data. *Categorical*, or nominal, data come from measures that have no inherent numeric value to them; they are simply categories such as gender, department, teaching method used, and so forth. Although researchers may assign a coding number to these categories for ease of computer analysis (e.g., female = 1; male = 2), the number has no real meaning. The codes could have just as easily been "A" or "B."

   Continuous, or interval, data, on the other hand, are data that have an intrinsic numeric value. Examples might include a person's salary, output in units, scrap or rework rates, performance rating, test score, or rating in a simulation exercise. *Ordinal*, or rank order, data are less descriptive than interval data. For example, five people could be rank ordered in height as 1, 2, and 3. While this approach lets you know that 1 is taller than 2—one rank order position apart—stating that the tallest person is 76 inches tall, the second tallest is 66 inches, and the third tallest is 65 inches is much more descriptive of the true heights and differences. It is important never to collect ordinal data when interval data can be just as easily obtained. One common example of HRD research data is that obtained from survey data asking for responses on a Likert scale (1–4; 1–5; 1–9). Statistically these data can be handled as continuous data.

   The result is that measures can be viewed in a 3 × 2 matrix. As shown in Figure 3.1, independent variable data may be categorical, continuous (inter-

	Independent Variable	Dependent Variable
Categorical		
Continuous (Interval)		
Ordinal		

Figure 3.1   Types of Variables

val), or ordinal. Similarly, dependent variable data may be either categorical or continuous.

Constructing Measurement Tools.   So far we have been talking about "measures" as if they were easy to come by. In fact, a large part of conducting good research is obtaining or building good measures of the variables in a research study. The quality of the research results is as much dependent on good measures as anything else researchers do. The best analysis in the world can't make up for poorly constructed measures.

Four basic types of measures are used in HRD studies:

- *Observational measures*—measures recorded by a person observing something. Performance ratings, 360° feedback, and checklists are examples.
- *Self-report measures*—a person in the study's own report. Examples include a trainee's report of use of training on the job or knowledge gained.
- *Objective measures*—measures taken by instruments or highly accurate measuring devices. Examples might include cost data, quality measures from equipment, or knowledge tests.
- *Estimates*—estimates of measures, usually by subject matter experts

To evaluate any of these, researchers must be clear on two concepts: *validity* and *reliability*. Measures are said to be *valid* if they measure what they are supposed to measure. Thus, self-report measures of performance on the job tend to not be very valid because people tend to overrate themselves. A *reliable* measure is one that yields consistent results. A measure can be very reliable (consistent) but not valid (measure inaccurately or the wrong thing). For example, self-ratings are very often reliable but not valid.

These concepts are significant ones for practitioners. For one thing, you will see both of them discussed at length in most research articles. And, before you accept research findings, you want to be sure valid and reliable measures are used. If you are conducting or sponsoring research in your organization, you want to be sure that you have valid and reliable measures so the conclusions you report to your boss are the correct ones. Finally, if you create research partnerships, you may spend considerable time discussing these concepts and need resources devoted to developing valid and reliable measures.

There are three common types of validity. *Content validity*, the minimum requirement for acceptable research, means that the content of your measure matches the content of what you are trying to measure. For example, a performance rating instrument is content-valid if the items on the instrument match what is really required to do the job. This is usually established by subject matter experts and is done logically, not statistically.

Criterion validity asks whether the measure really predicts the dependent variable it is supposed to predict. Thus, we would expect our performance rating instrument to be able to predict, or distinguish, high performers from low performers. If we find that successful people in an organization have widely varying scores on the performance rating instrument, then it would not have good criterion validity. An instrument could have good content validity (appear to have the right content) but not good criterion validity, probably because important things were left off the instrument.

The third type of validity is *construct validity*. A *construct* is something that cannot be directly observed or measured. Job commitment or motivation is an example. We can measure behaviors that are believed to represent commitment or motivation, but we cannot directly measure them like we can scrap or sales. Because indirect measures must be used, researchers have to establish that what they actually measure is really the construct they believe they are measuring. This is usually done by comparing the measure to similar or related measures.

Building Valid Scales.   Some measures are obtained from single objective and numerical data. For example, the number of sales made in a day, scrap rate, or age are all single numbers that are relatively easy to obtain. Other variables need to be measured more indirectly. Examples might include a supervisor performance rating, personality type, job commitment, or motivation. In these cases, researchers develop *scales* that consist of multiple questions that are mathematically grouped together to measure a variable. Chapter 10 discusses scale development in detail.

The development and testing of valid measurement scales is a special type of research. Researchers use a tool called *factor analysis* to build valid measurement scales. In this approach, researchers generate items for instruments, usually with the help of subject matter experts. A group of people then respond to the instrument, and factor analysis is used to look at the relationship between the items. By looking at the results, researchers can tell which items seem to be measuring the same thing so they can then be grouped into scales for further analysis. Chapter 11 will discuss factor analysis methods.

Research Designs
The design of an experimental or quasi-experimental research study refers to the way in which the data will be collected. There are really three basic design deci-

sions to be made, though they are often combined into many different variations. These three design tools are pretests, control groups, and time series. Each of them enables researchers to answer additional questions from the data.

Question 1: Is what we are observing now a change? Suppose we have measured individual performance after learning and find that it is at acceptable levels. Was the money invested in learning worthwhile? It could have been completely wasted because performance was just fine before the learning! The only way to be sure is to use a *pretest*. A pretest does not necessarily mean a traditional classroom test; it simply means taking a measure of whatever we are interested in before our intervention. These are sometimes referred to as *baseline measures*.

Question 2: Is a change due to our intervention? Continuing this example, let's suppose that we include a pretest and find that yes, performance did go up, and our statistics tell us that it was a significant change. Can we now say that our learning intervention worked? No, not yet. It could have been that everyone got a raise or a new supervisor at the same time as the intervention. If we want to control for the possibility that something else caused what we observe, we have to use a control group. A *control group* is nothing more than a group who is as close as possible to being the same as the people we are studying, but who do not get the learning intervention. The idea is that anything else that might affect our study group will affect the control group similarly. We won't know what it is, but we will know that the difference between the control group and our study group should be just the learning. Of course, it is often hard work to get a control group that is the "same" as our study group. Sometime we have a control group that is almost the same (trainees who come on Wednesday vs. those coming in 2 weeks) or similar but not identical (two plant sites). In HRD research, it is often hard to get a true control group, so researchers spend a great deal of time measuring and establishing the degree to which two groups are similar.

Question 3: Are the changes consistent over time? If your work performance is measured today, will it be the same as tomorrow, or 1 month from now, given the same task? Probably not. Often researchers are not satisfied with just one measure before or after the learning. Measures taken at a single point in time tend to be somewhat suspect. When measuring performance, for example, a person could be ill or simply have a bad day. If we took a measure once a week and averaged them, it might be more valid. Or, it might be easy to implement the same new process when we measure performance one month after learning it. However, will the employee continue to do it 3 months or 6 months after the learning? These are all applications for *time series* or repeated measures.

Creating the Design.   Researchers combine these three basic building blocks to create many different designs for research, depending on the purpose of the research (see chapter 6 for further discussion of research designs). The combinations are many: control group with pretest, single-group pretest with time series, and so on. By knowing these three basic components, you can understand just about any design.

Step 4: Selecting Analysis Tools

Many statistical analysis tools are available. This section will orient you to the most common ones that you will encounter when reading research or working with researchers.

Beginning researchers often equate certain analytical tools with the different types of research studies. Although there is some relationship, data analysis tools can be used for different purposes and in different types of studies. For example, analysis of variance might be used in an experimental or nonexperimental study. Insights into the decisions researchers make about quantitative analysis tools can be gained by understanding two things: what the basic questions being asked by the researcher are and whether the data from the measures being used are *continuous (interval)*, *ordinal*, or *categorical*.

It is convenient to think of quantitative tools as being used to answer one of five core questions:

Description: What are the characteristics of some group or groups of people?

Comparison of groups: Are two or more groups the same or different on some characteristic?

Association: Are two variables related and, if so, what is the strength of their relationship?

Prediction: Can measures be used to predict something in the future?

Explanation: Given some outcome or phenomenon, why does it occur?

Purpose: To Describe

At least part of most studies is simply to describe certain aspects of a group of people. If it is the entire purpose, the study is called a *descriptive study* (see chapter 7 on survey research methods). Consider, for example, a researcher who conducts a mail survey to investigate training needs of HRD professionals in a particular area. The survey might include certain demographics such as age, gender, and type of company. These data are categorical data. They would be analyzed using *frequencies*, which are simply percentages. Along with these data, the researcher might list six different training needs and ask people responding to indicate on a scale from 1 to 5 how badly they need each training program. These responses are continuous data, so the researcher would first report simple *means* or averages to describe the average level of need. These two tools are the basic measures used to describe a group of people.

Suppose that the mean response to the need for training in instructional design is "3.3." We know that the average level of need is a little above the midpoint, but it raises another question: Was everyone about at that level, or did some people answer with a 5 and others 1? Researchers look at another measure called a *standard deviation* to answer this question. A standard deviation tells you how widely the responses vary around the mean. In this case, a standard deviation of .2 would indicate that everyone responded pretty close to 3.3, whereas a standard deviation of .8 would indicate that answers varied much more widely. It turns out that, on average, about 66% of the responses will be within ±1 standard deviation of a mean, and 95% will be within ±2 standard deviations.

Purpose: To Compare

Once people see the means, they inevitably want to compare them between groups. For example, we might want to compare the mean responses of males and females to the earlier question. If males had an average response of 3.2 and females 3.25, we might be satisfied to "eyeball it" and say there is no real difference. Similarly, if males responded 3.2 and females 4.2, we would be fairly confident there is a real difference. But suppose males had an average response of 3.2 and females an average response of 3.5. Is that difference a real difference or close enough to say they are about the same? Researchers use a statistical tool called a *t-test* to compare means between two groups. This is simply a tool to indicate whether the difference is likely to be a "real" difference.

Now, suppose that instead of comparing the means between males and females we want to compare the means between three groups such as those in three different departments. For example, suppose that Department A's mean response is 3.2, Department B's is 3.5, and Department C's is 3.7.

A *t*-test will not work because it only works with two groups, so instead researchers use a technique called *analysis of variance*, or more commonly ANOVA. This technique tells you the same thing as a *t*-test, but with more than two groups. If the result is "significant" (a statistical concept explained later), the researcher knows that there is a difference among the three scores.

In this case, the dependent variable is the mean response that is continuous. The independent variable is the department because we are asking whether department predicts the mean response. It is a categorical variable. Analysis of variance always has categorical independent and continuous dependent variables. If the independent variable is continuous, you have to use regression, which is explained later. Analysis of variance is a very commonly used technique in HRD. Comparisons among different teaching methods, departments, or types of interventions would all require ANOVA as an analysis tool.

You will see other variations of ANOVA. One is called *factorial ANOVA*, which simply means that instead of one category as an independent variable, there are two or more. This is quite common because usually at least two categorical variables are involved as independent variables in a study. For example, when comparing three different training methods, we might also include job level as another independent variable because it could affect trainees' response to the teaching method. *Analysis of covariance*, or ANCOVA, is a close cousin that allows for one of the independent variables to be continuous. For example, we might use ANCOVA if we were comparing three departments using two different teaching methods in each one and wanted to include age (a continuous variable) in the study. *Multiple analysis of variance* (MANOVA) is used if there are more than one dependent variable (see chapter 8 for further discussion of MANOVA). All help us answer the same question: Are there differences among groups or categories?

Purpose: To Associate

Suppose now that instead of looking at different groups, we are more interested in the association between measures. For example, suppose that you want to know whether salary level is associated with test scores. Note the question is not whether one *causes* the other but whether there is some association between them. The tool researchers use to investigate association between two measures is *correlation*. A correlation will always range from −1.0 to +1.0 and tells us two things: the direction of the association and the strength of the association. The sign of the correlation tells us whether it is a positive association (e.g., when one variable goes up, the other one does, too) or negative (when one goes up, the other one goes down). The strength of the association is indicated by the actual number and how close it is to ±1.0, which is a perfect correlation. Suppose the correlation between salary and test scores is −.50. This tells you that people with higher salaries tend to score lower on the tests (a negative relationship) and that this association is moderately strong (.5 is halfway between 0 and 1.0). The graphs in Figures 3.2 and 3.3 show examples of a high positive correlation (Figure 3.2) and a low negative correlation (Figure 3.3).

Correlations do not tell us anything about causation, which is a mistake frequently made when interpreting them. In our example, does the −.50 correlation mean that making more money makes you less smart so you do worse on tests? Or, conversely, that doing well on tests causes you to make less money? No to both. Some other variable (time available to study, relevance of the material to

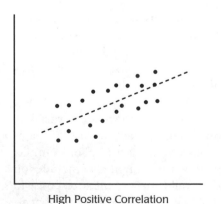

High Positive Correlation

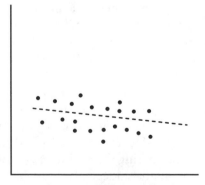

Low Negative Correlation

Figure 3.2   High Positive Correlation   **Figure 3.3**   Low Negative Correlation

their job, etc.) probably explains the relationship. Correlation only tells us that a relationship exists, not whether it is a causal relationship.

The correlation just described can only be used with two continuous variables. Other correlations can be used with categorical variables, though they are less common in HRD research. Some you might see include *Spearman's rho*, the *phi coefficient*, and the *point-biserial correlation*. They do the same thing as the Pearson correlation (described earlier—i.e., determine the correlation of the relationship between two variables) but with different types of categorical data.

Purpose: To Predict

The logical extension of correlation is to try to predict some dependent variable, such as performance or learning. Instead of examining simple correlations between two variables, the next step researchers take is to combine multiple independent variables together to examine their joint association with the dependent variable. The analysis tool they use is *regression* or, more specifically, *multiple regression* when there is more than one independent variable. It turns out that the output from this analysis is an equation that can be used to predict the outcome given a new set of values for the independent variables. For example, we might investigate whether a combination of measures of job commitment, supervisor support for training, and salary level could be used to predict test scores, and, if it does, how strong that relationship is. This is an example of multiple regression analysis. Chapter 8 discusses multivariate research methods, including multiple regression, in more detail.

Regression analysis is typically used when most of the independent variables are continuous variables, although techniques exist (called *dummy coding*) that allow some categorical variables to be included. Actually, correlation, ANOVA, and regression are essentially the same mathematical process, but ANOVA works best when most of the independent variables are categorical, whereas correlation and regression works best when most of them are continuous.

A note of caution: Prediction still does not imply a causal relationship. That is, we might have measures that successfully predict a dependent variable but do not cause it. A simple example illustrates this. We can probably predict salary level by measuring square footage of people's houses, the neighborhood they live in, and the price of the cars they own, but these factors do not cause the salary. They are merely associated with it and will probably mathematically predict it.

Purpose: To Explain

The highest level of research is explanation, or establishing causality. This is very demanding and often costly research. Research for the purpose of explanation seeks to understand why some phenomenon occurs. If we want to intervene and affect outcomes, it is not enough to say that it does or that it can be predicted. We need to explain *why* something occurs. Continuing the example about house size and salary, we have no idea from that research what factors lead to higher salaries, so we have no idea how to help young people develop their careers. If we are in advertising and simply want to know who to mail our ads to, that doesn't matter, but if we are educators wanting to help young people, it matters a great deal.

The tools discussed can be used to suggest possible causal relationships, but researchers seeking explanations have to use much more sophisticated tools. The best approach to determine causality is to conduct experimental research (see chapter 6). Nonexperimental research can be used to strongly infer causal relationships if tools such as structural equation modeling (e.g., LISREL) or path analysis are used (see chapter 9). Hierarchical regression is a more simple but useful approach. These tools typically require larger samples and more rigorous methodology.

Research for explanation is an area that practitioners tend to be less tolerant of when partnering with researchers. In business, intuitive understandings are often sufficient for decisions. Thus, when faced with the time and cost demands for explanatory research, practitioners tend not to want to support it. However, to advance the field of HRD and to provide solid theoretical foundations for practice, it is essential that organizations invest in explanatory research. Researchers need field sites that understand the long-term value of this research and are willing to do more than is required for their immediate decision-making purposes.

Step 5: Understanding and Interpreting the Results

The concept of significance is critical in understanding and interpreting results. Research never really "proves" anything. What researchers do is use elaborate sets of procedures to reduce the probability of an error to a small enough amount that one can be extremely confident that the answer is the real answer and not just a fluke occurrence. That is why researchers talk and write a lot about "p values." When reading research studies, you will see many references to "$p \leq .05$" or "$p \leq .01$." This is the standard way that researchers examine results. What they mean is that the researcher is 95% or 99% confident that whatever was found is real, and not just a chance occurrence. By convention, "$p \leq .05$" is the level at which a finding is considered *significant*. This is a very important concept because findings may look meaningful but not be statistically significant (and vice versa).

For example, suppose that one class has an average test score of 85% and another has an average score of 89.3%. You would like to know whether the one group really learned more than the other. The question that researchers have to answer is whether they can be certain that the difference is "real" or just a chance occurrence. It looks real, but is it? Statistical procedures actually approach this task backward by starting with the hypothesis that the difference is really equal to zero and try to disprove it. If the appropriate test results in $p \leq .05$, this means that there is less than a 5% chance that the difference is zero. Said differently, there is a 95% chance that the group with an average test score of 89.2% actually learned more than the group with an 85% average score.

More recently, researchers have emphasized the importance of calculating *effect sizes* in addition to or instead of using statistical significance. Chapter 5 elaborates on why effect sizes are so important. Basically, statistical significance does not tell us anything about the magnitude of the finding. For example, consider two groups whose mean responses on a scale are 3.4 and 3.5. The problem with significance tests is that they are highly sensitive to sample size. With a sample size of 1,000, this difference of .1 would likely be statistically significant, but with a sample size of only 100, it might not be statistically significant. This is due to the difference in *statistical power* between the two tests (see chapter 4 for further discussion of statistical power). With a large enough sample, even tiny differences between groups can be found to be statistically significant. Thus, statistical significance tests don't tell us anything about the magnitude of the difference and therefore how meaningful the difference is. Effect sizes tell us how meaningful the difference is.

CONCLUSION

While the tools and methodologies available for research continue to expand to embrace new paradigms and approaches, quantitative approaches to research will always remain a core approach to HRD research. Without them, the ability of researchers to provide guidance across multiple organizations and groups of employees would be limited. Together with qualitative tools, they enable research to advance HRD practice.

Reading and understanding quantitative approaches is much like learning a foreign language. At first, these methods can be intimidating and confusing, but with a little persistence and some help translating unfamiliar words, they become quite a bit more clear. Subsequent chapters will elaborate on all the concepts introduced in this chapter.

REFERENCES

Ary, D., Jacobs, L. C., & Razavieh, A. (1996). *Introduction to research in education* (5th ed.). Fort Worth, TX: Harcourt Brace.
McCall, M. W., & Bobko, P. (1990). Research methods in the service of discovery. In M. D. Dunnete & L. Hough (Eds.), *Handbook of industrial and organizational psychology* (pp. 381–418). Palo Alto, CA: Consulting Psychologist's Press.

FOR FURTHER READING

Bobko, P. (1995). *Correlation and regression.* New York: McGraw-Hill.
Borg, W. R., & Gall, M. D. (1992). *Educational research* (4th ed.). New York: Longman.
Campbell, D. T., & Stanley, J. C. (1963). *Experimental and quasi-experimental designs for research.* Boston: Houghton Mifflin.

Huck, S. W., & Cormier, W. H. (1996). *Reading statistics and research*. New York: Harper-Collins.

Kerlinger, F. N. (1986). *Foundations of behavioral research* (3rd ed.). Fort Worth, TX: Holt, Rinehart & Winston.

Sampling Strategies and Power Analysis

David L. Passmore and Rose M. Baker,
The Pennsylvania State University

CHAPTER OUTLINE

Sampling in research is a tightrope act that requires a fine balance between information and its costs. Information from a complete enumeration of a population seems desirable. For example, managers might require feedback to improve the quality of a trust-building workshop from all 10,000 of the company's workshop participants. Yet, each piece of information collected, organized, analyzed, and reported exacts costs. The available budget might support obtaining feedback only from far fewer than all workshop participants. Sampling—selection of *some* elements from a population containing *all* elements—helps obtain information within budget. Using a sampling strategy, perhaps managers can afford to obtain feedback about workshop improvement from a sample of 300 of the population of 10,000 participants.

Sampling can contain costs for obtaining information, but often at the expense of the quality of the information obtained. Information about the entire population inferred from the sample contains error because a sample does not contain all members of a population. Consider estimating the feedback of all 10,000 participants in the trust-building workshop gained from the survey responses of 300 sampled participants. One survey item could apply a Likert-type format (with, let's say, "strongly agree" to "strong disagree" scale points) to obtain respondents' agreement with the statement "I enjoyed the workshop exercise that required each participant to handle live snakes." Suppose that the most common response to this item by sampled workshop participants is "disagree." Does this mean that all 10,000 participants would respond most commonly with "disagree"? Not necessarily. Differences could exist between the responses of the particular sample of 300 workshop participants and all 10,000 company participants because the sample does not contain every member of the population.

One way to improve the quality (i.e., reduce the error) of the estimate of all 10,000 workshop participants' response to the "live snakes" statement is to increase the number of workshop participants sampled beyond 300. However, a larger sample size increases costs. Just how much accuracy in estimating all workshop participants' reactions to handling live snakes can the company afford? This trade-off between information and costs is the balance on which sampling decisions teeter in research in organizations.

In this chapter, we review briefly sampling theory and methods applicable to research in organizations to answer the practical question "How can I select a sample to produce the information I need for decision making?" A related question asks, "How large must my sample be to obtain the information I need accurately enough to make decisions?" This related question falls under the technical topic in statistics called *power analysis*.

We provide, first, an overview of terminology used in sampling and power analysis. Next, we consider sampling strategies that researchers in organizations could apply. Then, we consider practical recommendations for power analysis. Although these topics are quite technical, our approach is to provide a largely nontechnical discussion of sampling and power concepts, methods, and issues.

FUNDAMENTAL TERMINOLOGY

The acquisition of technical vocabulary is part of mastering methods useful in research on organizations. Technical jargon is efficient and useful because it allows rapid and precise communication with other researchers.

Population/Sample

Formally, a *population* is "any collection of objects or entities that have at least one common characteristic" (Jaeger, 1990, p. 138). We generally think of people as comprising populations, but populations of, for example, books, houses, work units, teams, quality circles, or products are identified easily, too. Researchers typically do not have access to data about entire populations, except in rare circumstances. However, most researchers want to generalize their research findings beyond the focus of their studies to the entire population of interest, which includes generalization to other people, places, and times.

Researchers ordinarily do not have access to data about entire populations because resources are limited. Instead, *samples* from populations are selected. According to Jaeger (1990), "A sample is . . . just a part of a population" (p. 139). The special case in which a sample that includes the entire population is called a census. A variety of sampling strategies are possible to select a sample that represents a population well and stays within budget.

Parameter/Statistic

A *parameter* is a characteristic of a population. For example, the average number of protégés guided by all mentors assigned in an organization is a parameter. A *statistic*, on the other hand, is a characteristic of a sample. The average number of protégés guided calculated from a sample of 10% of all mentors assigned in an organization is a statistic. Samples from populations offer several potential advantages over a complete enumeration of all sample members: greater economy, shorter time lags between conduct and reports of research, and higher quality of work by virtue of spending available resources only on obtaining data from a sample.

We often speak of *population parameters* and *sample statistics*. Exact calculation of population parameters is possible because information about all members of a population is known. A population parameter is what it is. It is a constant, not a variable—no guesswork required. However, we describe sample statistics as *estimating* population parameters because information only about some members of a population is known. We must *infer* population parameters from sample statistics.

Error in Estimation

Statistics are based on information from samples, not from populations about which most analysts actually are interested. Therefore, inferring population parameters from sample statistics usually involves some degree of error. For instance, error of inference certainly is made by using the responses to a 360° feedback questionnaire from a sample of 5% of all employees in an organization to estimate the level of job satisfaction among all employees. Only some employees are used to represent all employees. There undoubtedly is error in inferring the job satisfaction of all employees from just some employees.

Error in estimation of population parameters from sample statistics always will exist. The practical analyst knows that there is no way to eliminate error in estimation. At best, error in estimation is kept to a minimum. The question, though, is, How much error is tolerable and affordable in the decision processes that the data collected are meant to serve?

Decision Processes

Estimation

At times, an analyst might wish to estimate some value of a population parameter using data from a sample of population members. For instance, a planner of organizational development outreach programs might wish to estimate the proportion of employees who will register for a diabetes management seminar. The planner desires a *point estimate* of the population proportion (a parameter) based on a sample of employees to decide whether to invest resources design, develop, implement, and evaluate the seminar.

The program planner obtains a point estimate of the population proportion. However, the point estimate is calculated from a subset of the population, not the entire population. Therefore, there is error in estimation of the population proportion. The planner needs to know how precise the estimate is.

The planner can calculate an *interval estimate* of the population parameter. First, the planner might obtain a point estimate from a sample of surveyed employees that 7% of employees would register for a diabetes management program. Then, the planner could calculate a *confidence interval* indicating a range of values within which the population parameter might reside.

The planner might calculate a confidence interval from the data showing that she is 95% confident that the population parameter is between 4% and 10%. This interval means that the planner is 95% confident that the population parameter actually is between 4% and 10%. The *lower confidence limit* is 4%, and the *upper confidence limit* is 10%. In other words, the proportion of employees who will register for the diabetes management program is 7% ± 3%. If asked, the planner could say that her best guess based on the data is the 7% of employees would register for the seminar but add that she was pretty sure that the figure is between 4% and 10%.

Decision makers might not find that interval between 4% and 10% tight enough because they believe, based on financial models, that the break-even point course enrollment is 6% of employees. They want to be sure. The chance that the true population parameter might be lower than 6% adds uncertainty to the decision to continue with seminar planning.

The decision makers might require a more precise estimate about the level of interest in the diabetes management seminar. One way to generate a more precise estimate—that is, to reduce the width of the confidence interval—is to sample additional workers. Of course, the need for reducing risks of making decisions by adding more employees to the same needs to be balanced by the added costs of increasing the sample size. Everything has its price.

Hypothesis Testing

Another approach to decision making with data sampled from populations is through *hypothesis testing*. A *hypothesis* is a proposition. For example, the researcher might hypothesize that an organization's diversity training reduces tort liability for employment discrimination. The researcher sets up a *null hypothesis* that asserts that completing diversity training is no better than doing without diversity training.

The researcher collects data about employees who have completed diversity training and those who have not. Deciding how the employees are assigned to receive the training or not to receive it requires special knowledge and skills in research design to ensure that a fair comparison is made. Then, the organization's legal records are followed to determine the incidence, consequence, and losses from discrimination cases associated with each trainee.

The data are analyzed to attempt to reject the null hypothesis of no effect of diversity training on tort liability. If the null hypothesis is rejected, an *alternative hypothesis* is accepted to conclude that tort liability differs between people who have and have not received diversity training. Failure to reject the null hypothesis means that tort liability is the same, no matter whether the employee received diversity training.

The organization cannot afford to conduct research to determine the efficacy of diversity training for reducing tort liability with data from all employees. In response, the researcher selects a sample of employees for the research. As a result, data about tort liability among research participants are sample statistics and do not represent population parameters. Calculating the simple difference in point estimates of tort liability between employees with and without diversity training would show the effects of diversity training. However, such an approach would fail to account for the error in estimating these point estimates. A formal statistical test would provide the rigor for deciding whether to reject the null hypothesis of no effect of diversity training and to accept the alternative hypothesis that employees with and without diversity training differ in tort liability. Such formal statistical tests take into account the error in estimating population parameters from sample statistics. However, the best way to reduce the decision error in hypothesis testing is to increase the size of the sample of employees used in the study so that error in estimating population parameters is minimized.

SAMPLING STRATEGIES

The roles of sampling strategies and power analysis are to obtain estimates of population parameters from sample statistics that are as accurate as necessary for decision making, while remaining within budget constraints placed on available resources. In this section, we describe simple sampling strategies that are common in organizational contexts. We stick with discussion of sampling strategies already evident in the published literature under the twin assumptions that (1) these strategies are a good fit with practical research in organizations and (2) researchers should consider benefits and limitations of strategies that are in so much favor in the literature.

Note that sampling involves financial risks and opportunities, too. The costs of research can rise when researchers fail to implement optimal sampling strategies. If sampling strategies are suboptimal, more members of a population are included in research than are really required to answer research questions competently, adding to the direct costs of carrying out research and potentially exposing more members of the population to lost work time, foregone productivity, or other risks of allocating their time and effort to research. Or, selection of too few sample members means that more noise than information influences the decisions made from data, thus making the entire effort nothing more than a useless pantomime of research.

Sampling strategies are highly technical matters. More prescriptive, detailed, and technical sampling approaches than we review in this chapter are provided by Cochran (1977); Kalton (1983); Kish (1995); Levy and Lemeshow (1999); Lohr (1998); and Schaeffer, Mendenhall, and Ott (1986). Seek the advice of a professional statistician if the stakes associated with a study are high—that is, if high costs will accompany decisions based on the research outcomes, or if risks to research participants, individuals as well as organizations, are high.

Dooley and Lindner (2003, Table 1) observed that 51% of 158 articles appearing in *Human Resource Development Quarterly* between 1990 and 1999 used some form of sampling strategy. None of these sampling strategies was highly complex. Over 80% of the 81 empirical articles appearing in print during this period applied one of three simple sampling strategies: convenience sampling (37%), purposive sampling (30.9%), and some form of simple random sampling (17.2%). Cluster sampling and stratified sampling were applied in fewer empirical articles (6.2%) than complete censuses of populations (7.4%). One of the 81 articles failed to report a sampling strategy at all. Certainly, the choice of sampling strategies was limited during the period covered by the decade of published work that Dooley and Lindner reviewed.

Convenience Sampling

Convenience sampling involves the selection of sample members based on easy availability or accessibility. For example, an analyst might go to the organization's cafeteria and select employees to interview about reaction to a benefits and compensation package just because the cafeteria is a short walk down the hall from the analyst's office. Such a sampling plan almost guarantees that the cafeteria sample selected will not represent the population of employees. Perhaps administrative and executive employees never use the cafeteria. Perhaps employees with the most interest, greatest knowledge, and strongest opinions about the organization's benefits and compensation package never leave their desks during the working day to sit in the cafeteria.

Information obtained from a convenience sample could still provide some fairly significant insights, and even could represent a useful source of data in exploratory research. However, the major disadvantage of this technique is that we have no idea how representative the information collected about the sample is about the population as a whole. It is interesting that convenience sampling, a sampling strategy with perhaps the least usefulness for generalizability of findings, was the most common sampling method in the empirical articles in *Human Resource Development Quarterly* reviewed by Dooley and Lindner (2003).

Perhaps the best-known example how a convenience sample can lead to biased findings is provided by the 1936 *Literary Digest* poll (Bryson, 1976). The 1936 U.S. presidential election pitted Alf Landon (a Republican) against Franklin D. Roosevelt (a Democrat). The *Literary Digest*, a popular periodical, sent out 10 million ballots to subscribers, people in the phone book, people based on auto registry records, and people listed in voter registration records. The *Literary Digest* sent so many ballots out under the assumption that more data are better data (by way of comparison, a modern Gallup poll samples about 1,000 people).

The return rate for the *Literary Digest* ballots was 23% (quite high for a volunteer survey), meaning 2.3 million ballots were returned. For reference, the U.S. Census counted 123 million Americans in 1930 and 132 million in 1940. The poll predicted Roosevelt would get 43% of the vote. However, Roosevelt won by a landslide, getting 62% of the vote.

Why was the *Literary Digest* poll so wrong? The sample selected was a sample of convenience, and the sample was not representative of the target population (American adults). In short, their sample overrepresented wealthier Americans (people with phones and cars) who, even then, tended to be Republicans.

Purposive Sampling

Purposive sampling targets a particular group of sample members. When the desired population for the study is rare or very difficult to locate and recruit for a study, purposive sampling may be the only option. Patton (1990) identifies the following types of purposive sampling, especially in the context of qualitative research designs:

- *Extreme or deviant case*—learning from highly unusual manifestations of the phenomenon of interest, such as outstanding success/notable failures, top of the class/dropouts, exotic events, crises, and so forth

- *Intensity*—studying information-rich cases that manifest the phenomenon intensely, but not extremely, such as good students/poor students and above average/below average

- *Maximum variation*—purposefully picking a wide range of variation on dimensions of interest; documents unique or diverse variations that have emerged in adapting to different conditions; identifies important common patterns that cut across variations

- *Homogeneous*—focusing, reducing variation, simplifying analysis, and facilitating group interviewing

- *Typical case*—illustrating or highlighting what is typical, normal, or average

- *Critical case*—permitting logical generalization and maximum application of information to other cases because if a phenomenon is true of one case, it is likely to be true of all other cases

- *Snowball or chain*—identifying cases of interest from people who know people who know people who know what cases are information-rich—that is, good examples for study or good interview subjects

- *Criterion*—picking all cases that meet some criterion, such as all children abused in a treatment facility

- *Theory-based or operational construct*—finding manifestations of a theoretical construct of interest so as to elaborate and examine the construct

- *Confirming or disconfirming*—elaborating and deepening initial analysis, seeking exceptions, and testing variation

- *Opportunistic*—following new leads during fieldwork, taking advantage of the unexpected, and demonstrating flexibility

- *Politically important cases*—attempting to select prominent cases that will resonate with political leaders who must make or ratify decisions. Of course, sample members could be *not* selected based on their political importance, thus avoiding attracting undesired attention.

Purposive sampling can be an obvious source of bias. Unscrupulous groups or individuals may wish to make a particular point and may choose their sample with this purpose in mind. Yet, if a researcher requires information from particular groups (e.g., only broadband network users in the organization), the purposive sampling has, well, a purpose.

Simple Random Sampling

Under a simple random sampling strategy, "Each member of a population has an equal chance of being selected for a sample. Also, the chance that any member of the population is sampled doesn't depend at all on what other members of the population have been or will be sampled" (Jaeger, 1990, p. 143).

Drawing a random sample is not the same as selecting sample members from a population in a haphazard, arbitrary fashion. The process for selecting a random sample is simple, but requires the use of a random number table. Scheaffer et al. (1986, p. 43) provide a full description of the random sampling process. A random number table is a set of integers generated so that in the long run the table will contain all 10 integers {0, 1, 2, . . . 9} in approximately equal proportions with no trends in the pattern in which the digits were generated (see, e.g., Beyer, 1968). Choosing the numbers is analogous to drawing a number out of a hat.

Selection of a random sample does not necessarily guarantee that the sample represents the characteristics of the population faithfully. Consider, for example, a population defined as all employees in a firm, 43% of whom are women. A random sample of employees probably will not yield 43% women. Rather, random sampling merely ensures that no systematic process was used to sample from a population.

Cluster Sampling

A *cluster sample* is a random sample in which members of the population sampled are embedded in a collection—that is, a cluster—of elements. For instance, instead of sampling employees, a researcher might sample work teams, which are composed of employees. A questionnaire could be sent to a work team instead of sent to individuals within work teams, which reduces the resources required. In many cases, cluster sampling is the only feasible sampling strategy when individual members of the population are not available. Cluster sampling typically is used when researchers cannot get a complete list of the members of a population they wish to study but can get a complete list of groups or clusters of the population.

Stratified Sampling

A stratified sample is obtained by dividing the population into nonoverlapping groups called *strata* and then selecting a sample (usually a random sample) from within strata. For instance, a study of job satisfaction might sample within strata such as administrative workers and technical workers. Stratified sampling techniques generally are used when the population is heterogeneous, or dissimilar, where certain homogeneous, or similar, subpopulations can be isolated (strata). Stratification is useful when it is necessary to obtain a sample that is representative of the population (e.g., when the same proportion by sex, race, or national origin is desirable in the sample as in the population).

Census

A *census* is a sample of 100% of the population. It is enticing to believe that higher-quality findings are obtained from a complete enumeration of a population than from a sample. Yet, limited resources must be distributed more thinly over collection, organization, and analysis of data from a full census than data from a survey.

According to Hansen and Pritzker (1956), the Current Population Survey (CPS) (a household sample survey) produced in April 1950 a more accurate count of the labor force in the United States than did the full census of the population, which occurred also in April 1950. The CPS observed 2.5 million more persons in the labor force, and 0.5 million more people unemployed, than did the census. Interviewers for the census were just not as well trained as those for the CPS. They had more difficulty identifying and securing the participation of marginal labor force groups than did experienced CPS interviewers. They also were more unfamiliar than experienced CPS interviewers with collecting data about occupation, industry, work status, income, and education. These considerations, as well as those of economies and timeliness of results, led to the adoption in the 1960 U.S. Census of a 25% sample of households to increase the quality of information gathered. So, a census of the population sometimes is not as accurate as a sample from a population.

POWER ANALYSIS

Statistical power is the ability to reject a null hypothesis when it truly is false. Failure to reject the null hypothesis when it actually is false is called *Type II error* in statistics. Power is maximized and Type II error is minimized directly by increasing the size of the sample selected. However, a sample that is larger than is needed merely wastes resources. Just how large should a sample be? The answer is, large enough to reduce the error in estimating population parameters to acceptable levels.

Consider, again, an organization interested in determining if a diversity training program really is effective in reducing tort liability compared with no program at all. The analytic aim is to minimize the error in estimating the difference between liability experienced by employees with and those without diversity training so that the difference we estimate is larger than the error in estimating the difference that has practical importance.

For instance, suppose that decision makers need to discern tort liability differences of $5 million between employees with and without diversity training before the diversity training can be assessed to break-even financially. The power of the statistical test of the null hypothesis of no difference between groups with and without diversity would need to be sufficient to discern this $5 million difference. Kraemer and Thiemann (1987, p. 24) describe as the *critical effect size* the difference in tort liability that, in this case, is important enough for deciding that diversity training is effective. They also provide (pp. 105–112) a master table displaying the sample size needed to discriminate various critical effect sizes. This master table is adaptable to a variety of specific statistical tests of hypotheses.

CONCLUSION

Selecting the right kind and size of a sample from a population is an important scientific and financial decision in the design of research. Sampling strategies common in literature include convenience sampling, purposive sampling, simple random sampling, cluster sampling, stratified sampling, and a 100% census of all members of a population. Each strategy offers advantages and disadvantages. However, the most problematic sampling strategy (i.e., convenience sampling) is most common in literature in research on organizations. On one hand, a sample must be large enough to estimate population parameters precisely enough to allow decisions to be made based on data. On the other hand, a sample that is too large wastes resources. Fortunately, a simple table is available to allow calculation of a sample size that optimizes decision making.

REFERENCES

Beyer, W. H. (Ed.). (1968). *Handbook on tables for probability and statistics.* Boca Raton, FL: CRC Press.

Bryson, M. C. (1976). The *Literary Digest* poll: Making of a statistical myth. *American Statistician, 30*(4), 184–185.

Cochran, W. (1977). *Sampling techniques* (3rd ed.). New York: Wiley.

Dooley, L. M., & Lindner, J. R. (2003). The handling of nonresponse error. *Human Resource Development Quarterly, 14*(1), 99–110.

Hansen, M. H., & Pritzker, L. (1956, May). *The post-enumeration survey of the 1950 Census of the Population: Some results, evaluation, and implications.* Paper presented at the Annual Meeting of the Population Association of America, Ann Arbor, Michigan.

Jaeger, R. (1990). *Statistics: A spectator sport* (2nd ed.). Newbury Park, CA: Sage.

Kalton, G. (1983). *Introduction to survey sampling.* Newbury Park, CA: Sage.

Kish, L. (1995). *Survey sampling.* New York: Wiley.

Kraemer, H. C., & Thiemann, S. (1987). *How many subjects? Statistical power analysis in research.* Newbury Park, CA: Sage.

Levy, P. S., & Lemeshow, S. (1999). *Sampling of populations: Methods and applications* (3rd ed.). New York: Wiley.

Lohr, S. (1998). *Sampling: Design and analysis.* Pacific Grove, CA: Duxbury.

Patton, M. Q. (1990). *Qualitative evaluation and research methods* (2nd ed.). Newbury Park, CA: Sage.

Scheaffer, R. L., Mendenhall, W., & Ott, L. (1986). *Elementary survey sampling* (3rd ed.). Boston: PWS Publishers.

Effect Sizes versus Statistical Significance

Bruce Thompson, *Texas A&M University and Baylor College of Medicine (Houston)*

CHAPTER OUTLINE

Statistical significance tests can be traced back to applications more than three centuries ago (Huberty, 1999). Work in the early 1900s, including Gossett's development of the *t*-test, Pearson's formulation of the product-moment correlation, and the later elaboration of ANOVA by Sir Ronald Fisher and others, all facilitated the use of this logic. However, the uptake of statistical significance actually occurred primarily beginning in the 1950s (Hubbard & Ryan, 2000).

Criticisms of statistical significance testing arose almost as soon as the applications themselves (cf. Boring, 1919). However, in recent years the frequency of published criticisms has grown exponentially, and these indictments have been published in fields as diverse as economics, education, psychology, and wildlife science (cf. Altman, 2004; Anderson, Burnham, & Thompson, 2000).

This chapter has three purposes. First, some of the criticisms leveled against statistical testing are briefly summarized. Second, effect sizes as a supplement or an alternative to statistical tests are explained. Third, uses of confidence intervals, and especially confidence intervals for effect sizes, are presented.

Although both statistical (i.e., *p* values) and practical significance (i.e., effect sizes) are considered here, a third type of significance—clinical significance—does not fall within the scope of the present treatment. For explanations of statistics associated with clinical significance, the interested reader is referred to Kendall (1999) or Thompson (2002a).

STATISTICAL SIGNIFICANCE TESTS

Among the most widely cited critiques of statistical testing are the commentaries of Carver (1978), Cohen (1994), Schmidt (1996), and Thompson (1996). Harlow, Mulaik, and Steiger (1997) provide a balanced and comprehensive treatment of these arguments in their book *What If There Were No Significance Tests?*

Some critics have even argued that statistical significance tests should be banned from journals. According to Schmidt and Hunter (1997), for example, "statistical significance testing retards the growth of scientific knowledge; it *never* makes a positive contribution" (p. 37, emphasis added). Rozeboom (1997) is equally empathic: "Null-hypothesis significance testing is surely the most boneheadedly misguided procedure ever institutionalized in the rote training of science students. . . . [I]t is a sociology-of-science wonderment that this statistical practice has remained so unresponsive to criticism" (p. 335).

Empirical studies also suggest that researchers think they understand statistical significance tests but actually do not correctly understand them (Mittag & Thompson, 2000; Nelson, Rosenthal, & Rosnow, 1986; Oakes, 1986; Rosenthal & Gaito, 1963; Zuckerman, Hodgins, Zuckerman, & Rosenthal, 1993). Consequently, Tryon (1998) laments:

> The fact that statistical experts and investigators publishing in the best journals cannot consistently interpret the results of these analyses is extremely disturbing. Seventy-two years of education have resulted in minuscule, if any, progress toward correcting this situation. It is difficult to estimate the

handicap that widespread, incorrect, and intractable use of a primary data analytic method has on a scientific discipline, but the deleterious effects are doubtless substantial. (p. 796)

Three misconceptions regarding statistical significance tests are summarized here. First, statistical significance tests do *not* evaluate the probability of sample results occurring in the population, and thus do *not* evaluate result replicability. Statistical significance assumes that the null hypothesis exactly describes the population, and given that premise, evaluates the probability of sample statistics deriving from this presumed population, given the sample size (Thompson, 1996). In other words, statistical tests evaluate the probability of the sample (S), given the assumed population (P; i.e., $p_{S|P}$), and *not* the probability of the population, given the sample (i.e., *not* $p_{P|S}$) (Cohen, 1994).

It is one thing to say (correctly) that all men (M) are animals (A; i.e., $p_{A|M} =$ 100%). It is a different (and an incorrect) argument to suggest that all animals are men (i.e., $p_{M|A} \neq 100\%$).

The fact that the statistical significance p is *not* $p_{P|S}$ is unfortunate, because if p values were about the probability of the population, then p values would inform judgment regarding replicability of results in other samples drawn from the same population. But wishing does not change reality, except for those researchers who are genies or leprechauns. Of course, as Cohen (1994) notes, the statistical significance test "does not tell us what we want to know, and we so much want to know what we want to know that, out of desperation, we nevertheless believe that it does!" (p. 997).

Second, statistical significance tests are *not* independent of sample sizes, and so p values *cannot* reasonably be used as inverse indices of practical significance. The calculated p values in a given study are confounded by the joint influences of the sample size and the specific statistics computed for the sample.

As I have explained (Thompson, 1999), "Because p values are confounded indices, in theory 100 studies with varying sample sizes and 100 different effect sizes could each have the same single $p_{\text{CALCULATED}}$, and 100 studies with the same single effect size could each have 100 different values for $p_{\text{CALCULATED}}$" (pp. 169–170). The implication is that

> statistical significance testing can involve a tautological logic in which tired researchers, having collected data from hundreds of subjects, then conduct a statistical test to evaluate whether there were a lot of subjects, which the researchers already know, because they collected the data and know they're tired. This tautology has created considerable damage as regards the cumulation of knowledge. (Thompson, 1992, p. 436)

Third, statistical significance tests do *not* inform judgment regarding the value of results. A valid deductive argument may not contain any information in its conclusions that is not present in its premises, and so "If the computer package did not ask you your values prior to its analysis, it could not have considered your value system in calculating p's, and so p's cannot be blithely used to infer the value of research results" (Thompson, 1993, p. 365).

Improbable events are *not* intrinsically valuable. If you flip a coin, and it lands on its edge, this result may be quite unusual. But it is not necessarily earth-shaking. Such a result is merely rare! The divergence between rareness and value is illustrated in Shaver's (1985) classic dialogue between two hypothetical doctoral students:

> CHRIS: I set the level of significance at .05, as my advisor suggested. So a difference that large would occur by chance less than five times in a hundred if the groups weren't really different. An unlikely occurrence like that *surely* must be important.
>
> JEAN: Wait a minute, Chris. Remember the other day when you went into the office to call home? Just as you completed dialing the number, your little boy picked up the phone to call someone. So you were connected and talking to one another without the phone ever ringing. . . . Well, that must have been a truly important occurrence then? (p. 58)

EFFECT SIZES

Effect sizes quantify the degree to which sample statistics diverge from the expectations specified in the null hypothesis (see Thompson, 2002a). For example, if the H_0 is that $Mdn_{\text{left-handed people}} = Mdn_{\text{right-handed people}} = Mdn_{\text{ambidextrous people}}$, and the three sample medians are 100, 100, and 100, the effect size is 0. If the H_0 is that $SD_{\text{freshmen}} = SD_{\text{sophomores}} = SD_{\text{juniors}} = SD_{\text{seniors}}$, and the four sample standard deviations are 10, 10, 10, and 10, the effect size is 0. If the null hypothesis is that $R^2 = 0$, and the sample R^2 is indeed 0, so is the effect size.

Conversely, if the null hypothesis is that the IQ score coefficient of skewness of males equals the IQ score coefficient of skewness of females, and the sample coefficients are .75 and .80, the effect size is *not* 0. And the effect size would be even bigger if the two sample coefficients were .70 and .85, and bigger still (all things equal) if the sample coefficients were .25 and 1.25.

Like statistical significance tests, effect sizes are not new (Huberty, 2002). And there are literally dozens of effect sizes that can be used to quantify how much sample results diverge from the null hypothesis (Kirk, 1996). Useful summaries have been provided by Snyder and Lawson (1993) and Rosenthal (1994), among others.

Three Major Types of Effect Sizes

Here we will consider only some of the most commonly used effect sizes: Glass's Δ; Cohen's d, η^2, and R^2; and ω^2 and adjusted R^2. To make the discussion con-

TABLE 5.1   Heuristic Outcome Data for Hypothetical Two-Group Intervention

	CONTROL		INTERVENTION	
Particpant	*Outcome*		*Particpant*	*Outcome*
Molly	44		Anne	48
Nancy	46		Susan	49
Geri	48		Amy	50
Murray	48		Donna	51
Jan	50		Barbara	53
Peggy	52		Kathy	55
Carol	52		Deborah	56
Eileen	54		Wendy	57
Dianne	56		Kelly	58
Mean	50.000			53.000
SD	3.651			3.464
Variance	13.333			12.000

crete, let us presume that a researcher randomly selected 18 workers in the hypothetical Hawthorne Lightbulb Plant in Cicero, Illinois. Perhaps the researcher was focusing on job satisfaction as an outcome variable.

If the researcher had empirical evidence that job satisfaction dynamics were gender related, to avoid confounds the investigator might limit the study to women. In our example, following random selection, the 18 hypothetical women were randomly assigned to one of two treatment groups: an intervention group where workers enjoyed higher pay, shorter hours, and a more pleasant physical work environment, or a control group.

The outcome variable was measured with the Hypothetical Job Satisfaction Survey (HJSS). Table 5.1 presents the postintervention outcome variable scores for these 18 hypothetical workers. These same data will be employed to illustrate effect sizes falling within three major types.

Standardized Differences

In a two-group experiment, an appealing effect size statistic is simply to subtract a central tendency estimate (e.g., mean, median) for the control group from the same estimate for the intervention group. For example, for the Table 5.1 data, the mean difference in the two posttest scores is 3.00 ($M_{EXPERIMENTAL} - M_{CONTROL} = 53.00 - 50.00$).

However, one potential problem with this *unstandardized* difference effect size is that the import of a difference of 3.00 in the two means is partly a function of the metric of the outcome variable itself. If we are measuring an outcome involving body temperature measured in Fahrenheit, such a difference would be quite large. But if we were measuring on the GRE or SAT scale, such a difference might be barely noticed. Thus, the standard deviations of the outcome variable must be considered when evaluating mean (or median) differences.

Researchers in some disciplines, such as medicine, often work with measures having intrinsically meaningful metrics (e.g., deaths per thousand in the new-drug group vs. the placebo group). For example, every medical researcher throughout the world studying cholesterol will measure cholesterol as milligrams per deciliter. Because all these researchers are working with a single common metric, and that metric is meaningful (i.e., deaths per thousand, milligrams per deciliter), comparisons of outcomes across their studies are apples-to-apples, and such researchers would not even consider expressing their effects in some other, unnatural metric.

But outcome variables in the social sciences have *no* intrinsically meaningful metric. For example, some IQ tests have standard deviations of 15, whereas others have standard deviations of 16. Different measures of self-concept may have standard deviations of 10, of 15, of 100, respectively. These are arbitrary decisions made by various test developers, perhaps subject only to stylistic preferences for what may be their personal lucky numbers (so long as the lucky numbers are positive).

And the fact that different measures ostensibly of the same construct may have different metrics means that unstandardized differences from different studies using different measures cannot be compared apples-to-apples. Fortunately, this problem of incomparability of unstandardized effects across measures can be resolved by removing the measurement metrics from *all* the effect sizes, so that they then may be compared apples-to-apples.

In statistics, we execute division to remove from the answer the influences of whatever we are dividing by. For example, if we want to compare central tendency, or variability, or shape, or relationship statistics across groups of unequal sizes, we execute a division by some function of n (i.e., n or $n - 1$) in each group, and then we can compare these data dynamics apples-to-apples, having removed group sizes from the respective estimates.

We can do the same thing with effect sizes. If we want to compute mean differences with the measurement metrics removed, we estimate the *standardized* difference by dividing the unstandardized difference by some estimate of the population standard deviation ($\sigma_{\text{POPULATION}}$):

Standardized Difference $= (M_{\text{EXPERIMENTAL}} - M_{\text{CONTROL}})/\sigma_{\text{POPULATION}}$.

The only difficulty is that there are several reasonable estimates of $\sigma_{\text{POPULATION}}$, only two of which will be considered here.

First, Glass (1976) proposed that we could estimate the standardized difference by using the standard deviation of the outcome scores of only the control group participants:

$$\Delta = (M_{\text{EXPERIMENTAL}} - M_{\text{CONTROL}})/SD_{\text{CONTROL}}.$$

For the Table 5.1 data, this yields

$$\Delta = (53.00 - 50.00)/3.65 = 3.00/3.65 = 0.82.$$

Glass reasoned that an intervention might impact both (1) the central tendency of the outcome scores and (2) their spread-out-ness. Logically, then, SD_{CONTROL} might be taken as the best estimate of $\sigma_{\text{POPULATION}}$, because the spread-out-ness of the outcome scores in the control group could not have been impacted by the intervention.

Second, Cohen (1969) takes the position that not all interventions might be expected to impact the spread of the outcome variable scores. Furthermore, because $n_{\text{Total}} = n_{\text{EXPERIMENTAL}} + n_{\text{CONTROL}} > n_{\text{CONTROL}}$, logically in such cases the estimated standard deviation based on both groups should yield a more precise estimate of $\sigma_{\text{POPULATION}}$.

A pooled variance is estimated as

$$\sigma^2 = [(n_E - 1)SD_E + (n_C - 1)SD_C]/(n_E + n_C - 2).$$

For the Table 5.2 data,

$$\sigma^2 - [(9 - 1)13.33 + (9 - 1)12.00]/(9 + 9 - 2);$$
$$\sigma^2 = [(8)13.33 + (8)12.00]/(9 + 9 - 2);$$
$$\sigma^2 = (106.67 + 96.00)/(9 + 9 - 2);$$
$$\sigma^2 = 202.67/(9 + 9 - 2);$$
$$\sigma^2 = 202.67/16;$$
$$\sigma^2 = 12.67.$$

When group sizes are equal, the σ^2 estimate can be computed more easily as $(13.33 + 12.00)/2 = 12.67$.

The associated σ would equal the square root of the estimated variance: $\sigma = \text{SQRT}(\sigma^2) = \text{SQRT}(12.67) = 3.56$. Using this estimated SD_{POOLED},

$$d = (M_{\text{EXPERIMENTAL}} - M_{\text{CONTROL}})/SD_{\text{POOLED}};$$
$$d = (53.00 - 50.00)/3.56;$$
$$d = 3.00/3.56;$$
$$d = 0.84.$$

The computational differences in Glass's Δ and Cohen's d are heuristically valuable, because the choices make clear that in the case of effect sizes, as elsewhere in statistics, often there are not universally correct choices. If the control group sample size is large, and the intervention is likely to impact outcome score spread-out-ness, then $\sigma_{\text{POPULATION}}$ will be estimated reasonably by Δ. However, if control group size is small, and the intervention is unlikely to impact outcome score spread-out-ness, then d might be the more reasonable estimate.

There are *not* bright-line boundaries that clearly distinguish definitively correct choices from each other. As Huberty and Morris (1966, p. 573) once noted, "As in all statistical inference, subjective judgment cannot be avoided. Neither can reasonableness!"

Variance Accounted For

As explained in detail elsewhere (e.g., Thompson, 1984, 1991, 2000), *all* commonly used parametric analyses (e.g., *t*-tests, ANOVA, ANCOVA, regression, MANOVA, MANCOVA, descriptive discriminant analysis, and canonical correlation analysis) are correlational. Therefore, effect sizes analogous to r^2 can be computed in *all* these cases, whether or not they are printed by the computer packages.

For example, Table 5.2 presents the ANOVA summary for the Table 5.1 data. In the present example, the sum of squares of the 18 outcome variables scores is 268.50. As reported in Table 5.2, if we know to which group each of the 18 workers belonged, we can explain 40.50 sum of squares.

Or, put differently, if we know to which group each of the 18 workers belonged, we can explain 15.08% (i.e., 40.50/268.50) of the variability in job satisfaction. This ANOVA effect size is called η^2, or the correlation ratio (*not* the correlation coefficient, which instead is in an unsquared metric!). Because the *p* values for an ANOVA or a *t*-test analysis of two-group data are identical, $\eta^2 = 15.08\%$ is also the related effect size for the *t*-test analysis of the Table 5.1 data.

Related variance-accounted-for effect sizes can be computed in other analyses. For example, if we have a single outcome variable with a sum of squares of 200.00, and three intervally scaled predictor variables yielding a sum of squares explained of 50.00, the R^2 is 25.00% (i.e., 50.00/200.00). This effect reflects the fact that if we know the scores of the participants on the three predictor variables, we could predict 25.0% of the variability of the participants' individual differences on the outcome (Courville & Thompson, 2001).

Similar variance-accounted-for effect sizes can be computed in multivariate analyses. For example, a multivariate η^2 can be computed by subtracting Wilks's lambda (λ) from 1.0. Thus, if two outcome variables had been measured in the Table 5.1 example, and lambda was 0.80, multivariate η^2 would be 20.00%. This

TABLE 5.2 ANOVA Summary Table

SOURCE	df	SUM OF SQUARES	MEAN SQUARES	F RATIO	P	η^2
Between	1	40.50	40.50	2.84	.1112	15.08%
Within	16	228.00	14.25			
Total	17	268.50				

result would mean that if we know to which group each of the 18 workers belonged, we can explain 20.00% of the variability on the composite of the two outcome variables in the study.

Corrected Estimates

Whenever we estimate effect sizes in the population, or in future samples, using sample data, we tend to overestimate the effects in these other locations. This is because samples are like people, each sample has its own personality, and to some extent every sample is weird. The weirdness in a given sample arises from outlier influences and generates what statisticians call *sampling error variance.*

There is *more* sampling error variance when (1) sample size is small, (2) more variables are measured in the study, and (3) the population effect is smaller. These dynamics are explained in more detail in Thompson (2002b). Snyder and Lawson (1993) present several additional formulas for computing corrected effect estimates.

Because we know our sample size and the number of measured variables we are using, and we can estimate the population effect using the sample estimate, we can "adjust" or "correct" the sample effect size using these study features. The corrected estimate will always be less than or equal to the uncorrected estimate.

One such estimate for ANOVA results is ω^2 (Hays, 1981), which can be computed as

$$\omega^2 = [SOS_{BETWEEN} - (k-1)MS_{WITHIN}]/[SOS_Y + MS_{WITHIN}],$$

where k is the number of levels in the ANOVA way and MS is the mean square. For the Table 5.2 data, we obtain

$\omega^2 = [40.5 - (2-1)14.25]/(268.5 + 14.25);$

$\omega^2 = [40.5 - (2-1)14.25]/282.75;$

$\omega^2 = [40.5 - (1)14.25]/282.75;$

$\omega^2 = [40.5 - 14.25]/282.75;$

$\omega^2 = 26.25/282.75;$

$\omega^2 = 9.28\%.$

The "uncorrected" η^2 of 15.08% has "shrunken" to $\omega^2 = 9.28\%$, once we remove the estimated positive bias due to sampling error from the original estimate.

Ezekiel (1930) proposed a similar correction often used with r^2 and R^2. Monte Carlo simulation work also suggests that this correction may be applied to the squared canonical correlation coefficient (R_C^2; Thompson, 1990). This correction is automatically produced when the SPSS REGRESSION procedure is executed. The "corrected" or "adjusted" estimate can be computed as

$$1 - [(n-1)/(n-v-1)] (1-R^2),$$

where n is the sample size and v is the number of predictor variables. The formula can be equivalently expressed as

$$R^2 - \{(1 - R^2)\ [v/(n - v - 1)]\}.$$

Converting across Effect Size Types

It should be noted that standardized difference and variance-accounted-for effect sizes are in different metrics (one squared, one not), and so cannot be directly compared to each other. However, formulas exist to convert effects such as d into r (or η), or vice versa.

Cohen (1988, p. 24) has provided the following formula for deriving r from d when the groups of interest are of approximately the same size:

$$r = d/[(d^2 + 4)^{.5}].$$

For our heuristic data, we have

$$r = 0.843/[(0.843^2 + 4)^{.5}];$$
$$r = 0.843/[(0.710 + 4)^{.5}];$$
$$r = 0.843/4.710^{.5};$$
$$r = 0.843/2.170;$$
$$r = 0.3884.$$

To convert what in this case is actually η, because we are doing an ANOVA, $\eta^2 = 0.3884^2 = 15.08\%$. See Aaron, Kromrey, and Ferron (1998) for more detail on these conversions for cases when group sizes are disparate.

Conversely, Friedman (1968, p. 346) proposed the following formula to derive d from r:

$$d = [2\ (r)]/[(1 - r^2)^{.5}].$$

For our heuristic data, we have

$$d = [2(0.388)]/[(1 - 0.388^2)^{.5}];$$
$$d = [2(0.388)]/[(1 - 0.151)^{.5}];$$
$$d = [2(0.388)]/0.849^{.5}];$$
$$d = [2(0.388)]/0.921;$$
$$d = 0.777/0.921;$$
$$d = 0.843.$$

Interpreting Effect Sizes

The Task Force on Statistical Inference of the American Psychological Association (APA), appointed in 1996 to recommend whether statistical significance tests should be banned from APA journals, states, "*Always* provide some effect-size estimate when reporting a *p* value" (Wilkinson & APA Task Force, 1999, p. 599, emphasis added). The APA Task Force further emphasizes, "Reporting and interpreting effect sizes in the context of previously reported effects is *essential* to good research" (p. 599, emphasis added).

The 2001 APA *Publication Manual*, used by more than 1,000 social science journals, labels the "failure to report effect sizes" as a "defect in the design and reporting of research" (p. 5). Today, because such encouragements to report effects have had demonstrably limited impact (Vacha-Haase, Nilsson, Reetz, Lance, & Thompson, 2000), 23 journals (see Harris, 2003; Snyder, 2000) have gone further and now explicitly *require* the reporting of effect sizes.

Indeed, as Fidler (2002) recently observed, "Of the major American associations, only all the journals of the American Educational Research Association have remained silent on all these issues" (p. 754). How, then, should effect sizes be interpreted by applied researchers? Here four interpretation precepts are recommended.

First, interpret effect sizes by taking into consideration how well the assumptions of the statistical procedures in which effects were generated were met. Such assumptions are never met perfectly, and violations are a matter of degree. But effect sizes do not magically overcome the limitations of studies.

If a statistical analysis (e.g., ANOVA, regression, and descriptive discriminant analysis) requires certain assumptions, and these are grossly violated, *all* results are compromised, including effect sizes. However, it does appear that certain effect sizes may be more robust than others to the violations of statistical assumptions (Hess, Olejnik, & Huberty, 2001; Huberty & Holmes, 1983; Huberty & Lowman, 2000).

Second, effect sizes should be generalized only to similar interventions or situations (Olejnik & Algina, 2000). For example, in our hypothetical Hawthorne Lightbulb Factory intervention, the nine workers in the intervention group were given higher wages, shorter work weeks, and more pleasant working conditions. The intervention produced a positive impact on worker satisfaction ($d = 0.843$; $\eta^2 = 15.08\%$).

This effect does not mean that only giving workers a candy bar each day would result in similar gains. This is merely common sense, but too often in research common sense is honored more in the breach than in the practice.

Third, effect sizes should be interpreted by taking into score reliability for the data being analyzed. Measurement error attenuates effect sizes. A finding of *d* or η^2 equals zero is very different when Cronbach's $\alpha = .0$ (or $-.75$, or -7.50) than when $\alpha = .93$ (Thompson, 2003).

Remember that tests are *not* reliable; scores are reliable (Thompson & Vacha-Haase, 2000). Analyze and report the reliability of your own scores as part of interpretation (Wilkinson & APA Task Force, 1999). Such improvement would stand in stark contrast with contemporary practices. In their meta-meta-analysis of the measurement meta-analyses called "reliability generalization," Vacha-Haase,

Henson, and Caruso (2002) found that in the preponderance of articles, authors never even mention reliability!

Fourth, do *not* interpret effect sizes by invoking Cohen's benchmarks for "small," "medium," and "large" effects, except in the rare (possibly impossible) case where no related prior effects have been reported. Instead, interpret effect sizes "via *explicit, direct* comparison with the prior effect sizes in the related literature" (Thompson, 2002b, p. 28, emphasis added).

Cohen intended these benchmarks as general guidelines and did not seek their thoughtless application. As noted elsewhere, "If people interpreted effect sizes [using fixed benchmarks] with the same rigidity that $\alpha = .05$ has been used in statistical testing, we would merely be being stupid in another metric" (Thompson, 2001, pp. 82–83). Glass, McGaw, and Smith (1981) suggest, at least as regards relatively established areas of research, "there is no wisdom whatsoever in attempting to associate regions of the effect-size metric with descriptive adjectives such as 'small,' 'moderate,' 'large,' and the like" (p. 104).

Ask these two questions: (1) Given what I am studying, is the effect size noteworthy? and (2) Are the effect sizes comparable across related studies? Finding an η^2 of 2% for the effects of smoking on longevity, when all related studies consistently report roughly the same effect, may be very noteworthy (Gage, 1978, p. 21). Finding an η^2 of 50% in a study of smiling and touching behaviors of adolescents in fast-food restaurants may be less noteworthy if you are an adult not particularly interested in fast-food environs or the behaviors of teenagers who are strangers with each other, and especially if the effect sizes in related reports are highly variable.

Confidence Intervals for Effect Sizes

The 2001 APA *Publication Manual* suggests that confidence intervals (CIs) represent "in general, *the best* reporting strategy. The use of confidence intervals is therefore *strongly recommended*" (p. 22, emphasis added). However, empirical studies of journals show that confidence intervals are reported very infrequently (Finch, Cumming, & Thomason, 2001; Kieffer, Reese, & Thompson, 2001). In addition, "It is conceivable that some researchers may not fully understand statistical methods that they (a) rarely read in the literature and (b) infrequently use in their own work" (Thompson, 2002b, p. 26).

Researchers may wish to derive (1) statistics (e.g., M_X, Mdn_X, SD_X, r_{XY}, and R_C^2), (2) confidence intervals for statistics, (3) effect sizes (e.g., Δ, Cohen's d, η^2 and R^2, and ω^2 and adjusted R^2), and confidence intervals for effect sizes. Formulas may be used to obtain the first three sets of results, but not confidence intervals for effect sizes. Instead, specialized (but readily available) computer software (Algina & Keselman, 2003; Cumming & Finch, 2001; Smithson, 2001; Steiger & Fouladi, 1992) must be used to estimate confidence intervals for effect sizes.

Although confidence intervals for effect sizes have great appeal, space precludes full discussion of these applications. Thompson (2002b) presents an overview. The excellent new book by Kline (2004) provides more detail, in addition to further treatment of both the limits of statistical significance tests and effect size choices.

CONCLUSION

Not every aspect of effect sizes has been covered here. Hopefully, this brief summary has been sufficient to give the reader a glimmer of the possibilities of effect size interpretation and some considerable motivation for delving deeper.

As to the question of using statistical significance tests versus effect sizes, there are a range of views within the field.

- Some have argued that statistical significance tests are never helpful and should be banned (Carver, 1978; Schmidt, 1996).

- Some have argued that effect sizes should be reported, but only for statistically significant effects (Robinson & Levin, 1997).

- Some have argued that effect sizes should *always* be reported, regardless of whether effects are statistically significant (Thompson, 1996, 2002b; Wilkinson & APA Task Force, 1999).

Some may feel that the *status quo ante bellum* was acceptable and that only statistical tests should be reported (but it is difficult to name any exemplars of this view).

The protection against overinterpreting the serendipitous result in a single study does *not* arise by invoking p values. Instead, the best protection occurs when effect sizes in a given study are interpreted in the context of direct, explicit comparison with the effects in related prior studies.

A new day is dawning when it is becoming normatively expected for scholars to report and interpret one or more effect sizes for their research results. Such reporting will facilitate the "meta-analytic thinking" (Cumming & Finch, 2001; Thompson, 2002b) so important to sound academic inquiry. This view emphasizes the value of effect sizes across a related literature as a whole, and recognizes the inherent limits of the single study (Schmidt, 1996). We are past the point where the p values in a single study are accepted as reasonable warrants that the study's effects are either replicable or valuable!

REFERENCES

Aaron, B., Kromrey, J. D. & Ferron, J. M. (1998, November). *Equating r-based and d-based effect size indices: Problems with a commonly recommended formula.* Paper presented at the annual meeting of the Florida Educational Research Association, Orlando, FL. (ERIC Document Reproduction Service No. ED 433 353)

Algina, J., & Keselman, H. J. (2003). Approximate confidence intervals for effect sizes. *Educational and Psychological Measurement, 63*, 537–553.

Altman, M. (2004). Statistical significance, path dependency, and the culture of journal publication. *Journal of Socio-Economics, 33*.

American Psychological Association. (2001). *Publication manual of the American Psychological Association* (5th ed.). Washington, DC: Author.

Anderson, D. R., Burnham, K. P., & Thompson, W. (2000). Null hypothesis testing: Problems, prevalence, and an alternative. *Journal of Wildlife Management, 64*, 912–923.

Boring, E. G. (1919). Mathematical vs. scientific importance. *Psychological Bulletin, 16*, 335–338.

Carver, R. (1978). The case against statistical significance testing. *Harvard Educational Review, 48*, 378–399.

Cohen, J. (1969). *Statistical power analysis for the behavioral sciences.* New York: Academic Press.

Cohen, J. (1988). *Statistical power analysis for the behavioral sciences* (2nd ed.). Hillside, NJ: Erlbaum.

Cohen, J. (1994). The earth is round ($p < .05$). *American Psychologist, 49*, 997–1003.

Courville, T., & Thompson, B. (2001). Use of structure coefficients in published multiple regression articles: β is not enough. *Educational and Psychological Measurement, 61*, 229–248.

Cumming, G., & Finch, S. (2001). A primer on the understanding, use and calculation of confidence intervals that are based on central and noncentral distributions. *Educational and Psychological Measurement, 61*, 532–575.

Ezekiel, M. (1930). *Methods of correlational analysis.* New York: Wiley.

Fidler, F. (2002). The fifth edition of the APA *Publication Manual*: Why its statistics recommendations are so controversial. *Educational and Psychological Measurement, 62*, 749–770.

Finch, S., Cumming, G., & Thomason, N. (2001). Reporting of statistical inference in the *Journal of Applied Psychology*: Little evidence of reform. *Educational and Psychological Measurement, 61*, 181–210.

Friedman, H. (1968). Magnitude of experimental effect and a table for its rapid estimation. *Psychological Bulletin, 70*, 245–251.

Gage, N. L. (1978). *The scientific basis of the art of teaching.* New York: Teachers College Press.

Glass, G. V. (1976). Primary, secondary, and meta-analysis of research. *Educational Researcher, 5*(10), 3–8.

Glass, G. V., McGaw, B., & Smith, M. L. (1981). *Meta-analysis in social research.* Beverly Hills, CA: Sage.

Harlow, L. L., Mulaik, S. A., & Steiger, J. H. (Eds.). (1997). *What if there were no significance tests?* Mahwah, NJ: Erlbaum.

Harris, K. (2003). Instructions for authors, *Journal of Educational Psychology. Journal of Educational Psychology, 95*, 201.

Hays, W. L. (1981). *Statistics* (3rd ed.). New York: Holt, Rinehart & Winston.

Hess, B., Olejnik, S., & Huberty, C. J (2001). The efficacy of two improvement-over-chance effect sizes for two-group univariate comparisons under variance heterogeneity and nonnormality. *Educational and Psychological Measurement, 61*, 909–936.

Hubbard, R., & Ryan, P. A. (2000). The historical growth of statistical significance testing in psychology—and its future prospects. *Educational and Psychological Measurement, 60,* 661–681.

Huberty, C. J. (1999). On some history regarding statistical testing. In B. Thompson (Ed.), *Advances in social science methodology* (Vol. 5, pp. 1–23). Stamford, CT: JAI Press.

Huberty, C. J. (2002). A history of effect size indices. *Educational and Psychological Measurement, 62,* 227–240.

Huberty, C. J., & Holmes, S. E. (1983). Two-group comparisons and univariate classification. *Educational and Psychological Measurement, 43,* 15–26.

Huberty, C. J., & Lowman, L. L. (2000). Group overlap as a basis for effect size. *Educational and Psychological Measurement, 60,* 543–563.

Huberty, C. J., & Morris, J. D. (1988). A single contrast test procedure. *Educational and Psychological Measurement, 48,* 567–578.

Kendall, P. C. (1999). Clinical significance. *Journal of Consulting and Clinical Psychology, 67,* 283–284.

Kieffer, K. M., Reese, R. J., & Thompson, B. (2001). Statistical techniques employed in *AERJ* and *JCP* articles from 1988 to 1997: A methodological review. *Journal of Experimental Education, 69,* 280–309.

Kirk, R. E. (1996). Practical significance: A concept whose time has come. *Educational and Psychological Measurement, 56,* 746–759.

Kline, R. (2004). *Beyond significance testing: Reforming data analysis methods in behavioral research.* Washington, DC: American Psychological Association.

Mittag, K. C., & Thompson, B. (2000). A national survey of AERA members' perceptions of statistical significance tests and other statistical issues. *Educational Researcher, 29*(4), 14–20.

Nelson, N., Rosenthal, R., & Rosnow, R. L. (1986). Interpretation of significance levels and effect sizes by psychological researchers. *American Psychologist, 41,* 1299–1301.

Oakes, M. (1986). *Statistical inference: A commentary for the social and behavioral sciences.* New York: Wiley.

Olejnik, S., & Algina, J. (2000). Measures of effect size for comparative studies: Applications, interpretations, and limitations. *Contemporary Educational Psychology, 25,* 241–286.

Robinson, D. H., & Levin, J. R. (1997). Reflections on statistical and substantive significance, with a slice of replication. *Educational Researcher, 26*(5), 21–26.

Rosenthal, R. (1994). Parametric measures of effect size. In H. Cooper & L.V. Hedges (Eds.), *The handbook of research synthesis* (pp. 231–244). New York: Russell Sage Foundation.

Rosenthal, R., & Gaito, J. (1963). The interpretation of level of significance by psychological researchers. *Journal of Psychology, 55,* 33–38.

Rozeboom, W. W. (1997). Good science is abductive, not hypothetico-deductive. In L. L. Harlow, S. A. Mulaik, & J. H. Steiger (Eds.), *What if there were no significance tests?* (pp. 335–392). Mahwah, NJ: Erlbaum.

Schmidt, F. (1996). Statistical significance testing and cumulative knowledge in psychology: Implications for the training of researchers. *Psychological Methods, 1,* 115–129.

Schmidt, F. L., & Hunter, J. E. (1997). Eight common but false objections to the discontinuation of significance testing in the analysis of research data. In L. L. Harlow, S. A.

Mulaik, & J. H. Steiger (Eds.), *What if there were no significance tests?* (pp. 37–64). Mahwah, NJ: Erlbaum.

Shaver, J. (1985). Chance and nonsense. *Phi Delta Kappan, 67*(1), 57–60.

Smithson, M. (2001). Correct confidence intervals for various regression effect sizes and parameters: The importance of noncentral distributions in computing intervals. *Educational and Psychological Measurement, 61*, 605–632.

Snyder, P. (2000). Guidelines for reporting results of group quantitative investigations. *Journal of Early Intervention, 23*, 145–150.

Snyder, P., & Lawson, S. (1993). Evaluating results using corrected and uncorrected effect size estimates. *Journal of Experimental Education, 61*, 334–349.

Steiger, J. H., & Fouladi, R. T. (1992). R^2: A computer program for interval estimation, power calculation, and hypothesis testing for the squared multiple correlation. *Behavior Research Methods, Instruments, and Computers, 4*, 581–582.

Thompson, B. (1984). *Canonical correlation analysis: Uses and interpretation.* Thousand Oaks, CA: Sage.

Thompson, B. (1990). Finding a correction for the sampling error in multivariate measures of relationship: A Monte Carlo study. *Educational and Psychological Measurement, 50*, 15–31.

Thompson, B. (1991). A primer on the logic and use of canonical correlation analysis. *Measurement and Evaluation in Counseling and Development, 24*, 80–95.

Thompson, B. (1992). Two and one-half decades of leadership in measurement and evaluation. *Journal of Counseling and Development, 70*, 434–438.

Thompson, B. (1993). The use of statistical significance tests in research: Bootstrap and other alternatives. *Journal of Experimental Education, 61*, 361–377.

Thompson, B. (1996). AERA editorial policies regarding statistical significance testing: Three suggested reforms. *Educational Researcher, 25*(2), 26–30.

Thompson, B. (1999). If statistical significance tests are broken/misused, what practices should supplement or replace them? *Theory & Psychology, 9*, 167–183.

Thompson, B. (2000). Canonical correlation analysis. In L. Grimm & P. Yarnold (Eds.), *Reading and understanding more multivariate statistics* (pp. 285–316). Washington, DC: American Psychological Association.

Thompson, B. (2001). Significance, effect sizes, stepwise methods, and other issues: Strong arguments move the field. *Journal of Experimental Education, 70*, 80–93.

Thompson, B. (2002a). "Statistical," "practical," and "clinical": How many kinds of significance do counselors need to consider? *Journal of Counseling and Development, 80*, 64–71.

Thompson, B. (2002b). What future quantitative social science research could look like: Confidence intervals for effect sizes. *Educational Researcher, 31*(3), 24–31.

Thompson, B. (Ed.). (2003). *Score reliability: Contemporary thinking on reliability issues.* Newbury Park, CA: Sage.

Thompson, B., & Vacha-Haase, T. (2000). Psychometrics *is* datametrics: The test is not reliable. *Educational and Psychological Measurement, 60*, 174–195.

Tryon, W. W. (1998). The inscrutable null hypothesis. *American Psychologist, 53*, 796.

Vacha-Haase, T., Henson, R. K., & Caruso, J. (2002). Reliability generalization: Moving toward improved understanding and use of score reliability. *Educational and Psychological Measurement, 62*, 562–569.

Vacha-Haase, T., Nilsson, J. E., Reetz, D. R., Lance, T. S., & Thompson, B. (2000). Reporting practices and APA editorial policies regarding statistical significance and effect size. *Theory & Psychology, 10,* 413–425.

Wilkinson, L., & APA Task Force on Statistical Inference. (1999). Statistical methods in psychology journals: Guidelines and explanations. *American Psychologist, 54,* 594–604. (Reprint available through the APA home page: http://www.apa.org/journals/amp/amp548594.html)

Zuckerman, M., Hodgins, H. S., Zuckerman, A., & Rosenthal, R. (1993). Contemporary issues in the analysis of data: A survey of 551 psychologists. *Psychological Science, 4,* 49–53.

Experimental and Quasi-experimental Designs

Darlene Russ-Eft, *Oregon State University*
Amy L. Hoover, *Central Washington University*

As chapter 3 states, "Quantitative methods and the scientific method are the foundation of modern science." Such methods typically employ a theoretical framework to derive hypotheses that are then tested and accepted or rejected using appropriate statistical techniques. The purpose of these studies typically is to draw some causal inference. Underpinning all such studies, however, are the research designs that are used—be they preexperimental, experimental, or quasi-experimental. This chapter will introduce some of the most commonly used designs and discuss the advantages and challenges of each design. Where appropriate, examples of these designs taken from the HRD research literature will be reviewed.

ISSUES OF CONCERN

Before launching into a detailed discussion of the various experimental and quasi-experimental designs that can be used, we need to address six general issues: internal validity, external validity, frame of reference, longitudinality, frequency, and nested factors. The following sections provide an overview of each of these issues.

Internal Validity

The internal validity of an information-gathering effort is the extent to which it actually (correctly) answers the questions it claims to answer using the data that were gathered. All data collection and analysis is carried out in the context of a model, or set of assumptions, about the process being observed. If those assumptions are wrong, then the findings of the research are meaningless. If those assumptions are correct, then the research is internally valid, and the findings are meaningful.

The main type of threat to internal validity is that unmeasured processes might account for the results that were observed. A second type of threat is that overt responses do not correctly reflect underlying dimensions. Campbell and Stanley (1963) point out numerous threats to internal validity and proposed quasi-experimental designs that would control for the confounding of at least some of these threats, if true experimental designs are not possible. In order to achieve internal validity, the researcher must exert a substantial degree of control over the data-gathering process.

The primary methods for achieving high levels of internal validity involve procedures that constitute the "scientific method." First, sample members should be randomly assigned to treatment and control conditions. Whenever control groups are used for comparison, any selection and assignment other than by randomization will introduce bias. In many HRD studies undertaken within organizational settings, treatment and control groups have not been randomly selected and assigned from a predetermined population. Whenever that occurs, potential bias is introduced. For example, those who volunteer for the treatment condition are more motivated than those in the control group. Second, confounding factors should be identified, measured, and controlled. For example, a factor like years of experience as a supervisor might represent a confounding variable. The researcher would need to identify this as a potential confounding variable, obtain that information from each participant, and then possibly control the variable matching the years of experience of participants in the treatment and control groups. Finally, the use of a multiple methods approach will help to obtain converging evidence in support of a particular finding. If a number of methods of measurement and analysis all produce similar results, one is more likely to accept the result as being real rather than dependent upon the particular method used.

Campbell and Stanley (1963) identify several confounding variables that can affect internal validity:

- Specific events that occur independent of the data collection and that affect the results, such as a reorganization (history)
- Changes in attitudes or behavior simply due to the passage of time, such as obtaining greater confidence because of time on the job (maturity)
- Effects of a data collection process on some later data collection process, such as learning from repeated tests (testing)
- Changes in the data collection instruments or the observers (instrumentation)
- Attrition or loss of sample members (mortality)
- Differences in selection for different groups, as in more motivated staff volunteering for training (selection)

If a research study lacks internal validity, it will lose credibility in the face of any serious criticism. One must recognize, however, that there are costs associated with ensuring high levels of internal validity. One cost for increasing internal validity includes the increased direct cost for identifying and measuring confounding variables. Other costs are the obtrusiveness involved in control and the loss of external validity, and therefore generalizability, if too much control is exercised in order to obtain internal validity.

A high level of internal validity is absolutely necessary if the study is to be useful at the national or international policy level. On the other hand, internal validity need not be as great for exploratory investigations. This is because the study can be replicated and extended more carefully in order to produce an internally valid test of conclusions that were tentatively reached from an exploratory study.

External Validity

The external validity of an information-gathering effort is the extent to which answers based on the observations correctly generalize to other unobserved situations. For example, a study might be conducted within a specific organization and location and then generalized to other locations of that same organization or even to other types of organizations. The level of external validity tends to be determined by sample selection, whereas internal validity is determined by sample assignment. To the extent that internal validity is achieved through obtrusive control over data collection processes, external validity will be reduced.

Increasing external validity depends on drawing a representative probability sample and avoiding obtrusive measures as much as possible. It is in fact more important to have a broad sample covering the spectrum of possible people and organizations; thus, the focus is on being qualitatively representative as contrasted with being quantitatively representative. The reason for this is that quantitative deviation from exact representativeness can be corrected for during analysis. One approach for achieving external validity is to develop a model for the population from which one has selected a sample, so that particular attributes being observed can be taken into account in generalizations to the population. Another approach to maximize external validity is to perform a cross-validation or replication. Basically, this means that a single study is considered to consist of two halves, and each half is used as a check on results tentatively arrived at from the other half of the study.

The value of external validity is the generality of the results to a population of people or organizations. The costs for achieving external validity are the direct costs of obtaining broad and representative samples. The other costs might occur in compromises made in controlling for confounding variable.

It would seem that external validity must be achieved at a level sufficient to make accurate statements about people, organizations, and program at a national or international level. Samples should be representative and broad across different subtypes of people and organizations. Cross-validation methods should be used to check on external validity, and efforts to achieve internal validity should be undertaken that avoid obtrusive control.

Frame of Reference

Studies using experimental and quasi-experimental designs involve comparisons of observed performance with some expectations or ideas for performance. The frame of reference for such a study refers to the type of comparison undertaken. *Relative* comparisons examine what would have occurred without the HRD intervention or possibly the differences between two or more interventions. *Absolute* comparisons focus on the degree to which the intervention reaches some particular desired outcomes. Relative comparisons tend to be harder to implement, because they require comparing effects with empirical estimates of what would have occurred without the intervention or with some other interventions. On the other hand, absolute comparisons require greater advance planning, because it is necessary to establish a consensus or some documented evidence on the particular criteria to be used in the absolute comparison.

Almost all experimental or quasi-experimental studies in HRD use relative comparisons as opposed to absolute comparisons. In contrast, medical research frequently involves absolute criteria; that is, a procedure is considered successful if it produces a cure with no adverse side effects. The development of criterion-referenced tests is one example of the use of absolute comparisons.

Undertaking a relative comparison involves two basic steps. First, one must obtain a control group or other form of comparison group (e.g., a comparison program). This control group is the alter ego for the treatment group. Its performance is taken as an indication of how the treatment group could be expected to have performed were there no treatment. Second, one must select and implement statistical methods for the comparison. All of the statistical tests, such as analysis of variance, t-tests, analysis of covariance, Mann-Whitney, sign tests, and so on, are designed to enable one to compare the performance of two groups. These statistical methods are all based on particular assumptions (e.g., random assignment) that must be met in the collection of data in order to achieve internal validity.

Two steps are also needed when conducting an absolute comparison. First, one must identify the outcome criteria and obtain consensus from the client or experts that the criteria are appropriate. Second, one must develop a test or some other measure to determine whether the criteria are met.

For relative comparisons, there must be a compromise between the goal of achieving internal validity and that of avoiding intrusion or control. On the other hand, the costs for absolute comparisons include the problem of establishing the credibility of the criteria. There is also a problem in assigning results to the intervention. Even though it can be determined that an intervention is operating at or above the criterion level, an absolute comparison does not indicate whether that success was due specifically to that intervention or whether it was due to some confounding factor.

Longitudinality

The *longitudinality* of a design is the extent to which measurements are repeated and extend over time. The main problem of longitudinal designs is attrition; that is, if one wishes to obtain before-and-after and subsequent measures on participants, one must keep track of those people and recontact them. It also applies, unfortunately, to attrition of whole interventions and even to attrition of research staff. In order to cope with the problem of attrition, the operations that are needed are extra record keeping, methods for recontacting the people for whom the data have first been gathered, and methods for correcting for the inevitable attrition that will occur—that is, both statistical methods and special methods for selecting, locating, and obtaining responses from a subsample of the recipients and volunteers who otherwise would have been nonrespondents.

One alternative to straight longitudinal designs is to use *retrospection*—selecting individuals at the age or stage of the final data collection step and asking them to report retrospectively how they would have responded in earlier steps. This kind of design depends on the validity of the memories of the subjects who are contacted, and that validity varies with the type of content to be remembered. While one can remember accurately what year one graduated from high school, memories of one's attitude toward the job and toward particular groups of people can be quite questionable. Another problem with retrospection is the sampling problem. If you sample individuals at age 50 and obtain retrospective data from them about when they were 20, those persons will be a biased sample of the population of 20-year-olds 30 years before. Some of the population will have died or will have changed since they were 20, with respect to some of the stratification variables used in the sampling, so that, even disregarding effects of history, the results will not generalize to a new sample of 20-year-olds sampled in the same manner as the 50-year-olds.

A second variant on longitudinal designs is the overlapping panel design. For example, if one wanted to measure growth in skill level from the first year on the job to the fifth year on the job, one could measure the growth of three cohorts beginning simultaneously in the first, second, and third years. From these three overlapping cohorts in a 3-year period, one could reconstruct a growth curve over the period from the first to the fifth year. One could also determine the skill levels at a particular date, leading to a cross-sectional analysis. Finally, one could determine the skill level for all cohorts at a particular year, such as the third year, leading to a time-lag design (Russ-Eft, 1999; Schaie, Campbell, Meredith, & Rawlings, 1988).

The direct cost of a longitudinal design is considerably greater than the cost of the same amount of data collection taking place at a single time. This is because of the seriousness of the attrition problem. Failure to deal with attrition will cause the entire study to lose validity. Not only must methods for keeping track of participants be implemented, but also participants' interest in the research effort must be maintained so that they will be inclined to respond to follow-up data collection efforts. The third cost, which can be crucial, is the loss of timeliness. A design that takes 5 years to execute may not produce any results relevant to decisions that have to be made next year. One solution to this problem of loss of timeliness is to include types of data gathering in the initial phase of a longitudinal study that are sufficient to produce meaningful information that can be used prior to the later data collection phases.

Frequency

The frequency of data collection involves the number of repetitions within a specified period. Some study designs require one or two data collection efforts. Others, particularly ones using a longitudinal design, may require multiple data collections. Furthermore, the reason for making observations with greater frequency, such as once a month, rather than less frequently, such as once a year, is that one believes that there is significant variation within the longer period. If there is not such variation, for example, within the year, then once-a-year observation is quite sufficient.

The annual reports to the stockholders represent an example of an annual data collection and analysis effort. On the other hand, economic measures of the well-being of our society, such as cost-of-living indicators, have seasonal fluctuations, so that measurements are made more frequently than annually. Most HRD studies appear to have been undertaken on a one-shot design, in which there is not plan for a frequent or even infrequent repetition. To make future longitudinal studies more cost-effective, however, it would seem appropriate for researchers who undertake many of these one-shot studies to plan them in such a way that they might be baselines for long-term studies—for example, by asking participants for the names of individuals who would be likely to keep track of their changes of position, change of employer, or even change in residence.

Any design that involves repetition of data collection should minimize the recurring costs, even though that may increase the development costs. For example, extra care in development of easy reporting forms should be undertaken, and standard forms of analyses (e.g., computer programs) should be developed that can be applied repeatedly at maximum efficiency. By doing so, frequency will not affect cost other than being proportional to the amount of data collected. Collecting twice as much data should cost approximately twice as much, after development costs are subtracted, and this should be true whether the doubling of the data collected is caused by a doubling of frequency or of sample size.

Nested Factors

The designs described here assume that each person is selected independently of another. Within HRD research, however, the effects being studied may be "nested" within some other factor. "Effects which are restricted to a single level of a factor are said to be *nested* within that factor" (Winer, 1962, p. 360). As an example, let us assume that we want to determine the effectiveness of two different methods for training customer service employees. We then use one method with employees located in New York and a different method for those located in San Francisco. In such a design, we cannot separate out the effects of the different methods from the locations; in other words, we cannot determine the interaction effect between the method and the location. The only way to separate out these effects would be to test each method in each location.

COMMONLY USED DESIGNS

Preexperimental Designs

Table 6.1 presents an overview of various preexperimental designs. This table includes a graphic depiction of each design along with the purpose, data analysis approach, some advantages, and some challenges. The following paragraphs provide further detail on each of these designs. Campbell and Stanley (1963),

TABLE 6.1 Preexperimental Designs

TYPE OF DESIGN	NOTATION	PURPOSE	DATA ANALYSIS	POTENTIAL ADVANTAGES	POTENTIAL CHALLENGES
One-shot design and retrospective pretest	X ——— O	To describe posttest behavior or measure	Observation of behavior or measure	Can be a simple and inexpensive way to attempt to explain a causal relationship between variables	Provides no control for internal validity
One group pretest-posttest	O — X — O	To compare a pretest behavior or measure to posttest behavior or measure	Matched pairs t-test of pre- and posttest measures	Similar to one-shot design; can be a simple and inexpensive way to attempt to explain a causal relationship between variables	Can provide a measure of observed change, but does not provide conclusive results
Static group comparison	X ——— O ——— O	To attempt to evaluate the influence of a variable or treat-ment on a behavior or measure	Comparison of the behavior or measure between groups	Could be used to evaluate the influence of a treatment, but only if there is a determination of a pretest comparison between groups from a source external to the experiment	Provides no control for internal validity, if there is no determination of pretreatment comparison of groups

O = observation of dependent variable; X = treatment by independent variable.

Cook and Campbell (1979), and Russ-Eft and Preskill (2001) present even greater detail on these and other designs.

One-Shot Design

The term *one-shot* refers to the fact that data collection occurs at one time only. This design is commonly used in studies of HRD interventions, such as the ubiquitous posttraining reaction forms. Thus, it assumes that the participants are reacting to the intervention and not to some other factor, such as a downsizing announcement. Another example appears in many college, university, and training courses in which some final exam is given. Here the assumption is that the participants have had no previous experience or knowledge of the subject matter, which may or may not be the case.

Clearly, a major advantage of this design is its simplicity and cost-effectiveness. Data are collected at one time only, leading to lower time and costs for data collection. Furthermore, these data can be gathered as part of the intervention or course. Finally, if undertaking an absolute comparison, such a design may be considered appropriate, since the comparison will be with some desired outcome.

One-shot design provides little in the way of control for issues related to internal validity. It fails to control for events that are independent of the data collection, such as the example of the downsizing announcement (or history). It fails to control for changes due to the passage of time; for example, participants may have learned some skill simply as part of their work on the job. Finally, it fails to control for the effects of attrition; perhaps only those participants who were successful are surveyed and tested at the end of the intervention.

Retrospective Pretest Design

In this variation of the one-shot case study design, data are collected from participants following the intervention; however, the participants report *retrospectively* on their attitudes or skills. As a result, the researcher can compare these retrospective "preassessments" to the postassessment.

This design depends on the accuracy of participants' recall, as well as their willingness to provide "truthful" data. For example, in communication skills training, trainees may or may not be aware of their prior skill level until after completing the training. In these cases, the retrospective design may provide a more accurate picture of pretraining skills than the data gathering before training.

As with the one-shot design, the appeal of the retrospective design is its simplicity and ease of data collection. In addition, one can obtain a comparison between posttraining data and the retrospective pretest data. Furthermore, the posttraining data are not contaminated by the experience of pretesting.

One drawback of the retrospective design is that it does not include a control group of people who did not participant in the intervention. Thus, there is a possibility that the results were due to history with the job or the organization (as is true with the one-shot design). In addition, distortions may occur in these retrospective reports, resulting from memory problems or changes in attitudes. Finally, the problem of attrition may affect the results from this design.

One-Group Pretest-Posttest Design

This design involves actual data collection prior to and following an intervention. Unlike the previously described retrospective pretest design, it gathers data before an intervention and so does not rely on participants' memory.

An example of the use of this design appears in Tan, Hall, and Boyce (2003). These researchers examined learning gains among 283 automotive technicians as the result of brakes training using a 39-item multiple-choice test administered before and after training. In addition, the researchers examined the relationships of posttraining reactions with learning and with behavior (as measured by supervisors' ratings of trainees' on-the-job performance 6 months after the training).

As with the previous designs, this design is relatively simple and cost-effective. Indeed, the participants could be asked to complete an instrument that focused on attitudes, opinions, knowledge, or skill level at the beginning of a training session, for example, and then again at its conclusion as occurred in the Tan et al. study. Because data are collected as part of the intervention, costs for data collection and the possibility of attrition from the sample would be reduced.

As with the previously described designs, however, several challenges exist with this design. Similar to those for one-shot and retrospective designs, results may be attributed to previous history with the organization and the job (*history* and *maturation*). In addition, the pretest itself may cause changes to occur irrespective of the training (*testing*). For example, a knowledge or skills pretest may contribute to improved knowledge or skills. If so, the posttest measurement not only reflects the effects of the intervention, but it reflects the effects of the pretest *plus* the intervention. Indeed, that may have occurred in the Tan et al. study. Another issue involves possible changes in the data collection tool from the pretest to the posttest (instrumentation). Also, participants may leave their positions or the organizations between the time of the pretest and the posttest, resulting in a smaller than expected sample (*mortality*). Thus, such a design will result in increased effort and resources for follow-up. Note that follow-up issues did arise in the Tan et al. study with regard to the data collection undertaken with supervisors.

Static Group Comparison

Unlike the previous designs, this approach does include a comparison with a supposed control group. Two important aspects of the design are that no random assignment to the two groups occurs and that data collection only takes place following the intervention.

This design is relatively cost-effective, in that it employs only one data collection period. As such, problems cannot arise with previous experience with the data collection (*testing*) or with changes in the instrument (*instrumentation*).

Challenges related to internal validity primarily arise with the lack of random assignment. Thus, the treatment group may be comprised of participants who are more motivated, more skilled, or more likely to be promoted that the comparison group.

Experimental Designs

Table 6.2 presents various options for true experimental designs. The key aspect to experimental designs involves the random assignment to a treatment or a control group. This helps to ensure that the two groups are equivalent in terms of history and other preexisting circumstances or conditions that may influence the results.

Posttest-Only Control Group Design

This represents the first of the true experimental designs. Although researchers usually emphasize the importance of a pretest, one might want to consider avoiding the use of the pretest in order to eliminate the effects of the pretest on the posttest results. One can do this by using the posttest-only control group design.

In such a design, two groups are randomly selected, with one group experiencing the intervention, and the other receiving no intervention. The groups are then given a posttest at the same time following the intervention.

On the positive side, as with the static comparison group design, this design enjoys simplicity and efficiency in data collection, since it takes place at one time only. Also, this design eliminates concerns with test experience. Of greatest importance, however, random assignment ensures that no systematic bias exists among the groups.

The major limitation, certainly within organizations, is the lack of feasibility of random assignment to various treatment conditions. This problem is exacerbated when you attempt to assign certain people to a "control" condition where they do not receive the intervention. That could actually be considered unethical. In the case of some developmental opportunity, however, one possible alternative would be to provide the intervention for the "control" condition at some later time. For organizations with the imperative of completing everything *now*, the notion of keeping some people from needed developmental experiences may be unacceptable.

Pretest-Posttest Control Group Design

This is the classic experimental design that entails random assignment of subjects to either an experimental or control group, with a pretest and posttest administered to each group. The treatment, or independent variable, is administered only to the experimental group. This allows the researcher to compare differences in reaction, learning, behavior, or performance between the two groups. To do this, the researcher can make comparisons of the posttreatment behavior between groups in addition to making a within-group pretest-posttest comparison for both groups. This is important for the statistical analysis of the resulting data, as well as for maximizing factors related to internal validity of the experiment. If

TABLE 6.2 True Experimental Designs

TYPE OF DESIGN	NOTATION	PURPOSE	TYPICAL DATA ANALYSIS	POTENTIAL ADVANTAGES	POTENTIAL CHALLENGES
Posttest only control group	$R — X — O$ $R ———— O$	To examine the influence of a variable or treatment on a behavior or measure	Simple t-test for significance	Can be a simple and inexpensive way to attempt to explain a causal relationship between variables	Sensitivity to effects on the dependent variable is low, particularly with small sample size. Randomness is critical.
Pretest-posttest control group	$R — O — X — O$ $R — O ———— O$	To determine the effects of a treatment by comparing a treatment group with a controlled group sample	Depending on the number of levels of the variable, paired comparison or analysis of covariance on posttest scores using the pretest as the covariate	Traditional design, widely used; if executed properly, can ensure a high level of control for internal validity	Sample size is related to effect size. If an effect size cannot be estimated from previous studies it might be difficult to determine without repeated measures.
Solomon four-group	$R — O — X — O$ $R — O ———— O$ $R ———— X — O$ $R ———————— O$	Elaboration of the pretest-posttest control group design that controls for pretest effects	Multiple analysis of variance on dependent variable combined with analysis of variance on posttest scores	The most powerful experimental approach; high level of internal validity and minimization of pretest effects	Requires large sample size, more time-consuming and possibly more expensive than classic pretest-posttest control design
Factorial	$R — A_1 — B_1 — O$ $R — A_1 — B_2 — O$ $R — A_2 — B_1 — O$ $R — A_2 — B_2 — O$ OR $R — O — A_1 — B_1 — O$ $R — O — A_1 — B_2 — O$ $R — O — A_2 — B_1 — O$ $R — O — A_2 — B_2 — O$	To examine simultaneous effects of more than one independent variable	Multiple analysis of variance on dependent, moderator, or control variables OR multiple analysis of variance with repeated measures	Allows for comparison of independent effects of two or more variables along with interaction effects between main, moderator, and control variables	Requires large sample size

R = random assignment to groups; O = observation of dependent variable; X = treatment by independent variable; A_1, B_1, A_2, B_2 = notation for multiple independent, moderator, or control variables in a factorial design. True experiments are characterized by randomization, use of some kind of control, such as manipulation, and use of control groups.

conducted effectively, this design controls for many threats to internal validity. Because the two groups are tested at the same time both before and after the intervention, differences between the groups cannot be attributed to (1) unexpected events or circumstances within the organization; (2) the passage of time in the organization or on the job; or (3) special attitudes, knowledge, or skills gained as a result of certain organizational changes. The reason is because both groups would have experienced the same events, circumstances, and passage of time.

One example of the use of such a design appeared in a study by Martocchio and Hertenstein (2003). The study was undertaken with clerical workers at a university who voluntarily participated in a computer software class. Prior to training, these workers completed a general cognitive ability test, a pretraining self-efficacy scale, and a dispositional goal orientation scale. Within the same class session, participants "received a packet with either learning or performance orientation inductions on a random basis" (p. 422). In the middle of the 4-hour training, they completed the self-efficacy scale again as well as a test of declarative knowledge of the subject matter. Then at the end of the 4-hour training, they completed the self-efficacy scale for the final time.

The strength of the pretest-posttest control group design depends on the assumption that the only relevant variability in experience between the two groups is the treatment itself—in the case of Martocchio and Hertenstein, the learning orientation induction as compared with the performance orientation induction. Additionally, and most critical, is the assumption that the two groups are comparable with respect to their behavior or measured performance on the dependent variable prior to the treatment. Comparability is approximated by the random assignment to groups and by selecting a large enough sample size to assure variability in behavior or performance approaches that of a normal distribution. The question of what constitutes a large enough sample size is related to effect size, or the strength of the correlation between the dependent and independent variables. The effect size may be known from previous experiments or from the literature, or it may need to be estimated based on some preliminary measure. If the researcher can assume the groups are comparable, then analysis of covariance on posttest scores can be used with the pretest score as the covariate, which allows for adjustment of the posttest scores for pretest variability.

Use of the pretest-posttest control group design does not address long-term effects of the treatment or experimental errors such as the Hawthorne effect. Additionally, it cannot answer questions that arise from the possible interaction of the treatment effects with different kinds of subjects, differing degrees of intensity, other treatments, or difference in the sequence or order of treatments. To answer those questions, researchers may find a factorial or repeated measures design more appropriate. Moreover, it cannot control for the possibility that the pretreatment observation or measurement itself may have caused a change in subsequent behavior or performance measure (*testing*). For example, the pretest alerting both groups as to what is most important in the intervention. Another problem arises with the use of a control group that does not participate in the intervention. In some organizations, everyone must participate in the intervention at one time, making the use of such a control group impossible. Finally, because the design takes place over time, one might expect some attrition from the two groups, given the mobility of today's workforce. If attrition from the two groups were unequal, this might render differences in the groups simply due to the attitudes, knowledge, and skills of the remaining participants. The Martocchio and Hertenstein study avoided this last problem by conducting all of the research within a single session; this may or may not be possible, if the research question focuses on issues related to long-term changes.

Solomon Four-Group Design

If the researcher suspects that the pretest observation or measure may have an influence on the dependent variable, then the Solomon four-group design would be appropriate. For example, a pretest measure can sensitize subjects to the treatment, or their performance can improve as a result of the pretest itself, known as a *practice effect*. The Solomon four-group design combines the classic pretest-posttest control group design and the posttest only control group design (Table 6.2) with random assignment of subjects to four groups so that pretest effects are eliminated. If comparison of the two experimental groups shows similar results and comparison of the two control groups shows similar results, then a pretest effect can be ruled out. However, if the two groups that had pretests (one experimental and one control) differ from the two groups that had no pretest, then there may have been an effect on the dependent variable caused by the pretest. Because the effects of the pretest can be filtered out, the data can be analyzed using an analysis of variance based on posttest scores.

Bretz and Thompsett (1992) present a study that used the Solomon four-group design to compare the learning and satisfaction with two different training methods: integrative learning training and traditional, lecture-based training. A total of 180 employees were randomly assigned to one of the four groups. In addition, a no-treatment control group existed composed of volunteers, because "the organization was unwilling to assign employees randomly to a no-treatment group" (p. 944).

The primary advantages of the Solomon four-group design are that it controls for the effects of history, maturity, and pretesting and increases the internal validity. Because of the use of the pretest-posttest feature, it also provides some longitudinal evidence.

It does, however, suffer from some of the same challenges as those of the pretest-posttest control group design. That is, the researcher must include two groups who do not receive the intervention. Bretz and Thompsett overcame that problem by providing the intervention but simply using different methods for presenting the information. Another major disadvantage of this design involves its complexity. Although appropriate for laboratory studies, it may be extremely difficult to obtain four randomly assigned groups and measure them over time within an organization. It should be noted that Bretz and Thompsett state that the research was conducted in such a rigorous manner "because of the scope of the training, the perceived importance of MRP-II (manufacturing resource planning) in Kodak's business plan, and the potential benefits of IL (integrative learning) purported to offer in terms of greater learning and attitudinal improvements" (p. 943). In particular, it will be difficult to have two control groups that are randomly selected not receive the intervention. Indeed, in the Bretz and Thompsett case, all groups participated in the intervention but experienced different methods. Also, because the design takes place over time, some unequal attrition from the groups will likely occur and may destroy the assumptions of random selection. Finally, with four groups, it requires many people and much administration and data collection.

Factorial Design

This type of design enables the researcher to compare two or more independent variables at the same time. An example of the use of a factorial design appears in Mattson (2003) in which the researcher compared three different types of reporting about a developmental program—utility analysis, critical outcome technique, and anecdotal evaluation reports—as well as three different levels of impact—low, average, and high. This resulted in a 3×3 (report type by impact level) factorial design. Participants were randomly assigned to one of nine groups, asked to read the assigned report, and then completed an instrument measuring the decision-making usefulness and ease of use of the report.

Note that this factorial design also borrowed from the post-only control group design. In that design, two groups are randomly selected, with one group experiencing the intervention, and the other receiving no intervention. Alternatively, as in the Mattson study described earlier, the researcher randomly assigned participants to different types of interventions. The groups were then given a posttest at the same time following the intervention. In the Mattson study, the intervention involved the different types of reports, and the posttest consisted of the instrument measuring the usefulness and the ease of use.

On the positive side, the factorial design enables the researcher to examine the independent effects of variables, such as type of report and level of impact, as well as the interaction effects. In the Mattson study, only the type of report had a significant effect on ratings of usefulness—a direct effect. An interaction effect might have been observed if, for example, the anecdotal evaluation report showed high levels of usefulness only with reports of high impact. As with the other experimental designs, the research controls for many of the biases of history and maturity. Of greatest importance, however, random assignment ensures that no systematic bias exists among the groups.

The major limitation, certainly within organizations, is the lack of feasibility of random assignment to various treatment conditions or to a no-treatment control group. Such concerns did not arise in the Mattson study, since it simply involved the reactions to different types of reporting. Another challenge involves the number of groups and the size of the sample. Such factorial designs simply cannot be used if the number of participants is limited.

Quasi-Experimental Designs

Table 6.3 outlines various quasi-experimental designs. These designs are appropriate when random assignment to treatment and control conditions are not possible, which is very typical with research conducted in organizational settings. Such designs can provide useful information, and there is some evidence from the Campbell Collaboration (C2) that results from quasi-experimental designs may be similar to that obtained from experimental designs.

Time Series Design

The designs discussed so far have been limited to two separate data collection times: a pretest and a posttest. Another possible design involves repeated data collections before, during, and following some intervention. This represents the first of several quasi-experimental designs to be discussed.

When using a time series design, we would graph the results obtained at each time. An example might focus on the effects of a safety awareness and training program. In charting the results of such a program, we might examine the frequency of safety violations over time. If these showed some dramatic change only from the time immediately before to immediately after the program, we could assume that the program had some impact on the results. Collecting data at several points prior to the program would establish a stable baseline to use for comparing postprogram results.

A strength of this design is that the baseline data helps counter the argument that time in the organization or on the job by itself (history and maturation) resulted in changes in attitudes or behavior. Also, it provides longitudinal data on the variable of interest.

This design has several problems, however. First, one cannot easily isolate various organizational influences, and that could interact with the results separate from the intervention. In addition, repeated data collection must be undertaken leading to additional costs. Also, the repeated measurement could result in changes in attitudes or behavior (*testing*). Since this design takes place over time, attrition from the sample may occur due to people being reassigned or leaving the job and the organization (*mortality*).

Another set of issues arises from the use of longitudinal designs. In some cases, different results have been obtained when using a longitudinal design (which tests the same people over time) from those obtained when using a cross-sectional design (which tests different people at different stages at the same time). When considering such designs, you may want to consult some literature on this topic (Russ-Eft, 1999; Schaie et al., 1988).

TABLE 6.3 Quasi-Experimental Designs

TYPE OF DESIGN	NOTATION	PURPOSE	DATA ANALYSIS	POTENTIAL ADVANTAGES	POTENTIAL CHALLENGES
Time series	O – O – X – O – O	To determine the influence of a variable or treatment on a single sample group	Measure of change between behavior or performance before and after the intervention or treatment	Provides longitudinal data	Cannot separate out interaction effects of some organizational or other environmental factor
Latin square	R – Xa – Xb – Xc – O R – Xa – Xc – Xb – O R – Xb – Xa – Xc – O R – Xb – Xc – Xa – O R – Xc – Xa – Xb – O R – Xc – Xb – Xa – O	To examine the effects of different factors in one study	Multiple analysis of variance on dependent variable or multiple analysis of variance with repeated measures	Allows for the use of smaller sample sizes than in complete factorial design; can counterbalance order effects when using repeated measures	Assumes lack of interaction effects through prior research or pilot studies
Regression Discontinuity	C — O — X — O C — O ——— O	Variation of the pretest-posttest control group design where assignment is based on a cutoff value	Regression analysis using discontinuity based on pre- and posttest distribution of data	Controls for many areas of internal validity	Requires a continuous, quantitative measure of the dependent variable

R = random assignment to groups; O = observation of dependent variable; X = treatment by independent variable; Xa, Xb, Xc = levels of the independent variable; C = groups assigned according to a cutoff score based on the pre- and postdistribution of values for the dependent variable from a regression of data without the treatment effect. Quasi-experimental designs lack random assignment and are used in situations where true experimental designs may not be possible. Inferring a causal relationship between variables is difficult with some of these types of designs.

Separate Sample, Pre-Post Design

The separate sample, pre-post design as described by Campbell and Stanley (1963) includes several variations. One design involves the random assignment of one group that receives a pretest, then the intervention, and then the posttest and a second group that receives the intervention and the posttest only. An example of such a study from the literature is that presented in Carter (2002). The researcher was interested in examining the effects of two methods (lecture-based training as compared with case-study-based training) using a repeated measures design, meaning that the same people received both types of training. Furthermore, the researcher wanted to control for pretest effects. Training participants were randomly assigned to receive a group that received both the pretest and the posttest or one that received only the posttest.

Such a design does achieve control of the testing effects. Furthermore, with random assignment, it controls for any biasing effects from selection. Depending on the actual procedures, it may also control for the effects of external events (*history*) or factors related to time in place (*maturation*) that may influence the results, since there is a comparison with a control group.

Latin Square Design

The Latin square or counterbalanced design is one in which all of the participants receive all of the various treatments. Let us take the example of the Carter study and assume that we want to test two different training methods—lecture and case study. A Latin square or counterbalance design added to the separate sample, pre-post design would result in the following four groups:

Group	Week 1 Topic Labor Law			Week 2 Topic Occupation Safety & Health		
Group 1	Pretest	Lecture	Posttest	Pretest	Case Study	Posttest
Group 2	Pretest	Case Study	Posttest	Pretest	Lecture	Posttest
Group 3		Lecture	Posttest		Case Study	Posttest
Group 4		Case Study	Posttest		Lecture	Posttest

The advantage of the Latin square design is that it allows for the testing of main effects of multiple variables without the inclusion of the many groups needed in a full factorial design. In addition, it provides for counterbalancing order effects within a repeated measures design.

This design is considered a quasi-experimental design, because it does control for several issues related to internal validity. These include history, maturation, testing, instrumentation, selection, and mortality. The greatest challenge with such designs revolves around interaction effects. Thus, one does not know what the effects might be of the interaction of the testing, selection, and history with the observed results. In the case of counterbalancing order effects, it really provides control only in a weak sense and does not control for carryover effects of a specific sequence. Only by using a true experimental design with separate groups for each of the topic and methods can one eliminate issues related to such interaction or carryover effects.

Regression Discontinuity Design

This design involves the use of some pretest and posttest with the assignment of groups based on a cut point. One example might be the assignment for specialized training in the military based on scores on the Armed Services Vocational Aptitude Battery (ASVAB). One could then examine the regression line of scores on the ASVAB against some later achievement test. If such training had an effect, then we would expect some discontinuity in the regression line.

Such a design does control for many issues related to internal validity, such as history, maturation, testing, and mortality. In addition, it deals with some issues related to external validity and appears appropriate in certain field settings.

Some challenges do exist, however, with this design. First, the cutoff criterion must be applied rigorously; otherwise, it would result in a "fuzzy" design and lead to complexities in the analysis. Second, the design requires a sufficient number of pretest and posttest values to estimate the regression line. Finally, both groups must come from a single continuous pretest distribution.

DEALING WITH ORGANIZATIONAL REALITIES

As has been described, one of the joys of using any of the experimental and quasi-experimental designs involves the fact that many of the limitations of the design have been previously examined and described. There are, however, major challenges, particularly when working in an organizational setting with executives, managers, and employees as contrasted with a laboratory setting using volunteers.

The first major challenge involves the assignment of treatment and control groups. In some cases, there may not be enough resources or people available to monitor multiple groups. Even if the resources and people do exist for multiple groups, most organizations and decision makers do not see the advantages of denying certain people and groups that intervention in order to provide a "control" group. After all, if the organization is undertaking some sort of change effort, it presumably wants to take advantage of timing the intervention for a certain short period rather than dragging it out over time. Then, even if sufficient resources exist and decision makers do see the value of examining groups that experience the intervention with those that do not, randomly assigning people to the treatment and control groups may not be feasible. After all, people function within groups, and introducing only certain people within a group to the intervention may not yield completely independent treatment and control groups. Of course, one possible alternative would be to use groups rather than people as the unit of analysis and then randomly assign groups to the treatment or control. That alternative would, however, require large numbers of groups and people.

With all these challenges, there is some "joy" and hope. As mentioned at the beginning of the section on quasi-experimental designs, recent work by the Campbell Collaboration (www.campbellcollaboration.org) has shown that many of the quasi-experimental designs function well in providing adequate controls. Furthermore, certain advantages exist in collecting data within organizational settings. In particular, such settings allow the HRD researcher the opportunity to use archival data and available employee records. The researcher can undertake time series designs or multiple-group time series designs using these previously collected data. In addition, the researcher can use these data, or even data from other employees, to undertake some cross-validation of or some examination of the effects of other variables on the study results. With large organizations, the researcher may possess sufficient numbers of participants and amount of data in order to undertake a study using the regression. Perhaps of greatest importance, the HRD researcher has some assurance that the results possess some degree of external validity and that that external validity is far greater than that achieved by using undergraduate volunteers randomly assigned to participate in some simulation of an HRD intervention.

CONCLUSION

Experimental and quasi-experimental designs can help advance HRD research by aiding researchers and practitioners to determine cause-and-effect relationships. The examples provided in this chapter indicate that it is possible to use these types of research designs within organizational settings. It behooves the HRD researcher to understand the many varieties of designs that have been developed in order to make an appropriate selection for testing hypotheses and answering research questions. In doing so, the researcher will also need to understand the joys as well as the challenges of each design. That will enable the researcher to celebrate with some new understanding and to enrich the field with new knowledge.

REFERENCES

Bretz, R. D., Jr., & Thompsett, R. E. (1992). Comparing traditional and integrative learning methods in organizational training programs. *Journal of Applied Psychology, 77*, 941–951.

Campbell, D. T., & Stanley, J. C. (1966). *Experimental and quasi-experimental designs for research.* Boston: Houghton Mifflin.

Carter, S. (2002). Matching training methods and factors of cognitive ability: A means to improve training outcomes. *Human Resource Development Quarterly, 13*, 71–87.

Cook, T. D., & Campbell, D. T. (1979). *Quasi-experimentation: Design and analysis issues for field settings.* Boston: Houghton Mifflin.

Martocchio, J. J., & Hertenstein, E. J. (2003). Learning orientation and goal orientation context: Relationships with cognitive and affective learning outcomes. *Human Resource Development Quarterly, 14,* 413–434.

Mattson, B. W. (2003). The effects of alternative reports of human resource development results on managerial support. *Human Resource Development Quarterly, 14,* 127–151.

Russ-Eft, D. (1999). Research methods for advancing performance improvement. In R. A. Swanson (Series Ed.) & R. J. Torraco (Issue Ed.), *Performance improvement theory and practice: Vol. 1(1). Advances in developing human resources.* San Francisco: Berrett-Koehler.

Russ-Eft, D., & Preskill, H. (2001). *Evaluation in organizations: A systematic approach to enhancing learning, performance, and change.* Cambridge, MA: Perseus.

Schaie, K. W., Campbell, R. T., Meredith, W., & Rawlings, S. C. (Eds.). (1988). *Methodological issues in aging research.* New York: Springer.

Tan, J. A., Hall, R. J., & Boyce, C. (2003). The role of employee reactions in predicting training effectiveness. *Human Resource Development Quarterly, 14,* 397–411.

Winer, B. J. (1962). *Statistical principles in experimental design* (2nd ed.). New York: McGraw-Hill.

C H A P T E R   7

Survey Research in Organizations

Kenneth R. Bartlett, *University of Minnesota*

To paraphrase Charles Dickens, it could be said that these are the best of times for survey research within organizations yet also the worst of times. Perhaps we are not experiencing the worst of times, but certainly numerous challenges now face the researcher using surveys despite the fact that the survey has achieved a well-established reputation for being the preferred method for data collection in organizations. Recent studies on survey research are providing new insights, requiring revisions on much of the conventional wisdom that has guided this research method for much of the past few decades (Krosnick, 1999).

This chapter will briefly describe the history and emergence of the survey as one, if not the, dominant method for doing research in organizations. A five-step process for conducting survey research will be summarized, with key principles and best practices highlighted. Major challenges facing survey research will be reviewed, including a summary of literature related to the rapidly evolving and increasing popular survey mode of the Internet.

DEFINITION OF SURVEY RESEARCH

Definitions of surveys range from the overly broad to more formal descriptions of the entire survey research process. Existing definitions include "a method for gathering information from a sample of individuals" (Scheuren, 2004, p. 9); "a method used to gather self-report descriptive information about the attitudes, behaviors, or other characteristics of some population" (Rosenfeld, Edwards, & Thomas, 1995, p. 548); and "relatively systematic, standardized approaches to the collection of information . . . through the questioning of systematically identified samples of individuals" (Rossi, Wright, & Anderson, 1983, p. 1). The noted sociologist and founder of the Survey Research Center at the University of California Berkeley, Charles Glock (1988), describes survey research "as being concerned with the study of variation" (p. 38). This is a useful addition to existing definitions as it highlights the underlying purpose of the survey and cautions against inappropriate application of the method.

HISTORY OF SURVEY RESEARCH
IN ORGANIZATIONS

The survey is now recognized as the most frequently used data collection method in organizational research for assessing phenomena that are not directly observable (Gall, Gall, & Borg, 2003; Schneider, Ashworth, Higgs, & Carr, 1996; Smith & Dainty, 1991). The advantage of the survey over many other research methods is that they are usually cheaper, quicker, and broader in coverage (Bennett, 1991). Consequently, their use has greatly increased with estimates that millions of employees complete at least one organizational survey each year (Gallup, 1988).

To trace the origins of survey research highlights the different definitions of what constitutes a survey. While some point to census surveys conducted by the ancient Romans, church- or nobility-sponsored surveys of parishioners and citizens in the Middle Ages (Babbie, 1992), or the first United States census of 1790 (Smith, 1990), most histories of survey research are limited to the last 100 years. Although censuses, surveys of voting preferences, and surveys of social attitudes tend to receive the most attention, this method of data collection has long been used in organizational settings. The Scottish philosopher and social reformer Henry Mayhew was conducting detailed survey studies of British factory workers in the early 1800s, whereas by the early 1840s, U.S. employers were being surveyed on their perceptions of the quality of labor supply. Bills (1992) and others tracing the history of surveys in organizations tend to identify the 1930s and 1940s as the first stage in the evolution of surveys.

The increased acceptance and use of surveys, starting in the 1930s, has been linked to changing societal attitudes, advances in technology, increased emphasis on cost and efficiency, and greater knowledge and understanding of survey error structure Dillman (2000). Summarizing the developments over the past 25 years, Kalton (2000) describes how the field of survey research grew considerably after World War II. By the 1970s, surveys of both households and organizations were well established as the best means for gathering statistical data for researchers and policymakers on a wide variety of topics (Kalton, 2000). In 1975 the academic journal *Survey Methodology* was launched. The research profession of practitioners engaged in conducting surveys continued to grow rapidly as policy makers and organizational leaders learned the value of survey data for making informed decisions. The widespread use of computers has furthered the application of surveys over the past two decades with the advent of the Internet opening a new chapter in the history of this method.

PURPOSE OF SURVEYS

The purpose of survey research in organizations is to collect information from one or more people on some set of organizationally relevant constructs. While surveys have traditionally been divided into two broad categories, questionnaires and interviews, at least five major survey modes are in use today: face-to-face interview procedures, telephone interviews, mail surveys, Internet surveys, and touch-tone entry (also known as Interactive Voice Response) (Dillman, 2002). This chapter concentrates on the development and implementation of self-administered surveys using the five modes rather than the procedures and strategies associated with interviewing.

Most survey research employs a cross-sectional design. Glock (1988) notes that in cross-sectional studies the variation of interest is how the units being surveyed differ from one another at a single point in time. However, various longitudinal survey approaches such as trend, panel, cohort, and time series studies are gaining in popularity as researchers can collect and compare data from two or more points in time (Bauer, 2004). *Trend studies* (repeated measures over time with equivalent but not the same samples) allow researchers to examine how variations differ from each other from one time period to another. In *panel studies* (repeated measures in which data are collected repeatedly from the same samples), variation between units and within units over time is the central interest (Glock, 1988, p. 38). Dillman (2000) reports that the future of self-administered surveys would no doubt feature panel studies of the same individuals in organizations or of the same businesses where the same survey procedures can be repeated year after year. Kalton (2000) also projects an increased use of panel design in the future. Finally, time series designs, which are popular in education for tracking student performance and the transition for school to work, are also being recognized for their ability to accommodate the study of change in organizational settings (Bauer, 2004).

MAJOR ELEMENTS OF SURVEY RESEARCH

Despite the ubiquitous role of surveys in most people's lives (Rosenfeld et al., 1995) and the perceived simplicity of survey design and administration (Fink, 1995), survey research poses many complexities and challenges. Survey research involves a multistep approach. Numerous frameworks and descriptions of the steps in doing survey research exist, yet all share commonalities. The total or tailored design method of Dillman (1978, 2000) and the total survey method of Fowler (2002) are well-known. Other more practical practitioner oriented approaches are also available (Bourque & Fielder, 2003; Salant & Dillman, 1994; Thomas, 1999). This chapter combines the major elements from these and other sources to present a five-step process for conducting survey research in organizations:

1. Defining the survey purpose and objectives
2. Determining the sample
3. Creating and pretesting the instrument
4. Contacting respondents throughout the survey process
5. Collecting, reducing, and analyzing data

Step 1: Defining the Survey Purpose and Objectives

A key first step in conducting a survey is often overlooked. This is the need to define in specific terms the purpose and objectives for a survey. The familiarity and perceived ease of the survey method has sometimes resulted in the failure to consider other potentially more appropriate research methods. Sapsford (1999, p. 10) reminds researchers to ask five important questions before considering using a survey for research:

1. Is research feasible at all in these circumstances?
2. Is survey research the right way to approach the problem, to obtain the kind of answers that are required?
3. Is a survey feasible—would it yield valid conclusions?
4. Is it ethically appropriate to use survey methods rather than some other approach?
5. Is it ethically and politically appropriate to carry out any form of research, given the research questions and the social context?

An organizational survey can serve a range of purposes, reflecting the variety of intended uses to which the data collected will be applied. Examples include pinpointing areas of concern; measuring employer, employee, or customer attitudes; monitoring program impact; and providing input for future decision making (Rogelberg, Fisher, Maynard, Hakel, & Horvath, 2001). The specific research problem or question(s) should play a major role in determining the purpose and objectives for the survey.

Sapsford (1999) states that survey research tends to require a higher degree of planning than other research approaches. All survey research involves an investment in resources, including time and money, and confusion or lack of clarity of the purpose can result in wasted resources if the final data are not what is needed to answer the research question. Determining the purpose of the survey will also determine the survey scope. *Survey scope* refers to the methodological requirements that are driven by the chosen purpose of the survey, such as the number and type of respondents needed, the content areas to be covered, logistical requirements such as language translation, and the timing of data collection (Rogelberg, Church, Waclawski, & Stanton, 2002).

Step 2: Determining the Sample

The second major step of survey research is determining and selecting who will complete the survey. In some instances, a census maybe preferable if data are needed from every individual in a population. However, usually a sample, a small subset of a population selected to be representative of the whole population, is chosen. Many advances in sampling strategies have been made since World War II when probability samples were first employed in large U.S. government–sponsored studies. A review of a more detailed discussion on sampling is recommended (see chapter 8).

Sampling methods are usually divided into two broad types: probability and nonprobability. *Probability sampling* provides a statistical basis for reporting that the sample drawn is representative of the entire population. Using probability sampling means that every individual in an organizational survey would have a known, nonzero probability of being included in the sample (Fink, 1995). Probability sampling uses random selection to eliminate any form of subjectivity in choosing who will be surveyed and who will not. Examples of probability sampling techniques include simple random, stratified random, systematic, and cluster sampling.

Nonprobability samples provide the advantage of being relatively convenient and economical to construct. They may be appropriate for some organizational research settings although their main drawback is that they do guarantee that all eligible members of a population will have an equal chance of being included in the sample. Nonprobability samples are often used for surveys of hard-to-identify populations and also for pilot tests of questionnaires (Fink, 1995). Examples of nonprobability sampling techniques include convenience sampling, snowball sampling, and quota sampling.

Deciding the size of the sample to be sent a survey is an issue where the highly technical field of sampling provides many potential pitfalls for the beginning survey researcher (Oppenheim, 1992). A statistical calculation can be made given a predetermined margin of error and a table of sample sizes for confidence ranges. These tables of calculating sample sizes can be found in most introductory-level research texts. However, Fowler (2002) advocates a more pragmatic approach, stating that the size of the sample should be based on the purpose and objectives of the survey. A second key aspect guiding the selection of a sample size should be based on the analysis plan. In other words, the plans for how the data are to be analyzed will provide guidance in determining the minimum number of respondents based on the planned analysis techniques the researcher intends to use. The underlying aim in selecting a sample size is to focus more on accuracy than the need for a large sample size.

Step 3: Creating and Testing the Instrument

The next step in the survey process is designing and pretesting the survey instrument.

Design

As with the selection of the sample, the determination of the type of instrument to be used is driven by the purpose and objectives of the survey. The quality of the data collected and, therefore, its utility for organizational decision makers are largely dependent on the quality of the items, instructions, and response scales used in the instrumentation (Rogelberg et al., 2002). For this reason, someone new to survey research should consult the literature on item construction theory (e.g., chapter 3 of this volume; Edwards, Thomas, Rosenfeld, & Booth-Kewley, 1997; Fowler, 1995; Krosnick, 1999; Nunnally, 1978).

If the topic to be surveyed already appears in published studies, it may be possible to use or modify existing items or questions. In fact, it is recommended that researchers use questions with known and acceptable validity and reliability measures from other studies whenever possible (Bourque & Fielder, 2003). A useful inventory of questions that may help survey researchers in organizations appears in the *Handbook of Organizational Measurement* (Price, 1997; Price & Mueller, 1986). The handbook classifies numerous measures and scales under headings such as commitment, job satisfaction, innovation, organization power, stress, and attitudes toward technology. A more recent text covers existing measures on job attitudes, work behaviors, and work values (Fields, 2002).

If no appropriate items exist, then questions need to be written. Dillman (2000) states that the goal of writing a survey question is "to develop a query that every potential respondent will interpret in the same way, be able to respond to accurately, and be willing to answer" (p. 32). Questions can be structured in a number of different formats, including open-ended, where the respondent writes in his answer, or a variety of closed-ended options with response categories provided. Dillman provides 19 principles to guide wording survey questions, including the following:

- Choose simple over specialized words.
- Choose as few words as possible to pose the question.
- Use complete sentences to ask questions.
- Avoid specificity that exceeds the respondent's potential for having an accurate, ready-made answer.
- Develop mutually exclusive response categories.
- Avoid double-barreled questions.

When writing questions with close-ended response options provided, many researchers prefer to use a Likert-type rating scale. First developed by Rensis Likert for measuring attitudes, this type of scale can be applied to numerous different response anchors such as disagree to agree, unsatisfied to satisfied, and frequency, among many others. Dillman (2000) recommends that consistency be used throughout the survey in the direction in which the scale response anchors are displayed so that scales always run from negative to positive or positive to negative. In addition, attention should be paid to ensure that an equal number of positive and negative categories are used for questions measured on a scale. Care is needed when using scale responses to distinguish between a neutral and an undecided category if these response options are provided. Furthermore, the placement of an undecided category is important given that research reported by Dillman has shown major differences in response patterns with the preferred placement being a "no opinion" or "undecided" category in the last position of the scale, whereas the neutral response category should be at the midpoint.

Once the questions are written, then considerable effort and thought should be paid to constructing the survey. Dillman (2000) notes that survey design should attempt to achieve two objectives: first, a reduction in nonresponse and, second, the reduction or avoidance of measurement error. Above all else, the elements considered in survey design should aim to motivate people to respond. One of the general criteria for survey design is to start with relatively easy, straightforward questions that help get the respondent into the survey, whereas questions regarding a great deal of thought or those considered sensitive are usually placed in later sections of survey instruments (Fowler, 1995). There should also be a logical ordering of the topics contained in the survey. Several texts are now available on the practical aspects of survey layout (e.g., Bourque & Fielder, 2003; Dillman, 2000; Fink, 1995; Thomas, 1999), and advances in word processing software have improved the ability for even a novice to design an effective survey.

Testing

Now that the survey is developed, it should be pilot tested or pretested. The pilot test should be used with a sample as similar as possible to that of the main study. Dillman (2000) proposes a four stage process for pilot testing:

STAGE 1. Review by knowledgeable colleagues and analysts

STAGE 2. Interview with potential survey respondents to evaluate the cognitive and motivational qualities of each question

STAGE 3. A small pilot test. Further to this stage, Oppenheim (1992) suggests that participants in the pilot study be informed that they are taking part in a try-out study with encouragements made for respondents to be critical, to ask about things that they don't understand, and to help make the survey better.

STAGE 4. A final check from a small group of people who have had no role in the development or revisions of the survey to catch the inevitable "silly mistakes" that a new pair of eyes usually catch

During the creating and testing stages, efforts must be paid to assess, and improve if necessary, the validity and reliability of the survey. Numerous resources are available to assist with the psychometrics—the branch of survey research that enables the researcher to determine the quality of the survey. A detailed, but not overly technical, overview is provided by Litwin (1995).

Step 4: Contacting Respondents throughout the Survey Process

The actual implementation procedures of the survey have a greater influence on response rates than any design or layout effort. As Dillman (2000, p. 149) summarizes, research has shown that multiple contacts with respondents, the contents of cover letters, appearance of envelopes, incentives, personalization, sponsorship and how it is explained, and other attributes of the communication process have a greater capability for influencing response rates than any aspects associated with survey design. Yet, experimental research has shown that of all the factors related to implementation, making multiple contacts is the best way to improve response rates for mail, interview, and Internet surveys (Dillman, 2000).

The Tailored Design Method of Dillman (2000, p. 1515) recommends that mail surveys make five contacts with respondents. The first four should all be first-class mail with an additional special contact if needed. More specifically:

- A brief prenotice letter sent to respondents a few days prior to the mailing of the survey
- The survey sent with a detailed cover letter explaining why a response is important
- A thank-you postcard sent a few days to a week after the first mailing of the survey. This mailing expresses appreciation for responding and indicates that if the completed questionnaire has not yet been mailed, it is hoped that it will be returned soon.
- A replacement survey sent to nonrespondents 2 to 4 weeks after the first survey mailing. It indicates that the person's completed survey has not yet been received and urges the recipient to respond.
- A final contact may be made by telephone (if telephone numbers are available) a week or so after the fourth contact. It may also be made by courier (Federal Express, DHL, etc.) or by priority U.S. mail. A different mode of contact distinguishes each type of final contact from regular mail delivery.

Although the contact sequence described by Dillman (2000) has been shown to improve response rates, he also acknowledges that human subject protection committees in universities and public agencies often place requirements on survey researchers to reduce harassment of respondents with repeated contacts. Despite these potential limits on respondent contact, Dillman offers four additional suggestions for improving response rates during the implementation stage:

- Design a respondent-friendly survey.
- Provide return envelopes with real first-class postage stamps.
- Personalize correspondence with stationery printed on high-quality paper, addressed to the real names of respondents (not "Dear Employee"), and real signatures signed in ink.
- Provide token prepaid financial incentives rather than promised incentives. Research has shown that the inclusion of one to five dollars will increase response rates (Roth & BeVier, 1998).

Step 5: Collecting, Reducing, and Analyzing Data

A system should be developed to track surveys going out and then their return. Attempts should be made to limit the chance of losing surveys in internal mail systems or due to a poor filing system after investing considerable effort and resources to date. Computer and software advances have greatly assisted the survey researcher in the storing, manipulation, and analysis of data. However, the arrival of returned surveys is not the time to explore how the data will be entered and analyzed. An analysis plan should be included in the first stage of designing the survey with consideration also given to data entry and storage. The aim of data entry is to ensure that every response to every question on every survey can be turned into data that can be analyzed. For quantitative studies, a code book should be assembled where every question is allocated a numerical value for every answer category. In addition, decisions on how missing data are to be treated should be resolved. Once the final and cleaned data set is analyzed, it should be presented in a format that meets the purpose of the study and the informational needs of those sponsoring the survey.

Although the five-stage process to surveys discussed here is appropriate to apply in a variety of research settings, a series of additional guidelines are provided to assist in the application of surveys in organizations and businesses. Dillman (2002) describes several unique characteristics to consider when conducting surveys of business and organizations that are quite different from the approach that would be used for consumer surveys, political surveys, and household surveys. Among these are the questions, What is the organizational entity to be surveyed (entire corporation, single location, division, etc.)? Who should be the respondent? Does an organizational survey policy exist? Is it necessary to go through a gatekeeper? Who is the survey sponsor? and Does a reporting deadline for results exist?

More specific advice on gathering sensitive data in organizations on topics such as harassment, workplace violence, and employee theft is provided by Hosseini and Armacost (1990) and Pryor (2004). Many cross-organizational studies seek responses from top executive-level employees, and this population often produces low response rates. Cycyota and Harrison (2002) found that traditional techniques to increase response rates (advance notice, personalization, incentives, and repeated follow-up) were not effective with this population. In summarizing their findings, these authors suggest that much of what is known to work with organizational surveys has been tested with employee populations, not senior leaders, highlighting that there is much still to be learned about survey research in organizational settings.

NEW DEVELOPMENTS IN SURVEY RESEARCH

The final section of this chapter reports on new developments in survey research that are likely to be of interest to those conducting surveys in organizational settings. These include doing cross-cultural and international surveys, reaction to the well-documented trend of falling response rates, and the emergence of Internet surveys.

Cross-cultural and International Surveys

Given the global nature of business today many people conducting survey research in organizational settings find the need for extending their work across cultural or international boundaries. Yet, cross-cultural and international organizational research presents many challenges. Researchers now understand that studies of comparative management and international management require far more than the application of what works locally (Punnett & Shenkar, 2004). Although surveys remain the preferred method for cross-cultural organizational research, a growing body of literature now illustrates the greater understanding of the numerous methodological issues involved (Gelfand, Raver, & Ehrhart, 2002).

Strategies and recommendations of translation techniques for survey instruments have dominated discussion for doing survey research where different native languages are involved (Brislin, 1986; Harkness, 2003). However, more recent research has explored the specific impact that language has on the ways people respond to surveys (Harzing, 2003). Furthermore, new insights have been gained into how different cultures interpret work-related measures (Riordan & Vandenberg, 1994) and cross-national variation in response rates (Harzing, 2000). Researchers considering cross-cultural and international survey studies are suggested to examine one of the comprehensive guides now available on the topic (e.g., Harkness, Van de Vijver, & Mohler, 2003; Punnett & Shenkar, 2004; Usunier, 1998).

Falling Response Rates

It is noted that as the demand for survey research has increased in recent years so too has an increase in survey nonresponse (Atrostic, Bates, Burt, & Silberstein, 2001; Baruch, 1999; de Heer, 1999). Dillman (2000) notes that survey methods that seemed to work well in the 1980s are now less effective. Several U.S. government agencies that conduct research and collect statistics on organizations have noted falling response rates and have initiated coordinated efforts to further understand issues of nonresponse (Atrostic et al., 2001; Petroni, Sigman, Willimack, Cohen, & Tucker, 2004). A theoretical model for survey nonresponse in organizational studies has been advanced by Tomaskovic-Devey, Leiter, and Thompson (1994). The continuing trend of falling response rates has also been reported in survey research studies published in human resource management and organizational behavior journals (Roth & BeVier, 1998).

A variety of potential explanations for survey nonresponse are offered, including changing cultural norms for cooperation; an increase in frequency with consequent overexposure and frustration at academic and marketing surveys; and increased concerns of confidentiality and anonymity with technology used to collect, store, and analyze findings (Porter, 2004b). However, it is the issue of oversurveying that is attracting increasing attention. Goyder (1986) found that attitudes toward surveys were negatively related to the number of survey requests. Research has also begun to explore how personal attitudes toward surveys relate to responses (Rogelberg et al., 2001). Results showed that feelings about the act of completing a survey, called *survey enjoyment*, and perceptions of the value of survey research both relate to key respondent behaviors such as following directions, timeliness to respond, and willingness to participate in other survey research.

The concern with raising nonresponse rates has been highlighted by Groves (1989) in that nonresponse is usually nonrandom, which then in turn may introduce a bias into the results. A number of theories and explanations have been advanced for why people do and do not respond to surveys. Porter (2004b) categorizes these theories as belonging to two general groups: those that focus on the reasoned action of respondents and those that focus on psychological aspects to explain how a potential participant makes the decision to complete a survey.

Dillman (2000) has advocated that reasoned action of a potential survey participant is the driving determinant with individuals making calculations on the costs and benefits of completing the survey. This approach uses social exchange theory to explain why someone fills out a survey. Dillman and others (Tomaskovis-Devey et al., 1994) have focused on different techniques in the implementation stage, such as contacting respondents throughout the survey process phases to increase the likelihood that an individual will complete the survey. Examples such as making prior notice of survey arrival, offering a monetary incentive with the survey, and reducing the survey length are now known to positively impact response rates so respondents can more readily see the benefits while also reducing the perceived costs of participation (Roth & BeVier, 1998). While these are encouraging developments, the finding that these techniques do not apply to all populations of interest in organizational research (Cycyota & Harrison, 2002) calls attention for the need for further study on this issue.

Internet Surveys

In recent years, Internet and intranet surveys have experienced an explosive increase in usage to perhaps challenge the dominance of paper-and-pencil surveys in organizational settings (Stanton & Rogelberg, 2002). While e-mail was explored as a survey mode during the late 1980s and early 1990s (Sheehan, 2001; Yun & Trumbo, 2000), the rapid growth of the Internet has seen Web-based surveys emerge as one of the most dramatic changes in survey research (Umbach, 2004).

Birnbaum (2004) summarizes some of the benefits of Internet surveys in that this new technology allows researchers to collect data from participants all over the world 24 hours a day and 7 days per week. Surveys can be delivered quickly to anyone connected to the Web, and data can be saved automatically in electronic form, reducing costs in space, dedicated equipment, paper, and mailing, and labor. Finally, once a survey is properly programmed, data can be stored in a form ready for analysis, saving costs of data coding and entry that used to be an expensive and time-consuming part of the research process (p. 804). Others have suggested additional advantages of Internet surveys including flexibility in design and implementation (Dillman, 2000). It is also possible that Internet surveys provide a less threatening approach for collecting sensitive data (Umbach, 2004) and offer a novel medium for participation to avoid the "survey fatigue" reported with paper-and-pencil modes (Stanton & Rogelberg, 2002).

Yet, a number of disadvantages of Internet surveys also exist. Umbach (2004) notes the three most important relate to sources of error, ethical issues, and the expertise required. All survey researchers are concerned with minimizing sources of error but coverage error (sample is not equal to intended target population), sampling error, and measurement error introduced by the Internet delivery mode remain potential limitations. Although Dillman (2000) correctly predicted that the percentage of the population with the hardware, access, and skills needed to respond to Internet surveys is continually increasing, the general population coverage still does not equal that achieved by using conventional survey modes. Internet surveys also raise potential ethical issues regarding invading privacy to contact respondents then protecting participant privacy and confidentiality (Simsek & Veiga, 2001; Stanton & Rogelberg, 2002). Finally, while significant advances have been made in the hardware and software needed for creating and hosting Internet surveys, a level of technical expertise far greater than for traditional survey modes remains a necessity for developing and administering a survey on the Web (Porter, 2004a; Zhang, 1999).

Dillman (2000) points out that a fundamental difference exists between the design of paper and Internet surveys. In a paper survey, the designer completes the questionnaire that is then viewed by the respondent so that both see the same visual image. In an Internet survey, the designer and respondent may see different images of the same survey because of different computer operating systems, browsers, network connections, screen configurations, and individual designer decisions such as the use of color and text wraparound. The technology associated with the Internet does offer some exciting options for survey designers. Multimedia surveys can now be developed that incorporate audio and video. Advances in mobile computing and wireless technology are allowing investigations of surveys delivered to personal digital assistants (PDAs) and cell phones (Couper, 2002). Internet surveys also offer the opportunity to improve on skip patterns where respondents can be presented with questions based on previous answers. Expertise as well as literature on Internet survey layout and design should be consulted for a researcher new to this delivery mode (Birnbaum, 2004; Couper, 2001; Couper, Traugott, & Lamias, 2001; Dillman, 2000).

CONCLUSION

This chapter has reviewed the use of the survey method in organizational research. In briefly summarizing the purpose and history of survey research, it has highlighted the adaptability of this method of data collection. The five-step process for conducting survey research presented is based on a comparison of the most frequently used approaches (Bourque & Fielder, 2003; Dillman, 1978, 2000; Fowler, 2002; Salant & Dillman, 1994; Thomas, 1999). This indicates that several approaches to conducting surveys exist to guide researchers. Ongoing research continues to further identify and extend knowledge associated with the key principles and best practices with each step of the survey process. Major issues continue to shape the continued evolution of survey research. Recent studies and new literature are providing needed information for organizational researchers interested in cross-cultural and international surveys, issues associated with increased nonresponse, and the emergence of Internet surveys.

It is this last issue, Internet-based surveys, that perhaps presents the greater challenge and opportunity for advancing the application of survey research in organizations. It would appear that with continued development, refinement, and modification of all the strategies, techniques, and modes of delivery, the survey is likely to continue to provide a most-valued data collection method for conducting research in organizations.

REFERENCES

Atrostic, B. K., Bates, N., Burt, G., & Silberstein, A. (2001). Nonresponse in U.S. government household surveys: Consistent measures, recent trends, and new insights. *Journal of Official Statistics, 17*(2), 209–226.

Babbie, E. (1992). *The practice of social science research* (6th ed.). Belmont, CA: Wadsworth.

Baruch, Y. (1999). Response rate in academic studies: A comparative analysis. *Human Relations, 52*(4), 421–438.

Bauer, K. W. (2004). Conducting longitudinal studies. *New Directions for Institutional Research, 121*, 75–90.

Bennett, R. (1991). How is management research carried out? In N. C. Smith & P. Dainty (Eds.), *The management research handbook* (pp. 85–103). London: Routledge.

Bills, D. B. (1992). A survey of employer surveys: What we know about labor markets from talking with bosses. *Research in Social Stratification and Mobility, 11*, 1–31.

Birnbaum, M. H. (2004). Human research and data collection via the Internet. *Annual Review of Psychology, 55*, 803–832.

Bourque, L. B., & Fielder, E. P. (2003). *How to conduct self-administered and mail surveys* (2nd ed.). Thousand Oaks, CA: Sage.

Brislin, R. W. (1986). The wording and translation of research instruments. In W. J. Lonner & J. W. Berry (Eds.), *Field methods in cross-cultural research* (pp. 137–164). Beverly Hills, CA: Sage.

Couper, M. P. (2001). Web surveys: A review of issues and approaches. *Public Opinion Quarterly, 64*(4), 464–494.

Couper, M. P. (2002). *New technologies and survey data collection: Challenges and opportunities.* Paper presented at the International Conference on Improving Surveys. Available January 11, 2005, from http://www.icis.dk/ICIS_papers/Keynote1_0_3.pdf.

Couper, M. P., Traugott, M., & Lamias, M. (2001). Web survey design and administration. *Public Opinion Quarterly, 65*(2), 230–253.

Cycyota, C. S., & Harrison, D. A. (2002). Enhancing survey response rates at the executive level: Are employee- or consumer-level techniques effective? *Journal of Management, 28*(2), 151–176.

de Heer, W. (1999). International response trends: Results of an international survey. *Journal of Official Statistics, 15*(2), 129–142.

Dillman, D. A. (1978). *Mail and telephone surveys: The total design method.* New York: Wiley-Interscience.

Dillman, D. A. (2000). *Mail and Internet surveys: The tailored design method* (2nd ed). New York: Wiley.

Dillman, D. A. (2002). *Navigating the rapids of change: Some observations on survey methodology in the early 21st century.* Presentation to the American Association for Public Opinion Research, May 18. Available January 11, 2005, from http://survey.sesrc.wsu.edu/dillman/papers/AAPOR%20%Presidential%Address.pdf.

Edwards, J. E., Thomas, M. D., Rosenfeld, P., & Booth-Kewley, S. (1997). *How to conduct organizational surveys: A step-by-step guide.* Thousand Oaks, CA: Sage.

Fields, D. L. (2002). *Taking the measure of work: A guide to validated scales for organizational research and diagnosis.* Thousand Oaks, CA: Sage.

Fink, A. (1995). *The survey handbook.* Thousand Oaks, CA: Sage.

Fowler, F. J., Jr. (1995). *Improving survey questions: Design and evaluation.* Thousand Oaks, CA: Sage.

Fowler, F. J., Jr. (2002). *Survey research methods* (3rd ed.). Thousand Oaks, CA: Sage.

Gall, M. D., Gall, J. P., & Borg, W. (2003). *Educational research. An introduction* (7th ed.). Boston: Allyn & Bacon.

Gallup, G. (1988). Employee research: From nice to know to need to know. *Personnel Journal, 67*(8), 42–43.

Gelfand, M. J., Raver, J. L., & Ehrhart, K. H. (2002). Methodological issues in cross-cultural organizational research. In S. G. Rogelberg (Ed.), *Handbook of research methods in industrial and organizational psychology* (pp. 227–247). Malden, MA: Blackwell.

Glock, C. Y. (1988). Reflections of doing survey research. In H. J. O'Gorman (Ed.), *Surveying social life: Papers in honor of Herbert H. Hyman* (pp. 31–59). Middletown, CT: Wesleyan University Press.

Goyder, J. (1986). Surveys on surveys: Limitations and potentials. *Public Opinion Quarterly, 50*, 27–41.

Groves, R. M. (1989). *Survey errors and survey costs.* New York. Wiley.

Harkness, J. A. (2003). Questionnaire translation. In J. A. Harkness, F. J. R. Van de Vijver, & P. P. Mohler (Eds.), *Cross-cultural survey methods* (pp. 35–56). Hoboken, NJ: Wiley.

Harkness, J. A., Van de Vijver, F. J. R., & Mohler, P. P. (2003). *Cross-cultural survey methods.* Hoboken, NJ: Wiley.

Harzing, A. W. (2000). Cross-national mail surveys. Why do response rates differ between countries? *Industrial Marketing Management, 29*(3), 243–254.

Harzing, A. W. (with country contributors). (2003). *The use of English questionnaire in cross-national research: Does cultural accommodation obscure national differences.* Conference proceedings of the ANZIBA annual meeting, November 7–8, Dunedin, New Zealand.

Hosseini, J. C., & Armacost, R. L. (1990). Gathering sensitive data in organizations. *American Behavioral Scientist, 36*(4), 443–471.

Kalton, G. (2000). Developments in survey research in the past 25 years. *Survey Methodology, 26*(1), 2–10.

Krosnick, J. A. (1999). Survey research. *Annual Review of Psychology, 50,* 537–567.

Litwin, M. S. (1995). *How to measure survey reliability and validity.* Thousand Oaks, CA: Sage.

Nunnally, J. C. (1978). *Psychometric theory* (2nd ed.). New York: McGraw-Hill.

Oppenheim, A. N. (1992). *Questionnaire design, interviewing and attitude measurement* (2nd ed.). New York: St. Martin's.

Petroni, R., Sigman, R., Willimack, D., Cohen, S., & Tucker, C. (2004). *Response rates and nonresponse in establishment surveys—Bureau of Labor Statistics and Census Bureau.* Washington, DC: Federal Economic Statistics Advisory Committee. Available January 11, 2005, from http://www.bea.doc.gov/bea/about/fesac/Responseratesnonresponse inestablishmentsurveysFESAC121404.pdf.

Porter, S. R. (2004a). Pros and cons of paper and electronic surveys. *New Directions for Institutional Research, 121,* 91–97.

Porter, S. R. (2004b). Raising response rates: What works? *New Directions for Institutional Research, 121,* 5–21.

Price, J. L. (1997). Handbook of organizational measurement. *International Journal of Manpower, 18*(4/5/6), 305–558.

Price, J. L., & Mueller, C. W. (1986). *Handbook of organizational measurement.* Marshfield, MA: Pitman.

Pryor, J. H. (2004). Conducting surveys on sensitive topics. *New Directions for Institutional Research, 121,* 29–50.

Punnett, B. J., & Shenkar, O. (2004). *Handbook for international management research.* (2nd ed.). Ann Arbor: University of Michigan Press.

Riordan, C. M., & Vandenberg, R. J. (1994). A central question in cross-cultural research: Do employees of different cultures interpret work-related measures in an equivalent manner? *Journal of Management, 20*(3), 643–671.

Rogelberg, S. G., Church, A. H., Waclawski, J., & Stanton, J. M. (2002). Organizational survey research. In S. G. Rogelberg (Ed.), *Handbook of research methods in industrial and organizational psychology* (pp. 141–160). Malden, MA: Blackwell.

Rogelberg, S. G., Fisher, G. G., Maynard, D. C., Hakel, M. D., & Horvath, M. (2001). Attitudes towards surveys: Development of a measure and its relationship to respondent behavior. *Organizational Research Methods, 4*(1), 3–25.

Rosenfeld, P., Edwards, J. E., & Thomas, M. D. (1995). Surveys. In N. Nicholson (Ed.), *The Blackwell encyclopedic dictionary of organizational behavior* (pp. 548–549). Cambridge, MA: Blackwell.

Rossi, P. H., Wright, J. D., & Anderson, A. B. (1983). Sample surveys: History, current practices, and future prospects. In P. H. Rossi, J. D. Wright, & A. B. Anderson (Eds.), *Handbook of survey research* (pp. 1–20). Orlando, FL: Academic Press.

Roth, P. L., & BeVier, C. A. (1998). Response rates in HRM/OB survey research: Norms and correlates, 1990–1994. *Journal of Management, 24*(1), 97–117.

Salant, P., & Dillman, D. A. (1994). *How to conduct your own survey.* New York: Wiley.

Sapsford, R. (1999). *Survey research.* London: Sage.

Scheuren, F. (2004). *What is a survey?* Alexandria, VA: American Statistical Association.

Schneider, B., Ashworth, S. D., Higgs, A. C., & Carr, L. (1996). Design, validity, and use of strategically focused employee attitude surveys. *Personnel Psychology, 49,* 695–705.

Sheehan, K. (2001). E-mail survey response rates: A review. *Journal of Computer Mediated Communication, 6*(2).

Simsek, Z., & Veiga, J. F. (2001). A primer on Internet organizational surveys. *Organizational Research Methods, 4*(3), 218–235.

Smith, N. C., & Dainty, P. (1991). *The management research handbook.* London: Routledge.

Smith, T. W. (1990). The first straw? A study of the origins of election polls. *Public Opinion Quarterly, 54*(1), 21–36.

Stanton, J. M., & Rogelberg, S. G. (2002). Beyond online surveys: Internet research opportunities for industrial-organizational psychology. In S. G. Rogelberg (Ed.), *Handbook of research methods in industrial and organizational psychology* (pp. 275–293). Malden, MA: Blackwell.

Thomas, S. J. (1999). *Designing surveys that work.* Thousand Oaks, CA: Corwin.

Tomaskovic-Devey, D., Leiter, J., & Thompson, S. (1994). Organizational survey nonresponse. *Administrative Science Quarterly, 39*(3), 439–457.

Umbach, P. D. (2004). Web surveys: Best practices. *New Directions for Institutional Research, 121,* 23–38.

Usunier, J. C. (1996). *International and cross-cultural management research.* London: Sage.

Yun, G. W., & Trumbo, C. W. (2000). Comparative response to a survey executed by post, e-mail, and web form. *Journal of Computer Mediated Communication, 6*(1).

Zhang, Y. (1999). Using the Internet for survey research: A case study. *Journal of the American Society for Information Science, 51*(1), 57–68.

CHAPTER   8

Multivariate Research Methods

Reid A. Bates, *Louisiana State University*

CHAPTER OUTLINE

Research questions in organizational research rarely involve only two variables. For example, we would not (hopefully) try to predict or explain learning in training, efficacy beliefs, team performance, or climate for safety in an organization from a single independent variable. Although it would often be more convenient (but far less interesting) if the study of human behavior and performance in organizations were this simple, we are nearly always faced with trying to explain, predict, or understand phenomenon that are influenced by a plethora of potentially important variables. Good theory is an indispensable tool for guiding and interpreting research. But, in conjunction with solid foundation in theory, competent researchers must also understand and be able to use appropriate analytic strategies that can handle data on at least two but probably more variables. Multivariate analysis methods are key tools for organizational researchers because of their ability to incorporate multiple variables and to help us in our quest to understand complex behavioral and organizational phenomenon.

Modern point-and-click statistical packages for personal computers have made multivariate analysis in organizational research much more accessible to seasoned as well as novice researchers. However, when any data analytic strategy is taken for granted, becomes too routine or too easy to use, or is used without an adequate understanding of its potentialities—both pro and con—the result can be problematic. A mismatch between research questions and analytic methods, the use of analytic strategies with data that violate critical assumptions and undermine the validity of results, the misinterpretation of statistics and results, and misguided research-to-practice recommendations are just some of the adverse consequences that can occur. The bottom line is that in order to lead our profession through research, organizational researchers must have a sound fundamental understanding of multivariate data analysis to be able both to competently conduct and to interpret and evaluate research.

This chapter briefly reviews some fundamental multivariate analysis techniques available to organizational researchers. The goal is to identify appropriate research questions for each technique, outline fundamental guidelines for use, and discuss key theoretical and practical considerations in the use of these techniques in organizational research. The aim is to minimize discussion of the statistical and computational issues and focus on presenting straightforward and conceptually meaningful descriptions of the issues related to the use of multiple regression, multivariate analysis of variance, logistic regression, and discriminant analysis.

VARIABLE SELECTION

Before discussing these multivariate techniques, it is important to talk briefly about a process common to all the techniques: variable selection. Maximizing the value and utility of multivariate research starts with the careful and thoughtful selection of independent and dependent variables. Variable selection is, in short, one of the most fundamental and crucial steps in multivariate research.

In general, variable selection involves three key considerations: theory, measurement error, and specification error (Hair, Anderson, Tatham, & Black, 1998). First, theory or some other substantive rationale should guide the selection of variables in multivariate analyses. Selecting variables that have a firm footing in theory is critical, particularly in research with explanatory goals, because theory provides a framework for guiding construction of the multivariate models, interpreting the results of the analysis, and explaining the observed relationships. As Pedhazur (1982) says, explanatory research is "inconceivable without theory" (p. 174). In other words, multivariate statistical models can only represent or approximate the phenomena we are studying. They cannot by themselves provide meaningful insight into the reality of those phenomena in the absence of substantive theory (Brannick, 1993).

Second, variable selection should be done with careful attention to minimizing measurement error. *Measurement error* refers to the degree to which the observed (measured) values in a study are not equal to the true values of those variables in the population. For example, measurement error is present if our observed measure of learning transfer overestimates employees' true learning transfer levels. Measurement error has many sources in organizational research, and we typically assume that all variables measured in multivariate research in organizations contain some measurement error. This is problematic because it will inevitably provide a distorted view of the relationships we are trying to study, and it will weaken the power of the statistical techniques being used. Thus, researchers should always be concerned with using the measures that are most concordant conceptually with the concept(s) under study and that have the best psychometric qualities.

Finally, researchers should seek to minimize the inclusion of extraneous or nonessential variables in multivariate research. Including such variables effectively reduces model parsimony, increases the complexity of interpretation, reduces statistical power, and can mask the effects of more important variables. In addition, the exclusion of important variables should also be avoided. Excluding pertinent variables can bias results when those that are omitted are correlated with the variables that were included. For example, if, in a study of learning transfer, supervisor support is omitted from the analysis (even though previous research suggests it is meaningfully correlated with transfer-related efficacy beliefs), then the combined effects that these two variables share (efficacy beliefs and supervisor support) will be left out of the analysis. The effect would be to negatively bias the results of our study to the extent we are unable to fully assess the effects of transfer-related efficacy beliefs on learning transfer.

It is often easy to be less concerned with variable selection in multivariate research than is required. Variables may be selected indiscriminately, for the sake of convenience, or perhaps solely on an empirical basis. However, it is important to remember that the success of any multivariate research is ultimately contingent upon the identification and selection of the most conceptually and empirically sound variables possible given the goals of the research effort.

MULTIPLE REGRESSION: EXAMINING THE
DEGREE OF RELATIONSHIP AMONG VARIABLES

Multiple regression analysis examines the relationship between a single dependent variable and two or more independent variables. It is a widely used analytic technique in organizational research and has been the most popular statistical technique for hypothesis testing for at least two decades (Weinzimmer, Mone, & Alwan, 1994). Multiple regression analysis functions to estimate the extent to which the proportion of variance in a specific dependent variable is associated with variation in multiple independent variables. In so doing, it strives to minimize the sum of squared errors (i.e., deviations) from a regression line in order to produce a linear equation that best fits the observed data points. In other words, multiple regression analysis seeks to find the best combination of multiple independent variables that can predict or explain the variance in a single dependent variable with some degree of accuracy and precision.

Multiple regression analysis is a dependence technique in the sense it is concerned with how scores on the independent variables depend on the dependent variable scores. Thus, it is commonly said that Y (the independent variables) are regressed onto X (the dependent variable). For example, we might be interested in how learning transfer from training (the outcome variable) is dependent on several predictor variables such as transfer-related efficacy beliefs, perceived level of supervisor support for transfer, or reward contingencies. A unique aspect of multiple regression analysis is that it determines the relative predictive importance of each independent variable by simultaneously assessing the relationship between each independent variable and the dependent variable. Each of the independent variables is weighted by the multiple regression analysis procedure to maximize predictive accuracy. The weighted independent variables are formed into a linear combination called the *regression variate* or, more commonly, the *regression model* or *equation*.

Multiple regression can be used to provide insight into the independent and combined effects of a set of predictor variables, and it provides information about the direction and strength of their effects. It can be used to model main and interaction effects, observe improvement in a model's predictive ability through the incremental addition of variables, and examine curvilinear effects through various types of data transformations. In more advanced applications it can also be used to test causal models and to examine mediator and moderator effects. Because of this flexibility and usefulness, multiple regression analysis has earned its status as the analytic "workhorse of behavioral science researchers" (Henderson & Denison, 1989, p. 251).

In general, multiple regression analysis is used to address research questions concerned with prediction and/or explanation. On one hand, organizational research is often concerned with practical issues that focus on prediction. (It is important to note here that "prediction" in the context of multiple regression refers simply to the amount of variance $[R^2]$ in the dependent variable accounted for by the independent variables.) For example, we may want to find a set of biodata elements that can be used in the selection of new hires to predict those that will be "good" employees (however we choose to define and measure "good"). From a multiple regression analysis perspective, our research objective would be to maximize the predictive ability of a set of biodata elements. We could do this using a stepwise entry method to select only those variables that contribute substantially to the predictive accuracy of the biodata model. Or we could compare the predictive ability of two or more regression models, determine the predictive power of each, and choose the one that did the best job of predicting "good" employees.

On the other hand, multiple regression is perhaps more often used in organizational research for explanatory purposes. From this perspective, the concern is for understanding the nature of the relationship between a set of predictors and an outcome variable. For example, in the learning transfer example presented earlier, our interest may be in the importance of the variate as a whole in explaining variation in learning transfer, the type of relationships found between the independent variables and the dependent variables, and the interrelationships among the independent variables themselves.

The Analytic Process

After the research questions have been identified and the variables selected, another key decision the researcher faces is how to enter the independent variables into the regression model. There are three fundamental types of variable entry methods: simultaneous, stepwise, and hierarchical. The choice of which method to use ultimately depends on the goal of the research and the research questions being asked.

Simultaneous Variable Entry

In *simultaneous* entry, all of the independent variables are entered into the regression model at the same time. This method seeks to fit a prediction line as close as possible to all of the variable scores using a least squares fit approach that minimizes the distance between the variable scores and the prediction line. Researchers using simultaneous entry are generally concerned with identifying an optimal set of predictors capable of producing a statistically significant regression model. If the model is significant, then an examination of the standardized regression coefficients (beta coefficients) for each independent variable is undertaken. These values provide information about the relative predictive power of the independent variables. Simultaneous entry is typically used when the interest is purely in prediction and when the researcher is unsure how the predictors might work together as a set or what factors might need to be controlled. It is also possible to use this method to test hypotheses about the predictive power of individual variables.

Stepwise Variable Entry

Stepwise entry adds predictors (forward) to or drops them (backward) from the regression model in a step-by-step fashion depending on their statistical importance. This method focuses on identifying a regression model that contains only those predictors that will maximize R^2 and minimize the sum of squares error. Stepwise entry uses statistical results, usually correlations between the independent variables and the dependent variable, to select which predictors to retain and analyze. In effect, researchers using this method rely on the computer to make decisions about which and how many predictors to retain in the analysis (Leech, Gliner, Morgan, & Harmon, 2003).

This method is often used to "mine data" when there is a large number of predictors and a priori model specification is not possible, when there is no theory on which to base variable selection, or when the researchers have failed to use theory to guide model development (Henderson & Denison, 1989). Although commonly used, its application has come under intense criticism for a number of reasons (for a complete discussion of the problems with stepwise entry, see, e.g., Cohen, Cohen, West, & Aiken, 2003; Huberty, 1989; Snyder, 1991; Thompson 1989, 1995). For example, because variables entered later in a stepwise analysis are dependent on variables already entered, it is not uncommon for researchers to make inappropriate conclusions about the relative importance of the independent variables. Stepwise entry methods also tend to produce sample-specific results. In addition, the data-driven nature of stepwise entry, which seeks to maximize R^2, means that researchers should be extremely cautious when interpreting the retained variables as if they had theoretical importance. Because of these and other serious limitations, this entry method is best used only when

- researchers thoroughly understand its shortcomings;
- the research goal is primarily predictive (not explanatory);
- the sample size is very large relative to the number of variables (an observation-to-variable ratio of at least 40:1); and
- the results can be cross-validated with another sample, either a new or split sample (Cohen et al., 2003).

Hierarchical Variable Entry

A third method of entry is hierarchical entry. Like stepwise, *hierarchical* entry introduces predictors into the regression model in steps. A key difference, however, is that the order of entry is decided ahead of time by the researcher and is based upon a careful conceptualization of the research question(s) and a substantive theoretical or conceptual rationale. The a priori specification of variable order of entry is critical because different variable orderings can produce substantially different results. Three generally accepted criteria on which to base order-of-entry decisions are (1) the causal priority of the variables (cause variables are entered before effect variables), (2) research relevance, and (3) the structural or functional properties of the variables themselves (see Cohen et al., 2003, for a more complete description of these parameters). In addition, when reporting research results, the rationale underlying order of entry decisions should be clearly described.

Hierarchical regression is used to answer questions about how variance is partitioned among independent variables or sets of independent variables. It allows us to understand how predictors entered later in the model affect predictive power over and above that of the predictors entered earlier. The focus of the analysis is on the change in R^2 with each successive addition of predictors to the regression model. For example, if we were interested in learning how each of the transfer predictors mentioned earlier (transfer-related efficacy beliefs, perceived level of supervisor support for transfer, and reward contingencies) influenced overall learning transfer, we could enter each as a separate step in the analysis and examine the change in R^2 that occurred with the entry of each variable.

As you might expect, hierarchical regression is used for primarily explanatory research. It can be used to test theory-driven hypotheses, causal models, and moderated or mediated relationships. Because of its theory-driven nature, it is seldom appropriate as an exploratory tool.

Model Fit

Model fit in multiple regression is evaluated by examining values for the coefficient of determination (R^2). R^2 is a measure of the proportion of variation of the dependent variable about its mean that is explained by the independent variables. R^2 values vary between 0 and 1, and it is assumed that the higher the R^2 value (the closer to 1), the better the explanatory power of the regression model and the better its ability to predict the criterion. To determine whether R^2 is statistically significant (significantly greater than 0), an F statistic is calculated. In hierarchical regression, for example, an R^2 value and an F statistic would be calculated after each entry step in the analysis. It is commonly recognized when using multiple regression that the R^2 calculated in a sample overestimates the true R^2 in the population. Therefore, most studies report both R^2 values and "adjusted R^2" values because the latter tends to avoid the overestimation problem and provides a more unbiased estimate of the population R^2 (Darlington, 1990). In addition, because adjusted R^2 values make adjustments for the number of predictors and variations in sample size, they are helpful in making comparisons across regression models that included fewer or more predictors or were applied in a different sized sample (Hair et al., 1998).

Regression analysis also produces *regression coefficients* for each independent variable. These are numerical values that estimate the amount of change in the dependent variable for each unit change in the independent variable. In multiple regression, these are referred to as *partial regression coefficients* because each value takes into account the relationships between each of the independent variables and between each of the independent variables and the dependent variable. Partial regression coefficients are a function of both the degree of correlation in these relationships and the scale used to measure the independent variable.

Because partial regression coefficients are expressed in terms of the scale units used to measure the associated independent variable, it is often inappropriate to compare partial regression coefficients from independent variables measured with different scales. To overcome this problem, researchers typically rely on the beta coefficients. *Beta coefficients* are standardized regression coefficients (i.e., they have a mean of 0 and a standard deviation of 1), can have both positive and negative values, and are routinely produced in every regression analysis. Beta coefficients provide insight into the nature of the relationship between an independent variable and the dependent variable. For example, when a beta coefficient is negative, it tells us that a unit increase in the independent variable results in an expected decrease in the dependent variable. Beta coefficients also provide information about the relative predictive power of the independent variables by allowing a direct comparison across the independent variables in terms of the extent to which each contributes to R^2 (e.g., higher beta values indicate more predictive power).

Diagnostic Analysis

A number of authors make a strong case that some kind diagnostic analysis should be run as a routine part of every multiple regression analysis used in organizational research (Bates, Holton, & Burnett, 1999; Fox, 1991; Venter & Maxwell, 2000). Diagnostic analysis is done as a first step in multiple regression by simultaneously entering all the predictors in the regression model and examining several different output elements to address a number of issues. First, this analysis should test for violations of regression assumptions. In multiple regression analysis, four assumptions are made: linearity of the relationship between criterion and predictor variables; constant variance of the error terms (homoscedasticity); normality of the error term distribution; and the independence of residuals. Satisfying these assumptions is required in order for the normal probability density function to be used in testing the null hypothesis about parameter estimates. The extent to which the data confirm these assumptions can be evaluated by examining various residual plots, a method that provides more clarity over a range of diagnostic tests (Netter, Wassermann, & Kutner, 1989). Scatterplots of residuals are preferred over those of observed values because the latter can mask violations of assumptions, particularly when the regression slope is steep (Weinzimmer et al., 1994).

Second, the presence of substantial intercorrelations (multicollinearity) among predictors should also be examined. Multicollinearity can limit the size of the coefficient of determination (R^2) and make determination of the unique contribution of each predictor difficult to assess because the effects of the predictors are confounded due to their intercorrelation. (For more information on how to find multicollinearity in multiple regression analysis and what to do about it, see Belsley, Kuh, & Welsch, 1980; Chatterjee & Yilmaz, 1992; Hair et al., 1998; Morrow-Howell, 1994.)

Finally, most researchers agree that regression summary statistics such as R^2 or beta coefficients can present distorted pictures of sample data. This may easily occur when "good" data points are mixed with observations that are both inappropriate and influential. *Influential* observations refer to a broad category of data points that includes outliers, leverage points and other data points that have a disproportionate impact on estimates in a multiple regression analysis. This influence may result from substantial differences in the predictor values, extreme values for the criterion variable, or both. Therefore, a complete diagnostic analysis in multiple regression analysis should also test for the presence of outliers or influential observations, both of which are commonly found in organizational research. For more information on identifying and dealing with outliers and influential observations, see Hair et al. (1998) or Bates et al. (1999).

Data Considerations

Multiple regression analysis allows the use of a wide range of independent variables in attempting to make predictive equations. Although multiple regression analysis is used primarily when both the independent and dependent variables are metric (interval level), it can also accommodate categorical data (nominal or ordinal) through proper dummy coding (see Hardy, 1993, for more information on coding categorical variables in multiple regression analysis). The dependent variable in multiple regression analysis must be metric, although a specialized regression technique (logistic regression) can accommodate binary dependent variables.

Sample size is an important consideration in multiple regression because the size of the sample affects statistical power as well as the generalizability of the results. General guidelines can be found that recommend an observation-to-independent variable ratio of at least 5:1 or 10:1, but these can be deceiving because of the complexity of the issues involved in identifying appropriate sample size. Wampold and Freund (1987) suggest that the sample size in multiple regression "should be sufficiently large so that there is a reasonable chance (some say 80%) of detecting a relation (i.e., reaching statistical significance) when a true relation exists in the population" (p. 378). Using this criterion, observation-to-variable ratios less than 10:1 may often be inadequate (Maxwell, 2000). Thus, in addition to the number of independent variables, researchers should also consider expected effect size, power requirements, and level of accuracy desired when settling on a desired sample size. For more information on these issues, see Cohen (1988) or Maxwell (2000). Additional guidance can be found by consulting published sample size tables (e.g., Algina & Olejnik, 2003).

For More Information

The "standard" reference guides to multiple regression include Cohen and Cohen (1987), the nicely updated version of that text (Cohen et al., 2003), and Pedhazur

(1997). In addition to these, there are also a number of other informative and highly readable sources. Bobko (1995), for example, makes statistical theory in regression (and correlation) accessible to readers through the use of extensive applied examples from I/O psychology and management. Hair et al. (1998) provide a very comprehensive and readable treatment of multiple regression (and other multivariate techniques). For a more thorough discussion on the use of regression in the examination of mediators and moderators, see Baron and Kenny (1986) or Judd, Kenny, and McClelland (2001). For guidance in interpreting and reporting regression results, see Huberty and Allen (1999) and Huberty and Hussein (2001).

LOGISTIC REGRESSION: REGRESSION WITH A DICHOTOMOUS DEPENDENT VARIABLE

As we have seen, there are many cases in organizational research in which linear regression is appropriately used to assess the predictive power of a set of continuous independent variables on a single continuous dependent variable.

Logistic regression is ideally suited for situations in which the assumptions of linearity or and homoscedasticity (equal variance of residuals across independent variable values) cannot be met and a dichotomous dependent variable is involved (Hosmer & Lemshow, 2000). Dichotomous or binary variables are those with values restricted to two options, typically coded as 0 and 1. Logistic regression is based on the assumption of a binomial distribution and therefore cannot use the ordinary least squares approach to model estimation, as does multiple regression. The method of estimation for logistic regression is maximum likelihood. Maximum likelihood estimation takes an iterative approach to finding coefficients that maximize the likelihood of obtaining the observed values for the dependent variable. Put somewhat differently, in logistic regression, the maximum likelihood procedures estimate coefficient values for the independent variables that have the highest probability of generating the sample values of the dependent variable.

Logistic regression can thus be understood as a distinct form of regression analysis that is specifically designed to predict and explain dichotomous dependent variables. Like multiple regression, logistic regression also creates a variate with coefficients (logistic coefficients) that show the influence of each independent variable in predicting or explaining the dependent variable. The coefficients represent measures of the changes in the odds ratio and, like multiple regression coefficients, have signs (+ or −). Positive coefficients indicate an increase in the odds ratio (an increase in the probability of an event occurring); negative coefficients indicate a decrease in the odds ratio (a decrease in the probability of an event occurring) (Hair et al., 1998).

The Analytic Process

The analytic process in logistic regression involves the transformation of a binary dependent variable into a continuous variable (the logistic transformation) that is the natural logarithm of an odds ratio. The odds ratio is the comparison of the probability of a value for the dependent variable occurring versus it not occurring. An odds ratio says that, given the values of the independent variables in the model, the probability of a certain outcome (high/low, in/out, belongs to this type/that type) occurring can be calculated. In the example given earlier, the dependent variable is the likelihood of enrolling versus not enrolling in remedial training given basic skills assessment scores. The dependent variable in logistic regression is thus treated as a probability value, or the odds that a randomly selected case from a population has a particular combination of predictor values (Dattalo, 1994). The value of the odds ratio can then be studied to assess how it changes as values for the predictors change (for more details on this process and the mathematics involved, see Hosmer & Lemshow, 2000).

Like multiple regression, there are multiple options when it comes to the entry of variables in logistic regression—and the choice of which method to use is similarly dependent on the analytic objectives. One option is *simultaneous entry* (also called *direct entry*), when all the predictors are entered at once. This entry method allows researchers to evaluate the predictive contribution of each variable as if it were entered last in the model. It is typically used when hypotheses about the order or importance of predictors have not been made and the researcher wants to gain insight into the predictive power of each predictor.

Sequential or *hierarchical entry* is also possible in logistic regression. This approach runs multiple models each representing a different step in the sequential entry of variables and is appropriate if the researcher has a substantive rationale for specifying the order of entry of the predictors.

Another common alternative is *stepwise entry*, which, again like multiple regression, includes or removes predictors from the model based solely on statistical criteria. Consequently, it suffers from many of the same criticisms as do stepwise methods in multiple regression and is best used as a preliminary screening device when there are a large number of predictors. Readers are directed to Hosmer and Lemshow (2000) for a discussion of inclusion/exclusion criteria if the stepwise method is used. For more information about entry methods in logistic regression, see Menard (1995).

Model fit in logistic regression is evaluated by comparing logistic models with a null model (the model containing the intercept or constant only) and assessing the extent to which the logistic model improves fit. The baseline statistic of interest is the initial log likelihood function or the -2 log likelihood goodness-of-fit statistic ($-2LL$). Smaller values for $-2LL$ indicate better fit, and if this value decreases with the addition of independent variables, then model prediction has improved. The most commonly used fit statistic, the *chi-square statistic*, indicates whether the predictive improvement of the logistic model (containing the independent variables) over the null model is statistically significant. Another approach to the evaluation of model fit involves the construction of classification matrices (an approach similar to that used in discriminant analysis) or other classification tests (see Hosmer & Lemshow, 2000). Various measures (e.g., Cox & Snell R^2 and Nagelkerke R^2) analogous to the coefficient of determination (R^2) in multiple regression have also been developed as indicators of overall model fit and are often reported in published research. However, these cannot be easily interpreted (they don't accurately capture the meaning of variance explained or correspond to predictive efficiency) and are best used as supplements to overall goodness-of-fit test statistics (Peng, Lee, & Ingersoll, 2002).

A significant chi-square indicates that at least one coefficient in the logistic model is significantly different from zero (i.e., changes the odds ratio). The *Wald statistic* is used to determine whether this change is due to chance or not. Output from logistic regression analyses also includes R statistics that represent partial correlations between the predictors and the dependent variable while holding other predictors constant. These values are interpreted to show the level of association between the predictor and the dependent variable after the influence of the other predictors has been removed. Another approach for examining the contribution of a single independent variable is to run two models, one with the predictor of interest and one without. The chi-square difference between the models would represent the contribution of the independent variable to improved model fit.

Data Considerations

Logistic regression is used in the study of binary dependent variables and can be used with independent variables that are continuous, ordinal, dichotomous, or some combination thereof. Although logistic regression is not subject to assumptions of multivariate normality or linear relationships between predictors (as is multiple regression), researchers should be aware that these data characteristics can improve statistical power. Logistic regression is bound only by the assumption that the distribution of errors conforms to a binomial distribution. This assumption is typically taken as robust if the sample is random or there is no reason to believe that independence of observations has been violated (i.e., each response comes from a different case) (Peng et al., 2002). Also, logistic regression is sensitive to high correlations among the independent variables, so data should be screened for sources of multicollinearity. In terms of sample size requirements, recent recommendations suggest a minimum case-to-variable ratio of 10:1 with a minimum sample size of 100 (Tabachnick & Fidell, 2001).

As you will see in the next section, both logistic regression and discriminant analysis are used when the dependent variable is categorical. Like discriminant analysis, the fundamental goal of logistic regression is to predict group or category membership for individual cases (Tabachnick & Fidell, 2001). Despite this equivalence, there are several reasons why logistic regression is often preferred over discriminant analysis if the dependent variable is binary. First, logistic regression can potentially be applied in more situations because it is not bounded by assumptions of multivariate normality or equal covariance matrices across groups. Second, logistic regression can accommodate an extremely skewed distribution of dependent variables whereas discriminant analysis cannot (Morrow-Howell & Proctor, 1992). Finally, the straightforward statistical tests; ability to include continuous, ordinal, or categorical independent variables (the latter two typically require dummy coding); the capacity to incorporate nonlinear effects and provide familiar diagnostic measures (residuals, residual plots, measures of influence) make logistic regression a relatively user-friendly technique.

For More Information

The texts written by Hosmer and Lemshow (1989, 2000) are the standard references for researchers using logistic regression. In addition, Kleinbaum and Klein (2002) have produced a self-study guide to logistic regression that uses examples from biology and epidemiology. The chapters in this resource are arranged in a "lecture book" format that includes learning objectives, an outline, illustrations, key mathematics and formulae with explanations, practice exercises, and tests. Tabachnick and Fidell (2001) offer an in-depth and understandable description of logistic regression. Their text also includes a number of analysis examples and a comparison of popular statistical software programs designed especially for logistic regression in SPSS, SAS, and SYSTAT.

DISCRIMINANT ANALYSIS: PREDICTING GROUP MEMBERSHIP AND DESCRIBING GROUP DIFFERENCES

Discriminant analysis is a multivariate technique used for the study of group differences. It has two fundamental purposes: to predict or classify subjects (people, behavior, judgments, etc.) into groups and to describe and explain group differences following a statistically significant MANOVA. Within these two broad applications, discriminant analysis is a potentially useful multivariate technique when our interest is in classifying objects into groups based on scores on a set of independent variables, identifying which combination of independent variables from a larger set can best account for group differences, describing the key dimensions of group differences, or testing theories or models that incorporate stages or taxonomies (Betz, 1987).

As noted in the previous section, discriminant analysis is comparable in some ways to logistic regression. Both are concerned with identifying, predicting, or explaining group membership and both are used when the dependent variable is categorical and the independent variables are continuous. Logistic regression and discriminant analysis also use comparable diagnostic measures and, when used in two group analyses, can provide similar results when the assumptions of each technique are met.

There are also some key differences in these analytic techniques. The purpose of each is distinct: discriminant analysis is most often used to identify a set of predictors that best discriminates between two or more groups whereas logistic regression is concerned with making inferences about the relationship between a set of independent variables and a binary dependent variable (Morrow-Howell & Proctor, 1992). Logistic regression is more robust when variable distributions deviate from normality, and it can be used with nonmetric (categorical) independent variables when those are dummy coded. Categorical independent variables cannot be used in discriminant analysis because they violate the assumption of multivariate normality and consequently yield biased estimators (Cleary & Angel, 1984). On the other hand, logistic regression is limited to two groups, whereas discriminant analysis can handle two groups (two group discriminant analysis) but is generally the preferred method when or three or more groups (multiple discriminant analysis) are involved.

Discriminant analysis is most widely used as a predictive tool to classify subjects into groups. In so doing, discriminant analysis works to create linear combinations of a set of independent variables so that the different levels of the dependent variable (categories) differ as widely as possible. Thus, discriminant analysis is very similar to multiple regression in that both strive for prediction of a dependent variable using a linear combination of continuous independent variables (the independent variables in discriminant analysis are often referred to as *discriminant* or *discriminator variables*). A key difference is that multiple regression is used to predict a metric or continuous dependent variable. Discriminant analysis is used when predicting nonmetric or categorical dependent variables that have at least two but generally three or more levels (e.g., high performers/moderate performers/low performers, certification success/failure, employees who stay for 2 years or less/employees who stay for 5 years/employees who stay for 10 or more years, etc.).

A less widespread use of discriminant analysis, albeit one strongly advocated by some researchers (Huberty & Morris, 1989), is as a follow-up technique to a significant MANOVA. This has been termed descriptive discriminant analysis and is oriented toward "describing the effects of some grouping variables on a set of criterion variables" (Huberty & Barton, 1989, p. 159). Descriptive discriminant analysis is seen as providing at least two key advantages to the multiple univariate tests that follow a significant MANOVA. First, by simultaneously examining all the variables in the model, it avoids the experiment-wise error that comes with the use of repeated univariate tests. Second, it can provide more information and a richer understanding of group differences by examining the nature of the underlying dimensions represented by the multivariate differences between groups. For example, it can give insight into the relative ordering or importance of variables. Third, its use may lead to a more parsimonious explanatory model. In effect, it can provide what Brannick (1993) characterizes as a "data reduction function." That is, discriminant analysis allows the combination of a large number of independent variables into a smaller number of weighted combinations so that the differences between the categories of interest can be accounted for by a reduced set of variables.

For example, assume that a significant MANOVA indicated that two groups differed on 8 of the 12 variables under study; discriminant analysis may identify a significant discriminant function that effectively describes group differences using only five of the eight variables. Researchers interested in learning more about descriptive discriminant analysis are encouraged to consult Bray and Maxwell (1982, 1985), Huberty (1984), or Huberty and Wisenbaker (1992). Adsit, London, Crom, and Jones's (1997) study of cross-cultural differences in attitude survey ratings provides a good example of descriptive discriminant analysis used in organizational research.

Data Considerations

Discriminant analysis requires that the dependent variable be categorical with two or more levels. The levels can be formed on any basis such as demographic variables (gender, ethnicity), individual attributes (personality, cultural orientation, career interest), or some type of behavior (achieve certification/do not achieve certification, job leaver/job stayer). The independent variables in discriminant analysis are typically continuous (metric).

Because of the sensitivity of discriminant analysis to the observation-to-independent variable ratio, sample size is an important issue. From the perspective of overall sample size, a ratio of 20 cases to each independent variable is recommended, not to fall below a minimum ratio of 5:1. Group size is also an issue. The smallest group should not contain fewer than 20 cases. In situations with large discrepancies in group sizes, some effort should be made to equalize the group sizes through random sampling (Hair et al., 1998).

Discriminant analysis assumes that all relationships between independent variables and the dependent variable are linear. The other data requirements necessary for predictive discriminant analysis include independence of observations, multivariate normality of the independent variables, and equal covariance matrices. Multicollinearity should also be assessed, especially if the stepwise entry method is being used, since correlated independent variables can mask each other's effects making interpretation of the discriminant function difficult. For this reason, it is suggested that independent variables selected for discriminant analysis *not* be highly correlated (Brown & Wicker, 2000). Outliers can also have a substantial influence on the results of predictive discriminant analysis and outlier detection should be a part of every discriminant analysis. Hair et al. (1998) provide very user-friendly descriptions of methods for testing for violations of basic assumptions, checking multicollinearity, and identifying and dealing with outliers in discriminant analysis.

The Analytic Process

Like multiple regression, one of the first decisions to be made in the use of discriminant analysis is the method of entry of variables into the analysis. Options include simultaneous and stepwise, both forward and backward. Simultaneous entry puts all variables into the model at the same time and calculates the discriminant function using all of the independent variables. This method is useful if the number of independent variables is limited and the researcher has little interest in discovering how well certain variables perform as discriminators in the absence of others.

By far the most popular entry method in discriminant analysis is the stepwise approach, often called *forward selection*. This approach puts independent variables into the discriminant function one at a time to find the best one-variable model, the best two-variable model, and so on, until all variables have been entered. The order of entry is based on the variables' relative importance to group separation with the most powerful discriminators entered first (see Huberty, 1984, for a description of different indices for ordering and selecting variables in discriminant analysis). This method of entry is a common variable selection device particularly when a relatively large number of independent variables are being examined and the researcher is interested in selecting and removing those variables that don't add to the power of the model to discriminate between groups. However, as in multiple regression, the use of stepwise methods in discriminant analysis is not immune criticism (e.g., Thompson, 1989, 1995). It has been suggested this method should only be used as a preliminary analysis tool to discard some variables in situations with a large number of independent variables, or when a predetermined order of variable entry has been specified (Huberty, 1984).

The basic analytic strategy of predictive discriminant analysis is to create a variate (a linear combination analogous to a regression model) of the independent variables. The variate is referred to as the *discriminant function*. Discriminant analysis assigns values to the independent variables in the discriminant function that are weighted to maximize between-group variance. Predicted values produced by the discriminant function are used to assign observations to an a priori–defined category or group. Discriminant analysis then tests hypotheses about the equivalence of group means by adding the weighted values for the independent variables to produce a single score (the discriminant Z score) for each individual case in the sample. The mean Z score for all cases in each group is calculated to produce a *centroid* (group mean). The centroids are then compared and tested to determine whether the discrimination between groups is significant (i.e., the distance between group means is statistically significant) (Kleinbaum, Kupper, Muller, & Nizam, 1998). Wilks's lambda, Pillai's criterion, and Hotelling's trace are statistics typically used to evaluate the overall fit of the discriminant function. Mahalanobis D^2 and Rao's V are most appropriate when stepwise entry is being used (Hair et al., 1998).

If the discriminant function is significant, then the interest is in assessing the accuracy with which the discriminant function can predict group membership. For this purpose, discriminant analysis typically relies on the construction of classification matrices that assess the percentage of observations that are correctly classified (i.e., the hit ratio). To do so, a discriminant score is calculated for each individual case and compared to the centroid of each group. The case is predicted to belong to the group whose centroid is closest to the case's discriminant score. This then provides a basis for comparing the predicted group membership (based on discriminant score) with actual group membership (based on the a priori classification), and the percentage of correct predictions can be computed. The statistical test for the ability of the discriminant function to make statistically significant improvements in classification accuracy is the Mahalanobis D^2.

An interesting aspect of multiple discriminant analysis is that, unlike multiple regression, it calculates more than one linear combination of independent variables. In fact, it calculates $n-1$ discriminant functions, where n equals the number of groups in the analysis. So for a four-group discriminant analysis, three discriminant functions would be calculated; for five groups, four discriminant functions; and so on. Multiple discriminant analysis thus creates multiple models to reflect various dimensions of difference between groups.

The interpretation of predictive discriminant analysis results can be viewed "as a special type of factor analysis that extracts factors from the data for the specific task of displaying differences among criterion groups" (Watson, 1982, p. 125). Thus, the interpretation of predictive discriminant analysis results typically focuses on assessing the importance of the independent variables in discriminating between groups. This can be done through an examination of the size and sign (+ or –) of the *discriminant weights* (*also called discriminate coefficients*) for each variable. In general, larger values are seen as having more discriminating power, although multicollinearity among the independent variables can cloud this interpretative rule. As with beta coefficients in multiple regression, plus/minus signs on the coefficients indicate whether the variable makes a positive or negative contribution to the overall discriminant function (Hair et al., 1998). In another parallel with factor analysis, it can be useful in the interpretation of multiple discriminant analysis results to rotate the discriminant function. Like factor analysis, rotation is employed to make the discrimination easier to interpret, more meaningful, and more parsimonious (see Watson, 1982).

The interpretation of results can also be done through an examination of *discriminant loadings* (also known as *canonical variate correlations*). These loadings are conceptually similar to factor loadings in factor analysis and reflect the correlation between the independent variables and the discriminant function. In effect, they show the relative contribution of each independent variable to the discriminant function. There are no clear guidelines on which interpretative approach is superior (weights or loadings), and each provide different kinds of practical information. For example, discriminant weights are helpful in making decisions about what variables to retain whereas discriminant loadings are useful in interpreting the dimensionality of the function (Betz, 1987).

Validation of Results

As you may have deduced from the preceding paragraphs, discriminant analysis uses the same cases in the computation of the discriminant function as it does in the creation of the classification matrix. Because of this, predictive discriminant analysis models tend to overestimate (inflate) the hit ratio. Put somewhat differently, predictive discriminant analysis maximizes group differences by using an internal classification analysis that reclassifies cases with known a priori group membership and, in so doing, capitalizes on sample specific error (Betz, 1987). Although some researchers accept this as partial validation of the discriminant function if the sample size is large (the smallest group size is at least five times the number of independent variables) (Huberty & Barton, 1989), most agree that the internal and external validity of predictive discriminant analysis results will be improved if the discriminant weights are applied in a new sample. The simple reason is that the hit ratio generated from the new sample is seen as a better approximation of the predictive accuracy of the discriminant function. This validation step is considered particularly essential if the discriminant function is to be used for prediction in new populations. For more information on methods of cross-validation in predictive discriminant analysis, see Hair et al. (1998) or Brown and Wicker (2000).

For More Information

Hair et al.'s (1998) text, cited throughout this chapter, is an excellent resource that provides a very user-friendly and practical guide to discriminant analysis and other multivariate techniques. Brown and Wicker's (2000) chapter in Tinsley and Brown's (2000) text provides a thorough overview of both predictive and descriptive discriminant analyses. Tabachnick and Fidell (2000) present a more detailed and advanced discussion of the mechanics of discriminant analysis. For specific guidance in the reporting of discriminant analysis results, see Huberty and Hussein (2003). Huberty and Lowman (1998) provide helpful information about reporting results as well as a review of the popular statistical packages that perform discriminant analysis.

MANOVA: EXAMINING THE SIGNIFICANCE OF GROUP DIFFERENCES

As an organizational researcher, we might be interested in studying how different personality traits (e.g., task oriented vs. person oriented) of production unit team leaders influence individual team member performance across a number of criterion measures (e.g., absenteeism, coworker performance ratings, or accident rate). In analyses like this, where the researcher is interested in finding out whether there are significant differences in a set of two or more dependent variables across two or more groups formed by one or more categorical independent variables, multivariate analysis of variance (MANOVA) is the appropriate analytic choice. MANOVA, in effect, represents an extension and generalization of ANOVA to situations with multiple dependent variables. Whereas ANOVA tests whether mean differences on a single dependent variable are statistically significant, MANOVA creates a linear combination of dependent variables to maximize group differences and tests whether those differences are statistically significant. In our leadership style example, MANOVA is used to ask whether a combination of the three outcome measures (absenteeism, coworker performance ratings, and accident rate) varied as a function of the grouping variables (task- vs. person-oriented team leaders).

Although this research question could be addressed by performing separate ANOVA or *t*-tests for each dependent variable, this approach would create an experiment-wise error rate problem. Experiment-wise error rate is the probability of making one or more Type I errors (the probability of finding a significant difference in group means when in fact there isn't one) in multiple dependent-variable tests. For example, in a series of separate ANOVAs, as the number of dependent variables increases, the experiment-wise error rate increases exponentially (for more about this phenomenon, see Leary & Altmair, 1980). This problem is further exacerbated if the dependent variables are correlated (as they probably are in our example and often are in organizational research). If we do not control for the increased probabilities of Type I errors, we are faced with the difficulty of determining which of the effects in our study are "true" and which are not. It should also be noted that as Type I error rates increase, Type II error rates (the probability of *not* finding one or more significant differences across a multiple test when there are some) also increase. Thus, "separate univariate analyses of multiple dependent variables in the same experiment can be doubly disastrous" (Haase & Ellis, 1987, p. 405). In most circumstances, MANOVA controls for the inflation of both these error rates (for a more information on conditions in which MANOVA is less effective in controlling experiment-wise error, see Huberty & Morris, 1989, or Maxwell, 1992). It does so by performing a single multivariate test on the combined dependent variables.

MANOVA is able to use a single multivariate test (often called the *omnibus test*) to examine differences across multiple dependent variables because it combines multiple dependent variables into a single value (or variate) that maximizes group differences and the subsequent F value. As we have seen, the concept of a *variate* is central to discussions of many multivariate techniques and refers, in general, to a set of weighted variables identified by the researcher that are combined to meet the research objectives. In multiple regression, for example, a variate of independent variables is used to predict a single dependent variable. In the case of MANOVA, the linear weights of the dependent variables in the variate are formed so as to maximize the difference between two or more groups (the independent variables). By treating the dependent variables as a whole across groups, MANOVA provides a means for detecting an overall difference between the grouping variables even though there may be no differences based on single univariate tests. This is because a series of separate ANOVA tests do not take into account the correlation between dependent variables. They therefore use less information to assess group differences. By combining dependent variables into a variate, MANOVA capitalizes on the possibility that some linear combination of the dependent variables may identify combined differences that could not be found in separate univariate tests (Hair et al., 1998).

MANOVA has a wide range of potential uses in organizational research and can be used to address several different kinds of multivariate questions. We have already seen that MANOVA can be used to analyze overall differences between groups across multiple independent variables while controlling for experiment-wise error rate. MANOVA is also useful if a researcher is more interested in studying the collective effect of a set of dependent variables than in studying differences on dependent variables individually. In the example presented earlier, our interest may be in an examination of the three criterion measures as a single underlying construct representing individual team member performance (rather than the individual criterion measures separately). Because MANOVA creates a variate of the dependent variables, researchers can use it to examine multiple dependent variables as if they were a single construct or to gain insight into how the criterion variate might be reduced to a smaller number of dimensions (Bray & Maxwell, 1982).

MANOVA can also be used in repeated-measure designs. These designs involve subjects on which multiple data points on the same dependent variable have been collected at multiple points in time. For example, by taking multiple measures of performance at various time intervals (2, 4, and 6 weeks after training) MANOVA could be used to study the application and maintenance of learned skills over time. Readers interested in learning more about the use of MANOVA in repeated measures designs are encouraged to see O'Brien and Kaiser (1985).

Typical causal-comparative studies in organizational research include a number of variables. For example, the study of learning transfer systems often involves examination of motivation variables (e.g., expectancies; efficacy beliefs), support factors in the work environment (e.g., supervisor and coworker support), and elements related to the training program itself (e.g., content; delivery methods). With MANOVA, the researcher has the capacity to group these different variables into related clusters (e.g., all motivational variables, all work environment variables, and all training-related variables) and use a separate MANOVA to analyze each. The use of multiple independent variables (called a *factorial design*) can also include the addition of control variables or covariates. This transforms MANOVA into MANCOVA (multivariate analysis of covariance), in which the effect of the independent variables(s) can be examined after controlling for the effect of other variables (one or more covariates) that are predicted to be related to the dependent variable. This added dimension of MANOVA can, for example, control for (remove or partial out) the influence of potentially confounding variables or control for prior group differences when random assignment is not possible (Tabachick & Fidell, 2001).

The Analytic Process

MANOVA is typically a two-step process. The first step tests whether there are significant differences between groups on the combined dependent variables. This is the omnibus test. The precise meaning of a statistically significant omnibus test in MANOVA is that there is a difference between groups (two or more) on a linear combination of the dependent variables. In the example used earlier, this test would tell us if the personality orientations of the two groups of team leaders (task oriented and person oriented) had an effect on team member performance. Most statistical packages provide the researcher with multiple criteria against which to evaluate the multivariate differences across groups. The most common are Roy's gcr, Wilks's lambda, Hotelling's trace, and Pillai's criterion. These four test statistics are computed in different ways, often yield different answers, and each has its advantages and disadvantages (for a more thorough discussion of the pros and cons, see Hasse & Ellis, 1987). The most commonly used are Hotelling's trace and Pillai's criterion.

Post Hoc Tests

However, a significant omnibus test provides only a partial answer. Because MANOVA combines the dependent variables into a single variate, it is not possible to determine from a statistically significant omnibus test where the differences lie. In our example, we would only know that team leader personality orientation had an effect on team member performance. Thus, a significant finding to the question "Are there significant differences in a set of two or more dependent variables across two or more groups formed by one or more categorical independent variables?" leads to the second important question: "Where do these differences lie?"

A unique dimension of MANOVA is that this second step can be conducted in a number of ways. In general, the different approaches can be categorized as those focusing on analysis of the criterion variables (using univariate F test, discriminant analysis, step-down analysis, etc.), the analysis of the classification variables (using multivariate or univariate contrasts), or both (Bray & Maxwell, 1982). A complete review of all the possible approaches to analyzing a significant MANOVA is beyond the scope of this chapter. Readers wishing to learn more about the various options should see Bray and Maxwell (1982) or any of the texts listed at the end of this section. For present purposes, a brief overview will be provided of three of the most commonly used procedures for analyzing the criterion variables: univariate ANOVA tests with post hoc comparison tests, step-down analysis, and discriminant analysis.

Univariate ANOVA Tests

The most commonly used approach is to follow up a significant MANOVA with a series of univariate ANOVAs to show which dependent variables on which groups differ. Using this approach in our team example, we might use three separate ANOVAs to show on which outcome measures (absenteeism, coworker performance ratings, or accident rate) the two groups of team leaders differed. Significant ANOVAs on absenteeism and coworker ratings, for example, would suggest that the multivariate effect identified in the omnibus test was a function of these two factors and not accident rate. The most commonly used test for follow-up ANOVAs is Wilks's lambda, which yields an F value that can be used to determine the level of statistical significance.

With only two groups we could stop here. But if we had three or more groups (e.g., add a third personality orientation for team leaders), the follow-up ANOVAs would only tell us that the three groups differ along the outcome variables, but not which groups differ on which variables. Multiple t-tests can't be used here because the repeated comparison would inflate the Type I error rate. In order to make multiple comparisons between all the groups being studied (e.g., group 1 vs. 2, 1 vs. 3, 2 vs. 3, etc.), a number of specialized tests have been developed for this purpose. The most conservative and perhaps most commonly used are Scheffe's and Tukey's LSD.

Step-down Analysis

Step-down analysis can be used to find out whether a particular variable contributes unique information about group differences. It is similar to stepwise regression in that an F statistic is computed for a variable after the effects of the other variables have been eliminated. The results parallel those that would emerge if a MANCONVA were performed with all the "other" dependent variables entered as covariates. A critical requirement of this approach is that the researcher must have some theoretical or substantive support for the order of dependent variable entry to make the procedure valid (Hair et al., 1998). For more information on step-down analysis in MANOVA, see Koslowsky and Caspy (1991).

Discriminant Analysis

Discriminant analysis, as we have seen, uses a linear combination of dependent variables to maximize the separation of groups. When used in a descriptive mode as a follow-up to a significant MANOVA, the discriminant function and the associated beta coefficients can provide insight into the nature of group differences. For example, when used as a follow-up procedure in our team leader study, it would provide information about which linear combination of performance measures best differentiated among team leader orientations and which contributed the most to that differentiation.

Data Considerations

For a valid MANOVA, the capacity of the data to satisfy three assumptions should be verified prior to data analysis. These assumptions are independence of observations, equal covariance matrices of the dependent variables for all groups, and multivariate normal distributions for the dependent variables. The assumption of independence is often problematic in time series or repeated-measures MANOVAs. Researchers should therefore pay special attention to the use of such measures and be aware that there are repeated-measures models that can accommodate these situations. For more information on repeated-measures MANOVA models, see Keselman and Algina (1996), Crowder and Hand (1990), Tabachick and Fidell (2001), or Stevens (1992). More information on testing for covariance equality and multivariate normality can be found in Huberty and Petoskey (2000).

Sample size is important in MANOVA because, with small samples, the standardized discriminant weights become unstable (Huberty, 1975). Sample size requirements per cell in MANOVA must, at a minimum, exceed the number of dependent variables. Exact recommendations for the optimal sample size range from a minimum of 20 observations per cell to one in which the sample size of the smallest group is somewhere between 6 and 10 times the number of dependent variables. Maxwell (1992) suggests limiting the number of dependent variables to fewer than 10 unless the sample size is large. Regardless of the sample size guidelines used, researchers should make sample size decisions based on multiple factors including the statistical power desired, the number of groups, the number of dependent variables, and the expected size of the effect of interest. All of these factors should be considered in the planning stages of a MANOVA design.

Consistent with many other multivariate techniques, MANOVA is sensitive to the presence of outliers and the capacity of outliers to disproportionately affect results. Outliers can produce both Type I and II errors yet give no indication about which is occurring. Consequently, one of the first steps in the use of MANOVA should be an examination of the data matrix for outliers. In general, an *outlier* is a data value that is relatively distant from the overall group mean for a particular variable. There are no standard rules about how to make retention/

deletion decisions about outliers. The best recommendation is to run the analyses with and without them, or to delete them one at a time as a means of evaluating their influence (Huberty & Petoskey, 2000). Whatever evaluative route taken, commonsense judgments must be made about what to do with outliers, and a thorough and complete description of the procedures used in appraising and handling outliers should be included with the analysis.

Finally, it is often the case that insufficient attention is devoted to the selection of dependent variables in MANOVA. For example, high levels of correlation (multicollinearity) among dependent variables introduces variable redundancy and can reduce statistical power. The choice of outcome variables should therefore be done carefully and be firmly grounded in theory or a substantive rationale (Huberty & Petoskey, 2000).

For More Information

A number of very good texts provide thorough treatments of MANOVA, when it is useful, and the mechanics and the processes involved in using it (e.g., Stevens, 1992; Tabachnick & Fidell, 1996; Hair et al., 1998). To learn more about the multitude of potential uses of MANOVA in social science research, see Keselman et al. (1998). For more specific guidance in reporting MANOVA results, see Huberty and Petoskey (2000).

CONCLUSION

This chapter has provided an overview of some of the most useful and commonly employed multivariate statistical techniques in organizational research. The focus was to highlight, in accessible language, the fundamental conceptual and practical issues to be considered when using multiple regression, logistic regression, discriminant analysis, and MANOVA in organizational research. Guidelines for variable selection in multivariate analysis were discussed, and the importance of theory in providing guidance and insight into the meaning of statistical models has been emphasized. The types of research questions appropriate to these different multivariate techniques were discussed, with examples. For each analytic technique, fundamental issues with regard to the nature of the data required, the analytic process, and model evaluation were presented. Finally, a number of key references have been provided for readers who want to learn more.

REFERENCES

Adsit, D. J., London, M., Crom, S., & Jones, D. (1997). Cross-cultural differences in upward ratings in a multinational company. *International Journal of Human Resource Management, 8*(4), 385–401.

Algina, J., & Olejnik, S. (2003). Sample size tables for correlation analysis with applications in partial correlation and multiple regression analysis. *Multivariate Behavioral Research, 38*(3), 309–323.

Baron, R. M., & Kenny, D. A. (1986). The moderator-mediator variable distinction in social psychological research: Conceptual, strategic, and statistical considerations. *Journal of Personality and Social Psychology, 51,* 1173–1182.

Bates, R. A., Holton, E. F., III, & Burnett, M. F. (1999). The impact of influential observations on multiple regression analysis in human resources research. *Human Resource Development Quarterly, 10*(4), 343–364.

Belsley, D. A., Kuh, E., & Welsch, R. E. (1980). *Regression diagnostics: Identifying influential data and sources of colinearity.* New York: Wiley.

Betz, N. E. (1987). Use of discriminant analysis in counseling psychology research. *Journal of Counseling Psychology, 34*(4), 393–403.

Bobko, P. (1995). *Correlation and regression: Principles and applications for industrial/psychology and management.* New York: McGraw-Hill.

Brannick, M. T. (1993). Regression and discriminant analysis for analyzing judgements. In I. VanMechelen, J. Hampton, R. S. Michalski, & P. Theuns (Eds.), *Categories and concepts: Theoretical views and inductive data analysis* (pp. 247–263). London: Academic Press.

Bray, J. H., & Maxwell, S. E. (1982). Analyzing and interpreting significant MANOVAs. *Review of Educational Research, 52,* 340–367.

Bray, J. H., & Maxwell, S. E. (1985). *Multivariate analysis of variance.* Beverly Hills, CA: Sage.

Brown, M. T., & Wicker, L. R. (2000). Discriminant analysis. In H. E. A. Tinsley & S. D. Brown (Eds.), *Handbook of applied multivariate statistics and mathematical modeling* (pp. 209–235). New York: Academic Press.

Chatterjee, S., & Yilmaz, M. (1992). A review of regression diagnostics for behavioral research. *Applied Psychological Measurement, 16*(3), 209–227.

Cleary, P. D., & Angel, R. (1984). The analysis of relationships involving dichotomous dependent variables. *Journal of Health and Social Behavior, 25,* 334–348.

Cohen, J. (1988). *Statistical power and analysis for the behavioral sciences* (2nd ed.). Hillsdale, NJ: Erlbaum.

Cohen, J., & Cohen, P. (1987). *Applied multiple regression/correlation analysis for the behavioral sciences.* Hillsdale, NJ: Erlbaum.

Cohen, J., Cohen, P., West, S. G., & Aiken, L. S. (2003). *Applied multiple regression/correlation analysis for the behavioral sciences* (3rd ed.). Mahwah, NJ: Erlbaum.

Crowder, M. J., & Hand, D. J. (1990). *Analysis of repeated measures.* London: Chapman & Hall.

Darlington, R. B. (1990). *Regression and linear models.* New York: McGraw-Hill.

Dattalo, P. (1994). A comparison of discriminant analysis and logistic regression. *Journal of Social Service Research, 19*(3/4), 121–144.

Fox, J. (1991). *Regression diagnostics.* Beverly Hills, CA: Sage.

Haase, R. F., & Ellis, M. V. (1987). Multivariate analysis of variance. *Journal of Counseling Psychology, 34*(4), 404–413.

Hair, J. F., Anderson, R. E., Tatham, R. L., & Black, W. C. (1998). *Multivariate data analysis* (5th ed.). Englewood Cliffs, NJ: Prentice Hall.

Hardy, M. A. (1993). *Regression with dummy variables.* Newbury Park, CA: Sage.

Henderson, D. A., & Denison, D. R. (1989). Stepwise regression in social and psychological research. *Psychological Reports, 64,* 251–257.

Hosmer, D. W., & Lemshow, S. (1989). *Applied logistic regression.* New York: Wiley.

Hosmer, D. W., & Lemshow, S. (2000). *Applied logistic regression* (2nd ed.). New York: Wiley.

Huberty, C. (1989). Problems with stepwise methods—Better alternatives. In B. Thompson (Ed.), *Advances in social science methodology* (Vol. 1, pp. 43–70). Greenwich, CT: JAI.

Huberty, C. J. (1984). Issues in the use and interpretation of discriminant analysis. *Psychological Bulletin, 95*(1), 156–171.

Huberty, C. J. (1975). Discriminant analysis. *Review of Educational Research, 45,* 543–598.

Huberty, C. J., & Allen, J. B. (1999). Interpreting regression analysis results: An example. *Multiple Linear Regression Viewpoints, 25,* 29–32.

Huberty, C. J., & Barton, R. M. (1989, October). An introduction to discriminant analysis. *Measurement and Evaluation in Counseling and Development, 22,* 158–168.

Huberty, C. J., & Hussein, M. H. (2001). Reporting information in multiple correlation and multiple regression studies. In E. I. Farmer & J. W. Rojewski (Eds.), *Research pathway* (pp. 192–211). Lanham, MD: University Press of America.

Huberty, C. J., & Hussein, M. H. (2003). Some problems in reporting use of discriminant analysis. *Journal of Experimental Education, 71*(2), 177–191.

Huberty, C. J., & Lowman, L. L. (1998). Discriminant analysis in higher education research. In J. C. Smart (Ed.), *Higher education: Handbook of theory and research* (Vol. XIII, pp. 181–234). New York: Agathon.

Huberty, C. J., & Morris, J. D. (1989). Multivariate analysis versus multiple univariate analyses. *Psychological Bulletin, 105,* 302–308.

Huberty, C. J., & Petoskey, M. D. (2000). Multivariate analysis of variance and covariance. In H. E. A. Tinsley & S. D. Brown (Eds.), *Applied multivariate statistics and mathematical modeling* (pp. 183–208). New York: Academic Press.

Huberty, C. J., & Wisenbaker, J. M. (1992). Discriminant analysis: Potential improvements in typical practice. In B. Thompson (Ed.), *Advances in Social Science Methodology* (Vol. 2, pp. 169–208). Greenwich, CT: JAI Press.

Judd, C. M., Kenny, D. A., & McClelland, G. H. (2001). Estimating and testing mediation and moderation in within-subjects designs. *Psychological Methods, 6*(2), 115–134.

Keselman, H. J., & Algina, J. (1996). The analysis of higher-order repeated measures designs. In B. Thompson (Ed.), *Advances in social science methodology* (Vol. 4, pp. 45–70). Greenwich, CT: JAI Press.

Keselman, H. J., Huberty, C. J., Lix, L. M., Olejnik, S., Cribbie, R. A., Donohue, B., Korvalchuk, R. K., Lowman, L. L., Petoskey, M. D., Keselman, J. C., & Levin, J. R. (1998). Statistical practices of educational researchers. *Review of Educational Research, 68,* 350–386.

Kleinbaum, D. G., & Klein, M. (2002). *Logistic regression: A self-learning text* (2nd ed.). New York: Springer.

Kleinbaum, D. G., Kupper, L. L., Muller, K. A., & Nizam, A. (1998). *Applied regression analysis and other multivariate methods* (3rd ed.). Pacific Grove, CA: Duxbury.

Koslowsky, M., & Caspy, T. (1992). Stepdown analysis of variance: A refinement. *Journal of Organizational Behavior, 12,* 555–559.

Leary, M. R., & Altmaier, E. M. (1980). Type I error in counseling research: A plea for multivariate analysis. *Journal of Counseling Psychology, 27,* 611–615.

Leech, N. L., Gliner, J. A., Morgan, G. A., & Harmon, R. J. (2003). Use and interpretation of multiple regression. *Journal of the American Academy of Adolescent Psychiatry, 42*(6), 738–740.

Maxwell, S. E. (1992). Recent developments in MANOVA applications. In B. Thompson (Ed.), *Advances in social science methodology* (Vol. 2, pp. 137–168). Stamford, CT: JAI Press.

Maxwell, S. E. (2000). Sample size and multiple regression analysis. *Psychological Methods, 5*(4), 434–458.

Menard, S. (1995). *Applied logistic regression analysis.* Thousand Oaks, CA: Sage.

Morrow-Howell, N. (1994). The M word: Multicollinearity in multiple regression. *Social Work Research, 18*(4), 247–252.

Morrow-Howell, N., & Proctor, E. K. (1992). The use of logistic regression in social work research. *Journal of Social Service Research, 16*(1/2), 87–104.

Netter, J., Wassermann, W., & Kutner, M. H. (1989). *Applied linear regression models.* Homewood, IL: Irwin.

O'Brien, R. G., & Kaiser, M. K. (1985). MANOVA method for analyzing repeated measures designs: An extensive primer. *Psychological Bulletin, 97*(2), 316–333.

Pedhazur, E. J. (1982). *Multiple regression in behavioral research* (2nd ed.). Chicago: Holt, Rinehart, & Winston.

Pedhazur, E. J. (1997). *Multiple regression in behavioral research* (3rd ed.). New York: Holt, Rinehart, & Winston.

Peng, C. J., Lee, K. L., & Ingersoll, G. M. (2002). An introduction to logistic regression analysis and reporting. *Journal of Educational Research, 96*(1), 3–14.

Snyder, P. (1991). Three reasons why stepwise regression methods should not be used by researchers. In B. Thompson (Ed.), *Advances in educational research: Substantive findings, methodological developments* (Vol. 1, pp. 99–105). Greenwich, CT: JAI Press.

Stevens, J. (1992). *Applied multivariate statistics for the social sciences* (2nd ed.). Hillsdale, NJ: Erlbaum.

Tabachnick, B. G., & Fidell, L. S. (2001). *Using multivariate statistics* (4th ed.). Boston: Allyn & Bacon.

Thompson, B. (1989). Why won't stepwise methods die? *Measurement and Evaluation in Counseling and Development, 21*(4), 146–148.

Thompson, B. (1995). Stepwise regression and stepwise discriminant analysis need not apply here: A guidelines editorial. *Educational and Psychological Measurement, 55*(4), 525–534.

Tinsley, H. E. A., & Brown, S. D. (2000). *Handbook of applied multivariate statistics and mathematical modeling.* San Diego: Academic Press.

Venter, A., & Maxwell, S. E. (2000). Issues in the use and application of multiple regression analysis. In H. E. A. Tinsley & S. D. Brown (Eds.), *Handbook of applied multivariate statistics and mathematical modeling* (pp. 151–182). New York: Academic Press.

Wampold, B. E., & Freund, R. D. (1987). Use of multiple regression in counseling psychology research: A flexible data-analytic strategy. *Journal of Counseling Research, 34*(4), 372–382.

Watson, C. J. (1982). Approaches for the interpretation of multiple discriminant analysis in organizational research. *Academy of Management Review, 7*(1), 124–132.

Weinzimmer, L. G., Mone, M. A., & Alwan, L. C. (1994). An examination of perceptions of usage of regression diagnostics in organization studies. *Journal of Management, 20*(1), 179–192.

C H A P T E R   9

Structural Equation Modeling (SEM): An Introduction to Basic Techniques and Advanced Issues

Jeni L. Burnette and Larry J. Williams,
Virginia Commonwealth University

CHAPTER OUTLINE

Structural equation modeling (SEM), a statistical modeling technique offering a comprehensive approach to research questions, has become increasingly popular in the behavioral sciences. The ease of a simple bivariate experiment is often not a feasible option when researchers investigate human behavior in its natural setting. Consequently, over the years, researchers have developed advanced statistical techniques to handle multiple independent and dependent variables, some of which are measured and others of which are unobserved. Researchers in areas of organizational behavior, management, business, and applied psychology are often interested in multivariate relationships among some or all of the variables in a specified model, and SEM provides a viable statistical tool for exploring all of these relationships. The models investigated typically depict processes presumed to underlie values obtained with sample data, and these processes are assumed to result in measures of association (e.g., correlation) among the variables in the models (Williams, Edwards, & Vandenberg, 2003). SEM tests models of predicted relationships among observed and unobserved variables and offers numerous advantages over traditional approaches to model testing.

As the substantive use of SEM in organizational research becomes more prominent, it is essential to be familiar with the techniques and language of SEM. The aim of this chapter is to offer a succinct and clear introduction to SEM for readers familiar with regression and factor analysis techniques. The chapter is organized around the following preliminary themes: an introduction to SEM, an example of SEM, advanced SEM models, technical issues with SEM, recommendations for improved SEM analyses, SEM software, and furthering knowledge of SEM. Readers wishing to tackle advanced techniques of SEM beyond the topics covered can refer to the references at the end of the chapter. We take a conceptual rather than mathematical approach throughout the chapter and use a basic latent variable structural equation model to introduce topics and issues surrounding SEM.

AN INTRODUCTION TO STRUCTURAL EQUATION MODELING (SEM)

SEM is a technique for specifying and testing linear relationships among variables (MacCallum & Austin, 2000). It is usually considered to be a confirmatory tool rather than an exploratory procedure. That is, researchers are more likely to use SEM to establish the validity of a certain model rather than using SEM to "discover" an appropriate model. While structural equation modeling has become an increasingly popular form of data analysis in the last 20 years, Sewell Wright, a population biologist at the University of Chicago, first introduced the concept nearly 80 years ago. Since the 1970s, the development and use of SEM and statistical software had rapidly increased (for a review, see Bentler, 1986), and by the beginning of the early 1980s, SEM had become increasingly prevalent within the management and applied psychological literatures.

SEM is an extension of the general linear model (GLM) of which multiple regression is a part. Historically, multiple regression/correlation (MRC) analysis arose around 1900 in the study of the natural relation among a set of variables for a sample of subjects (Cohen, Cohen, West, & Aiken, 2003). Multiple regression helps the researcher discover more about the relationships between several independent or predictor variables and a dependent or criterion variable. The linear regression approach to data analysis can be especially useful when a relation between an observed dependent variable and a given observed independent variable is of interest. Regression can also be helpful when the researcher wishes to control for the influence of other independent variables. However, an assumption underlying the regression approach is that the dependent variable and independent variable(s) contain no measurement error.

Path analysis, an application of regression, refers to the steps of constructing and solving path diagrams. Path analysis is frequently used to represent causal relationships among a set of measured variables using linear equations (Millsap, 2002). Models often portray a graphical path diagram indicating how the variables are related to one another. In path analyses, the researcher typically explores the ability of more than one predictor variable to explain or predict multiple dependent variables. The path analysis equation is similar to a regression equation with each equation representing the value of a criterion variable as a linear function of one or more predictor variables (Millsap, 2002). Relative to path analysis, SEM has the advantage of not requiring the assumption of perfect measurement error, and both random and nonrandom measurement error can be modeled. More simply, path analysis is a subset of SEM that handles measured variables.

Factor analysis is an additional component of SEM. Factor analysis assumes that the covariances between a set of variables can be reduced to a smaller number of underlying latent factors (Hox & Bechger, 1998). Factor analysis is primarily used to examine data for patterns, to explore patterns among the interrelationships of the items, and to reduce a large number of variables into a smaller and more manageable number of factors. In exploratory factor analysis, the researcher proceeds with no prestated hypotheses about the number of latent factors and the relationship between the latent factors and the observed variables. In contrast, the researcher can use confirmatory factor analysis (CFA) when there is a clear picture about the factor structure. SEM combines the path analysis and confirmatory factor analysis approaches into a single integrated statistical technique. However, SEM can still be conceptualized as the analysis of two hypothetically distinct models. The measurement model is a confirmatory factor analysis model that indicates the relation of the observed variables to the proposed underlying constructs (Anderson & Gerbing, 1988). The structural model is also confirmatory in nature and is used to specify the causal relations of the constructs to one another based on a priori theory and hypotheses. Researchers can examine the measurement and structural model simultaneously, although this is not always the recommended approach (see Anderson & Gerbing, 1988, for a review).

SEM is unique from path analysis and factor analysis in that it handles both measured and latent variables. A *measured variable*, part of the measurement model, is a variable that can be observed directly and is measurable (also referred to as observed variables, indicators, or manifest variables). A *latent variable* is a variable that cannot be directly observed and must be inferred from measured variables. In summary, SEM is a combination of path analysis and confirmatory factor analysis that explores measured variables, establishes a measurement model linking latent variables to their indicators, and investigates the relations among latent variables in the form of a structural model.

AN EXAMPLE: PROCESSES ASSOCIATED WITH UNION PARTICIPATION

The basic latent variable structural equation model used to introduce topics and issues discussed in this chapter was taken from research on justice perceptions and union participation (Fuller & Hester, 2001) (see Figure 9.1). Terminology, notation, and application are illustrated using labels associated with the popular LISREL program (Jöreskog & Sörbom, 1996a, 1996b).

Before moving though the steps of SEM, let's briefly review relevant terminology. *Boxes* are the variables measured by the researcher and represent the observed variables (also referred to as manifest variables or indicators). Observed variables are often items, combinations of items (parcels), or complete scales

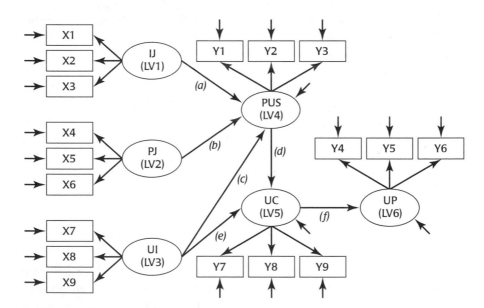

Figure 9.1   Basic Latent Variable Model (Fuller & Hester, 2001)

Note: This is a best-fitting model with standardized parameter estimates. All pathways are statistically significant (*p* < .05). The three exogenous variables are allowed to be correlated, but correlations were omitted for clarity.

Abbreviations: IJ = interactional justice; PJ = procedural justice; UI = union instrumentality; OPUS = perceived union support; UC = union commitment; UP = union participation.

from a survey instrument. A latent variable, representing the unobserved hypothetical construct, is usually represented by a *circle* in the model diagram. Latent variables may serve independent, mediating, and dependent roles and can be referred to as exogenous or endogenous. *Exogenous* variables are independent variables in all equations of which they are a part, whereas *endogenous* variables are dependent variables in at least one equation—although they may be independent variables in other equations in the system.

When using SEM, the researcher begins by developing the theoretical model and moves through three key steps: model specification, parameter estimation, and fit evaluation. We will use the theory and model from the Fuller and Hester (2001) example to walk through each of the three fundamental aspects of SEM. In specifying the model, the researcher's hypotheses are usually expressed in a drawing of the model (see Figure 9.1). The model describes how the indicators relate to the latent variables and details the associations among the latent variables. The second step entails obtaining parameter estimates for the relations proposed in the model and determining their statistical significance. The third step involves evaluating the adequacy of the model for explaining the data and potentially considering alternative models with paths added or deleted.

Model Specification

Model specification is the step in which the model is formally stated and the measurement and structural portion of the model are specified. Specification of the measurement model requires picking the number of common factors and the measured variables that are directly related to each common factor (Millsap, 2002). The measurement model, depicted in Figure 9.1, uses the data from Fuller and Hester (2001) on union participation. There are six hypothesized latent variables: union participation, union commitment, perceived union support, interactional justice, procedural justice, and union instrumentality. The authors represent each of the latent variables with three indicators. The arrows from the factors (circles) to the indicator variables represent factor loadings, and the second arrow heading to each indicator represents the influence of random measurement error.

The structural portion of the model specifies the directional relation among the latent variables. In the specific model presented in this chapter, interactional justice, procedure justice, and union instrumentality account for unique variance in perceived union support. The structural model also specifies that union instrumentality and perceived union support will have an effect on union commitment. Finally, the model proposes that union commitment influences union participation. The single-headed arrows linking the latent variables in the structural model represent parameters that are conceptually similar to regression coefficients (they represent the relationship between a dependent variable and an independent variable while controlling for the influence of other independent variables). The main difference between these estimates and traditional regression coefficients is that the former are not compromised by random measurement error through the use of the measurement model. Finally, the model permits unexplained variance in the latent dependent variables due to random error and unmeasured variables, represented by the additional arrow going to each latent dependent variable.

Parameter Estimation

Following model specification, the second step in SEM is parameter estimation, which occurs using the sample covariance matrix among the indicators. Numerous estimation methods are possible depending on the data and nature of the model. The method most commonly used and accepted for estimation is maximum likelihood estimation (MLE), which assumes a normal distribution and a reasonable sample size (Hox & Bechger, 1998). If your data are not normal, one of the more widely used and recommended approaches is the Satorra-Bentler chi-square correction (for a review, see Satorra & Bentler, 1994). Other available estimation methods may also be appropriate depending on the nature of the data and the sample size. In nearly all instances, the researcher is interested in the standard errors of the parameters estimated, which are used to determine confidence intervals for the estimates and/or to determine whether the estimates are statistically different from zero.

Evaluating Fit and Model Comparisons

Once the model has been specified using theory and the researcher has estimated the parameters, the next step is to evaluate the fit or adequacy of the proposed model. Goodness-of-fit estimates convey whether or not the proposed model "fits" (is a good representation of) the data, and they are used in the decision of whether or not to reject the model. There are numerous goodness-of-fit measures; for example, AMOS produces 25, and LISREL produces 15. Ultimately, these measures reflect the difference between the sample covariance used to obtain the parameter estimates and a predicted covariance matrix based on the parameter estimates. If the elements of the matrix are small, then the model is viewed as providing a good fit to the data, and the values for the fit indices will reflect this goodness of fit.

Of the available measures, the chi-square and degrees of freedom should be reported but deemphasized due to the influence of sample size and violations of normality. The comparative fit index (CFI) and the RMSEA are two of the highly recommended indices. They are scaled differently, with high values for the CFI indicating good fit (.95 has been offered as a threshold) and low values for the RMSEA indicating good fit (.08 and .05) have been proposed as cutoffs for indicating good fit. Finally, it should be noted that a very powerful way to compare competing models within the same data is through a chi-square difference test, if the models are nested. Two models are nested if one can be obtained from the other by constraining one of more paths to some predetermined value rather than estimating the coefficient for the path. Typically, the path(s) is constrained to zero to allow for a test of the significance of the path, and the key is whether the difference in chi-square values for the two models being compared exceeds the critical chi-square value associated with the difference in degrees of freedom. If the obtained chi-square difference exceeds the critical value, the hypothesis that the path (or paths) is zero is rejected.

Example Results

After confirming the factors in the measurement model, Fuller and Hester (2001) went on to test their proposed structural model. Results revealed that the model shown in Figure 9.1 was preferred among several evaluated (χ^2[126: = 230.96, $p < .05$; RMSEA = .037; CFI = .99). The structural paths in the model were all significant (paths a–f in Figure 9.1). The standardized parameter estimates revealed that of the antecedents of perceived union support, union instrumentality had the strongest effect (.52), followed by interactional justice (.38) and procedural justice (.10). The stronger predictor of union commitment was perceived union support (.47), while the effect from union instrumentality was slightly weaker (.44). The final path linking union commitment to union participation had a value of .21.

Fuller and Hester (2001) also compared the model in Figure 9.1 to other models that were nested. For example, they evaluated a model that forced the path from union instrumentality to perceived union support (path c) to zero. Results revealed that this alternative nested model fit the data more poorly (χ^2[127] = 408.54, $p < .05$; RMSEA = .060; CFI = .97). Note the lower RMSEAR and higher CFI reported above for the original model presented in Figure 9.1 reveal the better fit of this model. A chi-square difference test (χ^2 difference = 177.58, df = 1) resulted in rejecting the hypothesis that path c was equal to zero, again revealing that the model in Figure 9.1 is preferred.

The example from Fuller and Hester (2001) demonstrates the key steps in SEM. First, the authors specified their model and confirmed the measurement model. Once the authors proposed the model and estimated parameters, they were ready to test the fit of the proposed model. Systematic examination of alternative models is increasingly recommended, and the authors used theory to check their proposed models against potential competing models (Fuller & Hester, 2001). As illustrated by the better-fitting model with path c in the model, testing potential alternative models is a critical step in structural equation modeling. Finally, the best-fitting model in the Fuller and Hester (2001) example indicates the importance of union instrumentality in union support, an idea the authors had not necessarily proposed, but one that needs further exploration based on the fit indices for the best-fitting model.

ADVANCED APPLICATIONS OF LATENT VARIABLE TECHNIQUES

Reflective versus Formative Indicators

As noted earlier, Figure 9.1 specifies latent variables as causes of manifest variables, under the assumption that the latent variables produce behavior that is captured by the measures that constitute the manifest variables. Such indicator or manifest variable measures are termed *reflective*, because they are portrayed as reflections or manifestations of underlying constructs (Edwards & Bagozzi, 2000; Fornell & Bookstein, 1982). Reflective measurements are used in nearly all organizational applications of SEM. However, in some instances the direction of the relationship between latent and manifest variables is reversed such that measures are treated as causes of constructs (Bollen & Lennox, 1991; Edwards & Bagozzi, 2000; MacCallum & Browne, 1993). These measures are called *formative,* conveying that the measures form or produce their associated construct (Fornell & Bookstein, 1982). A frequently cited example of formative measurement is socioeconomic status, which is viewed as a composite of social and economic indicators such as occupation, education, and income (Hauser & Goldberger, 1971; Marsden, 1982). As noted by Williams et al. (2003), measures consistent with a formative approach from organizational research include group heterogeneity specified as the sum of differences on race, gender, and occupation (Jarley, Fiorito, & Delaney, 1997); job embeddedness as a function of fit, linkages, and sacrifice regarding the organization and community (Mitchell, Holtom, Lee, Sablynski, & Erez, 2001); and career success as a function of salary, job level, and number of promotions (Judge & Bretz, 1994).

Multidimensional Constructs

Many SEM studies involve designs where the latent variables include different dimensions of an overarching construct. For example, in the model from Figure 9.1, interactional justice and procedural justice can be seen as dimensions of an overarching global work justice construct. As reviewed by Williams et al. (2003), Edwards (2001) developed a framework for specifying and estimating multidimensional constructs that is organized around two key distinctions. The first is the direction of the relationships between the multidimensional construct and its dimensions. When the relationships flow from the construct (global work justice) to its dimensions (interactional and procedural justice), the construct is termed *superordinate,* conveying that the construct is a general entity that is manifested or reflected by the specific dimensions that serve as its indicators. When the relations flow from the dimensions to the construct, the construct is called *aggregate,* since the construct is a composite of its dimensions. The second distinction is whether the multidimensional construct is a cause or effect of other constructs within a larger causal model. These two distinctions combine to yield four prototypical models, and Edwards has identified an integrative analytic approach that can be used to investigate superordinate and aggregate constructs embedded in a structural equation model.

Method Variance

A third application of advanced SEM involves attempts to deal with problems associated with common method variance. As noted previously, the measurement model used in most SEM contexts acknowledges that the indicators contain measurement error. This measurement error is composed of two components, random and systematic. Under some research designs, advanced structural equation models yield estimates of both components, with the values for the systematic components being referred to as representing method variance. Method variance research that has used "measured" method effect variables involves social desirability and negative affectivity. Each of these constructs can be assessed with paper-and-pencil measures that can be included along with substantive variables in the questionnaire. With these studies, a latent variable associated with a method effect variable is linked via factor loadings with the indicators of substantive latent variables. This type of "complex" measurement model includes factor loadings linking the method effect latent variable to the substantive indicators, and these factor loadings represent the type of measurement contamination process associated with variables such as social desirability and negative affectivity. Williams, Ford, and Nguyen (2002) have discussed examples of this approach.

Another stream of research on method variance has involved designs in which multiple methods of measurement are used. In this literature, the multiple methods involved range from different scaling formats for the same questionnaire items (e.g., semantic differential vs. Likert response formats) to completely different sources of information (e.g., self-report; peer and supervisor ratings). This design is often referred to as *multitrait-multimethod* (MTMM), in that early applications were used with multiple measures of personality constructs.

Over the years there have been many applications of this design in organizational research, as described by Williams et al. (2002). Recently, Doty and Glick (1998) reanalyzed data from 28 of these studies using the SEM approach. Their results indicated that 46% of the variance in the indicators was accounted for by trait factors, whereas 32% was accounted for by method factors. They also compared the substantive factor correlations from models with and without the method factors and concluded that the method variance resulted in a 26% bias in observed relationships among the substantive factors. Doty and Glick note that this bias did not invalidate many of the research findings in these studies.

Measurement Equivalence or Invariance

A fourth type of advanced application of advanced causal modeling methods is relevant for designs in which the same measures or indicators are used in multiple groups or samples. Assume, for example, that there is an interest in whether the paths linking the latent variables in the model from Figure 9.1 are different for males when compared to females. Testing the equivalence of structural parameters without first establishing equivalence across gender groups in the measurement parameters (typically factor loadings and error variances) may result in inaccurate conclusions (Vandenberg & Lance, 2000). If the lack of invariance in factor loadings is unaccounted for, the researcher may draw an inaccurate conclusion concerning the difference between groups in the structural parameters. A thorough technical treatment of all of the measurement equivalence or invariance tests may be found in Vandenberg and Lance (2000). However, the crux of the issue is that cross-group comparisons, regardless of whether through testing for mean differences using traditional tests (e.g., ANOVA) or for differences in SEM parameters, should begin with testing the assumptions of invariant measurement operations across the groups being compared. This can be easily accomplished using the multisample capabilities of current SEM statistical packages, and more discussion of this can be found in Williams et al. (2003).

Moderators and Latent Variable Relationships

Moderation focuses on whether the strength of the relationship between an independent variable and a dependent variable depends on the level of a third variable, termed a moderator variable (Cohen, 1978). A historically popular method for testing moderation involved splitting the sample on the moderator variable and comparing correlations between the independent and dependent variables across the subsamples (Arnold, 1982; Zedeck, 1971). Hierarchical moderated regression has replaced this historical approach, and the independent and moderator variables are entered first followed by their product. The increment in variance explained by the product term provides evidence for moderation (Aiken & West, 1991; Cohen, 1978; Stone & Hollenbeck, 1984).

In SEM, methods for testing moderation parallel the subgrouping and moderated regression approaches. In particular, one approach often used for testing moderation in structural equation modeling involves creating subgroups based on a moderator variable and use of multisample techniques such as those previously discussed in the section on measurement invariance. However, whereas tests of measurement invariance entail the equality of measurement parameters, such as item loadings and error variances, tests of moderation with latent variables focus on the equality of structural parameters linking latent variables to one another. For example, a researcher could test the equivalence of the six structural parameters (a–f) shown in Figure 9.1 across two gender subgroups. Differences in these parameters across groups would constitute evidence for moderation.

Although the subgrouping approach works well for categorical moderator variables (e.g., gender and race), many moderator variables are continuous. As noted in a review by Cortina, Chen, and Dunlap (2001), structural equation models with continuous moderators present several difficulties. Cortina et al. reviewed and empirically evaluated various recommendations for this data analysis situation. Based on their assessment, they recommend an approach that is relatively simple to implement and easy to understand for researchers trained in classical test theory. This approach involves creating single indicators to represent the latent variables, accompanied by the fixing of the measurement parameters for these latent variables using classic measurement theory. Williams et al. (2003) present more information on this approach.

Analysis of Latent Variable Means

Thus far, the models discussed have yielded parameter estimates obtained from the covariances among the indicators in the models. There has been considerable recent development, however, involving models that incorporate information from the means of the indicators (the intercepts) and that include parameters representing the means of the latent variables. As noted by Williams et al. (2003), Vandenberg and Lance (2000) identified in their review several areas where latent variable means had been examined under a measurement invariance context, including changes in work-related perceptions during organizational entry, newcomer work adjustment, cross-cultural models of advertising, and race and gender differences in personality.

A second area of activity related to latent variable means emphasizes the analysis of experimental data. Ployhart and Oswald (2004) discuss the advantages of analysis of latent variable means relative to traditional approaches involving t-tests or ANOVAs on group means, and they also describe a series of models and model comparisons to guide researchers who want to test hypotheses about latent variable means. Ployhart and Oswald provide examples of latent mean analysis involving data from three independent groups and data from two independent groups with two repeated measures. They also discuss potential problems with latent mean analysis including larger sample size requirements (relative to traditional approaches), the required assumption of multivariate normality, and difficulties when the number of groups increases to greater than five.

TECHNICAL ISSUES

Model Evaluation

As noted earlier, researchers using structural equation techniques face the question as to whether a particular model provides a good fit to the data; this fit reflects the difference between the sample covariance matrix used in the analysis and one that is predicted based on the obtained parameter estimates. It was also noted that goodness-of-fit measures are used in this process. Unfortunately, these indices suffer from many limitations. McDonald and Ho (2002), among others, have discussed this issue and describe several problems. The most critical problem is that these measures summarize the *overall* fit and the *overall* degree of difference between the sample and predicted covariance matrices. However, as noted by McDonald and Ho, problems with a poorly fitting model "can be due to a general scatter of discrepancies not associated with any particular misspecification," or it "can originate from a correctable misspecification giving a few large discrepancies" (p. 72). Additionally, since a latent variable model includes both a measurement component (which links the factors to their indicators) and a structural component (which depicts the relationships among the latent variables), the model represents a composite hypothesis involving both components. As McDonald and Ho observe, "it is impossible to determine which aspects of the composite hypothesis can be considered acceptable from the fit indices alone" (p. 72).

This ambiguity associated with global fit indices suggests it might be important to determine what part of any model misfit is due to problems with the measurement versus the structural part of the model. This ambiguity results from the fact that problems with the measurement component can lead to inadequate fit values when the structural component is adequate, or the measurement model can be adequate and lead to acceptable fit values when the structural component is actually flawed.

Williams and Holahan (1994) have developed fit indices that isolate measurement and structural components of a composite model, and researchers may want to consider using these so that the adequacy of both components can be determined. McDonald and Ho also have proposed a supplementary two-stage procedure that begins with a confirmatory factor analysis for a measurement model that yields a set of factor correlations, followed by the use of these factor correlations as input into the evaluation of model with the same structural component (same pattern of relationships among the latent variables). With this process, the fit values of the structural model reflect only the structural model and are not contaminated by the measurement part of the model. Finally, McDonald and Ho also recommend examining (1) the standardized residuals for the measurement model to determine which covariances among the indicator variables are adequately accounted for, and (2) the residuals representing the difference between the factor correlations from the measurement model and the predicted correlations from the second step of their analysis process. The first set of residuals reflect the adequacy of the measurement model, while the second set provide evidence of the merits of the structural specifications.

Tests for Mediation

Another area in which methodologists are conducting research relevant to users of structural equation techniques involves procedures for testing mediational hypotheses. The previously discussed model in Figure 9.1 includes mediation, in that perceived union support and union commitment are mediators linking the three exogenous variables (interactional justice, procedural justice, and union instrumentality) to union participation. Over the years, many techniques for testing the significance of intervening variable effects have been developed and used. MacKinnon, Lockwood, Hoffman, West, and Sheets (2002) have recently provided a comparison of these methods, and their results are relevant for organizational researchers.

MacKinnon et al. began with a review of the literature that revealed that 14 different methods from a variety of disciplines have been proposed for use with path models that include intervening variables. They found that, in general, the widely used method of Baron and Kenny (1986) had very low Type I error rates and very low power unless the effect or sample size was very large. Specifically, the results indicated that with small effects the power was .106, even with a sample size of 1000, while with moderate effects the power was .49 with a sample size of 200. Thus, MacKinnon et al. concluded that studies using this approach were most likely to miss real effects as compared to other techniques. More details on this issue have been provided by Williams, Gavin, and Hartman (2004).

Data Requirements

Those interested in applying SEM techniques will need to be aware that these techniques carry several requirements in terms of the properties of the data being analyzed. Sample size requirements are often considered to be straightforward. Most common are recommendations or rules of thumb that focus on some minimum threshold for implementing SEM. Depending on the source, such minimums are thought to be 100, 200, or even more subjects (Boomsma, 1982; Marsh, Balla, & McDonald, 1988). More recent work suggests that methodologists have come to understand that the sample size issue is a little more complex. Because the addition of a single observed variable can add several estimated parameters to a model, one should consider the complexity of the model when determining an appropriate sample size. Specifically, it is now recommended that as models become more complex with more parameters being estimated, sample size requirements go up (Cudek & Henly, 1991), and rules of thumb have been offered suggesting minimum sample size to estimated parameter ratios (e.g., 5:1 as per Bentler & Chou, 1987). A simple recommendation is that if one is interested in a complex model with many parameters, one will need a large sample. With smaller samples, less complex models with fewer estimated parameters should be considered.

The use of SEM with maximum likelihood estimation carries an assumption of univariate and multivariate normality. Recent work shows that fit indices and standard errors, among other model parameters, are fairly robust to small departures from multivariate normality. However, where these departures start to get large, corrective measures may be needed. Potential corrections for nonnormality have been offered on everything from the fit indices and standard errors (e.g., Nevitt & Hancock, 2000; Satorra & Bentler, 1994, 2001) to the type of covariance matrix being analyzed and the estimator (i.e., other than maximum likelihood) utilized (e.g., Olsson, Foss, Troye, & Howell, 2000; West, Finch, & Curran, 1995). At a minimum, prior to moving into SEM analyses, researchers should examine their data using diagnostics relevant for the multivariate normality assumption. Where there are departures from it, results can be affected and options for dealing with it might be considered.

Missing data are a topic that has been receiving considerable attention lately within the SEM literature. Traditionally, the two most common options for dealing with missing data include pairwise and listwise deletion. Of the two, where SEM is concerned, listwise is the preferred method (Schafer & Graham, 2002). What is important to note is that researchers now have a wider range of better options for dealing with missing data than in past years, and these options can be invoked using specialized missing data software, a general statistical package (e.g., SPSS) prior to using SEM software or, in many cases, in the SEM software itself. When researchers face missing data, these options should be investigated.

RECOMMENDATIONS FOR IMPROVED SEM

The preceding two sections of this chapter reviewed advanced applications of SEM and technical issues related to SEM. We now provide a summary list of recommendations, described in more detail in Williams et al. (2004). First, researchers should consider the direction of relationship between latent variables and their indicators and use a formative approach if appropriate. If working with multidimensional constructs, researchers should consider the direction of their relations with their dimensions and choose the appropriate superordinate or aggregate model. If investigating moderators that are continuous in nature, consider the single indicator approach. Also, consider the use of latent variables when interested in variable means (as compared to covariances).

When assessing the fit of a latent variable model, researchers should examine the fit of both its measurement and structural components. If testing for mediation, beware of the low power of commonly used tests. When deciding on a sample size needed for SEM analyses, consider the complexity of the model. Check for violations of assumption of multivariate normality, and if this is a problem, investigate the most current recommended strategy. If missing data are a problem, consider the latest approaches available in SEM software.

SEM SOFTWARE PROGRAMS

A number of statistical programs are available once you are ready to test your specified models. LISREL, AMOS, and EQS are three of the more prevalent statistical packages used for SEM. LISREL is one of the more popular choices in the social sciences and is still the package of reference in most articles concerning structural equation modeling. Our aim in this section is merely to introduce the reader to the options and not necessarily to advocate one program over the other. Web sites are included in order to seek the information needed to make the decision about which software program is best for your specific needs (see Kline, 1998b, for a review of software packages).

LISREL, one of the more popular options in the literature, is one of the main contributors to the increased use of SEM. The Web site is www.ssicentral.com /lisrel/mainlis.htm. In October 2004, LISREL launched Windows 8.7, and new features include Generalized Linear Models for complex survey data and multivariate censored regression. A free student edition of LISREL 8.5 is available from the Web page.

AMOS, a statistical program that can be used to run structural equation models, is now distributed by SPSS. More information can be found on its Web site (www.spss.com/amos/). AMOS is an easy-to-use program and includes user-friendly features, such as drawing tools, configurable toolbars, and drag-and-drop capabilities that can help build structural equation models.

EQS was developed by Peter M. Bentler and provides researchers and statisticians with a tool for conducting a variety of structural equations models including multiple regression, multivariate regression, confirmatory factor analysis, structured means analysis, path analysis, and multiple population comparisons. Potential advantages of using EQS include no knowledge of matrix algebra is necessary, and EQS provides statistics for analysis on data that may not be normally distributed with the Satorra-Bentler scaled chi-square, robust standard errors, and the Yuan-Bentler distribution-free statistics (www.mvsoft.com/eqsintro.htm).

FURTHERING KNOWLEDGE OF SEM

As we bring this chapter to a close, we wish to leave readers with a number of resources for furthering their knowledge about SEM. Books are a good resource, as are journal articles and Web sites. A number of books on SEM have been written for an audience with some background in statistics but who are relatively new to SEM. The following are a limited selection of these types of books: Hoyle (1995), Kline (1998a), Kaplan (2000), Loehlin (2004), Maruyama (1998), and Schumacker and Lomax (1996). Some software-specific books for SEM include Arbuckle (2003) for AMOS; Bentler (1985, 1995) for EQS; and Jöreskog and Sörbom (1993) and Kelloway (1998) for LISREL. Several books touch on more advanced topics, including interactions in SEM (Jaccard & Wan, 1996; Schumacker & Marcoulides, 1998). A useful Web site for exploring SEM book options is Newsom's (2002).

Another useful resource is journal articles on SEM. *Structural Equation Modeling* is a journal devoted entirely to SEM and often presents articles on special topics. Journals taking both a theoretical and applied approach to SEM include, but are by no means limited to, *Psychological Methods, Applied Psychological Measurement, Research Methodology in Strategy and Management*, and *Psychometrika*.

REFERENCES

Aiken, L. A., & West, S. G. (1991). *Multiple regression: Testing and interpreting interactions.* Newbury Park, CA: Sage.

Anderson, J. C., & Gerbing, D. W. (1988). Structural equation modeling in practice: A review and recommended two-step approach. *Psychological Bulletin, 103,* 411–423.

Arbuckle, J. L. (2003). AMOS 5. (computer software). Chicago: Smallwaters.

Arnold, H. J. (1982). Moderator variables: A clarification of conceptual, analytic, and psychometric issues. *Organizational Behavior and Human Performance, 29,* 143–174.

Baron, R. M., & Kenny, D. A. (1986). The moderator-mediator variable distinction in social psychological research: Conceptual, strategic, and statistical considerations. *Journal of Personality & Social Psychology, 51,* 1173–1182.

Bentler, P. M. (1986). Structural modeling and psychometrika: A historical perspective on growth and achievements. *Psychometrika, 51,* 35–51.

Bentler, P. M. (1995). *EQS structural equations program manual.* Encino, CA: Multivariate Software.

Bentler, P. M., & Chou, C. P. (1987). Practical issues in structural modeling. *Sociological Methods and Research, 16,* 78–117.

Bollen, K., & Lennox, R. (1991). Conventional wisdom on measurement: A structural equation perspective. *Psychological Bulletin, 110,* 305–314.

Boomsma, A. (1982). The robustness of LISREL against small sample sizes in factor analysis models. In K. G. Jöreskog & H. Wold (Eds.), *Systems under indirect observation: Causality, structure and prediction: Part 1.* Amsterdam: North Holland.

Cohen, J. (1978). Partialed products *are* interactions: Partialed powers *are* curve components. *Psychological Bulletin, 85,* 858–866.

Cohen, J., Cohen, P., West, S. G., & Aiken, L. S. (2003). *Applied multiple regression/correlation analysis for the behavioral sciences* (3rd ed.). Hillsdale, NJ: Erlbaum.

Cortina, J. M., Chen, G., & Dunlap, W. P. (2001). Testing interaction effects in LISREL: Examination and illustration of available procedures. *Organizational Research Methods, 4,* 324–360.

Cudek, R., & Henly, S. J. (1991). Model selection in covariance structure analysis and the "problem" of sample size: A clarification. *Psychological Bulletin, 109,* 512–519.

Doty, D. H., & Glick, W. H. (1998). Common method bias: Does common method variance really bias results? *Organizational Research Methods, 1,* 374–406.

Edwards, J. R. (2001). Multidimensional constructs in organizational behavior research: An integrative analytical framework. *Organizational Research Methods, 4,* 144–192.

Edwards, J. R., & Bagozzi, R. P. (2000). On the nature and direction of the relationship between constructs and measures. *Psychological Methods, 5,* 155–174.

Fornell, C., & Bookstein, F. L. (1982). Two structural equation models: LISREL and PLS applied to consumer exit-voice theory. *Journal of Marketing Research, 19,* 440–452.

Fuller, J. B., Jr., & Hester, K. (2001). A closer look at the relationship between justice perceptions and union participation. *Journal of Applied Psychology, 86,* 1096–1106.

Hauser, R. M., & Goldberger, A. S. (1971). The treatment of unobservable variables in path analysis. In H. L. Costner (Ed.), *Sociological methodology 1971* (pp. 81–117). San Francisco: Jossey-Bass.

Hox, J. J., & Bechger, T. M. (1998). An introduction to structural equation modeling. *Family Science Review, 11*, 354–373.

Hoyle, R. H. (Ed.). (1995): *Structural equation modeling: Concepts, issues and applications.* Thousand Oaks, CA: Sage.

Jaccard, J., & Wan, C. H. (1996). *LISREL approaches to interaction effects in multiple regression.* Thousand Oaks, CA: Sage.

Jarley, P., Fiorito, J., & Delaney, J. T. (1997). A structural, contingency approach to bureaucracy and democracy in US national unions. *Academy of Management Journal, 40*, 831–861.

Jöreskog, K. G., & Sörbom, D. (1993). *LISREL 8: Structural equation modeling with the SIMPLIS command language.* Hillsdale, NJ: Erlbaum.

Jöreskog, K. G., & Sörbom, D. (1996a). *LISREL 8 user's reference guide.* Chicago: Scientific Software International.

Jöreskog, K. G., & Sörbom, D. (1996b). *Prelis 2 user's reference guide.* Chicago: Scientific Software International.

Judge, T. A., & Bretz, R. D. (1994). Political influence behavior and career success. *Journal of Management, 20*, 43–65.

Kaplan, D. (2000). *Structural equation modeling: Foundations and extensions.* Newbury Park, CA: Sage.

Kelloway, E. K. (1998). *Using LISREL for structural equation modeling: A researcher's guide.* Thousand Oaks, CA: Sage.

Kline, R. B. (1998a). *Principles and practice of structural equation modeling.* New York: Guilford.

Kline, R. B. (1998b). Software programs for structural equation modeling: AMOS, EQS, and LISREL. *Journal of Psychoeducational Assessment, 16*, 343–364.

Loehlin, J. C. (2004). *Latent variable models: An introduction to factor, path and structural equation analysis* (4th ed.). Mahwah, NJ: Erlbaum.

MacCallum, R. C., & Austin, J. T. (2000). Applications of structural equation modeling in psychological research. *Annual Review of Psychology, 51*, 201–236.

MacCallum, R. C., & Browne, M. W. (1993). The use of causal indicators in covariance structure models: Some practical issues. *Psychological Bulletin, 114*, 533–541.

Mackinnon, D. P., Lockwood, C. M., Hoffman, J. M., West, S. G., & Sheets, V. (2002). A comparison of methods to test mediation and other intervening variable effects. *Psychological Methods, 7*, 83–104.

Marsden, P. V. (1982). A note on block variables in multiequation models. *Social Science Research, 11*, 127–140.

Marsh, H. W., Balla, J. R., & McDonald, R. P. (1988). Goodness-of-fit indexes in confirmatory factor analysis: The effect of sample size. *Psychological Bulletin, 103*, 391–410.

Maruyama, G. (1998). *Basics of structural equation modeling.* Thousand Oaks, CA: Sage.

McDonald, R. P., & Ho, R. M. (2002). Principles and practice in reporting structural equation analyses. *Psychological Methods, 7*, 64–82.

Millsap, R. E. (2002). Structural equation modeling: A user's guide. In F. Drasgow & N. Schmitt (Eds.), *Measuring and analyzing behavior in organizations: Advances in measurement and data analysis* (pp. 257–301). San Francisco: Jossey-Bass.

Mitchell, T. R., Holtom, B. C., Lee, T. W., Sablynski, C. J., & Erez, M. (2001). Why people stay: Using job embeddedness to predict voluntary turnover. *Academy of Management Journal, 44,* 1102–1121.

Nevitt, J., & Hancock, G. R. (2000). Improving the root mean square error of approximation for nonnormal conditions in structural equation modeling. *Journal of Experimental Education, 68,* 251–268.

Newsorn, J. T. (2002). *Structural equation modeling books.* Retrieved from www.upa .pdx.edu/ IOA/newsom/sembooks.htm.

Olsson, U. H., Foss, T., Troye, S. V., & Howell, R. D. (2000). The performance of ML, GLS and WLS estimation in structural equation modeling under conditions of misspecification and nonnormality. *Structural Equation Modeling, 7,* 557–595.

Ployhart, R. E., & Oswald, F. L. (2004). Applications of mean and covariance structure analysis: Integrating correlational and experimental approaches. *Organizational Research Methods. 7,* 27–65.

Satorra, A., & Bentler, P. M. (1994). Corrections to test statistics and standard errors in covariance structure analysis. In A. von Eye & C. C. Clogg (Eds.), *Latent variable analysis: Applications for developmental research* (pp. 399–419). Thousand Oaks, CA: Sage.

Satorra, A., & Bentler, P. M. (2001). A scaled difference chi-square test statistic for moment structure analysis. *Psychometrika, 66,* 507–514.

Schafer, J. L., & Graham, J. W. (2002). Missing data: Our view of the state of the art. *Psychological Methods, 7,* 147–177.

Schumacker, R. E., & Lomax, R. G. (1996). *A beginner's guide to structural equation modeling.* Hillsdale, NJ: Erlbaum.

Schumacker, R. E., & Marcoulides, G. A. (Eds.). (1998). *Interaction and non-linear effects in structural equation.* Hillsdale, N.J.: Erlbaum.

Stone, E. F., & Hollenbeck, J. R. (1984). Some issues associated with the use of moderated regression. *Organizational Behavior and Human Performance, 34,* 195–213.

Vandenberg, R. J., & Lance, C. E. (2000). A review and synthesis of the measurement invariance literature: Suggestions, practices, and recommendations for organizational research. *Organizational Research Methods, 3,* 4–69.

West, S. G., Finch, J. F., & Curran, P. J. (1995). Structural equation models with nonnormal variables: Problems and remedies. In R. H. Hoyle (Ed.), *Structural equation modeling: Concepts, issues and applications* (pp. 56–75). Thousand Oaks, CA: Sage.

Williams, L. J., Edwards, J. R., & Vandenberg, R. J. (2003). Recent advances in causal modeling methods for organizational and management research. *Journal of Management, 29,* 903–936.

Williams, L., Ford, L., & Nguyen, N. (2002). Basic and advanced measurement models for confirmatory factor analysis. In S. Rogelberg (Ed.), *Handbook of research methods in industrial and organizational psychology* (pp. 366–389). Oxford: Blackwell.

Williams, L. J., Gavin, M. B., & Hartman, N. S. (2004). Structural equation modeling methods in strategy research: Applications and issues. *Research Methodology in Strategy and Management, 1,* 303–346.

Williams, L. J., & Holahan, P. (1994). Parsimony based fit indices for multiple indicator models: Do they work? *Structural Equation Modeling: A Multidisciplinary Journal, 2,* 161–189.

Zedeck, S. (1971). Problems with the use of "moderator" variables. *Psychological Bulletin, 76,* 295–310.

CHAPTER 10

Scale Development
Principles and Practices

Timothy R. Hinkin, *Cornell University*

CHAPTER OUTLINE

Stage 1: Developing the Measures
Stage 2: Testing the New Measures
Conclusion
References

The focus of research in organizational behavior is typically on the relationships between constructs. Often, however, much less attention is paid to the relationship between the construct and the manner in which the construct is measured. A *construct* is a conceptual term used to describe a phenomenon of theoretical interest that cannot be observed directly (Edwards, 2003). Examples include employee satisfaction, organizational commitment, and trust. A measure is a quantifiable assessment of the degree to which a respondent believes the construct exists, is felt, or is expressed. Questionnaires continue to be the most commonly used method for the collection of data in organizations using a variety of different measures (Hinkin, 1995). Data are collected today in several ways, including Web-based surveys, telephone surveys (IVR), and paper-and-pencil questionnaires.

A number of potential pitfalls are associated with collecting data such as negative attitudes about surveys on the part of respondents that may bias their responses (Rogelberg, Fisher, Maynard, Hakel, & Horvath, 2001) and poor response rates that do not adequately represent the population of interest (Baruch, 1999). The most important factor in obtaining valid, reliable, and generalizable results using questionnaire surveys, however, is ensuring that the measures used in the survey adequately represent the constructs under examination. Korman (1974) put it succinctly, stating that "the point is not that adequate measurement is 'nice.' It is necessary, crucial, etc. Without it we have nothing" (p. 194). Numerous studies have been published only later to have their results be questioned due to problems with measurement (e.g., Schriesheim, Powers, Scandura, Gardiner, & Lankau, 1993; Rafferty & Griffin, 2004). Unfortunately, problems with measurement continue to threaten our understanding of organizational phenomena (Hinkin & Tracey, 1999).

It is unclear whether measurement problems in the organizational behavior literature stem from unwillingness on the part of researchers to take the time and effort to develop measures with sound psychometric properties, or because reviewers and editors do not require that it be done, or from lack of knowledge about how to do so. Establishing evidence of construct validity in a measure does not necessarily require complicated, cumbersome analytical analyses or huge samples. Rather, the process can be quite straightforward to provide an efficient means for establishing the psychometric integrity of any measure.

The purpose of this chapter is to provide a guide for developing measures for field research in accordance with established psychometric principles. Regardless of the data collection methodology employed, it is crucial that the study begin with quality measures. The chapter is directed toward those readers who may have limited knowledge or methodological expertise in the scale development process, but who are somewhat familiar with many of the various statistical concepts and methods to be described herein. Other chapters in this book will go into the specific statistical techniques in more depth. The focus here will be on the process of scale development and the order in which the various analyses should be undertaken to assure the resulting measures possess sound psychometric properties. The chapter will describe the development of measures consisting of multiple scales. The process would be the same, although less complex, for developing a single multi-item scale. Since the vast majority of scales being used by behavioral scientists utilize continuous measurement with Likert scales (Cook, Hepworth, Wall, & Warr, 1981), such scales will also be employed in the following description.

Several criteria have been proposed for assessing the psychometric soundness of behavioral measures. They should demonstrate content validity, criterion-related validity, and internal consistency, and they should be parsimonious. All of these then contribute to providing evidence of construct validity, the relationship of the measure to the underlying attribute it is attempting to assess. *Content validity* refers to the adequacy with which a measure assesses the domain of interest. *Criterion-related validity* pertains to the relationship between a measure and another independent measure. *Internal consistency* refers to the homogeneity of the items in the measure or the extent to which item responses correlate with the total test score. *Parsimony* means that measures should be comprised of the fewest possible items that capture the domain of interest. Researchers can use specific practices to establish evidence of validity and reliability of new measures.

Each step of the process described here will contribute to increasing the confidence in the overall construct validity of the new measure. The process will be broken down into two primary stages, each of which consists of a number of steps. The first stage, "Developing the Measures," discusses the procedures that can be used to create sound scales using small samples prior to administering the measures to a field sample. It is in this stage that many measurement problems can be eliminated. The second stage, "Testing the New Measures," discusses the steps that are used to substantiate the quality of the new scales using a large sample in a field study. The scale development process is summarized as follows:

STAGE 1. DEVELOPING THE MEASURES
    Step 1: Item Generation
    Step 2: Item Wording
    Step 3: Number of Items
    Step 4: Item Scaling
    Step 5: Content Validity Assessment

STAGE 2. TESTING THE NEW MEASURES
    Step 1: Selecting a Sample
    Step 2: Preliminary Factor Analysis
    Step 3: Confirmatory Factor Analysis
    Step 4: Internal Consistency Assessment
    Step 5: Convergent and Discriminant Validity
    Step 6: Criterion-Related Validity
    Step 7: Replication

STAGE 1: DEVELOPING THE MEASURES

The scale development process begins with the creation of items that will eventually make up the scales. The most important idea here is that the scales should be evaluated and refined before they are used to collect data from a sample population. The greatest expense in conducting a field study is the cost of the survey administration, which includes the hard costs of data collection, as well as the time of the researcher and respondents. That, together with limited access to potential appropriate samples, makes it critically important that the survey measures taken into the field are psychometrically sound. There are a number of important factors to consider during this phase and specific steps to follow to aid in scale development, which will be discussed in the following section.

Step 1: Item Generation

The first stage of scale development is the creation of items to assess the construct under examination. At this point, the researcher's goal is to develop items that will result in measures that adequately sample the domain of interest to demonstrate content validity. A strong theoretical rationale that provides the conceptual definitions needed to be operationalized by the scales under development is a necessary but not sufficient condition for establishing construct validity of the new measure. Careful thought must go into item development, which can be a time-consuming and laborious effort.

There are two basic approaches to item development. The first is deductive, sometimes called *logical partitioning* or *classification from above*. The second method is inductive, known also as *grouping* or *classification from below* (Hunt, 1991). Both of these techniques have been used by behavioral researchers, and the scale developers must decide which is most appropriate in their particular situation. Each method will be briefly discussed here.

Deductive

Deductive scale development requires the use of a classification schema or typology prior to data collection. This approach requires an understanding of the phenomenon to be investigated and a thorough review of the literature to develop the theoretical definition of the construct under examination. The definition is then used as a guide for the development of items (Schwab, 1980). For example, *expert power* might be defined as "the ability to administer to another useful information." Items may then be generated based on this definition, being sure that they are worded consistently in terms of describing a single behavior or an affective response. Example items for expert power might include "he or she provides me with work-related advice" and "he or she is able to answer my questions about my work."

Inductive

Conversely, the inductive approach is so labeled because often little theory is involved at the outset, as one attempts to generate measures from individual items.

Researchers usually develop scales inductively by asking a sample of respondents to provide descriptions of their feelings about their organizations or to describe some aspect of behavior. An example might be "Describe how your manager communicates with you." Responses might include "I only hear from him or her when I do something wrong," or "He or she only communicates via e-mail." Responses are then classified into a number of categories by content analysis based on key words or themes (see Williamson, Karp, Dalphin, & Gray, 1982) or a sorting process such as the Q-sorting technique with an agreement index of some type, usually using multiple judges (see Kerlinger, 1986). From these categorized responses, items are derived for subsequent analysis.

Advantages and Disadvantages

An advantage of the deductive approach to scale development is that, if properly conducted, it will help assure content validity in the final scales. Through the development of adequate construct definitions items should capture the domain of interest. The disadvantages of the deductive approach are that it is very time-consuming and requires that researchers possess a working knowledge of the phenomena under investigation. In exploratory research, it may not be appropriate to attempt to impose measures onto an unfamiliar situation. In most situations where theory does exist, the deductive approach would be most appropriate.

The inductive approach may be very useful when there is little theory to guide the researcher or when doing exploratory research. The difficulty arises, however, when attempting to develop items by interpreting the descriptions provided by respondents. Without a definition of the construct under examination, it can be difficult to develop items that will be conceptually consistent. This method requires expertise in content analysis and relies heavily on post hoc factor analytic techniques to ultimately determine scale construction, basing factor structure and, therefore, scales on item covariance rather than similar content. Though items may load on the same factor, there is no guarantee that they measure the same theoretical construct or come from the same sampling domain (Nunnally, 1978). Because this technique lacks a theoretical foundation, the researcher is compelled to rely on some type of intuitive framework, with little assurance that obtained results will not contain items that assess extraneous content domains (Schriesheim & Hinkin, 1990). This technique also makes the appropriate labeling of factors more difficult (Conway & Huffcutt, 2003).

Step 2: Item Wording

One should follow a number of guidelines in writing items. Statements should be simple and as short as possible, and the language used should be familiar to target respondents. It is also important to keep all items consistent in terms of perspective, being sure not to mix items that assess behaviors with items that assess affective responses (Harrison & McLaughlin, 1993). An example of this would be including items such as "My boss is hardworking" and "I respect my boss" in the same measure. This is perhaps one of the most common mistakes researchers make in the development of measures. Items should address only a single issue; "double-barreled" items such as "My manager is intelligent and enthusiastic" should be not be used. Such items may represent two constructs and result in confusion on the part of the respondents. Leading questions should be avoided, because they may bias responses. Items that all respondents would likely answer similarly such as "This is a large organization" should not be used, as they will generate little variance. Individual items must be understood by the respondent as intended by the researcher if meaningful responses are to be obtained. Although some might argue that the use of reverse-scored items may reduce response set bias, it is suggested that they not be used. There have been too many examples of problems with reverse-scored items, and the use of a few of these items randomly interspersed within a measure may have a detrimental effect on psychometric properties (Harrison & McLaughlin, 1991).

Step 3: Number of Items

A very common question in scale construction is "How many items?" There are no hard and fast rules guiding this decision, but keeping a measure short is an effective means of minimizing response biases caused by boredom or fatigue (Schmitt & Stults, 1985; Schriesheim & Eisenbach, 1990). Additional items also demand more time in both the development and administration of a measure (Carmines & Zeller, 1979). Harvey, Billings, and Nilan (1985) suggest that at least four items per scale are needed to test the homogeneity of items within each latent construct. Adequate internal consistency reliabilities can be obtained with as few as three items (Cook et al., 1981), and adding items indefinitely makes progressively less impact on scale reliability (Carmines & Zeller, 1979). It is difficult to improve on the reliabilities of five appropriate items by adding items to a scale (Hinkin, 1985; Hinkin & Schriesheim, 1989; Schriesheim & Hinkin, 1990). It is also important to assure that the domain has been adequately sampled, because inadequate sampling is a primary source of measurement error (Churchill, 1979). These findings would suggest that a quality scale composed of four to six items could be developed for most constructs, though the final determination must be made by the researcher. It should be anticipated that approximately one-half of the items created using the methods described here will be retained for use in the final scales, so at least twice as many items as will be needed in the final scales should be generated to be administered in a questionnaire.

Step 4: Item Scaling

With respect to scaling the items, it is important that the scale used generate sufficient variance among respondents for subsequent statistical analyses. Although there are a number of different scaling techniques available, Likert-type scales are the most commonly used in survey research (Cook et al., 1981). Coefficient alpha reliability with Likert scales has been shown to increase up to the use of five points, but then it levels off (Lissitz & Green, 1975). Accordingly, it is suggested that the new items be scaled using five- or seven-point Likert scales. If the scale is to be assessing frequency in the use of a behavior, it is very important that the researcher accurately benchmark the response range to maximize the obtained variance on a measure (Harrison & McLaughlin, 1991). For example, if available responses range from "once" to "five or more times" on a behavior that is very frequently used, most respondents will answer at the upper end of the range, resulting in minimal variance and the probable elimination of an item that might in fact have been important but was scaled incorrectly.

There has been much discussion about the use of a neutral midpoint in the scale, such as "neither agree nor disagree." It is not clear whether the respondent is truly neutral or is answering in this manner for other reasons. Respondents must be given the opportunity to opt out of answering a question if it does not apply to his or her situation. This can be done using a neutral midpoint, which will be a data point used in the subsequent analysis, or a "does not apply" option, where the response would not then be included in the data.

Step 5: Content Validity Assessment

Once the items have been developed, they must be tested to assure that they adequately represent the domain of interest. Although procedures for assessing content validity have been widely publicized for many years, Hinkin (1995, 1998) notes that problems continue with the content validity of measures used in organizational research. Historically, content validity has been assessed using experts to sort items using a variety of indices, and then using factor analysis to aggregate items into scales. Unfortunately, there was subjectivity in this process as the researcher had to make a judgment regarding the number of factors to retain (i.e., use the scree plot, or Kaiser criterion) and about the magnitude of loadings for item retention. This type of judgment relies on heuristics and/or convention such as "positive and meaningful loadings" (Schriesheim et al., 1993, p. 400), and it subsequently introduces a degree of uncertainty into the interpretation and meaning of the focal construct(s). In addition, factor analytic techniques typically require larger sample sizes to achieve an adequate ratio of respondents to items, or the N-to-K ratio. Although sample size is not an inherent concern from a methodological standpoint, there may be administrative difficulties in obtaining enough data to yield robust results.

Recently a new methodology was developed to assess what is termed the *content adequacy* (a term similar to, though somewhat distinct from, *content validity*) of a new measure that overcomes some of the pitfalls of methods that rely on factor analysis (Hinkin & Tracey, 1999). This methodology uses an analysis of variance technique that can add a higher degree of confidence in item integrity and scale content adequacy. There are several advantages over factor analytic techniques. First, it virtually eliminates the use of subjective judgment for item retention. Analysis of variance provides a direct empirical test for determining item distinctiveness, and the only judgment call concerns the p value for determining significance. Second, it is very simple and straightforward. The procedure involves only one analytic procedure. Third, this technique can be used with small sample sizes of 30 to 50, which is desirable for addressing both practical and statistical differences (see Cohen, 1969). The use of small sample sizes is advantageous both because of convenience and also for statistical purposes. The use of small samples provides a more conservative means of distinguishing practical significance from statistical significance (Runkel & McGrath, 1984; Stone, 1978; Schmitt & Klimoski, 1991). Using small samples may result in the elimination of a few false-negative items that might be retained using factor analytic procedures, which may then require the development and assessment of additional items. However, it would be much more difficult to retain a false-positive item, a far worse consequence (Anderson & Gerbing, 1991). Schriesheim et al. (1993) point out that this type of process requires only that respondents are not biased and possess sufficient intellectual ability to perform the item-rating tasks. As such, university students are very appropriate for completing this task.

This methodology begins with definitions of the new constructs to be assessed and the six to eight items that have been generated using either the deductive or inductive methods described earlier. Then, measures of similar yet different constructs must be obtained and their definitions clarified. For each new measure being developed, at least one similar measure should be included in the analysis. The definition of one of the constructs is then presented at the top of each page of the questionnaire, followed by a randomized listing of all items. The number of pages will equal twice the number of constructs being developed. For example, if you were creating two new measures, there would be four individual pages, with a different definition at the top of each page.

Respondents then rate each of the items on the extent to which they believe that the items are consistent with each of the construct definitions. Response choices ranged from 1 (not at all) to 5 (completely). Two versions of the questionnaire should be administered, each with the pages presented in a different order, to control for response bias that may occur from order effects. The mean score for each item on each of the dimensions is calculated. Then, a comparison of means is conducted for each item across the definitions to identify those items that are evaluated appropriately (i.e., to identify items that were statistically significantly higher on the appropriate definition). One way analysis of variance and Duncan's multiple range test can be used is to compare item means across the five dimensions. Those items that are rated significantly higher on the appropriate dimensions should be retained for subsequent analyses.

At this point the researcher can be fairly confident that the new measures adequately represent the construct or constructs under examination. It is now necessary to administer them to a sample that is representative of the target population for further testing. Once the sample is identified, the new measures, together with those they could be hypothesized to correlate with and measures that they would not be expected to relate to, should be administered using one of the survey methodologies previously discussed.

STAGE 2: TESTING THE NEW MEASURES

Step 1: Selecting a Sample

Selection of an appropriate type and size of sample is very important to assure enough variance in responses and avoid the effects of an idiosyncratic context. It is important that the sample selected will demonstrate the behaviors or possess the attitudes under examination. For example, if you are studying leadership, the focal referent of the study should be in a position of responsibility and authority. There has been substantial debate over the sample size needed to appropriately conduct tests of statistical significance. The results of many multivariate techniques can be sample-specific, and increases in sample size may ameliorate this problem (Schwab, 1980). As sample size increases, the likelihood of attaining statistical significance increases, and it is important to note the difference between statistical and practical significance (Cohen, 1969). Very small statistically significant relationships may tell us very little about a particular phenomenon. Both exploratory and confirmatory factor analysis, discussed later, have been shown to be particularly susceptible to sample size effects. Use of large samples assists in obtaining stable estimates of the standard errors to assure that factor loadings are accurate reflections of the true population values.

At this stage of scale development, the researcher must ensure that data are collected from a sample of adequate size to appropriately conduct subsequent analyses. Recommendations for item-to-response ratios range from 1:4 (Rummel, 1970) to at least 1:10 (Schwab, 1980) for each set of scales to be factor analyzed. Based on the latter recommendation, if 30 items were retained to develop three measures, at least 300 respondents would be needed for data collection. It has been shown, however, that in most cases, a sample size of 150 observations should be sufficient to obtain an accurate solution in exploratory factor analysis as long as item intercorrelations are reasonably strong (Guadagnoli & Velicer, 1988). For confirmatory factor analysis, a minimum sample size of 200 has been recommended (McCallum, Widaman, Zhang, & Hong (1999). It is suggested that the more conservative approach of at least 200 respondents be adopted. As the number of items increases, it may be necessary to increase the number of respondents. With larger samples, smaller differences tend to be detectable as more than mere sampling fluctuation (Hayduk, 1987).

Step 2: Preliminary Factor Analysis

Once the data have been collected, it is recommended that exploratory factor analysis is used to further refine the new scales. The new measures, along with other measures included in the survey, should be subjected to factor analysis. This will confirm the a priori prediction of item loadings and also allow the reduction of a set of item variables to a smaller set of items to create a more parsimonious representation of the original set of observations providing evidence of construct validity (Guadagnoli & Velicer, 1988). Because the principal components method of analysis mixes common, specific, and random error variances, a common factoring method such as principal axis is recommended (Ford, MacCallum, & Tait, 1986; Rummel, 1970). Prior to conducting the factor analysis, the researcher may find it useful to examine the interitem correlations of the variables, and any variable that correlates at less than .4 with all other variables may be deleted from the analysis (Kim & Mueller, 1978). A key assumption in the domain sampling model is that all items belonging to a common domain should have similar average intercorrelations. Low correlations indicate items that are not drawn from the appropriate domain and that are producing error and unreliability (Churchill, 1979).

The number of factors to be retained depends on both underlying theory and quantitative results. When using the deductive approach, the researcher should have a strong theoretical justification for determining the number of factors to be retained and the examination of item loadings on latent factors provides a confirmation of expectations. Eigenvalues greater than one (Kaiser criterion) and a scree test of the percentage of variance explained should be used to support the theoretical distinctions (Conway & Huffcutt, 2003). If the items have been carefully developed, the number of factors that emerge on both Kaiser and scree criteria should equal the number of scales being developed. When using the inductive approach, the researcher may apply the same criteria at this stage to determine the number of factors to take into rotation. If the researcher believes that the factors will be largely uncorrelated, an orthogonal rotation should be used; if the factors are determined to be correlated, an oblique rotation should be used. It may be useful to conduct both types of analyses to determine which items to retain; however, if the intent is to develop scales that are reasonably independent of one another, more reliance should be placed on the orthogonal analyses when eliminating items.

Keeping in mind that parsimony and simple structure are desired for the scales, the researcher should retain only those items that clearly load on a single factor. The objective is to identify those items that most clearly represent the content domain of the underlying construct. There are no hard and fast rules, but the .40 criterion level appears most commonly used in judging factor loadings as meaningful (Ford et al., 1986). A useful heuristic might be an appropriate loading of greater than .40 and/or a loading twice as strong on the appropriate factor than on any other factor. It may also be useful to examine the communality statistics to determine the proportion of variance in the variable explained by each of the items, retaining the items with higher communalities. The percentage of the total item variance that is explained is also important; the larger the percentage, the better. Once again there are no strict guidelines, but 60% could serve as a minimum acceptable target. At this stage, inappropriately loading items can be deleted, and the analysis repeated, until a clear factor structure matrix that explains a high percentage of total item variance is obtained. If all items load as predicted then it will require some judgment in deciding which items to retain, remembering that the goal is four to six items per construct. The internal consistency assessment, described later, can also be used to reduce the length of scales.

Conway and Huffcut (2003) note that there are often problems in reporting factor analytic results, and Ford et al. suggest (1986) that the researcher should provide the following:

- Factor model
- Method of estimating communalities (if applicable)
- Method of determining the number of factors to retain
- Rotational method strategy for interpreting factors
- Eigenvalues for all factors (if applicable)
- Percentage of variance accounted for (if using orthogonal rotation)
- Complete factor-loading matrix
- Descriptive statistics and correlation matrix

Step 3: Confirmatory Factor Analysis

If the preceding steps are all carefully followed, it is highly likely that the new scales will be internally consistent and possess content validity. However, the researcher may further test the internal and external consistency of the measures through confirmatory factor analysis using a structural model approach for the items that have been retained from the preliminary factor analysis. It is also possible to skip the exploratory factor analysis step altogether, but this is not recommended when developing new measures.

One of the weaknesses of typical factor analytic techniques is their inability to quantify the goodness of fit of the resulting factor structure (Long, 1983). Items that load clearly in an exploratory factor analysis may demonstrate a lack of fit in a multiple-indicator measurement model due to lack of external consistency (Gerbing & Anderson, 1988). A computer program such as LISREL (Jöreskog & Sörbom, 2003) provides a technique allowing the researcher to assess the quality of the factor structure by statistically testing the significance of the overall model and of item loadings on factors. This approach affords a stricter interpretation of unidimensionality than does exploratory factor analysis (Lance & Vandenberg, 2002). In scale development, confirmatory factor analysis should be just that, a confirmation that the prior analyses have been conducted thoroughly and appropriately.

It is recommended that confirmatory factor analysis be conducted by using the item variance-covariance matrix. Differences in item variances are lost in the analysis of correlations because all variables are standardized to a common variance (Harvey et al., 1985). The purpose of the analysis is to assess the goodness of fit of rival models: a null model where all items load on separate factors, a single common factor model, and a multitrait model with the number of factors equal to the number of constructs in the new measure (Jöreskog & Sörbom, 2003). The multitrait model restricts each item to load only on its appropriate factor.

The chi-square statistic permits the assessment of fit of a specific model as well as the comparison between two models. The smaller the chi-square, the better the fit of the model. It has been suggested that a chi-square two or three times as large as the degrees of freedom is acceptable (Carmines & McIver, 1981), but the fit is considered better the closer the chi-square value is to the degrees of freedom for a model (Thacker, Fields, & Tetrick, 1989). A nonsignificant chi-square is desirable, indicating that differences between the model-implied variance and covariance and the observed variance and covariance are small enough to be due to sampling fluctuation. A model with a large chi-square may still be a good fit if the fit indices are high, as this measure is particularly dependent on sample size (Jöreskog & Sörbom, 2003). It is desirable to have a significantly smaller chi-square for the specified model than for competing models. An examination of root-mean-square-residuals may also be useful, with a value of less than 0.05 considered acceptable (Bagozzi, Yi, & Phillips, 1991).

There has been much discussion of goodness-of-fit indices, and more than 30 now are available for use, although there is still disagreement about which indices are most appropriate (Lance & Vandenberg, 2002). Muliak, James, Van Alstine, Bennet, Lind, and Stilwell (1989) recommend the use of the adjusted goodness-of-fit index (AGFI), normalized fit index (NFI), and Tucker-Lewis index (TLI) to determine the quality of fit of each model to the data. The use of relative fit indices such as the comparative fit index has been suggested to control for the effects of sample size. These indices measure the amount of variance and covariance accounted for in the model and range from zero to one. As there is no statistical test of fit, evaluation of these indices is somewhat subjective. As a heuristic, a value over .90 indicates a reasonably good model fit (Widaman, 1985).

Assuming that the multitrait model provides a better fit to the data based on these measures, the quality of the model can be further assessed by the item T values, which indicate the strength of the item loading, and modification indices. Once the overall fit of the model has been examined, each model coefficient should be individually examined for degree of fit. By selecting a desired level of significance, the researcher can use the T values to test the null hypothesis that the true value of specified parameters is zero, and those items that are not significant may need to be eliminated.

While the T values provide an estimate of fit for specified parameters, the modification indices provide information regarding unspecified parameters, or cross-loadings, with a large modification index indicating that a parameter might also contribute explained variance to the model. If large modification indices result, the model should be respecified and the analysis repeated, allowing the items with the largest indices to load on the specified corresponding factor. The output should then be examined, with special attention to T values for all specified loadings. Again, there are no strict rules, but the fewer modifications made to the initial model, the better. If all appropriate loadings are significant at $p < .01$ or less, and the magnitude and significance level of any inappropriate cross-loadings are relatively small, the researcher can be assured that the data fit the model quite well. If, however, an inappropriate item demonstrates a significant loading, then the item may not be tapping a single underlying construct and should be deleted and the model respecified. Performing this model respecification should result in a smaller chi-square and larger goodness-of-fit indexes.

Step 4: Internal Consistency Assessment

Following the recommended process to this point would assure unidimensionality of the new scales, but this approach is not enough to ensure the construct validity of the scale. The reliability of the measure should be assessed after unidimensionality has been established (Gerbing & Anderson, 1988). Reliability may be calculated in a number of ways, but the most commonly accepted measure in field studies is internal consistency reliability using Cronbach's alpha (Price & Mueller, 1986). At this step, the internal consistency reliabilities for each of the new scales is calculated. A large coefficient alpha (.70 for exploratory measures; Nunnally, 1978) provides an indication of strong item covariance and suggests that the sampling domain has adequately been captured (Churchill, 1979). If the number of retained items at this stage is sufficiently large, the researcher may want to eliminate those items that do not share equally in the common core dimension by deleting items that will improve or not negatively impact the reliability of the scales. This step is justified because the unidimensionality of individual scales has been established through the factor analyses previously conducted. Most statistical software packages produce output that provides reliabilities for scales with individual items removed.

At this stage it is simple to tailor scales to have the same number of items and still retain adequate domain sampling by carefully examining each item. Some subjectivity will be involved, as the researcher must assure that the retained items adequately capture the sampling domain. Because short scales reduce response bias and it is difficult to increase the reliability of five-item scales that have been properly developed, four or five items may be an appropriate number to use as a goal for each of the final scales. Reporting internal consistency reliability should be considered absolutely necessary.

Step 5: Convergent and Discriminant Validity

Up to this point, the researcher can be relatively assured that the new scales possess content validity and internal consistency reliability. Although the prescribed scale development process will build in a certain degree of construct validity, gathering further evidence of construct validity can be accomplished by examining the extent to which the scales correlate with other measures designed to assess similar constructs (convergent validity) and to which they do not correlate with dissimilar measures (discriminant validity).

Multitrait-Multimethod Matrix

Convergent and discriminant validity are most commonly examined by using the multitrait-multimethod matrix (MTMM) developed by Campbell and Fiske (1959; also see Schmitt & Klimoski, 1991). Although a number of researchers have criticized the original MTMM guidelines for use of unrealistic assumptions and reliance on a qualitative assessment of comparisons of correlations (e.g., Bagozzi et al., 1991), they are still useful in determining convergent and discriminant validity (Hollenbeck, Klein, O'Leary, & Wright, 1989; Marsh & Hocevar, 1988). The data from the additional measures obtained during the original questionnaire administration are used at this stage. A matrix is obtained by correlating the final scales with the other measures and by examining the magnitude of correlations that are similar and dissimilar.

Convergent validity is achieved when the correlations between measures of similar constructs using different methods (monotrait-heteromethod) are "significantly different from zero and sufficiently large" (Campbell & Fiske, 1959, p. 82). Discriminant validity is achieved when three conditions are satisfied: first, when correlations between measures of the same construct with different methods (monotrait-heteromethod) are greater than correlations between different constructs measured with different scales (heterotrait-heteromethod); second, when correlations between the same construct using different methods (monotrait-heteromethod) are larger than correlations between different constructs measured with common methods (heterotrait-monomethod); and, finally, when similar patterns of correlations exist in each of the matrices formed by the correlations of measures of different constructs obtained by the same methods (heterotrait-monomethod) and the correlations of different constructs obtained by different methods (heterotrait-heteromethod).

Structural Equation Modeling

Recent developments have been made in the use of confirmatory factor analysis for what Bagozzi et al. (1991) term "second-generation methods for approaching construct validity" (p. 429). The methodology is similar to that described in the "Confirmatory Factor Analysis" section with the addition of path specifications. These examine and test for significance the magnitude of relationships among the new constructs and additional measures with which they would be expected to relate to or not (Millsap, 2002). This methodology is discussed in greater detail in chapter 9 and in other sources (e.g., Williams, Ford, & Nguyen, 2002). Bagozzi et al. (1991) provide evidence that the use of confirmatory factor analysis in construct validation overcomes the weaknesses of the Campbell and Fiske (1959) technique by providing a quantitative assessment of convergent and discriminant validity and they recommend its use in future research. This technique has been adopted by other researchers (e.g., Shore & Tetrick, 1991; Becker & Cote, 1994) and may indeed eventually replace use of the MTMM. The use of the multitrait-multimethod matrix, however, has long been a well-accepted technique for establishing convergent and discriminant validity and should serve as a good starting point for establishing construct validity (Schmitt & Klimoski, 1991).

Step 6: Criterion-Related Validity

The researcher should also examine relationships between the new measures and variables with which they could be hypothesized to relate to develop a nomological network and establish criterion-related validity (Cronbach & Meehl, 1955). These relationships should be based on existing theory and may be examined using correlation, regression analyses, or structural equation modeling. If hypothesized relationships attain statistical significance, evidence of criterion-related validity is provided. Also, null relationships should exist where hypothesized.

Step 7: Replication

It may be argued that, due to potential difficulties caused by common source/common method variance, it is inappropriate to use the same sample both for scale development and for assessing construct validity. The factor analytic techniques that were used to develop the measures may result in factors that are sample-specific and inclined toward high reliability (Krzystofiak, Cardy, & Newman, 1988). The use of an independent sample will enhance the generalizability of the new measures (Stone, 1978). It is also recommended that when items are added or deleted from a measure, the "new" scale should then be administered to another independent sample (Anderson & Gerbing, 1991; Schwab, 1980).

The use of a new sample would also allow the application of the measure in a substantive test. It would now be necessary to collect another set of data from an appropriate sample and repeat the scale-testing process with the new scales. If the initial sample was large enough, it may be possible to split the sample randomly in halves and conduct parallel analyses for scale development (Krzystofiak et al., 1988). To avoid the common source problem, it is recommended that data from sources other than the respondent be collected where possible. The replication should include confirmatory factor analysis, assessment of internal consistency reliability, and criterion-related validity. These analyses should provide the researcher with the confidence that the finalized measures possess reliability and validity and would be suitable for use in future research.

CONCLUSION

Scale development clearly involves a bit of art as well as a lot of science. Anyone who has gone through a process similar to that described in this chapter will understand the difficulty of developing sound measures. Some may suggest a somewhat different approach than the process described here, and it is possible that a shorter, less time-consuming method could result in sound measures. Utilization of a process similar to this has, however, resulted in measures that appear to be psychometrically sound (e.g., Hinkin & Tracey, 1999; Kumar & Beyerlein, 1991; MacKenzie, Podsakoff, & Fetter, 1991). By carefully following the stages and steps outlined in this chapter, the researcher should end up with measures that demonstrate content validity, criterion-related validity, and internal consistency, and they should be parsimonious. All of these will contribute to the evidence of construct validity of the measure.

Particular attention should be paid to the "Developing the Measures" stage because it is here that subsequent problems with the measures can be most easily prevented. Once a researcher has taken a survey into the field and collected a large amount of data, measurement problems become much more serious. Using the method described here, researchers can develop measures efficiently that are also effective when put to use in field research.

REFERENCES

Anderson, J. C., & Gerbing, D. W. (1991). Predicting the performance of measures in a confirmatory factor analysis with a pretest assessment of their substantive validities. *Journal of Applied Psychology, 76*, 732–740.

Bagozzi, R. P., Yi, Y., & Phillips, L. W. (1991). Assessing construct validity in organizational research. *Administrative Science Quarterly, 36*, 421–458.

Baruch, Y. (1999). Response rate in academic studies: A comparative analysis. *Human Relations, 52*, 421–438.

Becker, T. E., & Cote, J. A. (1994). Additive and multiplicative method effects in applied psychological research: An empirical assessment of three models. *Journal of Management, 20*, 625–641.

Campbell, J. P., & Fiske, D. W. (1959). Convergent and discriminant validation by the multitrait-multimethod matrix. *Psychological Bulletin, 56*, 81–105.

Carmines, E. G., & McIver, J. (1981). Analyzing models with unobserved variables: Analysis of covariance structures. In G. Bohrnstedt & E. Borgatta (Eds.), *Social measurement: Current issues.* Beverly Hills, CA: Sage.

Carmines, E. G., & Zeller, R. A. (1979). *Reliability and validity assessment.* Beverly Hills: Sage.

Churchill, G. A. (1979). A paradigm for developing better measures of marketing constructs. *Journal of Marketing Research, 16*, 64–73.

Cohen, J. (1969). *Statistical power analysis for the behavioral sciences.* New York: Academic Press.

Conway, J. M., & Huffcutt, A. I. (2003). A review and evaluation of exploratory factor analysis practices in organizational research. *Organizational Research Methods, 6*, 147–168.

Cook, J. D., Hepworth, S. J., Wall, T. D., & Warr, P. B. (1981). *The experience of work.* San Diego: Academic Press.

Cronbach, L. J., & Meehl, P. C. (1955). Construct validity in psychological tests. *Psychological Bulletin, 52*, 281–302.

Edwards, J. R. (2003). Construct validation in organizational behavior research. In J. Greenber (Ed.), *Organizational behavior: The state of science* (2nd ed., pp. 327–371). Mahwah, NJ: Erlbaum.

Ford, J. K., MacCallum, R. C., & Tait, M. (1986). The application of exploratory factor analysis in applied psychology: A critical review and analysis. *Personnel Psychology, 39*, 291–314.

Gerbing, D. W., & Anderson, J. C. (1988). An updated paradigm for scale development incorporating unidimensionality and its assessment. *Journal of Marketing Research, 25*, 186–192.

Guadagnoli, E., & Velicer, W. F. (1988). Relation of sample size to the stability of component patterns. *Psychological Bulletin, 103*, 265–275.

Harrison, D. A., & McLaughlin, M. E. (1991). Exploring the cognitive processes underlying responses to self-report instruments: Effects of item content on work attitude measures. In *Proceedings of the 1991 Academy of Management Annual Meetings* (pp. 310–314), unpublished work.

Harrison, D. A., & McLaughlin, M. E. (1993). Cognitive processes in self-report responses: Tests of item context effects in work attitude measures. *Journal of Applied Psychology, 78*, 129–140.

Harvey, R. J., Billings, R. S., & Nilan, K. J. (1985). Confirmatory factor analysis of the job diagnostic survey: Good news and bad news. *Journal of Applied Psychology, 70*, 461–468.

Hayduk, L. A. (1987). *Structural equation modeling with LISREL.* Baltimore: Johns Hopkins University Press.

Hinkin, T. R. (1985). *Development and application of new social power measures in superior-subordinate relationships.* Unpublished doctoral dissertation, University of Florida.

Hinkin, T. R. (1995). A review of scale development practices in the study of organizations. *Journal of Management, 21*, 967–988.

Hinkin, T. R. (1998). A brief tutorial on the development of measures for use in survey questionnaires. *Organizational Research Methods, 1*, 104–121.

Hinkin, T. R., & Schriesheim, C. A. (1989). Development and application of new scales to measure the French and Raven (1959) bases of social power. *Journal of Applied Psychology, 74*, 561–567

Hinkin, T. R., & Tracey, J. B. (1999). An analysis of variance approach to content validation. *Organizational Research Methods, 2*(2), 175–186.

Hollenbeck, J. R., Klein, H. J., O'Leary, A. M., & Wright, P. M. (1989). Investigation of the construct validity of a self-report measure of goal commitment. *Journal of Applied Psychology, 74*, 951–956.

Hunt, S. D. (1991). *Modern marketing theory.* Cincinnati: South-Western.

Jöreskog, K. G., & Sörbom, D. (2003). *LISREL 8.53: A guide to the program and applications.* Chicago: SPSS.

Kerlinger, F. (1986). *Foundations of behavioral research* (3rd ed.). New York: Holt, Rinehart & Winston.

Kim, J., & Mueller, C. W. (1978). *Introduction to factor analysis: What it is and how to do it.* Beverly Hills, CA: Sage.

Korman, A. K. (1974). Contingency approaches to leadership. In J. G. Hunt & L. L. Larson (Eds.), *Contingency approaches to leadership.* Carbondale: Southern Illinois University Press.

Krzystofiak, F., Cardy, R. L., & Newman, J. (1988) Implicit personality and performance appraisal: The influence of trait inferences on evaluation of behavior. *Journal of Applied Psychology, 73,* 515–521.

Kumar, K., & Beyerlein, M. (1991). Construction and validation of an instrument for measuring ingratiatory behaviors in organizational settings. *Journal of Applied Psychology, 76,* 619–627.

Lance, C. E., & Vandenberg, R. J. (2002). Confirmatory factor analysis. In F. Dragow & N. Schmitt (Eds.), *Measuring and analyzing behavior in organizations: Advances in measurement and data analysis.* San Francisco: Jossey-Bass.

Lissitz, R. W., & Green, S. B. (1975). Effect of the number of scale points on reliability: A Monte Carlo approach. *Journal of Applied Psychology, 60,* 10–13.

Long, J. S. (1983). *Confirmatory factor analysis.* Beverly Hills, CA: Sage.

MacCallum, R. C., Widaman, K. F., Zhang, S., & Hong, S. (1999). Sample size in factor analysis. *Psychological Methods, 2,* 84–99.

MacKenzie, S. B., Podsakoff, P. M., & Fetter, R. (1991). Organizational citizenship behavior and objective productivity as determinants of managerial evaluations of salespersons' performance. *Organizational Behavior and Human Decision Processes, 50,* 123–150.

Marsh, H. W., & Hocevar, D. (1988). A new, more powerful approach to multitrait-multimethod analyses: Application of second-order confirmatory factor analysis. *Journal of Applied Psychology, 73,* 107–117.

Millsap, R. (2002). Structural equation modeling: A user's guide. In F. Dragow & N. Schmitt (Eds.), *Measuring and analyzing behavior in organizations: Advances in measurement and data analysis* (pp. 257–301). San Francisco: Jossey-Bass.

Muliak, S., James, L., Van Alstine, J., Bennet, N., Lind, S., & Stilwell, C. (1989). Evaluation of goodness-of-fit indices for structural equation models. *Psychological Bulletin, 105,* 430–445.

Nunnally, J. C. (1976). *Psychometric theory* (2nd ed.). New York: McGraw-Hill.

Price, J. L., & Mueller, C. W. (1986). *Handbook of organizational measurement.* Marshfield, MA: Pitman.

Rafferty, A. E., & Griffin, M. A. (2004). Dimensions of transformational leadership: Conceptual and empirical extensions. *Leadership Quarterly, 15,* 329–354.

Rogelberg, S. G., Fisher, G. G., Maynard, D. C., Hakel, M. D., & Horvath, M. (2001). Attitudes toward surveys: Development of a measure and its relationship to respondent behavior. *Organizational Research Methods, 4,* 3–25.

Rummel, R. J. (1970). *Applied factor analysis.* Evanston, IL: Northwestern University Press.

Runkel, P. J., & McGrath, J. E. (1972). *Research on human behavior: A systematic guide to method.* New York: Holt, Rinehart & Winston.

Schriesheim, C. A., & Eisenbach, R. J. (1991). Item wording effects on exploratory factor-analytic results: An experimental investigation. In *Proceedings of the 1990 Southern Management Association Annual Meetings* (pp. 396–398), unpublished work.

Schriesheim, C. A., & Hinkin, T. R. (1990). Influence tactics used by subordinates: A theoretical and empirical analysis and refinement of the Kipnis, Schmidt, and Wilkinson Subscales. *Journal of Applied Psychology, 75*, 246–257.

Schriesheim, C. A., Powers, K. J., Scandura, T. A., Gardiner, C. C., & Lankau, M. J. (1993). Improving construct measurement in management research: Comments and a quantitative approach for assessing the theoretical adequacy of paper-and-pencil and survey-type instruments. *Journal of Management, 19*, 385–417.

Schmitt, N. W., & Klimoski, R. J. (1991). *Research methods in human resources management*. Cincinnati: South-Western.

Schmitt, N. W., & Stults, D. M. (1985). Factors defined by negatively keyed items: The results of careless respondents? *Applied Psychological Measurement, 9*, 367–373.

Schwab, D. P. (1980). Construct validity in organization behavior. In B. M. Staw & L. L. Cummings (Eds.), *Research in organizational behavior* (Vol. 2, pp. 3–43). Greenwich, CT: JAI.

Shore, L. M., & Tetrick, L. E. (1991). A construct validity study of the survey of perceived organizational support. *Journal of Applied Psychology, 76*, 637–643.

Stone, E. F. (1978). *Research methods in organizational behavior*. Glenview, IL: Scott, Foresman.

Thacker, J. W., Fields, M. W., & Tetrick, L. E. (1989). The factor structure of union commitment: An application of confirmatory factor analysis. *Journal of Applied Psychology, 74*, 228–232.

Widaman, K. F. (1985). Hierarchically nested covariance structure models for multitrait-multimethod data. *Applied Psychological Measurement, 9*, 1–26.

Williams, L. J., Ford, L. R., & Nguyen, N. (2002). Basic and advanced measurement models for confirmatory factor analysis. In S. G. Rogelberg (Ed.), *Handbook of research methods in industrial and organizational psychology* (pp. 366–389). Malden, MA: Blackwell.

Williamson, J. B., Karp, D. A., Dalphin, J. R., & Gray, P. S. (1982). *The research craft* (2nd ed.). Boston: Little, Brown.

CHAPTER 11

Factor Analysis Methods

Baiyin Yang, *University of Minnesota*

CHAPTER OUTLINE

Factor analysis has just celebrated its centennial birthday in 2004. Its seminal idea was established by Spearman (1904) in discovering whether there is a common factor underlying a variety of branches of intellectual activity. *Factor analysis* nowadays is preferred as the common term representing several related statistical procedures that explain a set of observed variables in terms of a small number of hypothetical variables, called *factors*. It is a powerful statistical technique widely used for organizational research.

Two factor analysis techniques are commonly used: exploratory factor analysis (EFA) and confirmatory factor analysis (CFA). EFA is normally used to discover a set of a small number of latent constructs (i.e., factors) for a given larger number of observed variables, whereas CFA is more appropriate for confirming a predetermined factor structure based on theory or prior research. Factor analysis is a particularly useful research tool in developing and/or validating measurement instruments and in assessing theories on which instruments are established. Researchers can also use this tool in data analysis to discover new constructs in organizational study and thus to facilitate theory development.

Although factor analysis is widely used, researchers often make questionable decisions when applying this advanced research technique (Fabrigar, Wegener, MacCallum, & Strahan, 1999; Ford, MacCallum, & Tait, 1986). This chapter discusses specific methodological issues, principles, and processes for utilizing factor analysis in organizational study.

CONCEPTUAL BASIS OF FACTOR ANALYSIS

Situations of Using Factor Analysis

There are several situations in which factor analysis demonstrates its superior analytic capability that no other statistical technique can match. One situation in which factor analysis is the most suitable research tool involves the discovery of underlying dimensions for a phenomenon. The situation calls for an EFA approach based on several observable variables for the purpose of revealing underlying factors. For example, organizations tend to use various tests to make employee selection decisions. Human resource researchers may want to understand key competencies and their relationships based on available test scores. In this situation, EFA may be chosen to discover underlying factors that determine the correlation patterns of those observed scores on various tests such as aptitude tests and skill assessments.

Another situation in which factor analysis is widely used involves the development and validation of an instrument or an assessment tool to measure an abstract concept with either theoretical or practical interest. For instance, organizational researchers have been using the concept of "coaching" to describe certain behavioral characteristics showed by managers in their practice (McLean, Yang, Kuo, Tolbert, & Larkin, in press). Management by coaching as a concept cannot be directly assessed, but it can be inferred by various management behaviors (either self-reported or rated by subordinates or peers) in organizations.

Consequently, researchers may want to use factor analysis as a main statistical technique in discovering underlying factors of coaching behavior and identifying adequate measurement items. Although researchers can use another related technique, item analysis, in developing reliable and valid measurement items, factor analysis should be considered as a better tool for the development and validation of measurement tools in organizational study, particularly for the measurement of multidimensional constructs.

Yet another situation in which factor analysis is frequently used involves testing organizational constructs and theories. For example, researchers want to know whether job satisfaction is a unidimensional or multidimensional construct. Factor analysis can be used to examine the dimensionality of such a construct. Another example is the dimensionality of perceived organizational justice. While it has been widely accepted that organizational justice contains two factors— distributive and procedural justice (Greenberg, 1987)—this two-factor framework of organizational justice has been challenged with the introduction of two more factors, interactional justice (Bies & Shapiro, 1987) and informational justice (Colquit, 2001). In order to investigate the theoretical dimensionality of organizational justice, Colquit (2001) developed new measures of this construct based on seminal works in the field. The researcher used CFA and structural equation modeling (SEM) as data analysis techniques and confirmed the hypothesis of four dimensions for the construct of organizational justice.

Basic Ideas of Factor Analysis

The fundamental principle of factor analysis is to explain correlations among a large number of observable variables by identifying or confirming underlying factors that explain these correlations. Observed or measured variables may be single items on a survey instrument or other scale scores. However, in the most common application, the observed or measured variables will be single items from a survey-type instrument. The basic idea is that the mutual correlation of variables can be explained by their common dependence on a latent variable or factor. Researchers' task is to discover such factors with appropriate numerical analysis of the correlation matrix. Spearman (1904) demonstrated that the presence of an underlying factor would be revealed by a particular pattern in the correlation matrix.

Figure 11.1 shows a hypothetical situation in which six measured variables can be explained by two underlying factors. The basic idea of factor analysis is that the correlations among a set of observable variables can be accounted for by fewer unobservable variables (or factors). Common factor analysis seeks to partition variance of the observable variables into common variance (two factors noted by ξ_1 and ξ_2) and error variance (denoted as δs). The relationships between the observable variables and factors are called *factor loadings* and are noted as λs. The solid lines in the figure represent strong associations between a factor and some observable variables, and these variables are used to indicate the factor. The

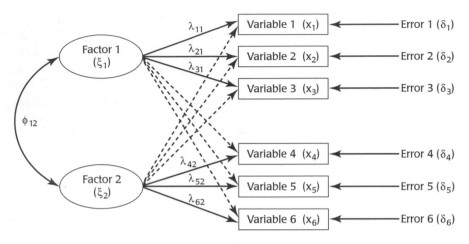

Figure 11.1   Basic Ideas of Factor Analysis

dashed lines represent weak associations between the factor and other observable variables that are not used to reflect the factor. As such, the correlations among a total of six observable variables are adequately explained by the presence of two hypothetical variables (or underlying factors) and the correlation between the factors. Figure 11.1 can also be regarded as a measurement model that indicates how a set of measured variables is determined by underlying factors (shared variance) and their uniqueness (unique variance). Such a model specifies the relationships between a set of measured variables and factors.

Exploratory versus Confirmatory Factor Analysis

Although different factor analysis techniques tend to share some basic ideas, they are different in identifying and determining the factors. Exploratory factor analysis is normally used to "explore" the underlying factors for a set of variables that indicate a phenomenon. In other words, researchers do not have a predetermined number of underlying dimensions of the structure before conducting actual data analysis. Researchers want the results of data analysis, rather than some predetermined concepts, to determine the study outcomes. The task of EFA is to discover the common factors that drive interrelationships among the observable variables. In CFA, however, researchers should have a prescribed number of underlying factors and the relationships between observed variables and designated factors. CFA is also often used to ensure some proposed factor structure prior to conducting structure equation modeling (see chapter 9 in this book). Therefore, EFA is normally used to uncover a correlation pattern among observed variables by identifying appropriate factors, and thus to reveal adequate associations between the factors and measured variables such as the ones suggested in Figure 11.1. CFA is used to test whether a predetermined correlation pattern such as the one in Figure 11.1 can be supported by the data.

Researchers planning to use factor analysis need to be aware of the applicability of both EFA and CFA in different situations. EFA is typically regarded as more appropriate than CFA in early stages of scale development where researchers' main purpose is to explore the underlying factor structure and to determine how measurement items load on factors that have not been clearly revealed. CFA would be an appropriate tool for data analysis where measurement models have a well-developed underlying theory for hypothesized loading patterns. Readers may want to consult some detailed discussions of differences between EFA and CFA (e.g., Hurley et al., 1997; Tinsley & Tinsley, 1987).

EXPLORATORY FACTOR ANALYSIS

Once researchers have determined that EFA is an appropriate tool to address the research question of interest, they need to make several critical decisions. These decisions include designing adequate factor analysis, selecting either common factor analysis or principal component analysis, selecting the extraction method, deciding on the number of factors, and choosing an adequate rotation method.

Design of Factor Analysis

In the process of determining the appropriate use of factor analysis, researchers must consider several key design issues (Fabrigar et al., 1999; Hair, Tatham, Andersen, & Black, 1998; Tinsley & Tinsley, 1987). First, researchers need to define the concept/construct to measure and develop adequate measured variables (sometimes called *measurement items* or *questions*) as the basis for factor analysis. Researchers need to select those variables related to the domain of interest and thus ensure that they share common variance in that domain. Researchers "should carefully define their domain of interest and specify sound guidelines for the selection of measured variables" (Fabrigar et al., 1999, p. 273). Inclusion of inadequate measured variables may not only cause the failure of uncovering important common factors but also bring some spurious factors irrelevant to the domain of interest. Normally, a content analysis is needed if factor analysis is used along with a process of instrument development.

Also, researchers need to ensure that each common factor is represented by multiple measured variables in factor analysis. Three to five measured variables per common factor are recommended for accurate results. When EFA is used for instrument development purposes, researchers should consider the nature of the measurement domain and anticipate the number of common factors to merge. In such a case, researchers should select multiple measured variables that reflect expected common factors. When there is little or no theoretical basis to anticipate the nature and number of common factors, researchers "should attempt to delineate as comprehensively as possible the population of measured variables for the domain of interest" (Fabrigar et al., 1999, p. 273). In this case, researchers should include a sample of observable variables, as many as feasible, reflecting the construct being measured.

Researchers must consider both the reliability and the validity of measured variables in including them in factor analysis. Variables with reliable measures are internally consistent and have low random error. Consequently, reliable variables can lead to adequate communalities in factor analysis. Communality is assessed as the squared multiple correlation for the variable using the factors as predictors. It reflects the percentage of variance in a given variable explained by all the factors jointly. Also, researchers need to ensure the face validity and convergent validity for the measured variables so as to have adequate loadings for the variables on their common factors. In addition, researchers need to ensure the independence of measures to be analyzed. Any dependency in the measurement of the variables may artificially increase the correlation and consequently appear together on the same factor.

Second, researchers who plan to use factor analysis need to ensure an adequate sample from a target population. One important consideration of such adequacy is the nature of the sample. Organizational researchers often use convenient sampling strategy. Although such a practice is unlikely to cause major problems so long as the sample represents the population and the size is large enough, researchers need to make sure that the convenience sample is not too homogeneous to cause attenuated correlations among measured variables. It is always desirable to select a sample that maximizes the variance on measured variables relevant to the constructs of interest and that minimizes the variance on measured variables irrelevant to the constructs of interest. Another consideration of sample adequacy is its size. While a big sample is always favored for better results (factor structure is stable and can be replicated), it is recommended to include 5 to 10 subjects for every variable to be analyzed, up to 300 participants.

Fabrigar et al. (1999) suggest that popular guidelines on sample size based on the number of measured variables have serious drawbacks, and researchers should use such guidelines with caution. They maintain that adequate sample size should be determined by the extent to which factors are overdetermined (i.e., at least three or more measured variables representing each common factor) and the level of the communalities of the measured variables. They advise that a sample size as small as 100 can be used to obtain accurate estimates when each common factor is overdetermined and the communalities are high (an average of .70 or above). Under moderate conditions of factor determination and commonalities, a sample size of at least 200 is needed. They also point out that samples as large as 400 to 800 might not be sufficient if these conditions are poor. In summary, users of EFA should consider both the number of measured variables and the associations between these variables and common factors. Five to 10 subjects per measured variable can be viewed as a practical guideline, and a sample of 200 or above is a minimum requirement for most factor analyses.

Third, researchers should be fully aware of adequate measures of association among variables. Although it is a common practice to use a correlation matrix in factor analysis because a correlation coefficient is the most frequently used measure of profile similarity, other indices measure the association between variables. Correlation coefficient is not an appropriate measure of profile similarity when the distributions of variables deviate significantly from normality. Researchers may want to consider using other association measures such as covariance, distance, and cross-product indexes. In addition, researchers need to conduct Bartlett's test of sphericity. This test assesses whether the correlation matrix comes from a population in which the variables are noncollinear (i.e., an identity matrix). A significant result suggests that the sample correlation matrix does not come from a population in which the correlation matrix is an identity matrix, and factor analysis can proceed.

Fourth, researchers need to make sure that the matrix to be analyzed is adequate. All measured variables to be analyzed must cover all subjects to be included in factor analysis. Submatrices from different data sources cannot provide a basis for factor analysis. Furthermore, researchers need to determine whether the data matrix contains meaningful information. Researchers can use Bartlett's chi-square test to examine whether the correlation matrix is an identity one or not. A statistically significant result suggests that the data may yield interpretable factors. Before performing EFA, researchers should check the correlation in order to make sure that common factors exist. Generally speaking, users of factor analysis do want moderate to strong correlations among measured variables, particularly among those variables expected to reflect the same latent factor. This is because such correlations explain common variance and provide the basis of the analysis.

However, sometimes high correlations can cause a problem for factor analysis. When two variables have a very strong correlation or one variable can be expressed in a linear combination of other variables in the matrix, factor analysis cannot proceed. Researchers facing such cases need to check the correlation matrix first and remove the variable with strong correlation with others from further analysis. Sometimes researchers need to identify which of the variables has been well represented by a combination of other variables. Researchers can conduct several multiple correlation analyses, correlating one of the measured variables with a set of other variables, and identify one variable with high multiple correlation coefficient with others. Then this variable can be excluded from further analysis because the high multiple correlation indicates that its meaning has been well covered by other variables.

Common Factor Analysis or Principal Component Analysis

The second important decision that factor analysis researchers have to make is judging the adequacy of using common factor analysis or principal component analysis (PCA). Park, Dailey, and Lemus (2002) observe that PCA is often mistakenly used when common factor analysis is more appropriate. Researchers should recognize both similarities and differences between common factor analysis and PCA (Velicer & Jackson, 1990). These two techniques share a similar purpose (i.e., explaining more variables with fewer factors/components) and some statistical procedures (i.e., extraction and rotation techniques). Nevertheless, they are quite different in terms of substantive implications for research. The purpose of common factor analysis is to uncover a latent structure of observed variables by identifying common factors that influence the measured variables. *Common factors* are unobservable latent variables that influence the measured variables and explain the correlations among those measured variables. The purpose of PCA is to reduce the measured variables into a smaller set of composite components that capture as many variations as possible among the measured variables with a small number of components.

These two techniques are also different in statistical procedures. The variance of a measured variable can be considered in three parts: common variance, unique or specific variance, and error variance. *Common variance* is the portion that a measured variable shares with other variables; *unique variance* represents the variation specific to a single variable; *error variance* is the one left or residual. Common factor analysis differentiates between common variance and unique variance. Theoretically speaking, factors represent the common variance of variables, excluding unique variance. Therefore, common factor analysis is a correlation-focused approach seeking to reproduce the correlation among the variables.

In contrast, PCA does not distinguish between common and unique variances. Components thus reflect both common and unique variances of the variables. PCA may be seen as a variance-focused approach seeking to reproduce both the total variable variance with all components and to reproduce the correlations. Such difference regarding common and unique variances is reflected in the statistical basis for common factor analysis, which uses estimated commonalities in the diagonal of correlation matrix. PCA simply uses the raw correlation matrix as the basis for component extraction. This statistical difference does have substantive implications for research in social and behavioral sciences. In addition, these two procedures are different in mathematical expressions: common factor analysis treats measured variables as a function of underlying factors, whereas PCA treats each extracted component as a function of the measured variables.

Although common factor analysis and PCA sometimes can produce comparable results in some situations, researchers should be fully aware of the conceptual differences and make right decisions in selecting the most appropriate data analysis procedure. For example, the term *factors* is often used interchangeably with *components*, and PCA is commonly regarded as a factor analysis. However, it should be recognized that PCA is not a true "factor analysis." Widaman (1993) reports that common factor analysis and PCA may generate quite different results when the ratio of the number of factors to the number of measured variables in common factor analysis is low. Restrictively speaking, only common factor analysis is a true factor analysis; PCA is not because it simply transforms the raw data into a set of orthogonal (unrelated) variables. PCA tends to be the appropriate data analysis technique when the purpose of research is to reduce the dimensionality for a set of direct measures. For example, for the purpose of discovering university professors' working patterns, a researcher may want to utilize PCA by analyzing some raw data on office hours, teaching load, advising time, time spent on job-related activities after working hours, and time dedicated to professional development so as to identify major components of professors' working patterns. PCA does not differentiate common and unique variance, and it assumes measured variables are adequate without measurement errors.

However, PCA is not an adequate data analysis technique when the research purpose is to reveal latent factors for a set of variables containing measurement errors. Many organizational studies involve measures such as attitudinal survey and ability assessments in either cognitive or affect domains, and thus the raw scores of such measures have measurement errors. Consequently, common factor analysis is generally the better choice because it allows researchers to interpret the meanings of data analysis results beyond observed variables (Conway & Huffcutt, 2003).

In summary, PCA is generally used when the research purpose is data reduction and the main interest is to reduce the information in many measured variables into a smaller set of components. Common factor analysis is generally used when the research purpose is to identify latent and underlying variables that contribute to the common variance of the set of measured variables.

Extraction Methods and Number of Factors

Once a decision has been made to use common factor analysis instead of PCA for data analysis, researchers have to select an adequate factor extraction method. Unfortunately, popular statistical programs such as SPSS use PCA as their default option in the extraction procedure, and some users fail to pay adequate attention to the extraction method and number of factors to be extracted. Users of factor analysis or any other statistical techniques should not mindlessly follow the default set by those popular statistical packages. The SPSS program sets PCA as its default for the factor extraction method and the number of eigenvalues greater than one as the default number of extracted factors. Researchers should recognize a variety of extraction methods and the rationale behind them.

Extraction Methods

There are several extraction methods for common factor analysis, including least square, maximum likelihood, principal axis factoring, alpha factoring, and image factoring. These extraction methods are either descriptive or inferential, depending on certain assumptions (Tinsley & Tinsley, 1987). The descriptive extraction method assumes both subjects and variables to be populations. This method includes procedures of least square, principal axis factoring, and image factoring. It implies that generalization of results from these procedures to new samples or variables requires several studies with similar variables. Principal axis factoring is similar to PCA in terms of extract factors with largest variance. But they are different as the former is a common factor analysis (i.e., using commonality estimates in the diagonal of the correlation matrix) and differentiates common and unique variances. Two commonly used extraction methods are maximum likelihood and principal axis factoring.

Although different extraction procedures of factor analysis are established on distinctive conceptual bases and use somewhat different statistical processes, choosing an adequate extract procedure should not be difficult. Such a decision should be made in congruence with adequate assumptions about the sample and measured variables. Tinsley and Tinsley (1987) regard principal axis factoring as the preferred extraction procedure for common factor analysis. Conway and Huffcutt (2003) recommend that organizational researchers use either maximum likelihood or principal axis factoring.

Number of Factors

Another very important decision in EFA is the criterion used to decide the number of extracted factors. Different criteria often lead to different results. Two major categories of such criteria are statistical rules and substantive considerations. Statistical rules for the number of extracted factors include Kaiser's rule of eigenvalues greater than one, Cattell's scree test, parallel analysis, the test of the significance of the information in the remaining correlation matrix, and the proportion of variance explained by the extracted factors. Kaiser's rule extracts only those factors with eigenvalues larger than one. Although the rule of eigenvalues greater than one is simple and easy to use and has been set as the default in SPSS program, research has shown that this criterion often overestimates the number of factors, yielding too many factors (Conway & Huffcutt, 2003).

Cattell's scree test assumes that the residual matrix (correlations that cannot be explained by the factors) gradually represents error variance when adequate factors are extracted. Eigenvalues represent the proportion of variance explained by extracted factors. Adequate factors, corresponding to those large eigenvalues, represent large amounts of extracted variance; those residual factors tend to have equal and small contributions to the total variance as represented by small eigenvalues. A scree test contains a plot of eigenvalues and requires researchers to determine the shape of a curve linking all eigenvalues starting from the largest to the smallest. A *scree* is the point where the curve becomes horizontal, and those factors above the scree are considered to be real factors. All residual factors below the scree are viewed as error factors. Although the scree test makes much sense in terms of extracting factors with meaningful variances, this criterion suffers from two problems. The first problem comes from a subjective judgment in deciding where the scree is located; the second one occurs when there is occasionally more than one scree point.

Another technique of selecting the number of factors is called *parallel analysis*. In using this approach, researchers compare eigenvalues obtained from sample data with ones expected from completely random data. The later eigenvalues are the predicted means of eigenvalues produced by repeated sets of random data. This approach involves numerous statistical calculations and procedures that are not typically known by ordinary users, and it is not included in commonly used statistical programs. Research has shown that this technique functions fairly well in yielding an accurate number of factors (Conway & Huffcutt, 2003; Fabrigar et al., 1999). Some have suggested that the use of parallel analysis in conjunction with the scree test can provide the most powerful strategy in deciding on the number of factors (Ford et al., 1986).

Researchers may determine the number of factors based on the percentage of variance accounted for by the extracted factors and by the last factor. The rule of thumb is that adequate factors analysis should retain the factors that can explain at least 60% or 70% of total variance. By the same token, factors that explain a very small amount of the variance should not be retained.

Substantive consideration in deciding the number of extracted factors includes prior theory and interpretable results. When researchers have an a priori theory or conceptual framework about the domain in which certain measured variables are subject to factor analysis, then such theory or conceptual framework should serve as the guideline for selecting the number of factors. When there are several competing or alternative theoretical frameworks in the literature, then factor analysis researchers need to conduct a critical review of the existing concepts and subconcepts. A synthesis of the existing frameworks in the literature can not only provide a powerful guideline for factor analysis but also advance the knowledge base. For example, McLean et al. (in press) reviewed major models of managerial coaching skill in the literature and proposed a new theoretical framework with four dimensions that covers those previously suggested dimensions. The researchers then conducted factor analysis based on the newly proposed framework. If researchers get a strong feeling about the existing theory or conceptual framework, they should consider CFA, in which the number of underlying factors and associations between measured variables and factors are clearly defined.

Researchers also need to consider whether the factor analysis results are interpretable in deciding the number of factors and the final solution. It is desirable to see that measured variables loading on the same factor have the same meanings. Researchers also want to see a simple factor structure in which no measured variables have significant loadings (usually set at .40) on more than one factor and low loadings on other factors, and each factor has sufficient number of measured variables. The ultimate goal of EFA is to discover those meaningful underlying constructs. Researchers need to define each extracted factor based on the interpretable meaning of the measured variables loaded on that factor. Although this interpretation process seems to be quite subjective, researchers must consider both meaning judgment and some statistical evidence such as factor loadings.

Many recommend that EFA users employ a combination of different extraction criteria (Fabrigar et al., 1999; Ford et al., 1986; Tinsley & Tinsley, 1987). An adequate strategy in deciding the number of factors to be extracted is to use multiple criteria and carefully examine several factor solutions before making a final decision. Factor analysis researchers suggest that it is better to overestimate the number of factors rather than underestimate. It is also recommended to select a range of factor solutions after taking into account a multiple criteria and then selecting the best solution as the final result for factor analysis. Researchers should consider both statistical indices and substantive interpretations in deciding the number of factors to be retained.

Factor Rotation Methods

For any given solution with more than one factor, EFA users normally need to select an adequate factor rotation method. The purpose of factor rotation is to improve the psychometric properties (i.e., reliability and validity) and substantive meanings of extracted factors (Ford et al., 1986). Factor rotation implies the change of basic axes representing underlying factors so as to produce interpretable results. Rotation changes the associations (i.e., factor loadings) between measured variables and factors.

Thurstrone (1947) provided one important principle for factor rotation: simple structure. *Simple structure* refers to a solution in which each factor is defined by a set of measured variables with high loadings and the rest with low loadings, and in which each measured variable loads highly only on some factors and loads low on the rest. Thurstone suggested that factor rotation should be conducted to find the best simple structure.

A number of different factor rotation methods have been developed to discover the simple structure, and they can be classified into either orthogonal or oblique rotations. *Orthogonal rotations* assume orthogonal relations among axes and thus imply uncorrelated relations among factors. It is commonly used in PCA for data reduction purpose. Varimax rotation is most widely used and considered the best orthogonal rotation (Fabrigar et al., 1999). This rotation method attempts to maximize the variance of squared loadings on a factor in order to produce some high loadings and some low loadings for each factor. Although orthogonal rotation, particularly the varimax method, is widely used, it is believed that this rotation fails to capture the complexity of factor structure because factors are constrained to be uncorrelated.

Unlike orthogonal rotations, *oblique rotations* allow correlations among extracted factors. This does not mean that oblique rotations require factors to be correlated. When the best simple structure is identified as orthogonal factors, a successful oblique rotation is able to produce a solution that is quite similar to the one yielded by a successful orthogonal rotation (Floyd & Widaman, 1995; Harman, 1976). In such a case, successful oblique rotation will provide close-to-zero estimates for the correlations among extracted factors. When the best simple structure is a solution with correlated factors, then a successful oblique rotation will be able to identify meaningful correlations among extracted factors. A number of oblique rotations are available, such as direct oblimin and promax rotations. These commonly used methods generally produce satisfactory solutions (Fabrigar et al., 1999).

Regarding the selection of rotation method, many researchers recommend the use of oblique rotation instead of orthogonal rotation (Conway & Huffcutt, 2003; Fabrigar et al., 1999; Ford et al., 1986; Gorsuch, 1997). Studies have shown that oblique rotations generally result in superior simple and interpretable solution. Such results tend to be consistent with the logical argument regarding the differences between orthogonal and oblique rotations. Oblique rotation tends to be more realistic because factors tend to have some degree of correlations in most situations. Even if factors are really uncorrelated or show low correlations, then an orthogonal rotation seems to be appropriate, but oblique rotation can also be used as it will yield very similar results.

Reporting EFA Results

Many factor analysis researchers found that not all published EFA studies report sufficient information for readers to be able to evaluate reported EFA processes and practices (Fabrigar et al., 1999; Ford et al., 1986; Tinsley & Tinsley, 1987). Quite often, EFA users failed to report the decision criterion for the number of factors extracted. Rummel (1970) suggested that published factor analysis studies should include the following information: (1) critical evaluation of the research, (2) replication of the findings, and (3) advancement or accumulation of knowledge. As a common practice, researchers should report key decisions regarding their factor analysis process, including factor extraction method, criteria used to determine the number of factors, rotation method, how factors were defined, and the method used to compute factor scores (if used). In addition, researchers should report several essential results of EFA, including descriptive statistics and the correlation matrix of measured variables, eigenvalues, communalities, the factor-loading matrix, the percentage of item variance accounted for by each factor, and correlations among extracted factors if an oblique rotation is utilized. When an oblique rotation is used, researchers need to report both factor structure and factor pattern matrices. *Factor structure* refers to a matrix containing correlations between measured items and extracted factors. *Factor pattern matrix* indicates the correlation of each measured variable with each factor when other factors are partialed out. The factor pattern matrix contains the values commonly known as "factor loadings" when reported in the literature. Factor pattern matrix is the same as structure matrix when an orthogonal rotation is used, whereas they are different when pattern matrix is used to facilitate the interpretation of factor solution under oblique rotation.

CONFIRMATORY FACTORY ANALYSIS

As mentioned, EFA is used to *explore* underlying factors when there is little or no prior theoretical guideline for a domain of interest, and CFA is used to *confirm* or *disconfirm* a hypothesized factor structure of interest. This is not to say that they cannot be used together to produce powerful results. EFA may be used to develop a hypothesized measurement model, and then CFA can be applied for testing the model with new data. McLean et al. (in press) first used EFA to identify underlying factors of managerial coaching behavior, and then they applied CFA to test a proposed model on coaching behavior based on a synthesis of existing models and prior results from the EFA. Consequently, both EFA and CFA can be used for instrument development and validation.

For the purpose of evaluating existing instruments, however, some have argued that CFA may be preferable (Conway & Huffcutt, 2003). CFA is also preferred before conducting causal modeling analyses in order to make sure measurement models are adequate. (See chapter 9 on SEM for detailed guidelines.) Structural equation modeling contains two types of models: a measurement model and a structural model (Bollen, 1989). Researchers need to assess the adequacy of measurement models with CFA before testing the structural model. CFA is a complicated statistical procedure that involves numerous notations and indices. Users of CFA need to understand the following basic issues.

Hypothesizing Factor Structures

To conduct a CFA, researchers must first hypothesize a factor structure or set of alternative structures that they believe may underlie the measured variables. This process is known as *model specification*. The hypothesized structure(s) normally comes readily from prior research and theories. A factor structure is also referred to as a *measurement model* that determines the number of latent variables and the associations between measured variables and the latent factors. For example, Yang, Watkins, and Marsick (2004) conducted a careful analysis of the theory and research on the concept of learning organizations and developed an instrument measuring the construct. They identified several different measurement models and tested their fit with data using CFA. Examples include a null model that assumes that a newly developed instrument has no common factors, a one-dimensional model that assumes that the concept of learning organizations is a unidimensional construct, and a seven-dimensional model that was based on a theoretical foundation and critical literature review.

Understanding the Usage of CFA

CFA is a complex statistical procedure that contains many statistical notations. Users of CFA need to recognize these notations first in order to be able to understand and conduct EFA analyses. CFA uses matrices to specify measurement models in a form so that they can be tested. There are five essential matrices in CFA: Λ (lambda), Φ (phi), Θ (theta), S, and Σ (sigma). The first three are specified by researchers; S and Σ represent the covariance (or correlation) matrices of the measured variables in the sample and in the population, respectively. The meanings of these matrices are as follows:

- Λ is the factor pattern matrix. This matrix contains the loadings of measured variables on latent factors.
- Φ is the covariance/correlation matrix of specified factors.
- Θ is the matrix of residuals (or measurement errors) of the measured variables that cannot be accounted for by common latent factors.
- S represents the covariance/correlation matrix of measured variables.
- Σ is the estimated covariance/correlation matrix implied by the hypothesized measurement model.

Evaluating Factor Models

CFA is essentially a hypothesis-testing process, examining whether the correlation/covariance matrix of measured variables from the data is equal to that of a hypothesized factor model. The general factor model used in CFA uses the values from the three matrices, Λ, Φ, and Θ, to compute an estimate of the covariance/correlation matrix in the population, Σ (sigma). Specialized computer programs such as LISREL and EQS are then used to choose estimates of each of the free parameters in such a manner that the discrepancy between the model-implied covariance/correlation matrix (Σ) and observed matrix (S) in the sample is minimized. The process of estimating the parameters also produces an overall test of the goodness of fit of the model to the data, in the form of χ^2 distribution. A nonsignificant χ^2 test suggests that the hypothesized model fits the data adequately, and thus it is tentatively accepted as plausible. As sample size increases, even trivial residuals might increase the likelihood of falsely rejecting the model. Furthermore, the χ^2 test is established to determine a restrictive hypothesis that the model being tested is the true model with regard to a particular sample. In other words, the χ^2 test demands a perfectly reproduced covariance matrix based on the hypothesized model. In fact, most social/behavioral models are merely approximations of "reality" or "truth." Consequently, the χ^2 significance test is limited in model-testing practice, and a variety of alternative statistical indices are proposed to determine the adequacy of the measurement and structural equation models (Bollen, 1989). Therefore, most researchers rely on a variety of alternative fit indices to reduce the dependence on sample size when assessing model fit. Because the various indices differ on their specific assumptions, researchers advocate that the models be judged using multiple fit indices that represent different families of measures of fit. One must also take into account the degree of substantive meaning for a model (Bollen & Long, 1993).

In addition to the χ^2 test, researchers normally report other fit indices such as Jöreskog and Sörbom's (1989) root mean square residual (RMSR), goodness-of-fit index (GFI), and goodness-of-fit index adjusted for degree of freedom (AGFI); Bentler's (1990) comparative fit index (CFI); Bentler and Bonett's (1980) nonnormed fit index (NNFI); and Steiger's (1990) root mean square error of approximation (RMSEA). The RMSR indicates the average residuals of covariance/correlation matrix, and its value of less than .06 represents an adequate fit. The GFI and AGFI reflect the proportion of the joint amount of data variance and covariance that can be explained by the measurement model being tested. The NNFI is a relative fit index that compares the model being tested to a baseline model (null model), taking into account the degrees of freedom. The CFI indicates the degree of fit between the hypothesized and null measurement models. A value of .90 or above on these indices indicates adequate model–data fit. The RMSEA represents a real advance in the evaluation of model fit from both statistical and conceptual viewpoints. Browne and Cudeck (1993) argue that because theoretical models are at best approximations of reality, the null hypothesis for any measurement/structural equation model will rarely be true. Rather than testing the null hypothesis of *exact fit* between the covariance matrix of sample and that of model for population, RMSEA establishes a hypothesis of *close fit* between the model and population. RMSEA values of .05 or less indicate a very close fit between the sample and the theoretical model, accounting for degrees of freedom. Values less than .08 reflect reasonably good-fitting models (Browne & Cudeck, 1993).

When the fit indices suggest the model is not adequate, researchers need to conduct tests of other alternative models to see whether any of them produces an adequate fit. This strategy allows researchers to evaluate the hypothesized model among the set of alternative prior models that provides an adequate fit to the data with the minimum number of parameters, which is then chosen as the "best" model (Jöreskog, 1993). If no model adequately fits the data, researchers should use exploratory techniques to identify a model that adequately fits the data (Bentler & Chou, 1993; MacCallum, 1986, 1995). Researchers should use such an approach in a very cautious way because the model capitalizes on relations that are specific to the particular data set. If the sample size is sufficiently large, researchers can consider splitting the whole sample randomly in half and then use one half to conduct an exploratory study to identify an adequately fitted model. The other half will be used in a confirmatory study to test the model identified from the first half of the sample.

CONCLUSION

This chapter has identified most of the important issues researchers face when conducting a factor analysis. EFA is often used to discover a set of a small number of latent constructs for a given larger number of observed variables, whereas CFA is more appropriate for confirming a predetermined factor structure based on theory or prior research. Although many statistical programs are available and the advancement of personal computers has made it easier to perform most statistical procedures, researchers should not simply follow those default options set by commercial programs. Users of factor analysis should understand its principles and adequate procedures and apply this powerful technique with great care.

Those who are interested in EFA may want to read more detailed descriptions in well-written texts such as those by Harman (1976), Gorsuch (1983), Rummel (1970), and Thurstrone (1947). A number of journal articles have addressed practical issues of using EFA in applied fields (see, e.g., Conway & Huffcutt, 2003; Fabrigar et al., 1999; Ford et al., 1986; Hair et al., 1998; Hurley et al., 1997; Park et al., 2002; Tinsley & Tinsley, 1987). In addition, several authors address methodological issues of CFA, including Bollen (1989), Bollen and Long (1993), Hair et al. (1998), Hurley et al. (1997), and MacCallum (1995).

REFERENCES

Bentler, P. M. (1990). Comparative fit indexes in structural models. *Psychological Bulletin, 107*, 238–246.

Bentler, P. M., & Bonett, D. G. (1980). Significance tests and goodness of fit in the analysis of covariance structures. *Psychological Bulletin, 88*, 588–606.

Bentler, P. M., & Chou, C. P. (1993). Some new covariance structure model improvement statistics. In K. A. Bollen & J. S. Long (Eds.), *Testing structural equation models* (pp. 235–255). Newbury Park, CA: Sage.

Bies, R. J., & Shapiro, D. L. (1987). Interactional fairness judgments: The influence of causal accounts. *Social Justice Research, 1*, 199–218.

Bollen, K. A. (1989). *Structural equations with latent variables.* New York: Wiley.

Bollen, K. A., & Long, J. S. (Eds.). (1993). *Testing structural equation models.* Newbury Park, CA: Sage.

Browne, M. W., & Cudeck, R. (1993). Alternative ways of assessing model fit. In K. A. Bollen & J. S. Long (Eds.), *Testing structural equation models* (pp. 136–162). Newbury Park, CA: Sage.

Colquit, J. A. (2001). On the dimensionality of organizational justice: A construct validation of a measure. *Journal of Applied Psychology, 86*, 386–400.

Conway, J. M., & Huffcutt, A. I. (2003). A review and evaluation of exploratory factor analysis practices in organizational research. *Organizational Research methods, 6*, 147–168.

Fabrigar, L. R., Wegener, D. T., MacCallum, R. C., & Strahan, E. J. (1999). Evaluating the use of exploratory factor analysis in psychological research. *Psychological Methods, 4*, 272–299.

Floyd, F. L., & Widaman, K. F. (1995). Factor analysis in the development and refinement of clinical assessment instruments. *Psychological Assessment, 7*, 286–299.

Ford, J. K., MacCallum, R. C., & Tait, M. (1986). The application of exploratory factor analysis in applied psychology: A critical review and analysis. *Personnel Psychology, 39*, 291–314.

Gorsuch, R. L. (1983). *Factor analysis* (2nd ed.). Hillsdale, NJ: Erlbaum.

Gorsuch, R. L. (1997). Exploratory factor analysis: Its role in item analysis. *Journal of Personality Assessment, 68*, 532–560.

Greenberg, J. (1987). A taxonomy of organizational justice theories. *Academy of Management Review, 12*, 9–22.

Hair, J. F., Jr., Tatham, R. L., Andersen, R. E., & Black, W. C. (1998). *Multivariate data analysis* (5th ed.). New York: Prentice Hall.

Harman, H. H. (1976). *Modern factor analysis* (3rd ed.). Chicago: University of Chicago Press.

Hurley, A. E., Scandura, T. A., Shcriesheim, C. A., Brannick, M. T., Seers, A., Vandenberg, R. J., & Williams, L. J. (1997). Exploratory and confirmatory factor analysis: Guideline, issues, and alternatives. *Journal of Organizational Behavior, 18*, 667–683.

Jöreskog, K. G. (1993). Testing structural equation models. In K. A. Bollen & J. S. Long (Eds.), *Testing structural equation models* (pp. 294–316). Newbury Park, CA: Sage.

Jöreskog, K. G., & Sörbom, D. (1989). *LISREL 7: A guide to the program and applications* (2nd ed.). Chicago: SPSS.

MacCallum, R. C. (1986). Specification searches in covariance structure modeling. *Psychological Bulletin, 100*, 107–120.

MacCallum, R. C. (1995). Model specification: Procedures, strategies, and related issues. In R. H. Hoyle (Ed.), *Structural equation modeling* (pp. 16–36). Thousand Oaks, CA: Sage.

McLean, G. N., Yang, B., Kuo, C., Tolbert, A., & Larkin, C. (in press). Development and initial validation of an instrument measuring managerial coaching skill. *Human Resource Development Quarterly*.

Park, H. S., Dailey, R., & Lemus, D. (2002). The use of exploratory factor analysis and principal component analysis in communication research. *Human Communication Research, 28*, 562–577.

Rummel, R. J. (1970). *Applied factor analysis*. Evanston, IL: Northwestern University Press.

Spearman, C. (1904). General intelligence objectively determined and measured. *American Journal of Psychology, 15*, 201–293.

Steiger, J. H. (1990). Structural model evaluation and modification: An interval estimation approach. *Multivariate Behavioral Research, 25*, 173–180.

Thurstrone, L. L. (1947). *Multiple factor analysis*. Chicago: University of Chicago Press.

Tinsley, H. E. A., & Tinsley, D. J. (1987). Use of factor analysis in counseling psychology research. *Journal of Counseling Psychology, 34*, 414–424.

Velicer, W. F., & Jackson, D. N. (1990). Component analysis versus common factor analysis: Some issues in selecting an appropriate procedure. *Multivariate Behavioral Research, 25,* 1–28.

Widaman, K. F. (1993). Common factor analysis versus principal component analysis: Differential bias in representing model parameters? *Multivariate Behavioral Research, 28,* 263–311.

Yang, B., Watkins, K. E., & Marsick, V. J. (2004). The construct of learning organization: Dimensions, measurement, and validation. *Human Resource Development Quarterly, 15,* 31–55.

CHAPTER   12

Meta-Analysis Methods

Baiyin Yang, *University of Minnesota*

CHAPTER OUTLINE
Advantages and Disadvantages of Meta-Analysis
Conducting Meta-Analysis
Conclusion
References

Meta-analysis is a relatively new, but increasingly popular, quantitative research method for synthesizing findings across studies. Niemi (1986) defines *meta-analysis* as "the application of statistical procedures to collections of empirical findings from individual studies for the purpose of integrating, synthesizing, and making sense of them" (p. 5). It is a special approach to reviewing the research literature on a topic; it reviews and synthesizes empirical studies in the literature. Meta-analysis originated in the medical field where the demand to answer complex and multifaceted questions with sometimes quite disparate findings is high (Rosenthal & DiMatteo, 2001). The first meta-analysis can be traced to more than 100 years ago when Karl Pearson (1904) collected correlation coefficients to determine the extent to which inoculation against smallpox was related to survival.

Merriam and Simpson (2000) maintain that literature review is a crucial step in the research process, and its purpose is to summarize and integrate previous work and thus to offer suggestions for future studies. While most literature reviews tend to be descriptive and narrative, a carefully designed meta-analysis should be inferential and conclusive. It goes beyond the conventional literature review with the aid of sophisticated statistical methods. Consequently, meta-analysis is more than a narrative review of the literature. For example, hundreds of studies have examined the factors that influence the transfer of learning (Arthur, Bennett, Edens, & Bell, 2003; Baldwin & Ford, 1988; Ford & Weissbein, 1997). These studies have not only used diverse theoretical definitions, procedures, research methods and samples but also identified different predictive variables affecting the learning transfer from various domains of study, such as training design, individual differences, and organizational environment. Consequently, it is not uncommon that some of the research findings on learning transfer are at odds with each other, and researchers tend to have conflicting interpretations and conclusions. A meta-analysis can integrate results from the existing studies in order to reveal patterns of causal relationships between training effectiveness and its influential determinants.

Meta-analysis method uses formal statistical techniques to sum up a body of separate but similar empirical studies. The purpose of meta-analysis is to synthesize and organize the existing empirical findings into a coherent pattern. Glass, McGaw, and Smith (1981) distinguish among the primary, secondary and meta-analysis of research:

> Primary analysis is the original analysis of data in a research study. . . . Secondary analysis is the reanalysis of data for the purpose of answering the original research question with better statistical techniques, or answering new questions with old data. . . . . Meta-analysis of research invites one who would integrate numerous and diverse findings to apply the full power of statistical methods to the task . . . it is the statistical analysis of the summary findings of many empirical studies. (p. 21)

In other words, meta-analysis is "analysis of analysis" (Glass, 1976, p. 3).

Glass et al. (1981) further identify three characteristics of meta-analysis. First, meta-analysis is quantitative, using numbers and statistical techniques for organizing and extracting valuable information that is nearly incomprehensive by other methods. Second, meta-analysis does not tend to evaluate the quality of existing studies. However, it attempts to record various aspects of research methodologies for the existing studies in order to identify their relationship to study findings. Third, meta-analysis aims to compare existing studies and to seek general conclusions across studies.

ADVANTAGES AND DISADVANTAGES OF META-ANALYSIS

The quantitative procedure of meta-analysis can be used to address those challenges imposed by the existence of different research findings to a given question. It allows researchers to combine numerical results from a number of studies, to accurately estimate descriptive statistics, to explain inconsistencies of findings in the literature, and to discover moderate and mediate variables for a dependent variable of interest (Rosenthal & DiMattco, 2001). The major strength of meta-analysis comes from its capacity to help researchers reach accurate and credible conclusions that other research approaches cannot provide, such as one single primary study and qualitative or narrative literature review. Meta-analytic research design nevertheless has both advantages and disadvantages.

Advantages of Meta-Analysis

One advantage of a meta-analytic research design is its capacity to integrate and synthesize current empirical studies on a particular topic. There may be a series of empirical studies for a research question. Meta-analysis allows researchers to integrate the existing empirical findings with some sophisticated tools such as combined tests. Because different existing studies may come from various empirical areas, a combined test tends to cumulate the existing findings in a scientific way and thus to present results with more generalizability. Researchers understand that it is crucial to conduct a literature review, yet they often get inconsistent or even conflicting findings. Qualitative or narrative review of the literature cannot deal with such findings, and thus sometimes such a review can be quite confusing.

Meta-analysis provides a cumulative view of a specific research topic by carefully analyzing similarities and differences of methodologies and findings across many studies. In other words, meta-analysis aims at getting a whole picture. By coding exiting studies quantitatively, meta-analysis researchers can keep track of a large amount of potential information and then conduct a more detailed analysis. Meta-analysis can easily summarize multiple variables from hundreds of studies that most narrative reviews cannot handle. In addition, meta-analysis allows researchers to examine a wider range of relationships, interactions, and other such complex analyses that are normally not permitted under qualitative research techniques.

A second advantage of meta-analysis for getting solid research findings comes from its nature of "analysis of analysis." Meta-analysis not only cumulates results from individual studies but also can be used to test complex theories involving many variables. Because social and organizational phenomena tend to be complex, different theories from various domains have been put forward to explain such phenomena. There might be several competing theories or theoretical frameworks within one research domain. For example, researchers can identify different predictors for the effectiveness of training in organizations, including training design, training method, skill or task characteristics, and evaluation features (Arthur et al., 2003). Meta-analysis offers a useful method to estimate the relative impacts of existing predictors on the dependent variable and thus provides aggregated empirical results for reviewing and judging available studies.

A third advantage of using meta-analysis is its tendency to offer guidelines for variable selection and research design in future research. Meta-analysis reviews the selected literature with empirical evidence and thus provides a broad and updated outlook about the relations between theoretical ideas and empirical evidence. Such outlooks have wide utility. For example, researchers can use such information to reflect on the existing design and find some promising variables for future studies. They can also use it to develop new conceptual and theoretical ideas based on empirical evidence revealed in meta-analysis such as moderators and interaction effects. In sum, meta-analysis allows researchers to develop and verify new theoretical ideas based on possible attributes and characteristics of all possible existing studies. That is, meta-analysis can follow a "research-then-theory-strategy" of theory building (Reynolds, 1971). Compared with other approaches, the main advantage of meta-analysis is that it is based on a number of proven empirical studies (i.e., published or other ways of being thus judged) instead of a single piece of research.

A fourth advantage of using meta-analysis as a research technique comes from its role in the continuous refinement and development of the existing theory. By identifying and testing those influential moderators and possible interactions effects, meta-analysis offers concrete conclusions about including newly proven variables or discarding old, less influential variables in the existing theories and conceptual models. For example, meta-analysis of the effects of instructional method based on adult learning principles might yield varying estimates, some strongly positive, some moderate, and some close to zero. The research interest might then appropriately shift from assessing the effects of instructional method on training effectiveness to identifying moderating variables. Perhaps, for instance, the instructional method based on adult learning principles works well for self-directed adult learners but not so well for dependent learners. To test this hypothesis, researchers would need to examine the effect of learners' characteristics as a moderator on the effectiveness of training. Identifying and confirming the impact of important moderator variables can facilitate theory development and increase the richness of empirical evidence.

Disadvantages of Meta-Analysis

Although the advantages of using meta-analysis seem obvious, criticisms have been raised, including the possibility of introducing bias into the sampling of findings, mixing together good and bad studies, combining "apples" and "oranges," and overemphasizing individual effects (Rosenthal & DiMatteo, 2001). Meta-analysis researchers should be fully aware of disadvantages associated with this technique.

The first disadvantage of meta-analysis is personal bias in selecting and including existing studies in the analysis. There is no single database that includes all empirical studies on the topic of interest, and not every computer-assisted search can identify all journal articles on the topic. Many good studies are not available simply because they are not published. There might be a publication bias; that is, significant results are more likely to be published, whereas nonsignificant results are relegated into file drawers (Rosenthal, 1979). Meta-analysis researchers need to set a clear and consistent standard for including empirical studies and to make a great effort in including all valid studies that meet this standard. Researchers also must avoid personal bias in deciding which studies from the literature to include in the analysis.

The second disadvantage of meta-analysis comes from the great variation of existing studies. Even on the same research topic and question, existing empirical studies may vary considerably in theoretical foundations and methodological issues, such as sampling strategy, operationalization and measurements of interested variables, data analysis techniques, and the reporting formats and contents. We know there are considerable variations among published studies in terms of research quality. Consequently, some have criticized the practice of meta-analysis for mixing good and bad studies.

Another criticism has been raised regarding the comparison of different types of studies as being similar to mixing apples and oranges (Hunt, 1997). Rosenthal and DiMatteo (2001), however, have defended the superiority of the meta-analytic approach in synthesizing very disparate studies. They argue that although studies vary methodologically, a well-designed meta-analysis takes into account such differences by treating them as moderator variables. Meta-analysis researchers should be sensitive to aggregating diverse studies with different study participants, sampling methods, and the operationalization and measurement of variables of interest. When combining studies, researchers need to be attentive to relevant moderator variables that can cause differences in research findings.

The third disadvantage of meta-analysis is its reliance on individual effects on a set of predictors on a dependent variable. Meta-analysis systematically assesses only individual relationships between dependent and independent variables and cannot provide a broad picture. Rosenthal and DiMatteo (2001) argue that this simple, systematic approach is essential in most research domains, stating that individual effects and correlations provide a foundation for building a comprehensive model that integrates many individual variables. In addition, meta-analysis tends to be a powerful tool for examining the combination and interactions of individual predictor variables. Such examination is a necessary condition for discovering multilevel and multifactorial models. Meanwhile, meta-analysis researchers need to be aware of the information loss when they concentrate on a single effect at a time in the analysis, also considering possible interactions among predictor variables.

Finally, another disadvantage of meta-analysis lies in its limited capacity of including new variables that are dramatically different from the existing theory (Yang, 2002). Meta-analysis researchers cannot operationalize new theoretical ideas beyond the variables and study attributes that have not been included in existing studies. Even though researchers may be able to discover different effects and hypothesize possible moderator effects, they cannot confirm such effects unless existing studies have reported relevant features. Consequently, a meta-analytic approach to theory building tends to be more applicable to a "research-then-theory" than "theory-then-research" strategy of theory building. Meta-analysis, therefore, has its limitation in developing and validating a groundbreaking theory.

CONDUCTING META-ANALYSIS

Hall and Rosenthal (1995) suggest three basic principles to guide meta-analysis: accuracy, simplicity, and clarity. They believe that quality research is often one that poses straightforward questions that can be addressed with simple statistical techniques. Researchers can avoid serious misconceptions simply by keeping close to the original data. In utilizing meta-analysis, researchers need to understand some basic steps of conducting meta-analysis, methods of estimating effect size, and the process of testing heterogeneity. There are a number of books and methodological articles on meta-analysis, and most of them offer similar steps to employing this research method (e.g., Durlak & Lipsey, 1991; Glass et al., 1981; Rosenthal & DiMatteo, 2001; Wolf, 1986).

Basic Steps of Meta-Analysis

Although there is no single correct way to conduct a meta-analysis, certain procedures are essential to meta-analytic research. A typical meta-analysis has the following steps:

1. Define variables of interest, and formulate the research question(s).
2. Search the literature, and identify adequate empirical studies in a systematic way.

3. Code previous studies, and select appropriate index of effect size.

4. Analyze the data collected from previous empirical studies.

5. Interpret the results and draw appropriate research conclusions.

Step 1: Defining Variables of Interest and Formulating the Research Question(s)

Suppose a researcher wants to conduct a meta-analysis to examine the impacts of some influential variables on training effectiveness. Specifically, the researcher is interested in the relationships among *training design, instructional method*, and *learning style* and their impacts on *training effectiveness. Training effectiveness* can be the dependent or response variable, while those influential variables of interest will be treated as independent variables or predictors. A meaningful research question can then be formulated—for example, Does a trainee's *learning style* moderate the impact of *training design* and *instructional method* on *training effectiveness*?

Step 2: Searching Literature and Identifying Adequate Empirical Studies in a Systematic Way

The next task of the meta-analysis is to search related literature and to identify all the published (and often unpublished) empirical studies related to variables of interest. Using the previously mentioned hypothetical study as an example, the researcher needs to identify all available empirical studies in the literature that have studied the impacts of *training design, instructional method*, and *learning style* on *training effectiveness.* It is necessary to read each of the studies and associated research methods, and thus to assess how variables of interest were operationalized and measured. For example, the concepts of *training design, instructional method, learning style*, and *training effectiveness* are theoretical constructs that human resource development professionals have frequently used to represent certain observable organizational behaviors. Organizational scholars and practitioners are often interested in developing and verifying theoretical models that depict their relationships in order to guide and inform practice. The researcher in such a study needs to thoroughly understand conceptual meanings of these constructs and operational definitions and measurement in different empirical studies.

One challenge faced by the researcher is the multifaceted nature of these constructs. Different studies might have attached diverse interpretations to the same construct and thus operationalized differently. Another challenge often comes from the fact that existing studies might have used different measurements for the same construct (which may inspire the apples-and-oranges criticism; Rosenthal & DiMatteo, 2001). A meta-analysis researcher thus needs to be fully aware of the differences among all included empirical studies. These differences include but are not necessarily limited to the following: different types of sample (age, gender, ethnicity, etc.), varying treatment situations, instruments with different psychometric properties, and the study and/or publication time. A well-done meta-analysis should take these differences into account by treating them as possible moderator variables. Suppose there are 50 studies in the literature that have investigated the impacts of *training design, instructional method,* and *learning style* on *training effectiveness,* and 15 used new employees, 25 included skilled employees with some degree of prior knowledge and skills, and the other 10 studies did not report the characteristics of trainees. Let us further assume that the researcher has a hunch that trainees' prior experience in the subject matter has some impact on *training effectiveness* with the interaction of both *instructional method* and *learning style.* Then the variable of *prior experience* should be included in the meta-analysis even though it was not considered in the previous studies.

Step 3: Coding Previous Studies and Selecting Appropriate Index of Effect Size

Based on the research question(s) and appropriate conceptualization, the researcher needs to code variables of interest into the meta-analysis. Durlak and Lipsey (1991) note that "it is impossible to specify all the variables that should be coded in any meta-analysis" (p. 303). However, some have suggested that researchers code those substantive and methodological characteristics that might influence study findings. Also, existing theories should play an important role in the selection of coding variables and the determination of coding method.

Durlak and Lipsey (1991) contend that meta-analyses "have varied from coding just a few variables to coding over a hundred variables per study" (p. 303), and they suggest using research questions as a guide for variable selection and coding. One of the common key informational items that should be recorded for each empirical study is the effect size or correlation between variables of interest. Sample size of each study is another commonly recorded variable. To reduce and avoid coding error, meta-analysis researchers may want to develop clear coding standards and use multiple coders. It is also necessary to check intercoding reliability and clarify any differences. It is desirable to have agreement among coders through further exploration and discussion.

Step 4: Analyzing the Data Collected from Previous Empirical Studies

There are three major approaches to analyzing data in a meta-analysis. The first is known as the "vote-counting" method, in which researchers sort the results of each existing study into one of three categories: positive significant, nonsignificant, and negative significant. This is a descriptive approach as the conclusions are drawn based on the resulting tallies. Wolf (1986) concludes that "the vote-counting approach is no longer recommended because of the poor statistical properties associated with it" (p. 13).

In the second approach, combined test, researchers analyze the results of the same research hypothesis from different primary studies in order to conduct a summary overall test of the hypothesis. Suppose dozens of empirical studies have examined the impacts of *training design* and *learning style* on *training effectiveness*, some of them have demonstrated the significant relationship, and others have failed to do so. A meta-analysis can be conducted to test the statistical significance of the combined results across these primary studies. A number of statistical tests are available for conducting a combined test in meta-analysis; their results tend to be consistent with each other (Wolf, 1986).

Closely related to the combined test is a method of estimating the magnitude of the effect size across existing studies. Suppose 20 studies have examined the impacts of *collaborative learning* as a training design on *training effectiveness* in similar organizational settings, but they have revealed different effect sizes. A meta-analysis is needed to calculate a grand effect size in order to draw a conclusion about the extent to which *training effectiveness* is accounted for by *collaborative learning* method.

The third approach to meta-analysis is to explore and examine possible interaction and/or moderator effects. This approach starts with examining the variability among the effect sizes of the existing studies. It is possible that the variability of effect sizes is attributed to sample characteristics (e.g., gender, race) or other influences such as geographic location and the time the research study was conducted. In our fictional example, the researcher might want to examine whether trainees' *prior experience* has mediated the relation between *training design* and *training effectiveness*. Statistical tests such as the chi-square test can be used to test homogeneity of effect sizes across different types of studies. More sophisticated tests such as the homogeneity test (generally called the Q statistic) should be used (Hedges & Olkin, 1985). This approach allows researchers to examine the viability of any conceptual grouping of the existing studies. The variability among effect sizes points to the possibility of an existing moderator variable that might explain the variability in effect sizes. If studies with samples of experienced trainees yielded significantly higher effect sizes on average than those with inexperienced samples, then it can be inferred that *prior experience* moderates the relationship between *training design* and *training effectiveness*.

A regression method can also be used to test whether the impact of a moderator variable is statistically significant where the effect size is used as the response variable and the moderator as one of the predictors. The regression method is particularly useful when some simple grouping variables are found to insufficiently explain the heterogeneity nature of effect sizes between many empirical studies. In this approach, variables coded from various characteristics of previous studies are used to identify predictor variables to explain effect size.

In addition, the regression method can be used to explore and examine interaction effects of interested variables on the variability of effect size. Suppose some studies on learning transfer have been conducted for training with the collaborative learning method and others with the conventional training method. Researchers may suspect that there is an interaction effect of *learning style* and *training design* on the outcome variable of *training effectiveness*. In this fictional example, the sample characteristics (i.e., *learning style*) and treatment (i.e., *training design*) should be coded for each of the studies in the literature, and these two variables and their interaction terms will be treated as predictors with effect size as a response variable in a multiple regression analysis.

Step 5: Interpreting the Results and Drawing Appropriate Research Conclusions

Durlak and Lipsey (1991) suggest three cautions in interpreting meta-analysis results and drawing conclusions. First, nonsignificance should be interpreted adequately. They warn that "null results might accurately reflect the true state of affairs, but they can also be artifactual" (p. 323). Meta-analysis researchers should be aware of confounding factors suppressing the real impacts on substantive variables. Also, researchers need to note the limited statistical power of a small sample size of the analysis (i.e., the total and valid numbers of studies included in meta-analysis). Second, meta-analysis researchers should restrict their generalization to the literature reviewed. Lastly, researchers should recognize limitations in the database and thus interpret the results in relation to available studies.

Estimating Effect Size

As mentioned in the previous sections, one major approach of meta-analysis is to estimate the magnitude of the effect size across existing studies. There are two main families of effect size: the *d* family for group differences and the *r* family for correlational relationships.

Pearson product moment correlation, *r*, is a commonly used statistic that measures the association between continuous variables. Researchers need to use phi (ϕ) to examine the relation between two variables when both of them are dichotomous, point biserial *r* when one variable is continuous and the other is dichotomous, and rho (ρ) when both variables are ordinal. Other indices in the *r* family of effect size are r^2, omega squared (ω^2), epsilon squared (ε^2), and eta squared (η^2). These squared indices are problematic in meta-analysis because they lack directionality and may cause misinterpretation (Rosenthal & DiMatteo, 2001).

There are three indices in the *d* family of effect size: Cohen's *d*, Hedges' *g*, and Glass's delta (Δ). All three use the same numerator—the difference between two group means, M_1 and M_2. Cohen's *d* uses pooled standard deviation (σ_{pool}) of the two groups as the denominator, Hedges' *g* uses pooled sample standard deviation (S_{pool}), and Glass's delta (Δ) uses sample standard deviation of the control group only ($S_{control\ group}$). These indices of effect size can be expressed in the following mathematical equations:

$$\text{Cohen's } d = \frac{M_1 - M_2}{\sigma_{pooled}}$$

$$\text{Hedges' } g \; = \; \frac{M_1 - M_2}{\sigma_{\text{pooled}}}$$

$$\text{Glass's } \Delta \; = \; \frac{M_1 - M_2}{S_{\text{control group}}}$$

These two types of effect sizes (i.e., r and d) are based on different research designs and thus must be interpreted accordingly. Researchers need to know that these two indices are convertible in the following formulas:

$$r = \sqrt{\frac{d^2}{d^2 + 4}} \quad \text{and} \quad d = \frac{2r}{\sqrt{1 - r^2}}.$$

Although researchers can choose the index of effect size from either type, the effect size r has several advantages over d (Rosenthal & DiMatteo, 2001). First, converting d's to r's makes sense because d can be viewed as a special case of r (i.e., point biserial case), and the other way of converting tends to lose information. Second, while d can be used to contrast between two groups, r allows for the analysis of trends across more than two groups.

It should be noted that not all empirical studies report effect size needed for meta-analysis, and in most cases, researchers must compute (with the assistance of a computer program) effect size. The following formulas have been developed to convert various summary statistics into commonly used metrics, r (Cohen, 1988; McGaw & Glass, 1980):

$$r = \sqrt{\frac{t^2}{t^2 + t}}, \text{ if the primary study reports } t \text{ statistics;}$$

$$r = \sqrt{\frac{F}{F + df_{\text{error}}}}, \text{ if the primary study reports } F \text{ statistics;}$$

$$r = \sqrt{\frac{\chi^2(1)}{N}}, \text{ if the primary study reports chi-square statistics; and}$$

$$r = \frac{Z}{N}, \text{ if the primary study reports standard normal deviation.}$$

If the primary study reports no specific statistics but p values, then researchers can convert p to its corresponding one-tailed standard normal deviate Z and then use the preceding equations to obtain r. Often studies only provide the level of statistical test and do not report exact p value; then researchers may want to use the low bound of Z scores associated with reported p values. For $p < .05, Z = 1.645$; for $p < .01, Z = 2.326$; and for $p < .001, Z = 3.090$. Sometimes the primary study shows a statistically nonsignificant relationship for a test but fails to report the associated statistics. In that case, researchers have to assign an r of zero, acknowledging a loss of information and an underestimate of the effect size.

After converting all effect sizes of the primary studies in the literature into the same format, meta-analysis researchers need to follow several steps to calculate a combined effect size. First, they need to normalize the distribution by transforming each r to the Fisher's Z transformation of r. The sampling distribution of Pearson's r is not normally distributed; Fisher's Z transformation converts Pearson's r's to the normally distributed variable Z. The formula for this transformation is

$$Z = .5[ln(1 + r) - ln(1 - r)],$$

where ln is the natural logarithm. It is not necessary to understand how Fisher came up with this formula. What is important are two attributes of the distribution of the Z statistic: (1) it is normal, and (2) it has a known standard error of

$$\sigma_Z = \frac{1}{\sqrt{N-3}}.$$

Next, researchers calculate both the unweighted mean and the weighted mean of these Fisher-transformed r's ($N - 3$ of each primary study). Then, they convert these unweighted and weighted means back to r and report both weighted and unweighted means as combined effect size.

Meanwhile, researchers can calculate the confidence intervals around these two estimates and use the confidence intervals for the purpose of a significant test for combined effect size. If the resulting confidence interval (CI) contains zero, then researchers fail to reject the nonhypothesis that overall effect is not significant. Otherwise, if the resulting CI does not cover zero, researchers will reject the nonhypothesis and conclude that overall effect is significant. Unweighted mean is recommended for the purpose of generalizing the result to studies other than those included in the collected sample (Rosenthal & DiMatteo, 2001). This estimate normally uses the random effects confidence interval, and its 95% CI around the unweighted mean uses the Z_r transformation of the correlations:

$$\overline{Z}_r \pm t_{.05} S / \sqrt{k}$$

Here $\overline{Z}_r$ is the unweighted mean of the Z-transformed r's, $t_{.05}$ is the value of the t distribution for a two-tailed p value of .05 for the degree of $k - 1$, k is the number of studies that yield Z_r's, and S is the standard deviation of the kZ_{rs}.

Assessing Heterogeneity

Another major approach to meta-analysis is to explore possible moderator effects. This approach starts with studying the variability among the effect sizes of the existing studies. Rosenthal and DiMatteo (2001) suggest that it is least useful and least appropriate to give up on combining the effect sizes if the test of heterogeneity is significant. They recommend that meta-analysis researchers examine the standard deviation of the effect sizes, plot them, identify outliers and naturally occurring groups, and focus on finding blocking variables or moderators that explain the data variation. Researchers can identify moderators by comparing average effect sizes in different subgroups that comprise the levels of moderators. Rosenthal and DiMatteo also suggest that researchers look for moderators even though the heterogeneity test of effect sizes is not significant. This is similar to the case in analysis of variance (ANOVA): An overall F with more than one degree of freedom in the numerator can be nonsignificant, but a planned contrast can be highly significant. In the situation of assessing the heterogeneity of effect sizes, a distribution of nonsignificant heterogeneity test may contain one or more contrasts that are both substantial in magnitude and statistically significant. The formula used to calculate the effect size and significant level for moderator is

$$Z = \frac{\Sigma(Z, \lambda)}{\sqrt{\Sigma\left(\frac{\lambda^2}{N-3}\right)}}.$$

where Z_r is the Z-transformed effect size r, λ is the contrast weight associated with each of the k studies, and N is the number of subjects or other sampling units on which each Z_r is based.

Sometimes meta-analysis researchers cannot find significant effects of moderator variables, even though effect sizes vary greatly among a set of primary studies. This phenomenon is due to either conceptual or empirical reasons. Conceptually, some effects tend to vary to a large extent, and it is natural to accept a variety of effect sizes for certain relations. Empirically, fewer available studies cannot provide enough statistical power to detect the significant levels of the effects of the moderator variables being tested. In the latter case, researchers must await the emergence of sufficient studies in the future and then assess these moderator variables.

Correcting Errors and Bias

The prior discussions on meta-analysis in this chapter do not take into account the attenuating effects of measurement errors and other artifacts. In many, if not most, social and behavioral studies, research results are not as accurate as they appear to be because of sampling error, measurement artifacts, and other artifacts. Therefore, it is necessary to adjust the effects of these artifacts and subsequently estimate the true population parameters. Hunter and Schmidt (2004) suggest that the purpose of meta-analysis is not only simply to summarize and describe the studies in a research literature but, more important, to estimate as accurately as possible population parameters. These authors provide an extensive discussion of systematic methods of correcting errors and bias in meta-analysis. Due to space limitations, this chapter will describe only basic principles and procedures of correcting error and bias.

Again, suppose researchers are interested in the relationship between *learning style* and *training effectiveness*. They should be aware of the fact that several study artifacts such as measurement error can alter the value of correlation between these two constructs. Because both *learning style* and *training effectiveness* are constructs with some degree of measurement errors, researchers normally estimate the relationship between these two variables with the correlation coefficient at the raw-score level, not at the construct level. Although the correlation at the construct level tends to reflect the true relationship between the two variables, the more reliable the measures obtained for the variables are, the closer the correlation coefficient of the raw scores to the true relationship at the construct level.

In addition to measurement error, Hunter and Schmidt (2004) have identified a number of other study errors and biases that could alter the value of outcome measures, including sampling error, dichotomization of the dependent and/or independent variables, range variation in the dependent and/or independent variables, deviation from the perfect construct validity in the dependent and/or independent variables, reporting or transcriptional error, and the variance due to extraneous factors that affect the relationship. These two researchers have provided detailed methods of correcting study errors and bias in meta-analysis; meta-analysis users may want to consult their book for the details of correcting other errors and biases. The follow paragraphs will demonstrate basic methods for correcting sampling and measurement errors.

Sampling error is the difference between the statistic estimate derived from a sample and the true or actual value of the whole population. It arises from estimating a population characteristic by looking at only one portion of the population rather than the entire population. To correct the sampling error, researchers need to estimate the population correlation with a weighted formula:

$$\bar{r} = \frac{\sum[N_i r_i]}{\sum N_i},$$

where r_i is the relation in study i and N_i is the number of subjects in the study. The corresponding variance across studies can be estimated by

$$s_r^2 = \frac{\sum[N_i(r_i - \bar{r})^2]}{\sum N_i},$$

This is the estimate of the variance of sample correlation, σ_r^2, which can be expressed as the sum of the variance in population correlations and the variance due to sampling error. This relationship can be expressed as

$$\sigma_r^2 = \sigma_\rho^2 + \sigma_e^2.$$

Hunter and Schmidt (2004) have provided the estimate of the sampling error variance as

$$\sigma_e^2 = \frac{(1-\bar{r}^2)^2 K}{\sum N_i},$$

where K is the number of studies. The variance of population correlation can be estimated by

$$\sigma_\rho^2 = \sigma_\rho^2 - \sigma_e^2.$$

This is the formula used to estimate the variance of population correlation while correcting sampling error. Now let us consider the method of correcting measurement error. Suppose researchers are interested in the relationship between *learning style* and *training effectiveness* and treat the former as the independent variable (x) and the latter as the dependent variable (y). Let us use T_x to denote the true score of the independent variable and E_x to denote the measurement error; then the raw score (or what we have observed) of this variable can be expressed as

$$x = T_x + E_x.$$

Similarly, let us use T_y to denote the true score of the dependent variable and E_y to denote the measurement error; then the raw score of the dependent variable can be expressed as

$$y = T_y + E_y.$$

We further denote the reliabilities of these two variables by r_{xx} and r_{yy}, respectively. Because *reliability* is defined as the proportion of the variance of raw score (or observed score) that can be explained by the true score (i.e., had we been able to measure the construct perfectly), a reliability estimate is the square of the correlation between the true score and the observed score. We then have

$$r_{xx} = \rho_{xT_x}^2$$

and

$$r_{yy} = \rho_{yT_y}^2$$

Although researchers normally estimate the sample correlation between two observed variables, the desired correlation is the population correlation between perfectly measured variables (i.e., $\rho_{T_x T_y}$). Such desired correlation indicates the relationship between two constructs while correcting measurement errors. Because of the following correlation patterns,

$$\rho_{xy} = \rho_{xT_x}\, \rho_{T_x T_y}\, \rho_{T_y y} = \rho_{xT_x}\, \rho_{yT_y}\, \rho_{T_x T_y} = \sqrt{r_{xx}}\sqrt{r_{yy}}\, \rho_{T_x T_y},$$

we obtain the following classic formula for correction for attenuation:

$$\rho_{T_x T_y} = \frac{\rho_{xy}}{\sqrt{r_{xx}}\sqrt{r_{yy}}} .$$

This is the formula used to estimate the correlation between two constructs while correcting measurement errors. For the methods of correcting other study errors and artifacts in meta-analysis of correlations and methods used for the d family of effect size, readers may want to consult Hunter and Schmidt (2004).

CONCLUSION

Meta-analysis is a powerful, useful research technique in integrating and synthesizing existing empirical studies. This chapter described both advantages and disadvantages of meta-analysis, common procedures and major steps of conducting meta-analysis, and frequently used procedures to estimate and test combined effect size. In some situations, researchers need to assess the heterogeneity of effect sizes in order to discover moderator variables. Also emphasized is the importance of correcting study bias such as sampling and measurement errors in meta-analysis.

This chapter has included some basic formulas, analytic tools, thought processes, and cautions for conducting meta-analysis. It is a straightforward process that most researchers can carry out with a statistical calculator. The challenge for meta-analysis researchers, however, may come from not understanding the statistical concepts and conducting related calculations. Researchers need to thoroughly review primary studies in the literature and the theoretical foundations that guided these studies. When used appropriately, meta-analysis can not only summarize existing studies in the literature but also advance theoretical and conceptual development in a research domain.

REFERENCES

Arthur Jr., W., Bennett Jr., W., Edens, P. S., & Bell, S. T. (2003). Effectiveness of training in organizations: A meta-analysis of design and evaluation features. *Journal of Applied Psychology, 88,* 234–245.

Baldwin, T. T., & Ford, K. J. (1988). Transfer of training: A review and directions for future research. *Personnel Psychology, 41,* 63–105.

Cohen, J. (1988). *Statistical power analysis for the behavioral sciences* (2nd ed.). Hillsdale, NJ: Erlbaum.

Cohen, J. (1994). The earth is round ($p < .05$). *American Psychologist, 49,* 997–1003.

Durlak, J. A., & Lipsey, M. W. (1991). A practitioner's guide to meta-analysis. *American Journal of Community Psychology, 19,* 291–332.

Ford, K. J., & Weissbein, D. A. (1997). Transfer of training: An update review and analysis. *Performance Improvement Quarterly, 10,* 22–41.

Glass, G. V. (1976). Primary, secondary, and meta-analysis of research. *Educational Researcher, 5,* 3–8.

Glass, G. V., McGaw, B., & Smith, M. L. (1981). *Meta-analysis in social research*. Beverly Hills, CA: Sage.

Hall, J. A., & Rosenthal, R. (1995). Interpreting and evaluating meta-analysis. *Evaluation and the Health Professions, 18*, 393–407.

Hedges, L. V., & Olkin, I. (1985). *Statistical methods for meta-analysis*. New York: Academic Press.

Hunt, M. (1997). *How science takes stock*. New York: Russell Sage Foundation.

Hunter, J. E., & Schmidt, F. L. (2004). *Methods of meta-analysis: Correcting error and bias in research findings* (2nd ed.). Thousand Oaks, CA: Sage.

McGaw, B., & Glass, G. (1980). Choice of the metric for effect size in meta-analysis. *American Educational Research Journal, 17*, 325–337.

Merriam, S. B., & Simpson, E. L. (2000). *A guide to research for educators and trainers of adults* (2nd ed.). Malabar, FL: Krieger.

Niemi, R. G. (1986). Series editor's introduction. In F. M. Wolf, Meta-analysis: Quantitative methods for research synthesis. *Sage University Papers: Quantitative Applications in the Social Sciences, 59* (Series No. 07-059).

Pearson, K. (1904). Report on certain enteric fever inoculation statistics. *British Medical Journal, 3*, 1243–1246.

Reynolds, P. D. (1971). *A primer in theory construction*. New York: Macmillan.

Rosenthal, R. (1979). The "title drawer problem" and tolerance for null results. *Psychological Bulletin, 86*, 638–641.

Rosenthal, R., & DiMatteo, M. R. (2001). Meta-analysis: Recent developments in quantitative methods for literature review. *Annual Review of Psychology, 52*, 59–82.

Wolf, F. M. (1986). Meta-analysis: Quantitative methods for research synthesis. *Sage University Papers: Quantitative Applications in the Social Sciences, 59* (Series No. 07-059).

Yang, B. (2002). Meta-analysis and theory building. *Advances in Developing Human Resources, 4*, 296–316.

Qualitative Research Methods

CHAPTERS

Context, Lived Experience, and Qualitative Research

Yvonna S. Lincoln, *Texas A & M University*

CHAPTER OUTLINE

Organizations are made up of human beings, who bring with them attitudes, prior knowledge, values, beliefs, motivations, hopes, worries, prejudices, spiritualities, politics, standpoints, social locations, and other characteristics that mark their lives and ultimately affect their performance, both as individuals and within groups in the workplace. Thus, showing the impact of efforts to improve organizations is always a task left unfinished, because it cannot account for many things unseen.

Organizations and the people who work in them possess the same rough or uneven edges that are found mathematically on fractals. Given the history and development of Western colleges and universities (both European and U.S.), the legitimacy of those disciplines focused on research in organizations is frequently found in a field's approximation of scientific pursuits—"scientific" in the sense of proceeding with inquiries via use of hypothetico-deductive models, building theories for the purposes of hypotheses testing, establishing short causal chains for their explanatory power, and creating models of certain specified segments of the social world.

There are problems with these goals. In subsequent arguments, three critical organizational arenas will be explored for the purposes of suggesting movement toward a different, and fresher, vision of how to manage the acquisition of legitimacy. A part of that vision is a serious and urgent entreaty to adopt a catholic, eclectic, and open stance to methods and philosophical paradigms for inquiry, a stance that forbids foreclosing models for inquiry and that foments a healthy ecumenicism in approaches to foundational questions. A short note on each of the foundational issues will demonstrate what I mean when I encourage an eclectic approach to inquiry paradigms.

THREE PUZZLES AND A PICTURE

Three issues that drive a discipline's struggle for legitimacy are questions of how knowledge is created, the discipline's impact on practice, and whether theory development is important (S. Lynham & R. Visser, personal communication, February 10, 2003).

Because organizational development, human resource development, and management are inextricably intertwined, and because they are, at bottom, practice oriented (just as medicine without patients would cease to be a discipline, or as education without students would cease to be supported as a profession), each of these issues revolves in some critical manner around the contribution to organizational flourishing and the enhancement of the chief resources of organizations: the humans working in them.

How Knowledge Is Created

No question is more central to a discipline than how its knowledge is created or constituted. How we get what we think we know—as well as how we go about getting what it is we think we do not know, and how we approach the vast unknown of what we don't know that we do not know—is a central epistemological question, not only of formal academic inquiry but of life. To rephrase the point as gracefully as possible, we cannot afford, in a complex world, to discredit any formal epistemologies or paradigms (nor can we afford to discredit any less formal epistemologies) when we are beginning to accumulate and sift through "knowledges." To label some kinds of knowledge about the world as the "gold standard" (National Research Council, 2002; Mosteller & Boruch, 2002), and the other kinds as "scholarship" but not "scientific" knowledge, is to cut oneself off from richness, depth, and variety in knowledge.

It is more useful to understand different models of knowledge as contributing different snapshots of the same phenomena, such that positivist research (primarily quantitative and statistical, although not always) can give us broad trends and excellent demographic snapshots. It may even, in large enough samples, grant us some epidemiological (i.e., causative) information, although prominent philosophers of science would disagree. Its limits, however, begin to be demonstrably evident when we try to understand "black box" processes (Lincoln & Guba, 1985, 2000; Guba & Lincoln, 1994), when we seek deep understanding of "lived experience" (Turner & Bruner, 1986), when we want to understand how individuals and groups go about "sense making" in organizations (Weick, 1995)—a critical issue for understanding the impact of human resource development efforts—or when we try to comprehend the meaning(s) behind "performing" performance (Denzin, 2003).

Overreliance on a single model of knowledge accumulation—or knowledge creation—has deep historical roots, knotted in the histories of the disciplines in U.S. institutions, in the tight logic and suasion of logical positivism, in issues of legitimation (and therefore academic support), and in the power and prestige of the natural and physical sciences on campuses, in both the United States and abroad (Novick, 1988). Indeed, we might argue that the technocratic mode of statistical reasoning has crept into virtually every aspect of life, more deeply within the academy than virtually anywhere else. Postman (1993) suggests that this frame of reference is fairly new in historical terms and represents a vastly different means of "constructing" the world than other ways of seeing it. Postman says:

> The first instance of grading students' papers occurred at Cambridge University in 1792 at the suggestion of a tutor named William Farish. No one knows much about William Farish; not more than a handful have ever heard of him. And yet his idea that a quantitative value should be assigned to human thoughts was a major step toward constructing a mathematical concept of reality. If a number can be given to the quality of a thought, then a number can be given to the qualities of mercy, love, hate, beauty, creativity, intelligence, even sanity itself. When Galileo said that the language of nature is written in mathematics, he did not mean to include human feeling or accomplishment or insight. But most of us are now inclined to make these inclusions. Our psychologists, sociologists and educators find it quite

impossible to do their work without numbers. They believe without numbers they cannot acquire or express authentic knowledge.

    I shall not argue here that this is a stupid or dangerous idea, only that it
is peculiar. What is even more peculiar is that so many of us do not find the
idea peculiar. To say that someone should be doing better work because he
has an IQ of 134, or that someone is a 7.2 on a sensitivity scale, or that this
man's essay on the rise of capitalism is an A– and that man's is a C+ would
have sounded like gibberish to Galileo or Shakespeare or Thomas Jefferson.
If it makes sense to us, that is because our minds have been conditioned by
the technology of numbers so that we see the world differently than they
did. Our understanding of what is real is different. Which is another way of
saying that embedded in every tool is an ideological bias, a predisposition
to construct the world as one thing rather than another, to value one thing
over another, to amplify one sense or skill or attitude more loudly than
another. (p. 13)

    The shift to emergent models of knowing—primarily qualitative—is likewise
deeply implicated in the "culture wars" on campus (Graff, 1992), in the politics of
political correctness and identity politics (Bérubé & Nelson, 1995), and in the critique that argues that higher education is failing because it has fallen away from
"real" science (Gross & Levitt, 1994). None of the contemporary critiques holds
water, but scholars wishing to uncover what qualitative research can uncover
should at least know the kinds of criticisms that tarry abroad in the land.

    "Qualitative" is one way of describing this new knowledge, but it is not the
most accurate. A more accurate description consists of specifying the underlying
paradigm, or philosophical model, from which the enjoinder to use qualitative
methods proceeds. For this, we generally specify, for example, phenomenological
models, hermeneutics, or anthropological interpretivism. Each of these philosophical stances begins with an ontological premise that at least some knowledge
is created by means of intersubjective exchanges. That is, it does not exist prior to
its cocreation by two (or more) cognizing human beings. This differs significantly from the ontological premises of positivism, which assert that "reality" is
"out there" to be investigated, separate from the humans who inquire into it, and
distinct from the invented system we call science utilized to explore it.

    The epistemology of such a knowledge model contravenes conventional re-
search in that it further specifies that the knower and the to-be-known do not
exist in dualistic relation—that is, separate from one another—but rather exist as
a monistic unit, both teaching and learning from each other in active exchange,
or intersubjectively. Far from pursuing objectivity in research activities, researchers pursuing an interpretivist, phenomenological knowledge base look for
instances of knowledge creation, both in their research participants and in themselves, which instances are treated as new insight, new understanding, enlarged
sophistication, *verstehen.* Researchers seek instances of "invention and construc-

tion, activities that seemingly move away from objects and objectivity to subjects and subjectivity" (Weick, 1995, p. 36).

Such knowledge is valued because it permits meaningful entry into the black box of human cognitive processing, and individual and organizational sense making. Qualitative methods offer the best possibility for understanding how individuals both make sense of and enact their social (and organizational) worlds, while recalling that "enactment is first and foremost about action in the world, and not about conceptual pictures of the world (en*think*ment)" (Weick, 1995, p. 36). Tests and measurements, while useful for some purposes, do not permit us to ask how individuals and groups make sense of their worlds. Only by observing, and communicating with them face-to-face, can we understand the meaning-making apparatuses that individuals bring to, and create from, a dynamic stream of events. Both of those tactics are qualitative methods.

Understanding and Showing Impact

Another serious issue in organizations is understanding the impact of activities and demonstrating their effect(s) on performance, learning outcomes, and organizational effectiveness. However, two serious issues with "impact" need to be addressed: the issue of causality, an epistemological concern, and the necessity of having demonstrable "impact" itself.

As an epistemological concern, the ongoing need to demonstrate impact—forget for a moment the necessity for organizational decision makers to earn their daily bread by showing some needed change in an organizational context—constantly hurls researchers and theoreticians into the cauldron of causality, and the necessity of trying to argue for short causal links between their training and the behavior and performance of individuals and groups. The shortest circuit into this arena is simplistic, often statistical, models of correlation and/or causality. The easiest comparison is to think of an organizational intervention as a clinical trial: administer a trial drug, and have the subject and physician both note all signs and symptoms of its effects.

The problem with this metaphor, however, is that it is not a chemical administered on a living body but rather a complex set of enactments and intersubjective activities, accompanied and followed by almost endless sense-making activities. Statistical approximations of learning, as well as follow-up studies of performance, rarely capture well what has happened, what participants learned. For such questions to be answered well, only qualitative methods will serve. Furthermore, the anthropologists' tests for validity and reliability, persistent observation and prolonged engagement at the site, appear to be the best ways in which we can document long-term learning and organizational performance.

There is another problem with documenting or showing the impact of interventions: Such a definition is anchored soundly in the assumption that development will produce observable, preferably measurable, actions on the part of organizational participants. But not all learning results in observable, socially bracketed, and socially created activity. Action has multiple forms, not all of which are visible to organizational members or researchers. Weick (1995) observes about enactment/action that

> creating is not the only thing that can be done with action. Blumer (1969) was especially clear that, because people had the capability for reflection, self-indication, and interpretation, "given lines of action may be started or stopped, they may be abandoned or postponed, they may be confined to mere planning or to inner life of reverie, or if initiated, they may be transformed" (p. 16). Any one of these outcomes, all of which differ from creation, can still produce meaning. . . . Abbreviated actions, constructed in imagination and indicated solely to oneself, can also be made meaningful. The caution, then, is to be careful not to equate action with a simple response to a stimulus, or with observable behavior, or with goal attainment. To do so may be to miss subtle ways in which it creates meaning. The act that never gets done, gets done too late, gets dropped too soon, or for which the time never seems right is seldom a senseless act. More often, its meaning seems all too clear. (p. 37)

To paraphrase, an action—an enactment—that comes as a result of, say, human resource development training in an organization may have no "demonstrable" effects at all. This might be especially true if the participant is asked her response on a questionnaire or paper-and-pencil measure. The only way to discover that the participant is still processing the training, or has connected the training to other events in an ongoing, dynamic stream, or has stepped out of the "punctuated, subjective, bracketed world" of the organization to understand some larger meaning (and perhaps will revisit the training in a different way, at a later date), is to explore that issue via qualitative methods.

Thus, the foundational issue of impact is at least a two-pronged dilemma, if not even more complex. Its conscious or unconscious assumption of direct causal relationships leave researchers with few methodological choices that are not highly conventional. Impact bears with it a cautionary note for researchers not to blind themselves with limiting, bounding concepts of causality that dictate inquiry decisions that simply further reify those same limiting conceptual structures. Stepping outside impact to consider the dynamics of long-term change can refocus researchers on influences, forces, pressures, and the residues of sense making that lead to deeper understandings of what a profession is accomplishing. That stepping outside conventional boundaries, however, demands a different sense of organizational realities, and grasp of potential epistemologies circulating in the context, and different methods and methodological strategies.

The other prong of the dilemma is assuming that learning leads to visible action. As Weick's extended exploration of action and meaning creation makes clear, not all meaning making leads to action that is visible or immediate. Neither is all performance external. Focusing on the purely visible, or the reportable, will fail to capture impacts, a result that leaves theoreticians, practitioners, and clients alike frustrated and unsatisfied. Again, the best possibilities for exploring learning and the interior processes that accompany learning are the methods that enable researchers to tap into cognitive and discursive sense-making activities.

A further note here: All of us have had the experience of never being quite "settled" about some issue until we find ourselves discussing it with a friend or colleague. In the middle of such discussions, we suddenly hear ourselves "working out" the sense of it all and often arriving at conclusions as we talk. So it is with organizational learning and qualitative methods. Qualitative methods create the venue for a new reality as that reality is discursively constructed via the "conversation with a purpose" that is an active interview (Holstein & Gubrium, 2003; Gubrium & Holstein, 2002).

The Development of Theory

Theories are enchanting. Theories are magical mazes of enmeshed meaning. Theories are the pig Latin of Ph.D.'s. They are a kind of code that few can translate well, they permit shorthand communication between cognoscenti, they mark the learned from the unlearned, the insider from the outsider, and they permit among grown-ups endless play using vivid imaginary worlds. They "explain" some reality and consequently permit sense making around that reality. They "stand for" some reality until a smart aleck finds the black swan—or postulates one. If physics is the queen of the hard sciences, then theoreticians are the kings of their disciplines. Aside from full professor, there is no distinction higher than being known as a "great theoretician" in one's field. Theoreticians are sought and bought, traded more wildly than hot stocks in a lively market.

What is theory, though? *Theory* is a shorthand and highly abstract model for some reality, a way of understanding regularly recurring phenomena that does not involve long epistemological explanations, the long epistemological explanations having already been worked out by long hours of drudgery and (generally) others' hard work. In its more conventional (usually quantitative) sense, theory is a means of describing causally linked relationships that exist among and between atomistic pieces of some reality (usually termed *variables*, to further confuse the noncognoscenti). Kaplan (1964) postulates that the function of theory is that

> theory puts things known into a system. But this function is more than a matter of what the older positivism used to call "economy of thought" or "mental shorthand," and what today is expressed in terms of the storage and retrieval of information. It is true that the systematization effected by a theory does have the consequence of simplifying laws and introducing order into congeries of fact. But this is a by-product of a more basic function: to make sense of what would otherwise be inscrutable or unmeaning empirical findings. A theory is more than a synopsis of the moves that have been

played in the game of nature; it also sets forth some idea of the rules of the game, by which the moves become intelligible. (p. 302)

Frequently, theories or pieces of theories can be described as a form of mathematical logic, as in A + B > C, or, in narrative form, element A, in the presence of element B, will lead to the recurring regularity known as C. Element A—let us say, pure oxygen in a closed tank—in the presence of rising heat—say, a Bunsen burner—will lead to outcome C—increased pressure on the container or given enough time and heat, a massive explosion. The nomothetic, lawlike proposition that this theory describes is that gases, under pressure from containment and/or heat, will expand (with often untoward consequences). The formulation just described was first described by mathematician David Hume more than 400 years ago in Scotland. The problem with these kinds of theoretical linkages is that they are short and far too abstract to deal with human learning and human behavior and/or performance, and they fail to represent "lived experience" adequately for purposes of meaningful action in the real world. Although they are excellent for some forms of physical reality—gases under pressure, gravity, chemical catalysis—they are reluctant contributors to our knowledge about human behavior. They are even less informative about the complex discursive multiple realities being created in a dynamic, punctuated, ongoing manner in organizations.

There are, however, other formulations for theories that are less linear and that provide more complex and interactive causal and noncausal linkages. If the conventional model described earlier is a *deductive* form of theory (or hypothetico-deductive form, as it has been most often termed in the past generation), then its contrast is what Kaplan (1964) terms a *pattern* form of theory. In pattern theories, short causal linkages are not evident (nor are they expected to be). The hierarchical nature of deductive theories is absent; in its place is what Kaplan terms a "concatenated" theory. In pattern models, "something is *explained* when it is so related to a set of other elements that together they constitute a unified system. We understand something by identifying it as a specific part in an organized whole" (Kaplan, 1964, p. 333, emphasis added).

Pattern theories have as their great utility that they are sensitive to and reflective of human systems, including organizational forms. As a reconstructed logic, pattern theories lead us to expect certain elements in similar systems, even as they explain the necessity of those elements in like groupings or forms. One superb benefit of pattern theories is that they prompt researchers to see phenomena under study as pieces of more unified, interconnected, and holistic systems. Thus, while conventional research, with its inducement to choose relevant variables (and relegate others to the category of irrelevant), may prompt us to investigate holistic phenomena atomistically, pattern theories nudge us toward systems views of complex human organizations. When the intended explanatory function is the description of an elaborate and manifold human grouping, patterns ultimately prove more heuristic than partial deductions.

Pattern theories, however, are constructed of very different material than deductive theories. Rather than parsimony, pattern theories are informed by richness and redundancy. Slums become integrated, composite, and highly structured communities, with rules for inhabitants' permitted and forbidden behaviors. "Organizational slack," rather than being seen as unused, "wasted" human resources, becomes the means and method by which organizations can fail and recover (Pfeffer & Salancik, 1978). The struggle toward richness empowers researchers and theoreticians alike to unearth the hidden processes of structuration, sense making, and meaning construction in organizational human resource development ventures.

Pattern theories themselves are best formed with qualitative data, or with a mixture of qualitative and quantitative data,[1] because those data are conducive to collecting and preserving richness and complexity. My argument here is that organizational researchers need the same ecumenicism with respect to theories and theory building that they need in methods, especially as they are still forging the knowledge base for a discipline.

Another caution, however, is in order. We often forget that much of Western science prior to the telephone was built on the basis of 5,000 years' worth of observational and descriptive data. Mesopotamian astronomers and medieval astrologists had much to teach us about the movements of stars as the seasons changed. Medieval alchemists' journals taught modern-day chemists about catalytic properties of basic compounds. Arabic physicians, "green women," and hags of the Middle Ages knew the properties of foxglove, chamomile, and a variety of abortifacients, emetics, and other medicinal compounds. The point is not what they knew but that those specialists built descriptive systems on chemicals, plants, herbs, and stars—descriptive systems we still rely on today. Many of our "modern" theories are actually quite old, buttressed by careful, thoughtful observational data. Most good theory, likewise, is constructed of deep, comparative observational data. In the rush to develop and advance theory, it might be all too easy to forget the basis of sound theory: sound observation and solid description. In a normative sense, any field ought to consist of some efforts at theory building and other, equally strenuous efforts at observation and description. Put another way, theories without extensive and penetrating description are not explanatory, for they have nothing to explain; they are, rather, little more than untested conjectures.

PICTURING A PROPOSED FUTURE

Most of what precedes this conclusion sounds as though it were written to apply only to individuals, but that should not blind the reader to the fact that all contexts are nested. Individuals are the smallest units in organizations, but they are nested within work groups, quality circles, or teams. In turn, teams are nested within departments and organizational functions (research and development, advertising, sales, accounting, and the like). Departments and functions, in their own turn, are nested within the larger organization, and organizations are subsequently nested within organizational ecologies (e.g., auto manufacturers, textile producers, mining and extraction corporations, public research universities, baccalaureate liberal arts institutions, art museums, labor unions, and Presbyterian churches, to suggest several). The ease of taking the individual as the unit of analysis should not blind one to the necessity of examining, in the same way, the work unit or the entire organization. Indeed, policies, decisions, and actions spread effects throughout an organization, much as a pebble chucked along the surface of a pond carries ripples outward to every edge. Thus, when I write about individual learning and performance, I am simultaneously indicating group learning, group performance, and organizational learning and performance. I am fostering an image that applies equally to the individual and to the organization.

The picture proposed comes in several segments. First, I would like to propose a healthy mix of paradigms (overarching philosophical systems) to guide research. Such a mix would include, at a minimum, ontologies (theories of reality) that treat reality as fragmentable; ontologies that treat realities as holistic; and ontologies that take as their concern the sense-making, discursively constructed, mental models that individuals and groups (as well as entire organizations) create in their organizational lives. Although I have not included them in this brief work, I would also include ontologies that take as their central concerns historically reified realities, suitable for deconstructive efforts to discover where such realities could be reconstructed toward more democratic and egalitarian aims (much as the deconstruction of the historical role of women in corporations has permitted a new construction to arise, one that permits women entry into managerial roles). The latter ontologies are those highly suited to critical theorist examinations of human resource and organizational theory development.[2]

Second, those committed to research in organizations would be well served by incorporating the abundant variety of epistemologies circulating in other social science and applied disciplines. Such epistemologies would include standpoint epistemologies, race and ethnic epistemologies, feminist epistemologies, "border" epistemologies (epistemologies of bicultural peoples), and indigenous epistemologies, as well as the epistemologies represented by the rich theoretical formulations imported from other disciplines—for example, postmodernism, poststructuralism, Foucauldian analyses, and the like. A theoretically diverse literature holds the potential for creating a discipline little marked by the prejudices, biases, and authoritarian superiority of a discipline committed solely to some "gold standard" for research. Substantively and theoretically diverse streams of research enrich further theoretical development and lend comprehensiveness, depth, and fecundity to disciplinary understandings.

Third, a cultivated sophistication regarding methodological and design decisions around inquiry problems, including an inculcation to deploy qualitative methods when there is a strong fit between problem and method, will further enhance research efforts throughout the discipline. The choice of methods, like the choice of theoretical lens or filters referred to earlier, ought to proceed on the basis of problem fit, not paradigm prejudice. Enlarging the range of available (and appropriate) methods can only generate better and more complete pictures of phenomena.

Fourth, those committed to research in organizations have the opportunity to build a multiperspectival, "multilingual" body of knowledges about practice, about impact, and about the processes of sense making in organizations around human resources and their development. *Bricoleurism,* the process of adapting, fitting, and tailoring materials and methods to the task at hand (Lincoln & Denzin, 2000), provides a rare opportunity for scholars to craft a practice and a knowledge base unmatched in other applied disciplines at present. The danger lies in granting sacerdotal status to one set of methods over another, one paradigm over another, a single theoretical lens, rather than multiple fruitful lenses. Engaging cross-pollinations, fertile concepts and constructs, provocative metaphors—all are the products of equally fertile methodological approaches to problems. The chances for a fecund and magnetic body of knowledge for theory and practice can only be enhanced by a rich and diverse set of methods.

NOTES

1. Positivist researchers can and do utilize qualitative data. Phenomenological paradigm researchers can and do use quantitative data. The central point here is that most methods do not belong, as possessions, to any given paradigm or philosophical model's practitioners. The more critical point is the purpose to which methods are put, or the meanings to which they are deployed. The major reason that phenomenological paradigms have been associated with qualitative methods is their insistence on believing that sense-making and meaning construction activities on the part of research responders are as important as the physical realities that surround them. Qualitative methods are simply better suited for collecting, analyzing, and interpreting respondent constructions than are quantitative methods, because they are immediate, processual, elaborative, and amenable to intersubjective interpretation.

2. Particularly useful on the critical theorist perspective on organizational development and organizational life is Gareth Morgan's (1997) comprehensive chapter "Organizations as Instruments of Domination" in his *Images of Organization.*

REFERENCES

Bérubé, M., & Nelson, C. (Eds.). (1995). *Higher education under fire: Politics, economics and the crisis of the humanities.* New York: Routledge.

Denzin, N. K. (2003). *Performance ethnography: Critical pedagogy and the politics of culture.* Thousand Oaks, CA: Sage.

Graff, G. (1992). *Beyond the culture wars: How teaching the conflicts can revitalize American education.* New York: Norton.

Gross, P. R., & Levitt, N. (1994). *Higher superstition: The academic left and its quarrels with science.* Baltimore: Johns Hopkins University Press.

Guba, E. G., & Lincoln, Y. S. (1994). Competing paradigms in qualitative research. In N. K. Denzin & Y. S. Lincoln (Eds.), *Handbook of qualitative research* (pp. 105–117). Thousand Oaks, CA: Sage.

Gubrium, J. F., & Holstein, J. A. (Eds.). (2002). *Handbook of interview research: Context and method.* Thousand Oaks, CA: Sage.

Holstein, J. A., & Gubrium, J. F. (2003). Active interviewing. In J. F. Gubrium & J. A. Holstein (Eds.), *Postmodern interviewing* (pp. 67–80). Thousand Oaks, CA: Sage.

Kaplan, A. (1964). *The conduct of inquiry: Methodology for behavioral science.* Scranton, PA: Chandler.

Lincoln, Y. S., & Denzin, N. K. (2000). The seventh moment: Out of the past. In N. K. Denzin & Y. S. Lincoln (Eds.), *Handbook of qualitative research* (2nd ed., pp. 1047–1065). Thousand Oaks, CA: Sage.

Lincoln, Y. S., & Guba, E. G. (1985). *Naturalistic inquiry.* Thousand Oaks, CA: Sage.

Lincoln, Y. S., & Guba, E. G. (2000). Paradigmatic controversies, contradictions and emerging confluences. In N. K. Denzin & Y. S. Lincoln (Eds.), *Handbook of qualitative research* (2nd ed., pp. 163–188). Thousand Oaks, CA: Sage.

Morgan, G. (1997). *Images of organization* (2nd ed.). Thousand Oaks, CA: Sage.

Mosteller, F., & Boruch, R. (2002). *Evidence matters: Randomized trials in education research.* Washington, DC: Brookings Institution Press.

National Research Council. (2002). *Scientific research in education.* R. J. Shavelson & L. Towne (Eds.). Committee on Scientific Principles for Education Research, Center for Education, Division of Behavioral and Social Sciences and Education. Washington, DC: National Academy Press.

Novick, P. (1988). *That noble dream: The "objectivity question" and the American historical profession.* Cambridge: Cambridge University Press.

Pfeffer, J., & Salancik, P. (1978). *The external control of organizations: A resource dependence perspective.* New York: Harper & Row.

Postman, N. (1993). *Technopoly: The surrender of culture to technology.* New York: Vintage Books.

Turner, V. W., & Bruner, E. M. (Eds.). (1986). *The anthropology of experience.* Urbana: University of Illinois Press.

Weick, K. E. (1995). *Sensemaking in organizations.* Thousand Oaks, CA: Sage.

Analyzing Qualitative Data

Wendy E. A. Ruona, *University of Georgia*

CHAPTER OUTLINE

Good research, regardless of the mode or methodology, presents rationally compelling conclusions that are supported by evidence. In qualitative research, this can sometimes feel like a daunting and elusive challenge. Anyone who has attempted to analyze qualitative data has surely experienced that all too familiar feeling of being overwhelmed with the sheer volume of data to be explored or drowning in the data once immersed in it.

This chapter focuses on demystifying and simplifying the qualitative data analysis process to help researchers enhance their ability to work with qualitative data. It rests on the assumption that one of the keys to generating excellent qualitative research is to conduct a rigorous analysis of the data. It is meant to be a highly practical chapter focused on "the basics" that have been culled from leading scholars specializing in this area as well as my own experience. The first two sections will introduce some prerequisite concepts that are foundational to qualitative data analysis. Next, I outline four general stages of the data analysis process and briefly discuss specific strategies to enhance the trustworthiness of your analysis process.

Finally, the chapter closes with a specific methodology for analyzing qualitative data using Microsoft Word. It has become increasingly common for qualitative researchers to turn to software to aid in the process of data analysis. Although more complex and multifunctional software programs are widely available, I have found that a simple word processing program like Microsoft Word offers excellent functionality for organizing, coding, sorting, and retrieving data and can be used to greatly enhance analytic capacity and, most important, the rigor of data analysis.

A FEW PREREQUISITE IDEAS ON QUALITATIVE RESEARCH

Before we delve into the process of data analysis, a few prerequisite concepts are important to understand.

Defining Qualitative Data

Qualitative data deal with meanings. Meanings are mediated primarily through language and action (Dey, 1993). Qualitative data are thus data in the form of words.[1] These words are derived from observations, interviews, or documents. Viewing data this way, though, is far too simplistic and mechanistic. We must always remember that participants' words represent their social realities. Their words offer rich, vivid, concrete descriptions of the meaning that they ascribe to their worlds. Miles and Huberman (1994) remind us that our "main task is to explicate the ways people in particular settings come to understand, account for, take action, and otherwise manage their day-to-day situations" (p. 7). The primary charge during qualitative research is to capture, understand, and represent participants' perceptions and meanings *through and in* their own words.

The Role of the Researcher

The work of qualitative research demands a lot from the researcher, and this is particularly true during data analysis. It is vitally important for the researcher to acknowledge that the words we study in our analyses are influenced by ourselves. In qualitative research, it is impossible for the researcher to stand apart from the participant. Our personal histories, gender, social class, ethnicity, characteristics, beliefs, and biases influence every stage of the process. All of this affects what we hear, observe, and deem as important. Denzin and Lincoln (2000) remind us that "there are no objective observations, only observations socially situated in the worlds of—and between—the observer and the observed" (p. 19). Qualitative data analysis, then, is really about *interpreting* participants' meanings. Meaning is constituted through our interpretive lens.

To effectively interpret the words and meaning of the participants, we should ensure, to the extent possible, that our "lenses" stay as clear as possible so we can retain our focus on the voices of the participants. We can use tools to surface and clarify our worldviews and assumptions so as to not cloud our understanding of participants' meanings. Two specific methods I recommend are as follows:

- *Personal disclosure (or subjectivity) statement.* At the start of your study, you should take time to write a personal statement in which you strive to surface and reflect on yourself as it relates to the study. Doing so will help expose your assumptions and biases. You should revisit this statement often throughout the study to help you remain aware of how you influence what you hear, see, and understand.

- *Memos.* Throughout your study, and particularly during data analysis, you should write memos to yourself. These memos should be a receptacle for your learnings, musings, biases, hunches, speculations, puzzlings, and so forth. They are a place for you to step back from the data and reflect on what's going on—not only within the data but also within you. Writing and reflecting on memos will help you see yourself and how you are influencing the process, thus enabling you to keep your focus on the participants. They are also extremely useful in making sense of the data, which will be discussed later in this chapter. Memos can also become a source of data that you may choose to explore as a part of your analysis.

Qualitative Research as Bricolage

It is also vitally important for the qualitative researcher to acknowledge her role as a *bricoleur*. The interpretive bricoleur "produces a bricolage—that is, a pieced together set of representations that are fitted to the specifics of a complex situation" (Denzin & Lincoln, 2000, p. 4). To produce this bricolage, the research process itself becomes a bricolage. So, while the remainder of this chapter offers specific, "how-to" methods to guide your data analysis, you'll also find that you will make many principled choices throughout the process. You will use a variety of strategies and methods and make many subjective judgments to "piece together" a process that is uniquely your own. The methods described in this chapter are not meant to limit your personal intuition and creativity—for qualitative research is as much of an art as it is a science.

In addition, as an organizational researcher adopting specific research traditions and methodologies, you'll also have to adapt this generic process to address the specific requirements of your methodology. As qualitative research has become an increasingly accepted form of inquiry, the interpretive and critical paradigms have flourished. The result has been the emergence of new methodologies for the design and analysis of qualitative research. These include grounded theory analysis, narrative analysis, phenomenological analysis, ethnomethodological analysis, conversation analysis, poetic representation, ethnodrama, and more. These each outline their own specific and systematic steps that this chapter is not designed to address. Rather, this chapter is offered simply as a systematic approach to guide those beginning in qualitative data analysis by focusing on inductive analysis. Coffey and Atkinson (1996) remind us that "methods per se do not substitute for thorough disciplinary knowledge" (p. 13). It is incumbent on you, the researcher, to continue to widen and deepen your knowledge of qualitative research—to continually explore and experiment with different analytic strategies that help you engage with the data in increasingly diverse and rich ways.

WHAT IS QUALITATIVE DATA ANALYSIS?

Glesne and Peshkin (1992) state that "data analysis is the process of organizing and sorting data in light of increasingly sophisticated judgments and interpretations" (p. 130). The purpose of data analysis is to search for important meanings, patterns, and themes in what the researcher has heard and seen. Before exploring specific processes for analyzing data, it is important to highlight the key features that characterize the qualitative data analysis process. Qualitative data analysis is a process that entails (1) sensing themes, (2) constant comparison, (3) recursiveness, (4) inductive *and* deductive thinking, and (5) interpretation to generate meaning.

Sensing Themes

Qualitative data analysis is, in essence, "the process of making sense out of the data" (Merriam, 1998, p. 178). This meaning making necessarily involves perceiving patterns from seemingly random information. As Boyatzis (1998) states, "Observation precedes understanding. Recognizing an important moment (seeing) precedes encoding it (seeing it as something), which in turn precedes interpretation" (p. 1). Qualitative data analysis, therefore, typically demands immersion in the collected data, openness and conceptual flexibility to perceive the patterns, and a great deal of information processing. The remainder of this chapter will largely focus on identifying categories and coding processes; however, always remember that the process of data analysis begins with your ability to recognize the codable moment—that is, to sense the themes emerging from the data.

Constant Comparison: The Core of the Process

During the data analysis process, we are essentially organizing the data into meaningful categories so that we can more fully and cogently understand what the participant means. A key strategy we use to do this is the constant-comparative method originally developed by Glaser and Strauss (1967). It entails doing just what its name implies—constantly compare.

> The researcher begins with a particular incident . . . and compares it with another incident in the same set of data or another set. These comparisons lead to tentative categories that are then compared to each other and to other instances. Comparisons are constantly made within and between levels of conceptualization until a theory can be formulated. (Merriam, 1998, p. 159)

Basically, "as each new unit of meaning is selected for analysis, it is compared to all other units of meaning and subsequently grouped (categorized and coded) with similar units of meaning . . . or a new category is formed" (Glesne & Peshkin, 1992, p. 134).

Recursiveness

The analysis process is a simultaneous and recursive process. You should *not* wait to begin your analysis until after all of your data have been collected. Rather, you should begin your analysis with the first interview or observation. This will help you understand what is emerging in the data, reconstruct the data as needed, and inform your study as it progresses. According to Bodgan and Biklen (1992), conducting simultaneous data collection and analysis will also help you (1) make decisions that narrow or widen the study; (2) make decisions about the type of study that you want to conduct; (3) identify "leads" to pursue and plan further data collection; (4) develop additional questions to ask participants; (5) try out ideas and themes on other participants; (6) reflect on your observations, learnings, and biases; (7) play with metaphors, analogies, concepts, visual maps, and so on; and (8) stimulate your reading of the literature. It is also the surest way not to feel as if you're drowning in the data. Miles and Huberman (1994) state that "the ultimate power of field research lies in the researcher's emerging map of what is happening and why" (p. 65). This simultaneous process of data collection and analysis ensures that you are critically reflecting and continually learning throughout the data analysis process and that your learning is being used to conduct better research.

Of course, data analysis does become "more intensive as the study progresses, and once all the data are in" (Merriam, 1998, p. 155). So, the next logical question is, When do you stop? Although certainly practical concerns such as time and money factor into this decision, ideally more theoretical and methodological concerns will prevail. First, Miles and Huberman (1994) remind us that conceptual frameworks and research questions are our best defense against overload. "The challenge is to be explicitly mindful of the purposes of your study and of the conceptual lenses you are training on it—while allowing yourself to be open and reeducated by things you didn't know about or expect to find. . . . Resist overload, but not at the price of sketchiness" (p. 56). In addition, some of the best advice comes from Lincoln and Guba (1985), who offer the following criteria that can used to judge when you are approaching "done":

> *Exhaustion of resources* (although sources may be recycled and tapped many times); *saturation of categories* (continuing data collection produces tiny increments of new information compared to the effort expended to get them); *emergence of regularities*—the sense of "integration" (although care must be exercised to avoid a fast conclusion occasioned by regularities occurring are a more simplistic level than the inquirer should accept); and *overextension*— the sense that new information being unearthed is very far removed from the core of any of the viable categories which have emerged (and does not contribute to the emergence of additional viable categories). (p. 350)

Inductive and Deductive Thinking

Many people contrast qualitative and quantitative research on the basis that qualitative research is an inductive process and quantitative research is a deductive process. An *inductive research process* "builds abstractions, concepts, hypotheses from the data" (Merriam, 1998, p. 7) with the belief that themes will be revealed from the close inspection of accumulated observations and cases. A *deductive research process*, on the other hand, aims to test a theory by collecting data and testing whether those data confirm or disconfirm the theory.

In practice, however, qualitative data analysis relies on *both* inductive and deductive reasoning. A large and fundamental part of data analysis is inductive— that is, identifying themes that emerge directly from the data. However, as a researcher progresses in her analysis, "tentative categories, properties, and hypotheses continually emerge and must be tested against the data" (Merriam, 1998, p. 192). Thus, in reality, we are continuously shifting back and forth between inductive and deductive modes of thinking during the process of data analysis.

Interpretations to Generate Meaning

As noted in the remainder of this chapter, the data analysis process is largely driven by the act of categorizing and coding. What is important to understand is that the very act of categorizing and coding is the start of theory building. During data analysis, we identify themes/categories, and we use codes to represent those emergent concepts. Those codes are theory laden—implying some kind of idea you have about that concept (Richards & Richards, 1994). Furthermore, the way you construct the relationships among the categories implies some idea that you have about how these categories are related. The themes that you identify and the relationships that you see between those themes results in a theory, or a "coherent description, explanation, and representation of observed or experienced phenomena" (Gioia & Pitre, 1990, p. 587). Thus, theorizing cannot be divorced from analysis.

The emphasis during data analysis is on the *act* of theorizing. According to Coffey and Atkinson (1996), "One must always be prepared to engage in creative intellectual work, to speculate about the data in order to have ideas, to try out a number of different ideas, to link one's ideas with those of others, and to move conceptually from one's own research setting to a more general, even abstract, level of analytic thought" (pp. 142–143).

Thus, data analysis is about much more than manipulating data. We have to think deeply about the data. And, in doing that, we actually go *beyond* our data. Our important ideas are not "in" the data but in our ideas about the data (Coffey & Atkinson, 1996). During data analysis, we do (and must!) engage in the creative, intellectual work of *interpretation*—offering our own perspective of what is going on in the data. We thus engage with ideas at a more general level. This process is what Coffey and Atkinson (1996) refer to as *abductive reasoning*. This is when we

> start from the particular . . . and try to account for that phenomenon by relating it to broader concepts. We do so by inspecting our own experience, our stock of knowledge of similar, comparable phenomena, and the equivalent stock of ideas that can be included from within our disciplines (including theories and frameworks) and neighboring fields. In other words . . . we seek to go beyond the data themselves to locate them in explanatory or interpretive frameworks. (p. 156)

We are, in essence, engaging in theory building—a continuous process of generating, verifying, and refining our descriptions, explanations, or representations of social phenomena (Lynham, 2002). This theory is derived "inductively from the 'real world' to enhance our understanding" (Turnbull, 2002, p. 319).

All of this being said, the *type* of theory that is generated during qualitative data analysis is contested and varies depending on which expert you read and, most important, what epistemological orientation you adopt. In this area, not even qualitative researchers are a homogeneous group. Glaser and Strauss (1967) usefully distinguish between substantive and formal theory. *Substantive theory* makes sense of the particular—emerging from the conceptual categories yet firmly grounded in the data. They apply only to what is being studied. *Formal theory*, on the other hand, is more generic in scope—going beyond the case under study and relating to social settings of many kinds. Abductive reasoning pushes beyond the local and particular toward more formal theory. This is not to say that qualitative theories are in any way generalizable but rather that our *inferences* allow us to move conceptually across a wide variety of social contexts. We must realize that the nucleus of any theory is constituted by a set of concepts and their interrelationships. As soon as we begin to reduce and refine categories and then link those categories together in some meaningful way, the analysis is moving toward the development of theory to explain the data's meaning. Qualitative research thus enables a qualitatively new understanding of relevant fragments of social reality (Alvesson & Sköldberg, 2000).

CONDUCTING DATA ANALYSIS

Now that you conceptually understand what data analysis is, we can move on to exploring the practical process of doing it. This section outlines four general stages of qualitative data analysis: data preparation, familiarization, coding, and generating meaning.

Stage 1: Data Preparation

Before you can even begin data analysis, you must get the collected data into a form that is easy to work with. This typically involves transcription of your interviews, focus groups, field notes, and so forth. In addition, during this stage you will take steps to ensure that the data are as "clean" as possible. This task may include minor editing, general tidying up of the data, and formatting.

This is also the time in which you need to organize your data. If you've offered to protect the identity of the participants, interviewees will likely need to be given pseudonyms or code numbers (with a secure and confidential file that links these to the original informants for your own information). Names and other identifiable material would also need to be removed from the transcripts.

Finally, you should establish a filing system (printed or electronic or both) that allows you to back up and store transcripts at various stages in the process. These systems should be rigorously maintained throughout the research project.

Stage 2: Familiarization

In preparing the data, you'll already have begun the process of familiarization. This stage of the process involves you immersing in the data much more deeply. It typically involves listening to tapes (or watching video material), reading and rereading the data, and jotting notes and memos about what you see and what you think is going on in the data. During this process, you should *actively engage* with the data—have a "conversation" with the data by asking questions of it and making comments on it (Merriam, 1988, p. 181). This familiarization time will help you get a general sense of the information and reflect on its overall meaning

(Creswell, 2002). It will help you to "tune into" what the participant is saying. In this stage, you'll also begin to note interesting and potentially important data that you will use as you progress in your analysis.

Stage 3: Coding

Miles and Huberman (1994) suggest that coding is the "stuff of analysis" (p. 56). It is the first step we take toward organizing information into meaningful categories. During this stage, we are essentially "generating concepts from and with our data" (Coffey & Atkinson, 1996, p. 26). This process involves "segmenting sentences or paragraphs into categories, and labeling those categories with a term" (Creswell, 2003, p. 192).

On one hand, coding can be thought of as data simplification (or reduction) in that we break up and categorize the data into simpler, more general categories. On the other hand, coding can also be conceptualized as data complication. Rather than viewing coding as a process in which we simply reduce the data, we should also regard it as our mechanism to open up the data so that we can interrogate the data in order to formulate new questions and levels of interpretation (Coffey & Atkinson, 1996). Coding is ultimately about discovering and conceptualizing the data.

What Is a Code?

A *code* is a "tag or label for assigning units of meaning to the information compiled during a study" (Miles & Huberman, 1994, p. 56). It is a shorthand designator (letters, numbers, words, and/or phrases) that represents a theme or pattern you see in the data. Boyatzis (1998) asserts that a good code is one that captures the qualitative richness of the phenomenon and that a good code should have the following five elements:

- A label (i.e., a name). This should be (a) conceptually meaningful, (b) clear and concise, communicating the essence of the theme in the fewest words possible, and (c) close to the data.
- A definition of what the theme concerns (i.e., the characteristics constituting the theme).
- A description of how to know when the theme occurs (i.e., indicators on how to "flag" the theme).
- A description of any qualifications or exclusions to the identification of the theme.
- Examples, both positive and negative, to eliminate possible confusion when looking for the theme. (p. 31)

Sources of Codes

Boyatzis (1998) outlines three different types of code development: theory driven, prior data or prior research driven, and inductive. He places these on a continuum from theory-driven to data-driven approaches because they differ in the degree to which the analysis starts with a theory versus the raw information in the collected data. *Theory-driven codes* are derived by beginning with a specific theory and its elements or hypotheses. *Prior research–driven codes* are quite similar in that the researcher uses her knowledge of past research (rather than a theory) to derive categories. Both of these methods basically help us create a "start list" (Miles & Huberman, 1994) of codes prior to even reading the data. *Data-driven codes*, on the other hand, are created inductively directly from the data you collected. They are based entirely on what you find interesting and significant in the data—words, events, processes, or characters that you see and believe capture the essence of what you're seeking to understand.

How to Code

Data-driven codes are the most fundamental and widely discussed method for developing themes and codes. If you can effectively work with your data to generate data-driven codes, you can easily adapt the coding process if you choose to use theory-driven or research-driven codes.

During the familiarization stage, you immersed yourself in the data and hopefully allowed yourself to "see" the data creatively and generatively. During this process, you will undoubtedly begin to see recurring topics or patterns emerging from the data. Once you feel like you're getting a deep and rich understanding of the data, pull back from the data and make a list of the categories or themes[2] that have emerged (i.e., what you see in the data at a thematic level). This will likely be a long list because you're just getting started.

Now move on to another transcript or two and repeat this same process. By the time you've immersed yourself in two or three transcripts, you are ready to create your preliminary list of themes. To do this, compile the list of themes from each interview and spend quality time reflecting on them. Work with that compiled list to understand what is going on in the data—cluster similar topics together, create categories and subcategories, and so forth. Your goal is to create categories that cover or span the significant themes emerging from your data. This is also a great time to be memoing so that you capture your reflections.

How do you know what qualifies as significant themes? First, you might deem a category as important because the number of people who are discussing a theme (i.e., the frequency with which it is arising in your data). Second, the audience for your study may dictate the importance of a theme. Third, some categories will simply stand out as unique and worthy of retaining. Finally, certain categories may reveal "areas of inquiry not otherwise recognized" or "provide a unique leverage on an otherwise common problem" (Merriam, 1998, p. 185).

Bear in mind several important guidelines as you work with your categories:

- Categories should *reflect the purpose of the research*. In effect, categories are the answers to your research question(s).
- Categories should be *exhaustive*; that is, you should be able to place all data that you decided were important or relevant to the study in a category or sub-category.

- Categories should be *mutually exclusive*. A particular unit of data should fit into only one category. If the exact same unit of data can be placed into more than one category, more conceptual work needs to be done to refine the categories.
- Categories should be *sensitizing*. The naming of the category should be as sensitive possible to what is in the data. . . . [You] should be able to read the categories and gain some sense of their nature.
- Categories should be *conceptually congruent* . . . the same level of abstraction should characterize all categories at the same level. (Merriam, 1998, pp. 183–184)

Once you feel comfortable that you have identified significant categories, organize your list and assign shorthand designators to each topic/theme. These designators can be letters, numbers, words, and/or phrases. You've just created your preliminary coding system!

It's time to actually begin coding your data so that you can more easily organize, manage, and retrieve it (Coffey & Atkinson, 1996, p. 26). You now need to put that coding system to use and go back and "tag" or label (i.e., code) pieces of data that "fit" into the theme. Return to those initial two or three interviews that you began with and code each of them using your coding system. Then, as you feel ready, continue coding the rest of your transcripts.

What you will surely soon discover as you return to your data is that the coding system that you initially created will evolve. This is a good thing! Remember that the purpose of data analysis is to deeply understand the meaning that participants ascribe to their experience. It would be a disservice to the participants if you hold too tightly to your initial coding system. In addition, if you're recursively collecting and analyzing your data, and using that analysis to inform your subsequent data collection, there are likely many reasons that categories are changing or being added. You must remain open to the process. You will "see" and learn new things as you continue to collect data and immerse yourself in the data. Things that you initially thought fit into one theme will seem to fit better into a different one. Outliers will emerge that will have to be conceptually dealt with. Thus begins a highly recursive process of coding, editing your coding system, recoding, and so on. Each time you change or add a category (i.e., a code), you'll have to go back and recode all data that was initially tagged with this code. Although this process can feel tedious and time-consuming, this is the *only* way to ensure that you will be able to retrieve and organize the data that support that theme.

The challenge during this part of the process is managing and manipulating your data. Some people use index cards, slips of paper, file folders, sticky notes, mind maps, and computer programs. Qualitative researchers each seem to have their own unique methods for approaching this daunting task. You'll likely create a hybrid method that bests fits your learning style. For me, the use of computer software is immensely valuable and a "must" for rigorous, effective data analysis.

Thus, I offer my own method for organizing and managing data using Microsoft Word later in this chapter.

When do you stop coding? Lincoln and Guba (1985) suggest that the process is over when the analysis seems to have run its course—"when all the incidents can be readily classified, categories are 'saturated,' and sufficient number of 'regularities' emerge" (Miles & Huberman, 1994, p. 62). However, ultimately, only you will know. You will likely find that you will only see *more* layers, nuances, and meanings as you spend longer in the field and the longer you are immersed in the data. The choice of when to stop your quest for understanding and meaning—when to finalize that coding system and complete your analysis—will be challenging. You must trust yourself and your process to make it when the time is right.

A few reminders before we end this discussion of how to code. First, coding and analysis are *not* synonymous. While it can certainly feel that coding is driving your analysis, you must continually remind yourself that your key responsibility is to understand the meaning in the data and to generate concepts from and with the data. "The important analytic work lies in establishing the thinking about linkages (between data and concepts), not in the mundane process of coding" (Coffey & Atkinson, 1996, p. 27). Second, the categories or themes are your abstractions derived from the data, not the data themselves (Merriam, 1998). During data analysis, these categories begin to take on their own life apart from the data. You must work to stay close to the data and the "voices" of the participants. Third, coding and analysis are exhausting and time-consuming work. You will need to allow ample time for this process—including time for breaks to recharge! Finally, you should be actively reflecting during this entire process, by taking field notes, writing in the margins of your transcripts, memoing, journaling, and dialoguing with colleagues if possible. Capturing your thinking and learning will be invaluable to you as you engage in data analysis—whether you choose to use your memos as a source of data to be analyzed formally or simply as a way to be aware of yourself during this process.

Stage 4: Generating Meaning

The process of coding and analysis necessarily involves interpretation of the data. Each decision you've made about what questions to ask of the data, what things you found significant, what categories you used, and how you began to think of those categories and subcategories as related have revealed your understanding and interpretation of what's going on in the data. However, once your coding is complete and your data have been categorized, you need to move more fully into the interpretive mode. This is the stage in which you will transcend the factual data and your cautious analysis of it and attempt to offer your own interpretation of what is going on (Wolcott, 1994). You will be generating meaning from what you have seen and learned.

During this stage, you need to play a little! Wolcott (1994) encourages researchers engaged in this stage to be more freewheeling, generative, and impassioned. You must go *beyond* the codes, categories, and data bits and get to what the "whole" is or may be (Dey, 1993). You need to explore the codes and categories. How do the themes fit together? What happens if you combine some or splice some apart? What does it mean if you link themes together? What patterns emerge across the themes? What contrasts, paradoxes, or irregularities surface? What lessons have been learned? What would happen if . . . ? What further questions need to be asked? During this stage, you need to use the themes you've arrived at during your analysis and *think with them.* Miles and Huberman (1994) offer a compendium of tools that will inspire you to experiment with different ways to display data. These tools require you to engage in various tactics that can help you think with your data and, in the process, generate meaning. These 13 tactics are briefly introduced in Table 14.1. Ryan and Bernard (2000) also provide an excellent synopsis of valuable tools to use during data analysis.

During this stage of the data analysis process, you will move into generalizing and theorizing. Although still grounded in the data, you are not anchored in it. There is no one best approach to theorizing. Your aim is to engage in the creative and intellectual work of exploring how the themes that have emerged are connected to each other as well as how they may be connected to ideas you have, the literature, prior research, and so on. The rigorous data analysis that you have conducted will afford you the unique opportunity to "make discoveries and generate interpretations of the social worlds we investigate" (Coffey & Atkinson, 1996, p. 154).

Of course, a few risks must be managed during this stage of the process. You can reach *too* far beyond the case in speculating about its meanings or implications. You can go off on a tangent and miss the essence of the meaning(s) in the data all together. You may slip into using theorizing to forward your own arguments (i.e., get on a "soapbox") that really can't be supported by the data. You can force an interpretation even when it's just not happening for you. "When the claim is made that an interpretation derives from qualitative inquiry, the link should be relevant and clear" (Wolcott, 1994, p. 37). To contribute quality research, you must ensure that the meaning you're deriving has a discernible and explicable link to the data. You must interrelate the parts of the data to the whole. It is your responsibility to be reasonable in your interpretations, continually respect the meaning of the participants, and provide full disclosure of the basis for any claims you make (Brown, 1989). And, of course, rich, thick description will ultimately serve as a solid foundation on which you can tell your story (Wolcott, 1994).

ENHANCING THE TRUSTWORTHINESS OF YOUR DATA ANALYSIS

Researchers aspire to produce research that is trustworthy. A thorough consideration of the issues around the trustworthiness of qualitative research is beyond the scope of this chapter (see Kvale, 1996, for an excellent discussion of this

TABLE 14.1   Miles & Huberman's (1994) Tactics for Generating Meaning

TACTICS	UNDERSTAND A PHENOMENON BETTER BY . . .
What Goes with What	
Noting Patterns	→ Seeing evidence of patterns while subjecting those conclusions to conceptual and empirical testing.*
Seeing Plausibility	→ Surfacing plausible conclusions.*
Clustering	→ Grouping things together based on their similarities and differences.
Integrate What's There	
Making Metaphors	→ Focusing on how one thing is similar to another thing (e.g., X is *like* Y).
Counting	→ Tallying the numbers of time something happens.
Sharpen our Understanding	
Making Comparisons	→ Drawing contrasts between two things (e.g., X is *not like* Y).
Partitioning Variables	→ Differentiating, dividing, or "unbundling" variables.
See Things and Theirr Relationships More Abstractly	
Subsuming Particulars Into the General	→ Asking "What is this specific thing an instance of ?" "Does it belong to a more general class?"
Factoring	→ Scanning various items to see what "factor" might underlie them.
Noting Relations Between Variables	→ Exploring how concepts are related to one another.
Finding Intervening Variables	→ Looking for other variables that may be part of the picture.
Assemble a Coherent Understanding of the Data	
Building a Logical Chain of Evidence	→ Developing a logical chain of factors that may be leading to something (i.e., a series of "if-then" statements) and then verifying that the consequence actually appears in the data.
Making Conceptual/ Theoretical Coherence	→ Connecting discrete facts with other discrete facts, and then grouping these into lawful, comprehensible, and more abstract patterns.

Source: Adapted from Miles and Huberman, 1994.

point). However, the aim of this section is to remind you of the key issues that we, as qualitative researchers, must be aware of. This section also offers specific strategies that you can employ during data analysis to attend to these issues.

Challenges to the Trustworthiness of Qualitative Data Analysis

Qualitative researchers should be concerned with three key issues during the research process. The first is *internal validity or credibility* of the findings. This deals with the question of how research findings match reality. It probes the congruence between findings and reality, and the wholeness of that depiction. Internal validity addresses the extent to which the findings make sense and are credible to the people we study as well as to our readers.

The second issue is *consistency of the findings*. It is important in qualitative research to focus on "dependability" (Lincoln & Guba, 1985, p. 288) and consistency of the results obtained from the data. That is, rather than demanding that other researchers get the same results (as in quantitative inquiry), the standard in qualitative research is that research should be judged based on the extent to which other researchers concur that, given the purpose of the study, its methods, analysis, and the information collected, the results are consistent and dependable.

The third key issue is *external validity or transferability of the findings*. In positivistic research, external validity pertains to issues of generalizability to other settings, problems, and so on. This concept must be reframed to reflect the philosophical assumptions of qualitative research, the most important assumption being that the goal of qualitative research is to *understand*, not to generalize. Stake (1994) advocates reframing this traditional notion of generalization by focusing on *analytical generalization*, which "involves a reasoned judgment about the extent to which findings from one study can be used as a guide to what might occur in another situation" (cited in Kvale, 1997, p. 233). This judgment is based on logic and a comparison between situations. The researcher must specify evidence, make arguments explicit, and then allow the readers to judge the soundness of the claims. The burden lies on the reader, more so than on the researcher, to demonstrate the applicability and transfer the findings (Lincoln & Guba, 1985) to another setting. This final form of generalization is the only form that is possible in qualitative research.

Strategies to Enhance Trustworthiness during Data Analysis

We can do many things throughout our data analysis process to enhance the trustworthiness of the data. Tactics that can be used to test or confirm findings are briefly summarized in Table 14.2. They are all things we can do during the stages of coding and generating meaning to help ensure that we are being true to

TABLE 14.2 Miles & Huberman's (1994) Tactics for Testing or Confirming Findings

TACTICS	IMPROVE THE TRUSTWORTHINESS OF YOUR ANALYSIS BY ...
Assessing Data Quality	
Checking for Representativeness	→ Being critical of your tendency to over-generalize.
Checking for Researcher Effects	→ Examining your study for biases emerging from (1) researcher effects on the case and (2) effects of the case on the researcher. Mange these to the extent possible.
Triangulating	→ Using multiple sources of data, multiple methods, and even multiple investigators to confirm the emerging findings (Merriam, 1998).
Weighing the Evidence	→ Critically evaluating if the data on which a conclusion is based is strong or weak.
Looking at "Unpatterns"	
Checking the Meaning of Outliers	→ Seeking the outliers (discrepant case, atypical setting, unique treatment, or unusual event) and verifying whether how what is present in this outlier is different from the mainstream theme(s).
Using Extreme Cases	→ Honing in on the extreme outlier to see what you can learn.
Following Up on Surprises	→ Reflecting on why you felt surprised—what does this tell you about your assumptions and biases? Then, going back into your data to "rebuild" your theory.
Looking for Negative Evidence	→ Consciously looking for negative or discrepant information that runs counter to the themes that are emerging.
Testing Our Explanations	
Making If-Then Tests	→ Creating "If-then" propositions and going back into the data to verify whether the "then" has happened.
Ruling Out Spurious Relations	→ Considering whether a third variable might be underlying, influencing, or causing two variables that you believe are connected.
Replicating a Finding	→ Collecting new information from new informants, new settings, new cases to test the validity and generality of your findings.
Checking Out Rival Explanations	→ Creating and holding on to several, rival explanations and give each one a good chance at explaining your findings.

Source: Adapted from Miles and Huberman, 1994.

the data. In addition, some specific strategies you should incorporate into the analysis process include the following:

1. *Personal disclosure statement.* As discussed earlier in this chapter, it is important for you to examine your assumptions and biases as they relate to your research project.

2. *Memoing.* The memos that you've been encouraged to write will help you surface your assumptions and biases. They will also help you reconstruct and understand your research process, which can enhance your reporting of the process and the findings.

3. *Member checks.* You can take data and tentative interpretations back to your participants to ask them whether the appropriate meaning had been accurately captured and whether the emerging themes were plausible.

4. *Peer examination.* You can ask your colleagues to comment on the findings as they emerge. This will facilitate the raising of alternative views and help you to remain open to alternative meanings.

5. *Audit trail.* Independent judges may be recruited to authenticate the findings of a study by following the researcher's trail. In order for this kind of audit to take place, the researcher must describe in detail how data were collected, how categories were derived, and how decisions were made throughout the inquiry. Take excellent notes of your process.

6. *Evaluation of the effectiveness of the interviews.* Because you are conducting simultaneous data collection and analysis, the analysis of each interview provides you an excellent opportunity to reflect on your skills as an interviewer, to evaluate whether you are soliciting rich and valuable information, and gauge whether you are effectively achieving your research goals.

It is incumbent on you to reflect on what threatens the trustworthiness of your data analysis and to utilize strategies such as these to ensure that the findings you generate are credible, consistent/dependable, and transferable should the reader of the findings choose to do so.

USING WORD PROCESSING SOFTWARE TO ANALYZE QUALITATIVE DATA

The use of computer software to aid in qualitative data analysis has received increasing attention during the past 15 years (Dey, 1993; Richards & Richards, 1994; Tesch, 1990; Weaver & Atkinson, 1994; Weitzman & Miles, 1995; Weitzman, 2000). Although the computer cannot actually conduct the analysis for you, computer software has become a widespread and accepted tool that can be used for taking notes, transcribing, preparing data, coding, searching for and retrieving data, "linking" data, memoing, analyzing content, displaying data, interpreting and building theory, mapping graphics, and, of course, writing up findings (Miles & Huberman, 1994).

An array of software packages is now available for qualitative researchers to utilize. Weitzman and Miles reviewed 24 different programs in 1995, and there are many more today. In addition, researchers continue to experiment with new ways to use technology in the qualitative data analysis process. Some concern has been raised that the use of software locks one into a particular approach or epistemology (Lonkila, 1995). Although this concern is worthy of reflection and caution, there seems to be consensus that the use of software can be helpful and valuable if chosen well. Your use of software should depend on the kind of data you're analyzing, your objectives, your style and approach, and whether employing software will help you immerse in the data to the extent necessary to achieve your objective. The use of software, like any good tool, should never restrict you.

Even with the multifunction programs available on the market today, I have found that a basic word processing software, such as Microsoft Office Word 2002,[3] provides a great deal of the functionality needed to conduct data analysis. While this view is not universally endorsed (Weitzman & Miles, 1995), it is interesting to note that Stanley and Temple (1996) conducted an analysis of five specialized qualitative data analysis software packages (The Ethnograph, NUD.IST, askSam, ETHNO, and InfoSelect) and concluded that qualitative researchers should consider using a good word processing package as their basic analytic aid and use dedicated qualitative data analysis software only if they find that they cannot do something that they really want to do. Others have agreed, which has led to increased exploration of word processing programs to aid in data analysis (Pelle, 2004; Ryan, 2004).

For me, the use of a basic word processing software has been immensely helpful in managing, organizing, and manipulating data and is a "must" for rigorous, effective data analysis. It has allowed me to manage data efficiently and effectively so that I could ultimately "see" and interact with it better. Additionally, it will allow you to

- analyze within individual cases and merge data to analyze across cases;
- quickly and thoroughly recode your data as themes emerge and evolve and make other global changes;
- sort by theme, participant, question number, and so forth;
- use other features of Word to search for keywords or codes, memo, count, and so on;
- open multiple windows to view different data sets simultaneously;
- customize the tables according to your specific questions and approach;
- save money and the steep "learning curve" often required of specialized qualitative data analysis software.

The following sections walk through each of the four stages of qualitative data analysis introduced earlier in this chapter: (1) data preparation, (2) familiarization, (3) coding, and (4) generating meaning. This time, however, specific, step-by-step directions are provided on how to use Word to assist you during each stage. This process was inspired by a method created by Carney, Joiner, and Tragou (1997) for conducting data analysis using WordPerfect. I originally adapted their process in 1999 (see Ruona, 1999) and have continually improved the process since then. The process has been widely shared with colleagues and students who have reported that it was extremely helpful to them and who felt that it enhanced their analyses. Participants of our research studies who have been consulted through member checks have often agreed. Many of these people have contributed valuable feedback and suggestions to refine the process, for which I am most grateful.

The process basically entails you formatting your data into tables (see Figures 14.1 and 14.2[4]), which allows you to organize your data, segment the data into meaningful "chunks," merge data across participants, and sort in a variety of ways. The following instructions assume that you have a basic, working knowledge of building and using tables in Word (XP platform). If this is not the case, and you are new to Word or the table feature in this software, you will likely need to supplement these instructions with some basic "how-to" tips available in other resources and/or in your software's Help screens. You can also visit my Web site (see "About the Authors" in this book) for more detailed instructions that include computer commands and navigation. Of course, the instructions may vary

Code	ID	Q#	Turn	Interview Data	Notes
10100	6	3	2	HRD is a global concept, making sense to global organizations and to individuals around the world.	
10600	6	1	3	In 2001, organizations talk about learning and knowledge being the key levers in competing and performing. What were organizations talking about in 2006 and 2011, and how did HRD react to those?	
10900	6	7	4	As Martin Luther King was fond of saying, "you shall reap what you sow." HRD is a key tool in the sowing process, and in the caring for the crop. Those who choose to simply buy crops grown by others place themselves in a weak position. The wise organization is the one that knows what crops to buy, what crops to sow and when. The wise organization is also the one that tends those crops and reaps the rewards.	
11000	6	9	5	We maintain that advantage by ensuring that we apply those theories to improve the performance of individuals, groups, and organizations.	
11300	6	9	7	We specialize in improving workplace performance through the application of adult learning theories – no other profession does that, and it is what makes us distinctive. …	
12100	6	4	11	The number of stories about HRD practitioners who rise to VP or Senior VP positions in organizations, and the trickle of CLOs.	Pleasant surprise (#4)
12100	6	6	9	A relative lack of power in organizations.	
12100	6	9	10	...and well-placed in organizations to influence decision-making and change interventions.	
13100	6	2	16	Our inability to adapt to changing organizations that are more flexible, more technological, less patient (wanting more rapid progress), and more global	
13200	6	1	17	In 2015, how do organizations tell good practice, good practitioners, and good theories/research from the poor versions of all those?	
13600	6	3	22	We harnessed the energies of those who are coming up through the system and those who are entering the system right now.	
14100	6	4	24	The increasing willingness to look outside of the traditional line of vision, and explore theory and practice from emotions, spirituality, story-telling, etc., and see these as a potential source of material and inspiration for HRD professionals.	
14200	6	8	27	Practitioners know about cutting-edge HRD theories and research, understand them, and can apply them in their workplace.	
21300	6	10	24	HRM – and they are too focused on procedures, policies, and protecting the organization from its own employees.	

Figure 14.1   Sample of Interview That Has Been Analyzed and Coded through Stage 3

slightly if you are using a different version of the software. In addition, the term *data* is used here to generically mean any qualitative data that are collected through interviews, focus groups, video/audio recordings, field notes, and so on, and are in the form of words to be analyzed. These instructions assume an analysis of an interview transcript; however, this process can be easily adapted to field notes from observations, field notes, memos, and the like.

Stage 1: Data Preparation

The computer is perfectly suited for the work of Stage 1, which is to get the collected data into a form that is easy to work with. Your purpose during this stage is to organize and format your data so that you can begin the analysis process. Your desired output is one table per interview that documents the input of the participant. To ready your data for the rest of this process, complete the steps detailed here:

1. Transcribe your data using the simplest format possible. I recommend simply transcribing what the interviewer said in italics and what the interviewee said in plain text, separated by a line (paragraph insertion) between each section. For instance:

   This is a question that the interviewer asked or a statement that the interviewer made. It is in italics.

   This is the response of the participant. It is in plain text (i.e., not italic).

   This is what the interviewer said/asked. It is in italics.

   It is best not to use any additional formatting (tabs, columns, bullets, etc.).

2. Assign the participant a code number. Keep a separate record that will link the person's actual identity to this code number.

3. Save the transcribed interview as a document. Then, close the file. This will ensure that you have a "clean" electronic copy of the transcribed interview.

4. Reopen the file that is your transcribed interview. Create a copy by saving the file with a different file name. This will be the file in which you begin your analysis. The original file should be kept somewhere safe.

5. Prepare to create a table by deleting all blank lines that are between the paragraphs. You can do this manually or using the Find-Replace feature in Word (replacing all double paragraph marks with just one paragraph mark).

6. Set up the document. If it is not already in "landscape" format, change the page orientation to landscape. Also, set the left- and right-hand margins to 0.5 inch to maximize your working space.

7. Create the table by selecting all of the data. With all of the data selected, use the Convert Text to Table command.

8. Add columns to create a table that will look like the following by adding columns to the left and right of the data that you just converted. *Note:* The example below is not to scale but is indicative of the relative size of each column in relation to each other.

				Your data is in this column.	

Ultimately, the result should be a table that has six columns—four columns to the left of the column that contains your data and one column to the right of your data. *Note:* It is very important to use that the same column widths for each interview that you prepare so that you can merge and sort data later.

9. Create a header row. Go to the top row of your table, and insert a row. Label that top row as specified in the top row of the sample table here.

Code	ID	Q #	Turn #	Data	Notes
				Your data is in this column.	

Code: You will use this column during Stage 3 to label and code emerging themes in the data.

ID: You will use this column to label the participant that is speaking. You should use a code number that you have assigned and tracked accordingly.

Q #: In this column, you will record the number of the question that was asked to elicit the participant's response in that row.

Turn #: This column is very important: It will allow you to sequence the text of the interview so that you will be able to quickly locate and track information within the interview. This feature is akin to what many in qualitative research refer to as a line number. I prefer the term *turn*, because sometimes the "turn" will be a line, a sentence, a passage, or a whole paragraph, for example. This is, in essence, the indicator of where this "chunk" is in your data.

Data: This column will contain the actual text from the data, divided into meaningful segments.

Notes: This column provides you space to record you personal notes, hunches, insights, and so forth. You can also use this column to make explicit links to the research questions driving your project if that's helpful.

Note: These are the minimum recommended columns. You may find it useful to add additional columns depending on your research project and/or preferences.

When you have labeled each of the six columns, you might want to select that top row and set that row as the default header row on all following pages (under Table Properties in Word). This will ensure that the header row on page 1 will also be the top row on each subsequent page throughout the document.

9. Automatically number the Turn # column using the Bullets and Numbering function under Formatting or on your toolbar. Make it so that the numbering begins from 1 in the first row after your header row.

Stage 2: Familiarization

In preparing the data, you'll already have begun the process of familiarization. This stage of the process involves you immersing in the data much more deeply. Your purpose during this stage of analysis is to actively engage with the data, begin your analysis, and record your insights about what you "see" in the data. Your desired output is one table per interview that preliminarily partitions meaningful segments of data and captures your insights. To use Word to help you during this stage, complete the steps detailed here.

1. Working in the table you created during Stage 1, begin to analyze participant responses. *Note:* For now, you are not going to deal with the Code column. You'll get to that in Stage 3 described later. For each row you should complete the following:

   ▪ *Type in the ID number.* This column indicates who is speaking at the time. Most of the time it will be the participant and you should enter their identification number. You should also type your initials plus that participant's identification number in the column/row when it is you who is speaking (e.g., WER06 would indicate that I was speaking with participant number 6). Later when you have merged the data from multiple participants, this will enable you to easily link something you said to the actual interview in which you said it.

   ▪ *Type in the Q #.* Record the number of the question that was asked to elicit the participant's response in that row.

   ▪ *Analyze the data.* This is the most important part of the process. Take the time to read the data until you feel familiar with it. Ensuring your familiarity and "fluency" with the data is essential to ensuring an effective analysis. The purpose is to begin to see important meanings and patterns in what you have heard and seen.

   Your work in this step is to identify meaningful segments of data (a phrase, sentence, paragraph or passage). To do this, read the participant's responses. Segment out the response by dividing ideas/statements that are different from each other. For each meaningful segment of data, add a row into your table and move (Cut and Paste) that segment of data into the new row. Continue this process until the response you are working with is sufficiently divided into meaningful statements, adding as many new rows as you deem necessary.

- *Capture notes, insights, and so on,* about anything in that row that strikes you.

2. Before proceeding to the next section of data, be sure to fill in the ID # and Q # columns for your newly added rows. Also, check to be sure that the computer is automatically numbering each new additional row you add with increasing numbers in the Turn # column.

3. Repeat Steps 1 and 2 until you are completely finished with your initial analysis of this data.

4. Clean up the document as needed. Conduct a spell-check and do any formatting that will help you to further analyze and code in Stage 3. Save the document before you close it.

5. For now repeat this process on one or two more interviews, and then move on to Stage 3. After you've completed Stage 3, come back and complete Steps 1 through 4 of this stage on all interviews you must analyze. Ultimately, you want to create one, separate table per interview.

Stage 3: Coding

Now that you've become more familiar with your data and, in the process, begun your analysis, it's time to move on to coding. This process involves further segmenting your data into categories/themes and tagging those themes with a code number. Your objective during this stage is to continue your analysis—segmenting data and coding it thematically. Your desired output is one table per interview that codes the themes emerging from that participant's data—in a format that is highly usable for you. See Figure 14.1 for an example. To use Word to help you during this stage, complete the following steps.

1. Open up the document(s) that you were working with in Stage 2.

2. Compile your preliminary list of themes. If you are using a preestablished coding scheme, this should be relatively straightforward. However, if you're inductively analyzing your data (i.e., deriving data-driven codes), you will need to use your initial analysis of the first two or three interviews for this step. Once you feel like you're getting a good understanding of the data and can see recurring topics or patterns, pull back from the data and compile a list of the categories or themes that have emerged from each interview (on paper, sticky notes, or however you'd like). Reflect on and work with your list to understand what is going on in the data—cluster similar topics together, create categories and subcategories, and so on. Your goal is to create categories that "cover" or span the significant themes emerging from your data.

The following is an excerpt of a coding scheme used in the analysis of a set of data surveying HRD professionals' ideas on issues and trends affecting the profession. The codes provided are the ones needed to understand the coding of Interviewee #6 on *Appendix A: Analyzed & Coded Interview.*

10000 Driving Forces

    10100   International/Globalization
    10200   XXXX
    10300   XXXX
    10400   XXXX
    10500   XXXX
    10600   Changing Organizations
        10610 XXXX
        10620 XXXX
    10700   Changing Workforce
        10710 XXXX
        10720 XXXX
        10730 XXXX
    10800   War or tragedy
    10900   Value of Human Resources

11000 HRD Work/Competitive Adv.

    11100   E-Learning
    11200   XXXX
    11300   Learning
      11310 XXXX
      11320 XXXX

12000 Business/Orgl. Credibility

   12100   Boardroom (increased recognition)

      12200 XXXX
      12300 XXXX

13000 Future of HRD Profession

    13100   Keeping up with changes/future
    13200   Standards
    13300   XXXX
    13400   XXXX
    13500   XXXX
    13600   Recruiting (best & brightest)

14000 Scholarly Leadership

    14100   Multi-disciplinary
    14200   Theory/practice

21000 Competitors

    21100   XXXX
    21200   XXXX
    21300   HRM
    21400   XXXX
    21500   XXXX

Sample

Figure 14.2   Sample Coding Scheme

3. Create your initial coding system. Assign a four- to five-digit coding number to each category (see Figure 14.2 for an excerpted example). This numbering system allows you to create categories and subcategories and leaves ample room for multiple categories. Most important, later on during Stage 4 of this process, this numbering system will provide you with excellent sorting capability.

4. Use that preliminary coding system to code those initial two or three interviews. Starting at the top of the data within each interview, begin coding the rows, entering the appropriate code number for each segment of data (i.e., each row) in the Code column.

It is quite likely that you'll need to continue to further segment the data during this stage. Just as in Stage 2, as you need to further segment the

data, add a row below the current row in which the response was originally given. Cut and Paste the text you are dividing and assign the appropriate code number.

If you need to code the same passage with two different code numbers,
Copy and then Paste that row. Change the code number in the copied
row. I also highly recommend jotting a note to yourself in the Notes column that this has been coded with two different code numbers.

You will also find that your coding system will evolve as you analyze. As
mentioned, the analysis process is highly recursive. New themes and insights
will emerge. Things you initially thought fit in one category will seem to
fit better in another. You'll need to edit your coding system as it evolves.

And, of course, you'll need to recode your data as the coding system
evolves. Use Find-Replace as a simple and efficient way to make global
changes. All you need to do is specify the code that you want to replace
with the new code, and the software will automatically recode your data.

Continue this process until the data you are working with is adequately
divided into meaningful statements and coded accordingly.

5. Before proceeding to the next section of data to be analyzed, be sure to fill
   in the ID # and Q # columns for any newly added rows. Also, check to be
   sure that the computer is automatically numbering each new additional
   row you add with increasing numbers in the Turn # column. Finally, use
   the Notes column to capture any key information that you find helpful.

6. Proceed with the next rows, repeating Steps 2 through 4 until you have
   completely coded all of the data for this interview.

7. Clean up the document as needed. Be sure to conduct a spell-check and do
   any formatting that will enhance readability and understanding of the data.

8. After you have completely coded the interview and segmented data as you
   would like, turn off the auto-numbering tool. If left on, rows will be
   renumbered during the sorting process, and the numbers will become
   meaningless. Turn off the automatic numbering to lock in numbers as
   they are.

9. Save the document before you close it. You have now analyzed and coded
   an interview—congratulations!

10. Before you move on to Stage 4, complete Stages 2 and 3 on all interviews
    you must analyze, creating one coded table per interview.

Stage 4: Merging and Working with All of Your Data to Generate Meaning

Once each interview has been coded, it is necessary to merge all of the data together into a master document so you can conduct a group-level (or cross-case)
analysis. This further helps you move toward generating meaning and building

Code	ID	Q#	Turn	Interview Data	Notes
10100	6	3	1	HRD is a global concept, making sense to global organizations and to individuals around the world.	
10100	100	11	100	Support the globalization process in a morally appropriate way.	
10100	130	11	102	Globalization: We have always looked at the workplace as a more or less local scenario. As companies learn more and more about the advantages of global networks in their operations the "workplace" as such becomes more and more complex. Traditional scenarios don't count anymore. While one collaborates through e-conference technology with different co-workers on-line the social and cultural context of each individual involved is still "locally" experienced.	Relates to e-learning (11000) Relates to 10610 (changing orgs.)
10600	6	1	2	In 2001, organizations talk about learning and knowledge being the key levers in competing and performing. What were organizations talking about in 2006 and 2011, and how did HRD react to those?	
10600	142	11	103	In the past we would discuss loose coupling and tight coupling of organizations as an either/or dialogue. Today this dialogue is resurfacing. Prescribed as world views, rationalization, and functionality can lead to disenchantment. There is a pressing challenge to build an ethic of responsibility where we can incorporate the critical concepts and yet build upon the ideas within the organization.	
10700	108	11	104	Meeting the needs of an increasingly diverse audience (i.e., education levels, global cultural issues, and the less visible issue of generation gap).	
10700	109	11	105	The workforce, over the past several years, has become extremely diversified. A great challenge for any leader will be to motivate the workforce to function as a cohesive team, setting aside differences and barriers.	
10800	6	2	1	Atomic war or some pandemic, resulting in the destruction of current societies.	
10900	1	7	1	One can either build human capital or use it up. If you choose the latter course, the organization will soon become uncompetitive.	
10900	13	4	1	The general recognition that 'people matter"	
10900	14	4	1	The recognition by many business people that knowledge and learning are critical to their organizations' success.	
10900	3	4	1	Emphasis on the human dimension in organization has grown.	
10900	4	3	1	CEO's would believe (and act on the belief) that people are their most important asset.	

Figure 14.3   Sample of Master File Data through Stage 4

theory. Your desired output at this stage is one master table that contains data from all sources in your research. Figure 14.3 provides an example. This is an excerpt from a 2003 study on future trends in HRD. This example shows the data from 14 participants who discussed one theme (coded as 10100—internationalization/globalization). In this table, the data from multiple interviews is mixed together. It is helpful to be able to know what question number elicited this response for much-needed context. Also, the Turn # column helps to quickly locate that quote (row) back in the original transcript (analyzed and coded in Stages 2 and 3) in case you need to reference that source document. To use Word to help you during this stage, complete the steps detailed here.

1. Create a new document. Confirm page setup. If this document is not already oriented in "landscape" format, change the page orientation to landscape. Set the left- and right-hand margins to 0.5 inch.

2. Open up one transcribed and coded interview file completed in Stage 3. Copy this table and Paste it into the newly created document.

3. Repeat Step 2 with all interviews that you have transcribed and coded. Delete any extra rows or empty lines between the individual tables that you have pasted into this document, ensuring that each table is connected throughout the document so that it is now one, large table. Also, ensure that the columns align with each other.

4. Save. You now have a master table that contains all of your data. Now, on to the step that makes all this effort worth it.

5. Sort your data by whatever column(s) you would like. Go to Table and choose Sort. Select the name of the column you would like to sort by. If you'd like to see your data by code number, just tell the computer that's what you want. Then, if you want to see it by question number and then again resorted by participant number, just tell it to do it. Conduct this step as you continue to query and analyze your data—as often and as much as you need.

You will need to sort your data for at least three key reasons (and likely a few more that you'll discover on your own). First, you will want to group the data thematically (by code numbers) so you can reflect on the themes that are emerging across all participants.

As you do this, you may find you'll need to continue to further segment the data. Just as in Stage 2, as you need to further segment the data, insert a row below the current row in which the answer was originally given. Cut and Paste the text you are dividing. Continue this process until the data you are working with is sufficiently divided into meaningful statements and coded accordingly. Remember, though, that this additional partitioning will *not* be reflected in the tables of the individual participants completed during Stages 2 and 3. As you segment data in the master document, copy the ID number, the question number, and turn number from the source statement to all newly created rows. This will ensure your ability to link the context of the statements and tie it back to the original files as necessary. Remember, at this point, the auto numbering has been deactivated, and you want it that way.

You may also find that you'll need to continue to edit your coding system as you glean new insights into your data now that it's been compiled. Edit your coding system and recode your data as necessary using the Find-Replace feature to make global changes. Once again, these changes will *not* be reflected in your original source documents unless you go back to those documents and change the code numbers there.

The second key reason that you need this sorting feature is so you can more fully engage in interpreting and generating meaning. Remember that Stage 4 of the data analysis process is about you *thinking with your data*—interpreting and exploring how the themes that have emerged are connected to each other as well as how they are connected to the ideas you have, the literature, prior research, and so forth. Tables in Word are a bit too linear to really foster creative exploration of your data, especially lacking in its capacity to help you see connections *between* themes. You will undoubtedly want to find more innovative and generative ways to "see" the whole (such as those recommended by Miles & Huberman in Table 14.1 or in Ryan & Bernard, 2000). However, your capacity to sort and resort data during this stage will enable you to "query" and organize the data, which you will find immensely valuable as you work with your themes.

Finally, when your analysis is done and your coding system is finalized, you'll want to conduct final "sorts" according to the way that you want your final data set organized. This will enable you to easily retrieve key quotes as you write up the results of your research study.

6. Save. Save often!

Additional Useful Features in Word

Once you become adept at the basic procedure outlined here and continue to learn more about the features in Word, you will find that other features can be helpful to you during your data analysis. A few that I have used or that have been forwarded to me by people who have used this procedure and "discovered" these features are described in the next subsections.

Highlighting

If you are visually oriented, you might want to highlight key terms, take notes, or color-code elements of your document to help you keep things organized or emphasize key ideas. All you have to do to highlight things in Word is select the Highlight button on your Formatting toolbar or use Borders and Shading on the Formatting drop-down menu.

Bookmarking

A *bookmark* identifies a location or selection of text that you tag for future reference. You can easily use a bookmark to help you remember where you left off in your analysis before a break, which will save you the hassle of scrolling to find that spot when you return. Just select the word/section you want to bookmark, go to the Insert drop-down menu, and select Bookmark.

Finding

You can use the Find feature on the Edit drop-down menu to look for occurrences of keywords throughout a document.

Memoing

I tend to keep a separate document of my memos, but some people who have used this procedure have utilized the Insert Comments feature in Word as a receptacle for their emerging insights. You can use the Reviewing toolbar or the Insert drop-down to insert a marker in the text and open a window for your comment. You can then print the document with these comments showing or print them separately. If your computer is set up for it, you can now even insert a voice comment.

Counting

If you need to count the number of times a keyword or code occurs, you can simply use the Find-Replace feature on the Edit drop-down menu. All you have to do is specify the Find What and the Replace With fields as the same term or code number and Word will report how many replacements were made.

Facilitating Data Analysis Teams

Word allows multiple users to work with a document in innovative ways. First, if you e-mail it to other people, their changes can be tracked and viewed (see Track Changes). Additionally, the newer versions of Word allow teams to set up a document workspace centered around one or more documents (see Shared Workspace). Finally, Word is making it easier and more accessible to collaborate online.

CONCLUSION

This chapter was designed to demystify and simplify the qualitative data analysis process to help beginning researchers enhance their ability to work with qualitative data. It rests on the assumption that one of the keys to generating excellent qualitative research is to conduct a rigorous and systematic analysis of the data. The chapter has reviewed some prerequisite concepts foundational to qualitative data analysis and also outlined four general stages of the data analysis process in concept and then more specifically in step-by-step directions on how to use Word to assist you during each stage. In addition, specific strategies to enhance the trustworthiness of your analysis process were offered.

The processes outlined here are not the only ones an excellent qualitative researcher needs; they are simply a place to begin as you develop your qualitative skills, and many alternative analytic strategies are also available (see Denzin & Lincoln, 2000; Coffey & Atkinson, 1996). It is also important to acknowledge that the processes in this chapter are accompanied by their own assumptions and biases like any other tool. In using them, I reveal my biases for the sociological tradition that views text as a "window into the human experience" (Ryan & Bernard, 2000) and for constructivism, which emphasizes understanding and reconstruction. This chapter has also weighed heavily on procedural knowledge needed to organize and manage data, which also reveals my bias for a "nuts-and-bolt" approach that works. In this vein, I concur with Chenail (1995) that an invaluable approach is to keep the "method simple because in qualitative research the complexity is in the data" (p. 55). Do not overgeneralize my "prescription." Rather, use it as a basis on which you can explore and compare other qualitative approaches and methodologies for data collection and analysis. Qualitative research expects no less of you—you must be critical and reflexive in your inquiry.

Qualitative data analysis is ultimately about our quest to understand complex human beings and social systems—which is certainly anything but simple or straightforward. I consider qualitative research, and especially data analysis, to be an art. One of the primary functions of art is to *interpret* the subject matter at hand. When we conduct qualitative research, we have the privilege of shining light on the subjective meaning that people attach to their lives and experiences. True artistry must surpass mechanics. As an artist in your own right, you should embrace data analysis as a creative and generative process, engaging your powers of observation, dialogue, and learning. Only then will you be able to fulfill the hope of qualitative research: to see things that others may not see and help to show the world what you see.

NOTES

1. Although qualitative researchers increasingly are including still and moving pictures as qualitative data, this chapter does not deal with these forms of data.

2. The terms *category* and *theme* are interchangeable in this chapter.

3. Microsoft® is a registered trademark of the Microsoft Corporation. The software referenced in this chapter is Microsoft Office Word 2002, which will be referred to throughout the rest of the chapter simply as Word.

4. Figures 14.1–14.3 are samples derived from a research study conducted on future trends in HRD. For a complete write-up of this study, see Ruona, Lynham, and Chermack (2003). Thank you to my coauthors for allowing me to share some of our raw data and coding system.

REFERENCES

Alvesson, M., & Sköldberg, K. (2000). *Reflexive methodology*. London: Sage.

Bodgan, R. C., & Biklen, S. K. (1992). *Qualitative research for education: An introduction to theory and methods* (2nd ed.). Needham Heights, MA: Allyn & Bacon.

Boyatzis, R. E. (1998). *Transforming qualitative data: Thematic analysis and code development*. Thousand Oaks, CA: Sage.

Brown, M. (1989). What are the qualities of good research? In F. H. Holm & D. L. Hultgren (Eds.), *Alternative modes of inquiry in home economics research: Yearbook 1989*. Peoria, IL: Glencoe.

Carney, J. H., Joiner, J. F., & Tragou, H. (1997, March). Categorizing, coding, and manipulating qualitative data using the WordPerfect word processor. *The Qualitative Report, 3*(1). Retrieved December 18, 2004, from http://www.nova.edu/ssss/QR/QR3-1/carney.html.

Chenail, R. J. (1995, December). Presenting qualitative data. *The Qualitative Report, 2*(3). Retrieved December 18, 2004, from http://www.nova.edu/ssss/QR/QR2-3/presenting.html.

Coffey, A., & Atkinson, P. (1996). *Making sense of qualitative data*. Thousand Oaks, CA: Sage.

Creswell, J. W. (2002). *Research design: Qualitative, quantitative, and mixed methods approaches*. Thousand Oaks, CA: Sage.

Denzin, N. K., & Lincoln, Y. S. (2000). The discipline and practice of qualitative research. In N. K. Denzin & Y. S. Lincoln (Eds.), *Handbook of qualitative research* (2nd ed., pp. 1–36). Thousand Oaks, CA: Sage.

Dey, I. (1993). *Qualitative data analysis: A user-friendly guide for social scientists*. London: Routledge.

Gioia, D. A., & Pitre, E. (1990). Multiparadigm perspectives on theory building. *Academy of Management Review, 15*(4), 584–602.

Glaser, B. G., & Strauss, A. (1967). *The discovery of grounded theory.* Chicago: Aldine.

Glesne, C., & Peshkin, A. (1992). *Becoming qualitative researchers: An introduction.* New York: Longman.

Kvale, S. (1996). *Interviewing: An introduction to qualitative research interviewing.* Thousand Oaks, CA: Sage.

Lincoln, Y. S., & Guba, E. G. (1985). *Naturalistic inquiry.* Thousand Oaks, CA: Sage.

Lonkila, M. (1995). Grounded theory as an emerging paradigm for computer-assisted qualitative data analysis. In U. Kelle (Ed.), *Computer-aided qualitative data analysis: Theory, methods and practice* (pp. 41–51). London: Sage.

Lynham, S. A. (2002). The general method of theory-building research in applied disciplines. *Advances in Developing Human Resources, 4*(3), 221–241.

Merriam, S. B. (1998). *Qualitative research and case study applications in education.* San Francisco: Jossey-Bass.

Miles, M. B., & Huberman, A. M. (1994). *Qualitative data analysis: An expanded sourcebook.* Thousand Oaks, CA: Sage.

Pelle, N. (2004). Simplifying qualitative data analysis using general purpose software tools. *Field Methods, 16*(1), 85–108.

Richards, T., & Richards, L. (1994). Using computers in qualitative research. In Y. S. Lincoln & N. K. Denzin (Eds.), *Handbook of qualitative research* (pp. 445–462). Thousand Oaks, CA: Sage.

Ruona, W. E. A. (1999). *An investigation into core beliefs underlying the profession of human resource development.* Unpublished doctoral dissertation, University of Minnesota, St. Paul.

Ruona, W. E. A., Lynham, S., & Chermack, T. (2003). Insights on emerging trends and the future of human resource development. In D. Short & J. Bing (Eds.), *Shaping the Future of Human Resource Development: Advances in Developing Human Resources, 5*(3) (Special Issue), 272–282.

Ryan, G. W. (2004). Using a word processor to tag and retrieve blocks of text. *Field Methods, 16*(1), 109–131.

Ryan, G. W., & Bernard, H. R. (2000). Data management and analysis methods. In N. K. Denzin & Y. S. Lincoln (Eds.), *Handbook of qualitative research* (2nd ed., pp. 769–802). Thousand Oaks, CA: Sage.

Stanley, L., & Temple, B. (1996). Doing the business: Using qualitative software packages in the analysis of qualitative data sets. In R. G. Burgess (Ed.), *Using computers in qualitative research* (pp. 169–193). Greenwich, CT: JAI.

Tesch, R. (1990). *Qualitative research: Analysis types and software tools.* London: Falmer.

Turnball, S. (2002). Social construction research and theory building. *Advances in Developing Human Resources, 4*(3), 317–334.

Weaver, A., & Atkinson, P. (1994). *Microcomputing and qualitative data analysis.* Aldershot, UK: Avebury.

Weitzman, E. A. (2000). Software and qualitative research. In N. K. Denzin & Y. S. Lincoln (Eds.), *Handbook of qualitative research* (2nd ed., pp. 803–820). Thousand Oaks, CA: Sage.

Weitzman, E. A., & Miles, M. B. (1995). *Computer programs for qualitative data analysis.* Thousand Oaks, CA: Sage.

Wolcott, H. F. (1994). *Transforming qualitative data: Description, analysis, and interpretation.* Thousand Oaks, CA: Sage.

Grounded Theory Research Methods

Carol D. Hansen, *Georgia State University*

CHAPTER OUTLINE

The purpose of this chapter is to discuss the function and methodology of grounded theory research. For many, the term is synonymous with the use of qualitative research methods. The bond began in 1967 with a landmark publication by two clinical sociologists, Barney Glaser and Anselm Strauss, entitled *The Discovery of Grounded Theory*. Their text offered a new approach for qualitative researchers to make theoretical contributions to their domains of inquiry. Moreover, it appealed to naturalistic scholars who sought the empirical rigor found in quantitative study without sacrificing flexibility and the rich description associated with qualitative work. While grounded theory research emerged from the discipline of sociology, it is now employed in virtually all domains where the study of human interaction and organizational behavior is conducted. In particular, this approach to research has been embraced by scholars in management, education, and the health sciences.

This chapter focuses on four questions: (1) How did grounded theory originate? (2) What is its underlying logic and assumptions? (3) What is unique about the methodology? (4) How does theory emerge from data? It is organized into two major sections. The first describes the features of grounded theory research: its history, assumptions, and key aspects of the methodology. The second section reviews issues and procedures for the creation of theory from grounded data.

FEATURES OF GROUNDED THEORY RESEARCH

The term *grounded* refers to the systematic generation of theory from data that has been empirically collected and analyzed (Glaser & Strauss, 1967). It is, thus, the creation of theory that is based on data from fieldwork.

Grounded theory research is a general methodology that originated in quantitative research yet can be used in both qualitative and quantitative work. However, grounded theory is seldom used in quantitative studies, a trend that may be related to the difficulty in grounded theory of assuring the required statistical rigor associated with empirical research (Glaser & Strauss, 1967).

Grounded theory research is extremely useful to qualitative researchers because it is rich in meaning and relatively inexpensive to use. The intent is to generate new insight by discovering the social reality of those whose actions combine to impact a given set of human phenomena. In a video interview with Andy Lowe (1992) at the University of Sterling, Glaser describes the basic principle of grounded theory research as the following:

> All things are integrated at all times. And, things form patterns. People should trust in the patterns that emerge and reoccur. By definition patterns occur over and over again. Once you pick them up you can see their integration with other actions. It is all multivariable. It is always integrating. It is always in motion. The world does not occur in a vacuum.

The work of Glaser and Strauss is thus a break from the conventional deductive approach of empiricists; it opposes the notion of theory testing and a priori definition of concepts and hypotheses. While accepting the positivist's position that the ultimate function of theory is explanation and prediction, Glaser and Strauss advocate theory generation through the discovery of categorical themes that emerge from the data (Glesne & Peshkin, 1992). In the Lowe interview, Glaser explains that the role of grounded theory is to "discover what is relevant" rather than to "force relevancy" on the subject of study.

HISTORY

Glaser and Strauss developed the term *grounded theory* and its techniques from a hospital study in northern California in the late 1960s. They presented a formal description of how they collected and used data to develop a theoretical understanding of how the staff managed the care of its dying patients. The authors were frustrated with the divide between empiricists and theorists that characterized much of the research conducted at the time. They were especially dissatisfied with the prevalent hypothetico-deductive practice of testing "great man" sociological theories. In connecting the two techniques, Glaser and Strauss were able to build theory through a firsthand study of phenomena. They shared the conviction that new theory should be grounded in rich observational data.

Trained in the tradition and practice of fieldwork, Strauss saw the need to go into the field to discover what was really happening. Glaser, whose background was in the rigorous procedures associated with the inductive use of quantitative sociology, saw the potential to create theory from systematic data coding and the creation of conceptual categories. Strauss and Glaser agreed that the use of qualitative methods should result in the generation of theory that was systematically grounded in the reality of the informants. Meanwhile, they sought to enhance the legitimacy of qualitative methods through the increased codification of data.

ASSUMPTIONS

The basic assumptions that influenced Glaser and Strauss's creation of grounded theory research came from two schools of sociology: American pragmatism and symbolic interaction (Locke, 2001). American pragmatism emphasizes an understanding of human nature through the empirical study of people's everyday lives rather than through the broad creation of philosophy, a mode that dominated the social sciences at the beginning of the twentieth century. *Symbolic interaction* refers to the relationship between people's actions and the meanings people place on those actions. This thinking began to influence research as early as the 1920s and was led by scholars at the University of Chicago.

Pragmatically, Glaser and Strauss thought that helping hospital staff better understand how they socially evaluated patients would improve how they delivered care. Symbolic interaction, as a theoretical frame, emphasizes the importance of data based on reality. It signaled a departure from high theory, called "armchair philosophy" by many, which was dissociated from everyday organizational and individual behavior.

Assumptions that underlie symbolic interaction include the following:

- How people derive meaning informs and guides their actions.
- Meaning or sense making is learned from social interaction.
- Meaning is dynamic and capable of change.

These points suggest that the sense making that shapes perceptions of what is appropriate and inappropriate action is unique. Thus, a study's design and the theoretical relevance of its findings may be grounded in time and logic to a given social unit, situation, and period.

The arguments contained within symbolic interaction frame my own assumptions about the use of grounded theory:

- The study's focus question(s) must be considered important and problematic given the social unit.
- There are no predetermined hypotheses.
- The unit of analysis is the group, as relevant meaning making is shared and constitutes collective action.
- The findings and their theoretical implications are unique to a given social unit and given time period.

Although there are competing paradigms in qualitative research (Guba & Lincoln, 2004), I believe that grounded theory can be used in any form of qualitative inquiry whose ontology embraces the perspective of multiple realities and whose epistemology seeks to understand how interpretative meanings are constructed. Grounded theory may be found, for example, in case studies, action research, or ethnography. It is especially appropriate for studying organizational cultures (Glaser & Strauss, 1967; Strauss & Corbin, 1990), as will be illustrated in the second part of this chapter.

GROUNDED THEORY RESEARCH METHODOLOGY

By virtue of focusing on the nature of people's lives, inquiry originally required a prolonged field engagement of at least a year and employed the techniques found in anthropology such as participant observation, informal interviewing, and document examination. Today, similar methods are typically used; however, the time frame can be much shorter as grounded theory research may be used in rapid assessment studies of organizations.

A question that novice researchers often ask is whether grounded theory research is a process or a product of qualitative methodology. The answer is that it is both. Every step of the research is done systematically so that it is possible to trace the "process" from which the "product" (theory) is generated. The resulting theory is an explanation of categories, their properties, and the relationships among them. It provides structure that is often lacking in other qualitative approaches without forgoing suppleness or thoroughness. The distinguishing fundamentals of doing grounded theory research are the following (Strauss & Corbin, 1993):

- Simultaneous involvement in data collection and analysis phases of research
- Creation of analytic codes and categories developed from the data, not from preconceived hypotheses
- The development of middle-range theories to explain behavior and processes
- Memo making (i.e., the writing of analytic notes to explicate categories)
- Theoretical sampling for theory construction rather than for representation of a given population
- Delay of the literature review to compare emergent theory with extant literature

THE PROCESS OF GROUNDED THEORY RESEARCH

As with any process, the way of carrying out grounded theory research can be described as a set of steps. Eagan (2002) has broadly outlined the process as somewhat similar to traditional research methods; the five steps include the initiation of research, the selection of appropriate data, data collection, data analysis, and, finally, the conclusion of the study. What differentiates the process of grounded theory research from other methods is the interchange between data collection and analysis. In contrast to the rigidity of preestablished sampling procedures in traditional forms of research, the route taken in grounded theory research is particularly iterative. The various steps in the analysis of data weave back and forth in response to the need for adjustment in the research design. I will use Eagan's detailed model to explain this progression (see Figure 15.1).

In initiating a grounded theory study, the researcher must select an area of inquiry for the study and an appropriate site for the collection of the data. An area of inquiry may focus on specific phenomena, a place or location, or a certain context. A review of pertinent literature and the development of a set of hypotheses should be delayed. Instead, the researcher should begin the inquiry by

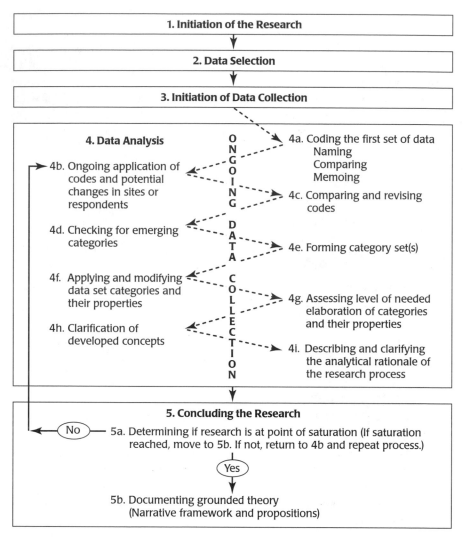

Figure 15.1 The Process of Grounded Theory Research
Source: Eagan (2002, p. 281).

refining the overall research question and determining what kind of data will most assist in exploring the study's purpose. In turn, the researcher must remain open to the possibility of the research design's veering in another direction as one piece of data leads to the next. Thus, it is difficult to develop a specific plan for sampling as ongoing decisions should be informed theoretically but will derive from the emergence of categories and grounded theory during the research process.

Eagan's model lists nine substeps that are constantly informed by ongoing data collection. These steps concern the initial coding of data, coding application, coding comparison, and revision. Coding involves three key tasks: naming, comparing, and memoing. Locke (2001, p. 47) defines these three activities. In *naming*, researchers attempt to develop concepts and abstract meanings for the incidents and observations that they record. *Comparing* leads to the creation of general categories by developing a common name or "category" for multiple incidents or observations in the data. *Memoing* consists of taking notes about the analysis process itself that may reflect insights or ideas sparked by a particular incident while in the field or as the categorical properties are generated and theoretical ideas emerge.

Analysis activities respond to ongoing data collection and comparison; the analysis continues until the researcher determines that the data are saturated. Data saturation indicates that a valid and reliable pattern has emerged that does not require confirmation through the collection of more data. Likewise, as the researcher considers new sources of data, it is critical to select those opportunities that will permit interesting contrasts to data already collected. For example, if the subject of innovation emerges as a key category in a given study, then the researcher may wish to compare the issue by collecting data in another organization. The final step in a grounded theory study is to convert patterns of saturated data into a narrative framework and a set of theoretical propositions that may be used in future research.

ASPECTS OF THE METHODOLOGY

Three aspects of the methodology that I wish to emphasize are constant comparison analysis, coding and categorical development, and theoretical sampling.

Constant Comparison Analysis

As a process, grounded theory is iterative, repetitive, and replete with comparisons. New data are compared with existing data, and a new theoretical hunch is compared with yesterday's ideas. This is the concept of constant comparison, which is critical to the collection and analysis of data via grounded theory (Glaser & Strauss, 1967; Lincoln & Guba, 1985; Torraco, 1997). The fact that the researcher is simultaneously involved in data collection and analysis permits continuous reflection on the meaning of what is heard and seen. Like any detective work, one clue leads to the next and suggests the direction for the next step in solving the mystery of the study. The approach is nonlinear, and the joining of the theoretical and the empirical leads to an increased blur between data collection and data analysis. In this way, grounded theory yields dense conceptual analyses of empirical problems (Charmaz, 2004). It is also through the constant comparison of data and their emerging patterns that coding protocols and categorical development can be reconsidered and refined.

A study of organizational change by Mohrman, Ramkrishnan, Tenkasi, and Mohrman (2003) used constant comparison as a cornerstone in their creation of theory. The study examined eight organizations to see whether, how, and what kind of social networks contribute to the sense-making and self-design processes through which organizational participants learn to operate differently in their local contexts. The investigation was an open-ended exploration that employed an exploratory research question instead of predetermined hypotheses and theory. Data were subjected to continuous, cyclical, evolving interpretation and reinterpretation that allowed patterns to emerge.

Of particular interest was the opportunity to discern differences in patterns between comparable units, discover categories that differentiated the units, and then generate hypotheses and theory about them. The authors first applied the method among the eight companies to discern differences in the types of networks that are created or emerge during the change process. Afterward, the focus was on comparing units within the four companies where organizational change persisted. After an initial round of high-level interviews, the interview protocol was redesigned and conducted with key informants and a representative sample of the worker roles within the selected units. These interviews led to a third redesign of questions and a round of interviews within the units of interest. Within-case analysis was conducted followed by across-case analysis. This permitted a detailed description of patterns for each organization and business unit before there was an attempt to generalize patterns across cases. The researchers then began to identify theoretical categories and make comparisons across categories at both levels of analysis. Their initial case comparisons were used to identify common dynamics and to refine the unique understandings of each case. Cases were further compared to develop the emerging constructs and logic of the conceptual framework. As more cases were folded into the analysis, the level of abstraction was elevated, and a conceptual model began to emerge.

Coding and Categorical Development

All grounded theory research studies use a data coding scheme. Coding is the process of simultaneously reducing the data by dividing it into units of analysis and identifying each conceptual unit. Once patterns in the coded data emerge, they form the basis for categorical development that is higher in level and more abstract than the concepts the categories represent. The categories are then modified and organized into sets. Grounded theory research is especially suitable for the study of processes, and so categories are often expressed as activities directed toward a similar process (Strauss & Corbin, 1990). An example would include a verb followed by a noun, such as "caring for patients" or "advising employees."

In multiple coding protocols, comments can fall into more than one category. Comments are used to categorize conceptual data rather than to quantify it.

Therefore, the number of times an individual comment is coded and categorized is less relevant. Strauss and Corbin (1990) recommend that the process of categorical development be conducted in three stages, which they respectively term *open* (the development of concepts and categories), *axial* (the development of connections between a category and its subcategories), and *selective coding* (the integration of categories to create a theoretical framework). The final stage should offer a theoretical explanation of how the categories interact and under what conditions they operate.

A grounded investigation of strategic marketing planning (SMP) by Ashill, Frederikson, and Davies (2003) offers a relevant example of categorical development. The study's purpose was to explore the organizational context in which SMP takes place, as perceived by SMP managers, so as to generate a frame of factors that characterized the process of SMP. The research was based on a field investigation of four large organizations drawn from a single industry using a multiple-case design.

The researchers began by collecting "grounded events," actual incidents describing the operation of the SMP process. Of concern was the worker's social construction and the way that they interpreted the reality of the process. Reliability was promoted by using the same questioning protocol with all informants, and construct validity was enhanced by using multiple sources of evidence (interviews, observations, and the review of pertinent process documentation) and by establishing a chain of evidence as each interview was concluded. External validity was promoted in that all organizations belonged to the same industry and were relatively similar in size and age. The data sets were first analyzed within a given organization and then compared across the four organizations.

The analysis and coding of interview data employed a three-step analysis procedure (Miles & Huberman, 1984). The transcripts were broken down into "thought units" that ranged from a phrase to several sentences. Second, in the categorizing phase, the thought units were organized into emergent categories and the category labels were adjusted to capture a sense of a shared message among the thought units. In the third and final classifying phase, the categories emerged into seven unifying themes or "core categories" that provided a storylike summary of "what was going on" in the data and what the SMP process looked liked to the study's informants.

Theoretical Sampling

A final, and important, aspect of the methodology is theoretical sampling. This form of sampling is not random and is not based on statistical probability. Moreover, the sampling frame may be modified as a result of constant comparison analysis. A determination of what data should be collected is recurrent and subject to revaluation in order to facilitate the theorizing process. This approach to data collection accepts that it is impossible to identify ahead of time with certainty all of the categories of data that the researcher needs to review. Theoretical sampling is thus purposefully designed to pursue data collection to support categorical development to the point of concept saturation, which occurs when the data are stable and the patterns unlikely to change (Locke, 2001).

An illustration of how theoretical sampling works can be seen in the study of occupational cultures. In an ethnography I led of human resource development (HRD) professionals as an occupational culture, the sampling frame used the theory of how occupational cultures form and bond to identify appropriate informants (Hansen, Kahnweiler, & Wilensky, 1994). Trice and Beyer's (1993) review of the literature informed the requirements of our sample. Membership in an occupational culture is first and foremost formed through one's occupational training. Likewise, cultural characteristics suggest that the greater the investment in one's training, the greater the sense of professional identity. Occupational cultures are reinforced through membership in professional associations and their influence is often stronger than the culture of the organization where one works. Given these findings, we collected data across a number of organizations. The specific sampling requirements for each informant were the following: (1) completion of a master's degree in HRD, (2) current work engagement in training, career, or organizational development, and (3) membership in a professional association such as the American Society of Training and Development (ASTD) or the International Society of Performance and Instruction (ISPI). Because culture is socially learned and sustained, my colleagues and I located informants by asking one HRD professional to identify another to participate in the sample. The expected bias from the social bonding of a shared cultural membership was considered theoretically desirable. Finally, by comparing evolving patterns in the data, we saw that we did not have enough information to theoretically understand differences between experienced and novice practitioners. This led to an enlargement of the sample size and a new direction in its frame.

GENERATING NEW KNOWLEDGE USING GROUNDED THEORY RESEARCH

In judging the usefulness of an emergent theory, four central criteria should guide its development (Glaser & Strauss, 1967; Strauss & Corbin, 1990). First, the theory must "fit" the topic of study. That is, it must be related to the problem of inquiry and in some way build on existing thought or offer theory where none exists. Second, it must be "understandable" to the study's informants as well as to those who research and practice in that area. This point asks whether the new theory is both feasible and reasonable.

Third, the theory must be "general" and abstract enough to be generalized to a broader theory (not a broader population) and applicable to a variety of settings. The concept "applicable" is more appropriately linked to the notion of transferability rather than the traditional notion of generalizing as found in empirical study. This is an important distinction. Transferability implies that the reader can "choose" to transfer or relate the general nature of the theory and findings of a given study to his or her own situation. Thus, the opportunity to draw applicable conclusions is the reader's choice and responsibility rather than the researchers.

Finally, theory should provide "control" of action by proposing relationships among concepts. This aspect of grounded theory research emphasizes its explanatory power. Researchers have likened the generation of theory to the development of models that are analogous to stories of cause and effect (Golden-Biddle & Locke, 1997; Strauss & Corbin, 1990). Other scholars discussed theory conceptualizations as behavioral rules or axioms (Spradley, 1979). For example, Spradley's ethnography of bars found gender differences in purchasing behavior. He surmised that female customers consider the purchase of drinks as an economic transaction, while male customers consider it as an opportunity to assert their masculinity.

In addition to developing novel explanations, new theory can confirm or deny a research perspective. In returning to my earlier example of occupational cultures, existing theory suggested that the nature of one's work is a more powerful determiner of work behavior than cultural membership in any one organization. Our findings confirmed and added ammunition to this theoretical perspective in our qualitative study of human resource development professionals (Hansen et al., 1994).

Developing Theoretical Points

The task of developing grounded theory occurs in three stages (Golden-Biddle & Locke, 1997). A problem must be first linked to a body of literature. This link is generally tied to other research that has attempted to study a similar question. Links may also reflect commonality of research perspectives (i.e., the importance of societal culture as a conceptual and behavioral referent in organizational life). Showing how new theory can expand or refute existing thinking is where qualitative research is often the weakest. It is this strain of theoretical development that truly sets grounded theory research apart from hypothesis testing.

Once the importance of studying the research problem is established, it is essential to highlight what is problematic about current research. Gaps imply that not enough is known or that current research is flawed. Many qualitative studies suggest, for example, that previous quantitative research was too narrow and that it failed to uncover critical issues.

Finally, new theory must make suggestions for how a current study will contribute to a better understanding, explanation, and solution to the problem. For example, my work on privatization in the Côte d'Ivoire (West Africa) suggests that current theories of cultural relativity are not enough to understand the adoption of new entrepreneurial behaviors. The fact that new management and work expectations were based on models that are culturally different from prevailing norms explains, only in part, the difficulty of changing employee behaviors. My findings offer new theory by illustrating the cultural importance of kinship and village solidarity. Family ties resulting in workplace favoritism is a norm that is not only culturally different but also culturally constraining to the development of trust and psychological ownership in one's company. These factors are critical for employees to exhibit the extra role behavior needed to break the cycle of conformity, compliance, and apathy that is characteristic of state-owned companies. This theoretical model is illustrated in the next section.

Illustrating New Knowledge

In illustrating theory, it is helpful to think of theory as a kind of narrative with its own plot development and characters whose actions theoretically influence the story's outcome. Strauss and Corbin (1990) refer to this process as *selective coding*; Golden-Biddle and Locke (1997) call it *model building*. Stories are helpful metaphors. They have a beginning that describes the problem and its setting. A middle follows that shows evidence to support change in the form of new theory. Theoretical stories conclude with an ending that shows how the present account contributes to the problem's resolution and the literature as a whole.

Stories can also be told from a variety of perspectives. The notion of different perspectives is linked to emic and etic traditions of reporting data (Pike, 1967). The emic perspective tells the story from the viewpoint of the informant and uses his or her own vocabulary and definitions in the form of raw quotes and stories to illustrate the grounding of emergent theory. A technique that I have developed to uncover an informant's emic perspective is to ask my interviewees to deconstruct their own stories (Hansen & Kahnweiler, 1993). As informants analyze their narratives, they reveal much of their own perspective in how they label characters and explain the moral of their tale.

Etic reporting tells the story from the perspective of the researcher. This story account may occur in the form of historical reporting of a case where the researcher attempts to find truth by triangulating and verifying all relevant sources. The perspective of the researcher may, in other cases, be critically interpretative and philosophical in tone by attempting to link emergent theory with associated literature.

There are also stories that report the "voices not heard" (Boje, 1991). These stories give expression to actors that may have been perceived to play a marginal role in driving the story's plot. Such stories question why these actors have traditionally played minor roles and theoretically ask whether the outcome could have been different and perhaps better had these characters played a stronger role in the development of the story.

Finally, in illustrating new knowledge, not only is it critical to use data as proof of how the theory emerged; it is also helpful to illustrate theory lines in the form of flowcharts and other visual displays. While such exhibits are typically associated with quantitative data from experimental or survey research, they can equally show relationships among key variables found in qualitative data. For example, a flowchart showing how one variable may influence another, which may then influence another, and so forth, may be a powerful aid in conveying a theoretical storyline. Likewise, visual displays can show the linear or nonlinear nature of related patterns.

Figure 15.2 illustrates the flow of theory development from my research in the Côte d'Ivoire. The model illustrates the interaction of workplace factors that appear to hinder the entrepreneurial transformation of newly privatized companies just prior to the December 1999 political coup and ensuing hostilities. These themes emerged from ethnographic interviews with more than 90 informants in 30 companies over a period of 3 years (Hansen, 2002). The data were triangulated with observations, document reviews and interviews with additional informants such as journalists and government officials.

The model begins and is driven by the solidarity of ethnic group obligations. Note that at the time of this study, the population of the Côte d'Ivoire consisted of four major ethnic groups that can be subdivided into more than 60 different clans and indigenous dialects. Ethnic groups, for the most part, reflected variance in religion, geography, and political and economic power. In addition, it was

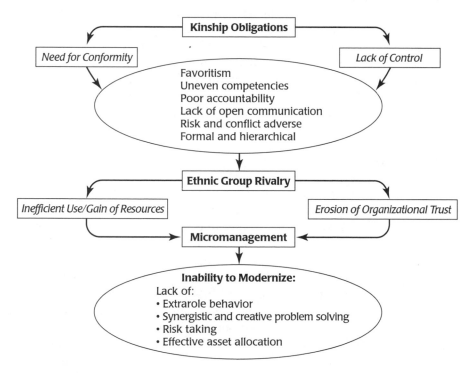

Figure 15.2 The Effects of Kinship Obligations

estimated that a third of the population were illegal immigrants from neighboring countries. Ethnic groups typically considered political borders to be less important than family lines. For example, the Akan live in both the Côte d'Ivoire and Ghana. When the Akan king died in Ghana in the late 1990s, Ivorians equally mourned his passing. At the time of this text's publication, the Côte d'Ivoire was geographically divided by a civil war that, in general terms, reflected differences in ethnic alliances and differences in external support.

Obligations were strongly related to the importance of family. They often led to a lack of personal control and a need for conformity that resulted in favoritism in the workplace, which led to uncertain managerial and employee competence and poor accountability of work processes and products. Protecting one's own (as in family ties) also meant that information was not openly shared within the organization and that the uncertainty of information coupled with the demands to ensure the survival of the ethnic group, led to an organizational culture that was risk and conflict adverse. Finally, in keeping with the norms of ethnic group socialization in a vertical collective, organizational structures tended to be formal and hierarchical (Triandis, 1995). These factors led to a workplace that had few rules based on objective performance criteria. A subtle form of rivalry then characterized the firm environment as each ethnic group vied for resource and power distribution resulting in the erosion of organizational trust and an inefficient use and gain of resources. Faced with an inept and even corrupt resource infrastructure and feeling that they often could not trust their employees' loyalty or competence, managers believed that they must micromanage to ensure that work goals were met. This tight control of the workplace countered modern management practices designed to encourage interdependence, synergy, openness and innovation. As an outcome, there was little evidence of extrarole behavior, creative problem solving, risk taking, or effective asset allocation.

CONCLUSION

As qualitative methods are employed in more and more studies of organizational issues, it is essential to remember that the primary use of grounded theory research is to build theory from data. Its introduction called into question our assumptions about scientific inquiry. Grounded theory research originated from a desire to use inquiry for practical reform and to explore the symbolic interaction of social reality. Thus, it studies real problems, is interpretative, recognizes the multiple facets of meaning making, and does not use predetermined hypotheses.

Although this use of qualitative methods acknowledges that the discovery of new theory is sometimes messy, it offers more rigor than typically found in other qualitative methods. Through the methodological aspects of focused coding and the constant comparison of data and theoretical sampling, grounded theory research offers a systematic approach to the creation of new propositions. Good emergent theory should do the following: (1) address a theoretical gap or need, (2) be feasible, (3) transfer to other settings, and (4) propose the emergence of a kind of story of how and under what conditions people see the interface of their actions.

REFERENCES

Ashill, H. J., Frederikson, M., & Davies, J. (2003). Strategic marketing planning: A grounded investigation. *European Journal of Marketing, 37*(3/4), 430–461.

Boje, D. (1991). The storytelling organization: A study of story performance in an office supply firm. *Administrative Science Quarterly, 36*(1), 106–126.

Charmaz, K. (2004). Grounded theory. In S. N. Hesse-Biber & P. Leavy (Eds.), *Approaches to qualitative research: A reader on theory and practice* (pp. 496–521). New York: Oxford University Press.

Egan, T. (2002). Grounded theory research and theory building. *Advances in Developing Human Resources, 4*(3), 277–295.

Glaser, B., & Strauss, A. (1967). *The discovery of grounded theory: Strategies for qualitative research.* Chicago: Aldine.

Glesne, C., & Peshkin, A. (1992). *Becoming qualitative researchers.* White Plains, NY: Longman.

Golden-Biddle, K., & Locke, K. (1997). *Composing qualitative research.* Newbury Park, CA: Sage.

Guba, E. G., & Lincoln, Y. S. (2004). Competing paradigms in qualitative Research: theories and issues. In S. N. Hesse-Biber & P. Leavy (Eds.), *Approaches to qualitative research: A reader on theory and practice* (pp. 17–39). New York: Oxford University Press.

Hansen, C. (2002). Organizational change and the village funeral in the Côte d'Ivoire. In *Proceedings of the Society for Organizational Culture and Symbolism.* Budapest: Author.

Hansen, C., & Kahnweiler, W. (1993). Storytelling: An instrument for understanding organizational dynamics. *Human Relations, 46*(12), 1391–1449.

Hansen, C., Kahnweiler, W., & Wilensky, A. (1994). Human resource development: A study of occupational culture through organizational stories. *Human Resource Development Quarterly, 5*(1), 55–74.

Lincoln, Y. S., & Guba, E. G. (1985). *Naturalistic inquiry.* Beverly Hills, CA: Sage.

Locke, K. (2001). *Grounded theory in management research.* Thousand Oaks, CA: Sage.

Lowe, A. (1992). Interview with Barney Glaser. Retrieved May 2004 from www.groundedtheory.com/vidseries1.html.

Miles, M. R., & Huberman, A. M. (1984). *Qualitative data analysis.* Thousand Oaks, CA: Sage.

Mohrman, S. A., Ramkrishnan, V., Tenkasi, A., & Mohrman, M. (2003). The role of networks in fundamental organizational change: A grounded analysis. *Journal of Applied Behavioral Science, 39*(3), 301–322.

Pike, K. (1967). *Language in relation to a unified theory of the structure of behavior.* The Hague: Morton.

Spradley, J. (1979). *The ethnographic interview*. New York: Holt, Rinehart & Winston.

Strauss, A., & Corbin, J. (1990). *Basics of qualitative research: Grounded theory procedures and techniques*. Newbury Park, CA: Sage.

Torraco, R. (1997). Theory building research methods. In R. A. Swanson & E. R. Holton III (Eds.), *Human resource development research handbook* (pp. 114–137). San Francisco: Berrett-Koehler.

Triandis, H. C. (1995). *Individualism and collectivism*. Boulder, CO: Westview.

Trice, H., & Beyer, J. (1993). *The cultures of work organizations*. Englewood Cliffs, NJ: Prentice Hall.

Ethnographic Research Methods

Pamela Crespin, Christine Miller, and Allen W. Batteau,
Wayne State University

This chapter describes the methods used and challenges encountered when conducting ethnographic research in organizations. After describing ethnographic methods, we present two case studies that use these methods in contemporary business organizations. We conclude with a general discussion of the challenges of organizational ethnography: framing appropriate research questions, gaining access, maintaining the research role, confronting ethical challenges, and accounting for issues of scale when using firsthand observation.

ETHNOGRAPHIC METHODS

Ethnographic methods originated in the encounter of European imperial powers with indigenous populations. Colonial administrators found that explorers' reports were often too superficial, and missionaries' narratives too colored by their own emotional biases, to present a useful accounting of the customs and modes of livelihood of the indigenous peoples that had become the administrators' responsibilities. From the two founders of the discipline, Franz Boas (at Columbia University) and Bronislaw Malinowski (at Cambridge), generations of ethnographers, following in the wake of explorers, set forth to remote locales to live for extended periods of time among the population they were studying. This extended immersion, which is the sine qua non of ethnographic research, was initially a practical necessity: the ethnographic locale was sufficiently remote that there was no alternative but to live among the villagers, eat their food, converse with their elders in the local patois, and participate in their rituals. Over time these extended encounters with the Other became the rite of passage for all fledgling social anthropologists. Through this encounter the ethnographer was able to return to civilization and create an account that familiarized the unfamiliar and lent a shared humanity to peoples that had heretofore been understood only as savages and troglodytes.

Immersion, however, is not enough, particularly if ethnography aspires to create scientific (i.e., replicable) results. "Deep hanging out" might appear to be an adequate description of the European observer sitting on a log doing nothing visibly useful, but her apparent inactivity is only a guise, an aspiration to interfere as little as possible with the activities and rhythms of the village. (This is sometimes more difficult than it might sound, if one's dress, skin complexion, and accent are markedly different; it is even more difficult if one maintains ties to colonial outposts such as mission schools or trading posts.)

Behind the apparent inactivity is, first, ongoing observation, both structured and unstructured. The ethnographer will conduct her observations with a protocol, but typically the protocol defines general domains, rather than specific behavioral items. More typically, however, the ethnographer will use participant observation, which means that she will participate at some level in the village activities, whether cultivating gardens, building houses, or participating in rituals (Spradley, 1980). In participant observation the ethnographer usually writes up her notes only back in her hut, perhaps at the end of the day. These notes are subject to analytic protocols that we will describe later.

Participant observation may be supplemented by unstructured interviewing, which to some may resemble little more than interesting conversations. Again, however, the ethnographer is guided by a protocol identifying what areas are of interest, whether kinship terminology, subsistence methods, or beliefs about the supernatural. The objective, however, is to elicit these in as naturalistic a manner as possible: forced-response questionnaires are rarely used until the ethnographer has acquired sufficient familiarity with the local milieu to understand what questions are meaningful and important to ask.

The ethnographer may also collect artifacts and documents, take pictures, record songs, or collect any other sort of data that intuitively seem pertinent. Always the ethnographer is watchful of imposing preconceptions on the villagers; for example, discussions of graduate education, one of us found out, had almost no meaning within a community where most persons' education stopped at the eighth grade.

No less important than collecting such field data is the return from the field. More than a few ethnographers have been known to go native: after a year in residence, it is not far-fetched to imagine that the ethnographer would find life on a Polynesian island more appealing than academic life in the northern latitudes. However, for the majority that do return from the field, the next several months are spent analyzing the data: going over interview transcripts and field notes, pulling out common themes, constructing narratives from snippets of stories, and using content analysis to identify patterns. Finally, the ethnographer writes the ethnographic account, which if well done creates for the (Western, educated) reader a familiarity and an immediacy for a people who would otherwise be exotic. This is what Margaret Mead accomplished with *Coming of Age in Samoa*, creating an understanding of adolescent sexuality that arguably had just as much impact as Freud and Kinsey.

Mead's accomplishment sums up the importance of ethnography, in its enlargement of our understanding of human possibilities. When one has lived for an extended period of time in an unfamiliar village, when cultural disorientation—an essential ethnographic experience—is embedded in one's daily routine, one acquires a profound conviction that all social forms are conventional. It is this experience and this conviction, more than any methodological or conceptual apparatus, that define an ethnographic view.

However, when the ethnographic gaze is turned toward contemporary institutions, a new set of opportunities and challenges arise (Schwartzman, 1993). These institutions, such as media companies and manufacturers, are not remote and exotic. Research in them lacks the primordial encounter with the Other that was the original hallmark of ethnography. Instead of being conducted at the sufferance of a colonial administrator, it is conducted with the permission and usually

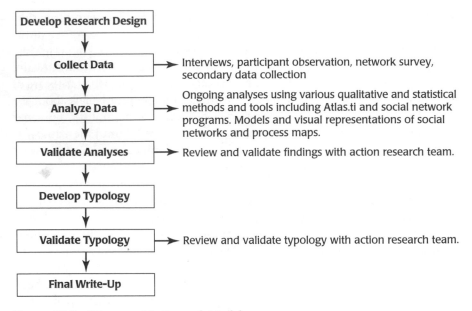

Figure 16.1 Ethnographic Research Model
Source: Adapted from G. H. Sengir, R. T. Trotter II, D. M. Kulkarni, E. K. Briody, L. B. Catlin, & T. L. Meerwarth (2004), "Modeling Relationship Dynamics in GM's Research-Institution Partnerships," *Journal of Manufacturing Technology Management*.

at the behest of management. Instead of an encounter with our Others, it is an encounter with our Selves.

We now turn, in ethnographic fashion, to two exemplary instances of this: a study at a broadcasting organization and a study of innovation at a manufacturer. Both generally followed the general ethnographic research model presented in Figure 16.1. Following the presentation of the two cases, we make some general remarks concerning the challenges and opportunities of ethnographic research in organizations.

CANADIAN BROADCASTER CASE

As Czarniawska-Joerges (1992) notes, a significant challenge inherent in organizational ethnography is access. Many organizational decision makers consider academic research disruptive, and they are concerned about the information that might be disclosed. Another source of resistance, particularly when compared to typical business and management research designs, is the initial absence of a definitive research question, a fundamental characteristic of ethnographic and grounded theory research models.

The researcher's goal was to conduct ethnography at a major facility of the Canadian Radio Broadcaster (CRB). Anticipating significant difficulty gaining access to the CRB, the researcher decided not to contact key decision makers until she had established her presence as a chair at a Canadian university and developed relationships with Canadians (and expatriate Americans) who could influence CRB decision makers. Through these efforts and contacts, she was able to meet with a member of the CRB board of directors and a nationally known CRB radio host, both of whom, after hearing her proposal, agreed to contact senior staff members at the CRB.

Within a few weeks of her arrival, the researcher was also meeting regularly with managers and staff in CRB's local office. She provided these local managers with a formal, written proposal for the project and responded to their concerns and objections in writing and in person. An initial condition to proceed, set by these local managers, was that all of them must agree to the project before she would receive open access. Within a few meetings, two managers agreed to the projects; however, the third continued to resist. The researcher had already been warned by some CRB employees that this manager might be fearful about the level of scrutiny inherent in the project design. His final condition before he would agree to the project was full editorial rights to all of the work involving CRB, which—as a journalist—he must have known an academic researcher cannot relinquish.

As a precaution, the researcher had already begun contacting and proposing the project to managers and staff in other CRB locations, as well as to members of CRB's senior management. After a systematic campaign of telephone interviews, e-mail, postal letters, meetings, and written proposals, several CRB managers expressed interest in the project, with some reservations. Among their explicit concerns was the project's potential demand on employees' limited time and energy. After massive layoffs in recent years, the remaining staff is stressed and overworked, and another nationwide budget cut was scheduled to occur during the on-site period of the study.

In December, Jess (pseudonym) notified the researcher that one show had agreed to participate in the project. After obtaining the approval of a CRB senior manager, Jess granted her access for a 3-month ethnography and reserved the option to extend the project (which he did). Because Jess was also concerned about the project's impact on his beleaguered staff's time and focus, he stipulated that the researcher hold formal interviews off-site and pay interviewees for their time. Although the researcher offered to pay each interviewee for his or her off-duty time, each refused; however, most accepted a complimentary meal during the interview.

Another condition Jess set forth for the project was the use of pseudonyms for the organization, its location, and employees' names. As an added precaution, the researcher elected to review photographic slides with Jess (who indicated which slides are appropriate for publication and use in public presentations). She also opted not to identify company publications and to omit descriptive details of places and speakers. In terms of the organization's identity, it is important to note that Jess acknowledged that people would undoubtedly be able to "read through the lines"; that is, despite the pseudonym, some would be able to identify the organization. Consequently, protecting employees' names and the location of the on-site portion of the study became paramount.

Fetterman (1989, p. 18) refers to the initial phase of fieldwork as the "survey period," during which the ethnographer gathers basic structural and functional information and learns the organization's language (Aguilera, 1996). When the formal ethnography began on January 5, 2000, an initial goal included charting the CRB's spatial and functional structures, the latter of which is derived from its division of labor and hierarchy. Other survey activities included gathering information on personnel and scheduled events (e.g., meetings, regular, and special programs). These data provided the researcher with a multidimensional map (organizational structure and physical plant), aided the formulation of a tentative research schedule, and initiated acquisition of the CRB's specialized lexicon.

From the moment of entry into the field site, building and maintaining trust is a crucial factor in any ethnography's success. At the CRB, imminent layoffs magnified employees' concerns about the researcher's motives, and throughout the project a few of these adept interviewers probed and challenged her motives and assessments, especially because she was moving freely across hierarchical boundaries. Her first few days at the CRB found most members of the radio show (who the director of radio said had agreed to be subjects of the research project) uncooperative and approachable. She quickly gravitated toward the personnel of other shows who were interested in the project and willing to participate. Soon, members of the show to which she was originally assigned invited her to include them in the study, and she ultimately gained access to the staff of four radio shows and several other departments associated with radio programming.

After a few weeks, the researcher knew she had gained an important level of trust when she was regularly invited to on-site and off-site events. She became, along with everyone else, a target of the continual stream of sarcastic barbs and jokes. Along with this favorable transition in her status at the CRB came another challenge: a number of people sought to co-opt her as a political ally and to harvest the politically sensitive information to which she had access. The critical test was then to reserve neutrality, while also maintaining the level of trust she had earned.

Participant observation involves the direct observation of and, when possible, participation in microevents and interactions as they occur. Unlike data collection and analysis techniques typical of most organizational research, participant observation enables ethnographers to develop a comprehensive understanding of the people and processes (Aguilera, 1996). By allowing the ethnographer and subjects to share every form of communication, participant observation builds trust and mutuality and enables the ethnographer to discover and understand what is important to the subjects (Reeves-Ellington, 1998). In this way, the data and the subjects define the project (Aguilera, 1996).

Ultimately, the ethnographer was able to observe during every weekday shift and in a variety of activities and venues at the CRB. This allowed her to meet and observe a large number of employees, to observe a full range of production activities, and to attend a broad selection of meetings, training sessions, and special events. The number of CRB employees she observed at each of these venues ranged between 2 and approximately 50. Additionally, she "shadowed" some people in each department or group, attended off-site work activities (e.g., remote broadcasts), and participated in off-duty social events. This varied schedule maximized the number and duration of observations and interactions, helped her build relationships with most of the approximately 50 people directly employed in this CRB broadcasting group, and enabled her to meet an additional 30-plus CRB employees in auxiliary production or support groups.

Many types and sources of data are important for the study of complex organizations. Some examples include rituals, stories, jargon, humor, physical arrangements, corporate structure, technology, archival documents, and population characteristics. The data include emic (interviews) and etic (observation) perspectives. The data may also be classified as formal and informal practices, themes, and forms (Martin, 1992, p. 37). Formal data are usually written and controlled by management (e.g., organizational charts, job descriptions, and technology). Informal data are seldom written and evolve through interaction (e.g., communication patterns and unwritten norms).

Organizational archives can be a rich source of data with which to "trace the path of evolution and cultural consequences" (Briody & Baba, 1994, p. 257). Generally, archived documents represent a formal and idealized view of the organization. They can be used to compare and triangulate data obtained from other sources (Briody & Baba, 1994; Fetterman, 1989) and to reveal contradictions in organizational values. A company's archives may contain a range of documents, such as announcements, annual reviews, articles, award announcements, brochures, business cards, company newsletters, employee rosters (with department and contact numbers), floor plans, functional flowcharts, interoffice memos, job titles and descriptions, labor contracts, management reports, mission and vision statements, maps, news and publicity releases, organizational charts, policy and procedure manuals, promotional material (e.g., lapel buttons, shirt with logo), recruitment material, schedules of regular and special events, training materials, and work and shift schedules.

At the CRB, the primary method used for recording data on-site was handwritten field notes, because it was not feasible to obtain prior permission from the stream of people continually moving in and out of recording range. Electronic recording can also exacerbate suspicion, especially in an organization under severe stress, such as the CRB. Consequently, with the exception of one formal interview, which was conducted and recorded over a 2-day period in the interviewee's private office, the researcher did not audio- or videotape on-site conversations. She recorded the CRB interior with still photography, and she used still photography and videotape to record the CRB's exterior and some off-site activities (e.g., remote broadcasts).

In addition to interviews and observations at the CRB, the ethnographer photocopied CRB written documents available on-site. While this CRB site did not have a library or archive of company documents, she was able to collect crucial material through individual employees and company Web sites. A wide range of material was obtained, including annual reviews, newsletters, mission and vision statements, technical and training manuals, and memos. She also obtained historical accounts of the CRB, written by employees, at local bookstores.

To understand the organization from the emic, or insiders', perspectives, she conducted formal and informal interviews with people within each of the CRB's departments and employee classifications. Informal interviews were ad hoc, conducted on-site, often involved more than one interviewee, and were recorded as handwritten field notes.

Formal interviews were semistructured and open-ended; in addition to providing data on predetermined topics, this format allowed interviewees to generate their own topics. A pattern of shared categories emerged from these topics, which delineate the members' leading concerns. These categories informed the questions the researcher prepared for formal interviews. She conducted all of the formal interviews with one interviewee (per interview) and, with one exception, off-site.

From the onset of an ethnographic project, data analysis is an inductive process, which is ideal for producing the models and theory necessary to comprehend complex organizations. Early into the on-site research, the ethnographer identified the themes of significant concern to many people at CRB. It quickly became apparent that technological upgrades are driving CRB's reengineering program. This program included conducting layoffs, breaking down functional barriers ("silos"), and increasing contingent labor. The indirect result for the CRB is declining programming quality. With rare exception, the approximately 50 CRB employees with whom she spent most of her time agree that these are serious problems, and public statements by CRB senior managers affirm their existence and severity. Additionally, the overwhelming majority of her informants (nearly 50) expressed great concern about some or all of the following topics: the increased presence of contingent labor, loss of institutional knowledge and industry experience, decentralizing silos, downsizing technical specialists, and generalizing workers and work processes.

In keeping with grounded theory, the subjects' primary concerns became the salient categories for her continuing data collection and analysis. Technological and organizational innovations became secondary categories for data collection. To gain a comprehensive understanding of these themes, she expanded her literature research to include communication technology and global labor trends.

The ethnographer developed a systemic model of these categories and, near the end of the formal ethnography, checked her preliminary model and understanding of the interrelatedness of the primary themes with CRB members.

ETHNOGRAPHY AT AN AUTOMOTIVE SUPPLIER

A second ethnographer conducted a study of Auto Tech, a supplier of automotive components. This is a company that also has been under severe pressure to innovate, even while controlling costs and reinventing its identity. Like several of its competitors, it had previously existed as a component within a large automotive firm. At the time of its spin-off, Auto Tech faced a series of major challenges, all of which needed to be addressed simultaneously. Reinventing itself as an organization capable of generating and commercializing innovative products and services was at the top of the list.

Recognizing that some organizational cultures are more conducive to innovation than others, top-level managers at Auto Tech set out to create a culture that was supportive of innovation. It was also recognized by management that this is far easier said than done. While new initiatives and processes can be implemented, culture cannot be dictated. Managers at Auto Tech confronted a common problem faced by managers everywhere: Given the limitations of their ability to see deeply into the organization, how could managers know what impact their decisions were having? How would they know that the behaviors they wanted to elicit were actually occurring deep in the organization?

The use of metrics to evaluate progress toward desired performance targets is common across all industries. This is also the case in measuring organizational performance along the dimensions of innovation and commercialization. However, the indicators used to measure performance typically provide a backward view. To use an analogy, they can tell you that you're losing altitude but may not be able to tell you why. Only by "popping the hood" on the organization—checking out the components and seeing how they're working together—can you begin to understand what's actually going on inside. Using ethnography to study organizations is analogous to popping the hood.

The work of the organizational ethnographer is usually not understood. Forsythe (1999) addresses this issue in detail in her article on ethnography as invisible work. Ethnographic data are gathered from numerous sources that are selected by the anthropologist based on the research question that she or he is attempting to investigate. The selection of what are considered data is an important but frequently overlooked part of ethnographic work in organizations and leads to the general impression that anyone can do ethnography (Forsythe, 1999). Consequently, members of the subject organization, especially those with technical backgrounds, tend to underestimate the skill sets required to produce good ethnography. Because these technical personnel also tend to devalue the social aspects and interactions of their own work, the work of the ethnographic researcher, which is largely focused on complex social phenomena, is marginalized.

Other aspects of ethnographic work tend to be invisible to anyone who is not trained in qualitative social science research techniques. For example, once collected, data must then be coded by the ethnographer, a process that requires specific skills and training in order to tease out and interpret reoccurring patterns and themes. A skilled ethnographer is able to take data collected from interviews and direct observation and compile a detailed narrative describing the inner workings (or nonworkings) of the organization. With a deep understanding of the philosophical grounding of the tools and techniques of ethnography, the anthropologist-researcher is able to detect underlying assumptions and values of organizational members. Using selected data, the researcher is able to juxtapose formal organizational charts with maps of the informal networks where work actually gets done.

An organizational ethnographer grounded in the theory and methods of qualitative research has a unique approach to his or her study that tends to "problematize" the subject(s) of research. This means that what subjects of the study would typically take for granted is routinely called into question by the ethnographer (Forsythe, 1999). Taking this approach will often reveal aspects of the organization that are unsettling or disturbing, yet it is just these findings that, if they can be accepted and processed by organizational members, prove to be the most profoundly significant.

Preliminary finding in the specific case of Auto Tech would only amount to speculation. However, some general observations can be cited regarding the dialectical tension that exists in most firms between pressures to maintain stability and control and typically disruptive pressures generated by emergent elements (Dougherty, 1996; Putnam, 1983; Seo & Putnam, 2002). The latter are often in response to the influence of changing conditions in the external environment. Thus, the organization is in the position of attempting to balance a dual nature, operating simultaneously and at different levels as both a closed and open system. Engaging in capacity-building planned change (e.g., building innovative capacity) evokes tension as the anticipated and unanticipated consequences of change initiatives are confronted by the forces of organizational control and stability. A wide variety of techniques are applied for the purpose of eliminating resistance to change, including voluntary terminations and process engineering or reengineering. The results of such efforts are mixed and can result in damaging effects to the organization's social fabric and networks, including depleted morale and disrupted social networks. According to one organizational informant, for a number of reasons, the negative effects must be taken in stride: "Well, I had to cut off my fingers, but at least I still have my arm." The appreciation and acceptance of qualitative social science research applied in tandem with traditional statistically based quantitative methods may lessen the need to resort to such drastic measures.

NEW CHALLENGES, NEW METHODS

As these two examples illustrate, organizational ethnography is so dramatically different from village-centered ethnography that our traditional training in field methods scarcely prepared us for some of its challenges. First and foremost is the challenge of what questions one should be asking. If one understands field research as a triangulation among theoretical questions, the factual opportunity afforded by the field site, and the priorities of the sponsor or gatekeeper, then the third of these probably looms more heavily in organizational ethnography than in other sorts of ethnographic studies. Questions posed in ethnographic field studies in organizations in some manner tend to connect with the distinctive cultural features of organization (Batteau, 2000); yet as both of these case studies demonstrate, organizations are not monolithic entities, regardless of the opinions or desires of their managers. Thus, once inside the organization, one discovers a universe of questions, contradictions, hidden agendas, and countercultures, many of which are ripe for up-close, in-person study.

However, one must first get inside. All groups have boundaries, but organizations uniquely invest resources in defining and maintaining boundaries, whether in the identification and control of members, assets, or physical spaces. Furthermore, unlike in the village setting where the ethnographer arrives (implicitly) representing a superior power, ethnographers approach organizations from positions of relative weakness: in our recollection, there has never been an ethnographer who successfully demanded access to conduct a study inside a contemporary corporation. More typically, as these accounts indicate, we persuade, form alliances, and in some manner buy into some management agenda. Again, however, noting the diversity of agendas within corporations, this is not always as large a problem as it might seem at first.

Often, if a corporation is willing to let an ethnographer in the door, it will be to study a problem that the corporation considers important. If the corporation considers the problem important, it may in fact be willing to put the ethnographer on the payroll to study the problem. Although this at times creates difficult compromises, at other times it is unavoidable, and the best the ethnographer can hope to do is to maintain her ethical and intellectual integrity in the face of potential pressures to disclose or modify her findings. The worst situation is where one corporate function (say, a headquarters) hires the ethnographer to conduct a study of another function, such as a branch plant or field office. In this situation the ethnographer may come to be perceived by either or both sides as a spy, regardless of the intentions of any party involved. If one is seen as or expected to be a spy, then the research is hopelessly compromised.

The American Anthropological Association has a code of ethics that is intended to prevent harm to the subjects of ethnographic research. Informed consent must be obtained from all participants, informants' identities must be kept confidential unless confidentiality is explicitly waived, and informants must be protected from any repercussions resulting from their participation in a study or the information that they disclose. When one is inside the organization at the sufferance of management, undue pressures might be brought to bear to disclose information that has been provided in confidence. In some instances, ethnographers inside organizations were forced to suspend their research rather than compromise their informants.

More typically, however, the pressures and counterpressures are more subtle than this. Given the diversity and political conflicts within most corporate workplaces, various groups may make efforts to "adopt" the ethnographer and enlist her help in getting their unique point of view across. If the group in question is a subaltern group, has been in some manner treated unjustly by corporate management, or is otherwise able to play on the ethnographer's sympathies, this role may be difficult to resist. These individuals or groups will open up to the ethnographer, having figured out that she needs information sources. It is easy for the researcher to lose sight of the fact that their information is as partial as anyone else's. The other side of this process is the no less typical process where groups conclude that they have nothing to gain from cooperating with this pesky person who is always asking questions. Inside an organization, the ethnographer is continually frustrated by sought-for informants who are too busy to talk to her. In short, even after the researcher is allowed on the premises or placed on the payroll, access problems remain.

A more difficult problem, however, is how to generalize or scale up findings that by their very nature are local and miniaturist. Ethnographic studies inside corporations are sometimes dismissed because of their small sample size, even though the hallmarks of ethnographic research—up close, in person, in depth—precludes any alternative. The sought-after ethnographic results—subtle behavior patterns, informal communication, informal processes that fly beneath management's radar—by definition cannot be studied on a larger scale. The response to this concern is that for certain scientific purposes, size does not matter, and there is no safety in numbers. Just as Margaret Mead enlarged our understanding of sexuality from her encounters with a few dozen Samoan teenagers (scarcely an adequate statistical sample), Kirk Cornell's (2004) ethnography of automotive suppliers created a new understanding of the use and misuse of technology within supply chains, based on his in-depth study of eight suppliers. An enlarged understanding derives less from piling up case after case and more from a few strategic questions posed in strategic locations.

Geertz (1973) has described ethnography as "thick description," an insightful comment that captures both the value (and difficulty when done well) of descriptive methods, as well as the multiple layers of meaning captured by naturalistic, empathetic research methods. Human behavior typically has multiple layers of meaning, particularly inside organizations, which bring together multiple functions, groups, and roles. Batteau (2000) gives examples of these multiple layers of meaning and ways that different parties within an organization can play them off against each other, manipulating multiple meanings for strategic advantage. These cannot be captured except through naturalistic methods such as ethnography.

In sum, the growing use of ethnographic methods both in academic studies of corporations and by corporate management should be ample testimony that value is being derived from methods that cut against the grain of standard, quantitative, large-sample surveys. These methods are welcomed both inside corporations and out wherever it is understood that social life has complexities that neither a single research method nor any singular viewpoint can encompass.

NOTES

1. Months later, after the researcher returned to the United States, this manager's resignation from the CRB was announced in the press.

2. Although these conditions make access more difficult, they create an opportune environment for studying the organization (Brannen, 1998). Under stress, the social order tends to break down, and the environment becomes less predictable (Brown & Starkey, 1994). Members can become defensive of their traditional beliefs and behaviors, which makes these elements more visible (Kleinberg, 1994).

3. In organizational ethnography, employees often view the decision maker who controls the researcher's access as responsible for the organization's problems. This creates a particular dilemma for researchers, for whom inclusion within an employee group may depend on his or her explicit expression of their shared values and beliefs.

4. In the 1990s, firms took advantage of technological innovations in digitally based computer-networking capabilities, and—under the banner of "reengineering"—a wave of organizational change profoundly altered the concept of the traditional job.

5. As an exception that proves the statement, we might consider the "Sociology Department" that Henry Ford established in the 1920s at Ford Motor Company. Ostensibly a social welfare enterprise to assist immigrant families in adjusting to their new life in the United States, agents of the Sociology Department visited the homes of factory laborers and reported on any signs of subversion or union activity among the workers.

REFERENCES

Aguilera, F. E. (1996). Is anthropology good for the company? *American Anthropologist*, *98*(4), 735–742.

Batteau, A. (2001). Negations and ambiguities in the cultures of organization. *American Anthropologist*, *102*(4), 726–740.

Brannen, M. Y. (1998). Negotiated culture in binational contexts: A model of culture change based on a Japanese/American organizational experience. In T. Hamada (Ed.), *The Anthropology of Business Organization: Anthropology of Work Review*, *18*(2–3) (Special Issue), 6–17.

Briody, E. K., & Baba, M. L. (1994). Reconstructing culture clash at General Motors: An historical view from the overseas assignment. In T. Hamada & W. E. Sibley (Eds.),

Anthropological perspectives on organizational culture (pp. 219–260). Lanham, MD: University Press of America.

Brown, A. D., & Starkey, K. (1994). The effect of organizational culture on communication and information. *Journal of Management Studies, 31*, 807–828.

Cornell, K. (2004). *An anthropological view of supply chain technologies in the automotive industry.* Unpublished doctoral dissertation, Wayne State University, Detroit, MI.

Czarniawska-Joerges, B. (1992). *Exploring complex organizations.* Newbury Park, CA: Sage.

Dougherty, D. (1996). Organizing for innovation. In S. R. Clegg, C. Hardy, & W. R. Nord (Eds.), *Managing organizations* (pp. 175–190). Thousand Oaks, CA: Sage.

Fetterman, D. M. (1989). *Ethnography step by step.* Applied Social Research Methods Series, Vol. 17. Newbury Park, CA: Sage.

Forsythe, D. E. (1999). "It's just a matter of common sense": Ethnography as invisible work. *Computer Supported Cooperative Work, 8*, 127–145.

Geertz, C. (1973). *The interpretation of cultures.* New York: Basic Books.

Martin, J. (1992). *Cultures in organizations: Three perspectives.* New York: Oxford University Press.

Putnam, L. L. (1983). The interpretive perspective: An alternative to functionalism. In L. L. Putnam & M. E. Pacanowsky (Eds.), *Communication in organizations: An interpretive approach* (pp. 31–54). Beverly Hills, CA: Sage.

Reeves-Ellington, R. H. (1998). A mix of cultures, values, and people: An organizational case study. *Human Organization: Journal of the Society for Applied Anthropology, 57*(1), 94–107.

Schwartzman, H. B. (1993). *Ethnography in organizations.* Newbury Park, CA: Sage.

Seo, M.-G., Putnam, L. L., & Bartunek, J. M. (2002). Dualities and tensions of planned organizational change. In M. S. Poole & A. H. Van de Ven (Eds.), *Handbook of organizational change and innovation.* New York: Oxford University Press.

Spradley, J. P. (1980). *Participant observation.* New York: Holt, Rinehart, & Winston.

CHAPTER 17

Historical Research Methods

Michael Rowlinson, *Queen Mary, University of London*

CHAPTER OUTLINE
Overview of the Historical Research Process
Organizational Studies and Business History
History as a Repository of Facts
Historical Analysis and Organizational Dynamics
Collection and Organization of Company
    Documentation
Periodization and Writing Strategies
Conclusion
Further Reading
References

There are increasing calls for a historical perspective in organization studies. The hope is that a "historic turn" might help make the study of organizations less deterministic and more ethical, humanistic, and managerially relevant (Clark & Rowlinson, in press). In this chapter, I quickly overview the historical research process and use the example of my own research on the extensive collection of historical documents held by Cadbury, the British chocolate company, to explore issues to be considered when analyzing company documents from a historical perspective.

My intention is to address the question of why historical analysis of company documents is rarely pursued as a research strategy by organizational researchers. The discussion is centered on the theme of exploring the differences between organization studies and business history, starting with a series of misconceptions concerning archival research on the part of organizational researchers. Then I contrast the problem of periodization in business history, with the focus on everyday life in qualitative organizational ethnography and how this affects writing strategies in history and organization studies.

OVERVIEW OF THE HISTORICAL RESEARCH PROCESS

Johnson and Christensen (2005) provide the following basic overview of the historical research process. This information is a distillation of Chapter 13 in their research textbook (Johnson & Christensen, 2003).

What Is Historical Research?

Historical research is the process of systematically examining past events to give an account of what has happened in the past. It is not a mere accumulation of facts and dates or even a description of past events. Rather, it is a flowing, dynamic account of past events that involves an interpretation of the events in an attempt to recapture the nuances, personalities, and ideas that influenced these events. One of the goals of historical research is to communicate an understanding of past events.

The following are five important reasons for conducting historical research (based on Berg, 1998, as cited in Johnson & Christenson, 2005):

- To uncover the unknown (i.e., some historical events are not recorded)
- To answer questions (i.e., there are many questions about our past that we not only want to know but can profit from knowing)
- To identify the relationship that the past has to the present (i.e., knowing about the past can frequently give a better perspective of current events)
- To record and evaluate the accomplishments of individuals, agencies, or institutions
- To assist in understanding the culture in which we live (e.g., education is a part of our history and our culture)

Historical Research Methodology

There is no one approach that is used in conducting historical research, although a general set of steps is typically followed. These include the following, although some overlap and movement back and forth occur between the steps:

1. Identification of the research topic and formulation of the research problem or question
2. Data collection or literature review
3. Evaluation of materials
4. Data synthesis
5. Report preparation or preparation of the narrative exposition

Identification of the Research Topic and Formulation of the Research Problem or Question

This is the first step in any type of educational research, including historical research. Ideas for historical research topics can come from many different sources such as current issues in education, the accomplishments of an individual, an educational policy, or the relationship between events.

Data Collection or Literature Review

This step involves identifying, locating, and collecting information pertaining to the research topic. The information sources are often contained in documents such as diaries or newspapers, records, photographs, relics, and interviews with individuals who have had experience with or have knowledge of the research topic. Interviews with individuals who have knowledge of the research topic are called *oral histories*.

The documents, records, oral histories, and other information sources can be primary or secondary sources. A *primary* source is a source that has a direct involvement with the event being investigated, such as a diary, an original map, or an interview with a person who experienced the event. A *secondary* source has been created from a primary source such as books written about the event. Secondary sources are considered less useful than primary sources.

Evaluation of Materials

Every information source must be evaluated for its authenticity and accuracy because any source can be affected by a variety of factors such as prejudice, economic conditions, and political climate. Every source must pass two types of evaluations:

External criticism. This is the process of determining the validity, trustworthiness, or authenticity of the source. Sometimes this task is difficult, but other times it can easily be done by analyzing handwriting or determining the age of the paper on which something was written.

Internal criticism. This is the process of determining the reliability or accuracy of the information contained in the sources collected. Firsthand accounts by witnesses to an event, for example, are typically assumed to be more reliable and accurate. This is done by positive and negative criticism.

- *Positive criticism* refers to assuring that the statements made or the meanings conveyed in the sources are understood. This is frequently difficult because of the problems of vagueness and presentism. *Vagueness* refers to uncertainty in the meaning of the words and phrases used in the source; *presentism* refers to the assumption that the present-day connotations of terms also existed in the past.

- *Negative criticism* refers to establishing the reliability or authenticity and accuracy of the content of the sources used. This is the more difficult part because it requires a judgment about the accuracy and authenticity of what is contained in the source.

Historians often use three heuristics in handling evidence to establish its authenticity or accuracy: corroboration, sourcing, and contextualization. *Corroboration* entails comparing documents to each other to determine whether they provide the same information. *Sourcing* involves identifying the author, date of creation of a document, and the place it was created. During *contextualization*, the researcher identifies when and where an event took place.

Data Synthesis and Report Preparation
Synthesis refers to selecting, organizing, and analyzing the materials collected into topical themes and central ideas or concepts. These themes are then pulled together to form a contiguous and meaningful whole.

Watch out for the following four problems that might arise when you attempt to synthesize the material collected and prepare a narrative account:

- Trying to infer causation from correlated events. Just because two events occurred together does not necessarily mean that one event was the cause of the other.

- Defining and interpreting key words so as to avoid ambiguity and to ensure that they have the correct connotation

- Differentiating between evidence indicating how people should behave and how they in fact did behave

- Maintaining a distinction between intent and consequences. In other words, educational historians must make sure that the consequences that were observed from some activity or policy were the intended consequences (Johnson & Christensen, 2005).

ORGANIZATIONAL STUDIES AND BUSINESS HISTORY

Considering their common interest in business organizations, dialogue between qualitative organizational researchers and business historians concerning theory and methods is relatively limited. This is partly because business history—defined as "the systematic study of individual firms on the basis of their business records" (Tosh, 1991, p. 95; see also Coleman, 1987, p. 142), which is virtually synonymous with the historical analysis of company documentation—is characterized by a lack of methodological reflection. This quality describes history in general, as Hayden White (1995), one of the most influential philosophers of history, observes: "History is rather a craft like discipline, which means that it tends to be governed by convention and custom rather than by methodology and theory and to utilize ordinary or natural languages for the description of its objects of study and representation of the historian's thought about those objects" (p. 243).

Qualitative researchers in organizational studies are expected to justify their methodology, whereas business historians do not have to contend with a high expectation that they can and will account for their methodological approach. Business history remains resolutely empiricist and atheoretical in the sense that its conceptualizations and claims are relatively unexamined, and, unlike organization studies, it lacks an ostentatiously theoretical language. Business historians verge on assuming that their interpretation of company documents is commonsense, and therefore their procedure needs no explanation (Rowlinson, 2001, p. 15).

The preference in qualitative organization studies, especially organizational culture studies, is for interviews and observation, which I refer to as organizational ethnography (e.g., Ott, 1989; Van Maanen, 1988), as opposed to the historical analysis of documents. Organizational researchers considering a historical perspective should be aware of a series of misconceptions in organization studies concerning archival research. These misconceptions can be summarized as follows (distilled from Strati, 2000, pp. 158–159; see also Martin, 2002, pp. 348, 352):

- History consists of a repository of facts that can be used to confirm or refute organizational theories.
- Historical analysis of company documentation does not interfere in the dynamics of an organization.
- Company documents have already been collected and organized by companies before a researcher can analyze them.
- Archival research is not a proper method of empirical organizational research because instead of being directly generated in the course of organizational research, historical data are merely collected.
- The validity and reliability of company documentation must be questioned more than other sources, since it has been collected and processed for the purpose of legitimating a company.
- History is synonymous with the organizational memory shared by members of an organization.

HISTORY AS A REPOSITORY OF FACTS

Organizational researchers tend to regard history as a repository of facts, or they castigate historians for holding such a naive view of history. However, philosophers of history have long recognized the ambiguity of history. As Hegel wrote, "The term *History* unites the objective with the subjective side. . . . It comprehends not less what has *happened*, than the *narration* of what has happened" (cited in White, 1987, pp. 11–12).

As a result of this inherent ambiguity, history has always had to tackle epistemological questions such as "How can we know about the past? What does it mean to explain historical events? Is objective knowledge possible?" (Fay, 1998, p. 2). However, historians often evade such questions by practicing a

> sleight of hand . . . hiding the fact that all history is the study, not of past events that are gone forever from perception, but rather of the "traces" of those events distilled into documents and monuments on one side, and the praxis of present social formations on the other. These "traces" are the raw materials of the historian's discourse, rather than the events themselves. (White, 1987, p. 102)

Historians seek to "reconstruct the past" mainly by studying its documentary "traces" (Callinicos, 1995, p. 65), whereas for organizational ethnographers, "The history that counts is . . . embedded in the daily practices and symbolic life of the group studied" (Van Maanen, 1988, p. 72). *What passes for history in organizational studies usually consists of interpretations of studies that have already been carried out by historians rather than original historical research.* This reinforces an impression that historical "facts" come ready-made and detracts from appreciating "the historian's almost alchemical gift of transmuting old records in archives into the struggles and passions of the once-living human beings of whom these documents are the traces" (Callinicos, 1989, p. viii).

HISTORICAL ANALYSIS AND ORGANIZATIONAL DYNAMICS

If history is merely required to frame contemporary research on an organization, then access to company documentation is probably not required. Sufficient information can often be found in publicly available sources such as published company histories, annual reports, prospectuses, newspapers, trade directories, house journals, trade press, trade catalogues, and parliamentary papers (Orbell, 1987, p. 9). Most of these sources can be consulted without having to contact the companies being researched, and they are a mainstay for comparative historical surveys of companies (e.g., Whittington & Mayer, 2000). But if history is to provide more than background information, and if the company being researched is still in existence, then access will probably be required to the historical documents held by the company itself. The situation facing researchers who propose to use company documentation is one that business historians are all too familiar with: "Many firms are conservative in their access policy . . . and normally they will insist on vetting any publication which results before it goes to press. This is understandable, for the records are the private property of the company, and businesses need to ensure customer and employee confidentiality—some, such as banks, especially so" (Armstrong, 1991, p. 25).

A small number of companies in the United Kingdom have archivists, but the majority have "no formal in-house provision for the care and administration of their historical records" (Orbell, 1987, p. 12). The *Directory of Corporate Archives*, produced by the Business Archives Council (Richmond & Turton, 1997), lists 88 British businesses that "offer access to their archives on a quasi-formal basis," most of which employ an archivist. However, noninclusion in the *Directory* should not be taken to mean that a company does not possess a significant collection of historical documents or that access will automatically be denied. Cadbury, for example, does not appear in the *Directory*.

In 1983, Sir Adrian Cadbury, then chairman of Cadbury Schweppes, granted access to the historical documents held by the company at its main Bournville site in southwest Birmingham, England, to a team of organizational researchers from Aston University in Birmingham. The purpose of the archival research was to provide a historical orientation for a case study of changes in work organization at Cadbury (Smith, Child, & Rowlinson, 1990). As the doctoral researcher in the team, I was assigned to the historical research and spent much of my time from 1983 to 1987 poring over documents in the Cadbury library (Rowlinson, 1987). In retrospect, I have come to realize that this was a rare opportunity for an organizational researcher to conduct a detailed historical study of company documents. Few researchers are ever allowed the level of access that I was granted to such an extensive private collection of company documents without being commissioned to write an authorized history of the company concerned (Coleman, 1987).

As with ethnographic research (Turner, 1988, p. 114), my historical research at Cadbury was the product of a relationship between me, as a researcher, and members of the organization. The staff in Cadbury's company library made access to documents a reality on a daily basis, allocating me space to work and often providing an understanding of the documents I was studying based on their long service with the company. It is inevitable that a researcher comes to identify with an organization and its members, and subsequently I have often felt duplicitous for disclosing an interpretation of my data that is critical of Cadbury. The ethnographic researcher who criticizes an organization can hide behind anonymity by using a pseudonym for the organization in which research took place. But the historical researcher is answerable to the organization members who granted access if, as is expected in business history, the company is named when the research is written up.

COLLECTION AND ORGANIZATION
OF COMPANY DOCUMENTATION

Business historians warn that the state of many collections of company documents is unlikely to match the expectations of organizational researchers. As an
organizational researcher, I found the sight of the historical documents held by
Cadbury daunting. The documents were stored in various places around the factory. Two large cupboards in a corridor in the basement were stuffed full of
papers and files. If there was any organization in these cupboards, it was not
apparent. I was allowed to rummage through the documents, which mostly consisted of large bound annual volumes containing minutes of committee meetings. When I found volumes that looked interesting, I could take them to the
Cadbury library to read through.

One set of documents was set apart from the rest. These were the Cadbury
board minutes and accompanying files, which were kept in a room of their own
on the top floor of the main office block, adjacent to the directors' offices, which
symbolized a reverence for the firm's history. The minutes start from 1899, when
Cadbury converted from a partnership to become a private limited company.
Each annual volume of board minutes has an accompanying volume of the board
file, containing correspondence and reports. In the earliest years, the board minutes and documents in the files were handwritten in an impressive style, which I
often found difficult to decipher. The historical documents held at Cadbury are
best described as constituting a "collection" rather than an "archive," as the term
archive carries connotations, for historians, of documents having been organized
and catalogued by an archivist.

Generation of Historical Data

Organizational ethnographers maintain that they "face the problem that their
texts . . . taken from the field must first be constructed," whereas the texts used by
historians and literary critics come "prepackaged" (Van Maanen, 1988, p. 76). But
historians maintain that their sources are *not* the same as literary texts, since historical texts have to be constructed (Evans, 1997, p. 110). Although the term *text*
can be taken to mean any written document, qualitative organizational researchers usually take historical documents to consist of published material, such
as books, magazines, and newspapers (Denzin & Lincoln, 2000, p. 375). Qualitative documentary research is equated with a deep and detailed analysis of a small
sample of such publicly available texts (Silverman, 2000, pp. 42–43). But this does
not correspond to the task that faced me when I was confronted with the historical documents in the Cadbury collection.

Just as the organizational ethnographer faces choices over what to record in
the field, so the historian has to decide which documents to consult and how to

take notes from them. After seeing the extent of the Cadbury collection, I decided to restrict my "primary" research to the documentation it contained and to forego documentary research in other libraries, such as the Birmingham public library. There were two pragmatic reasons for this decision. First, it limited my "archive" to manageable proportions. Second, in case access to the Cadbury collection was not extended beyond the duration of the research project, it seemed sensible to make the most of the access I had been granted while it lasted.

From the vast array of documents in the Cadbury collection, I selected for consultation those that appeared most likely to shed light on the management of labor. The procedure that I followed (if it can be called that) was to take a volume of minutes, such as the board minutes or the Works Council minutes, and to skim the pages trying to spot any item of interest. (Later volumes of the board minutes and of some committees included an index, and I could note any entries in the index that looked as if they might be of interest.) For each item of interest I made notes on a 5″ × 8″ record card. It was also possible to photocopy particularly interesting documents. What I now refer to as my "data" from the research on Cadbury consists of four boxes containing approximately 4,000 record cards and four indexed files full of photocopies, which I can consult when writing about Cadbury without revisiting the Cadbury collection. The record cards contain all my handwritten notes on the documents that I consulted during the research. In addition to the board minutes, I examined various volumes of minutes for other management committees, minutes for the separate Men's and Women's Works Councils, from their inception in 1918, and the *Bournville Works Magazine*. Of course, some of the cards have only a few lines, whereas others are filled with verbatim notes of what appears in the documents. My most detailed notes are from the board minutes. I have one full box of nearly 1,000 record cards in chronological order for all volumes of the board minutes from 1899 to 1929. To take one year as an example, board meetings in 1916 were more or less weekly, and more than 800 minutes were taken. Out of these my data consist of notes on 55 minutes from 35 meetings.

As with other qualitative methods in organization studies, only a small proportion of my data is ever likely to be used in published outputs. However, the versatility of the enormous volume of data I generated in the craftlike fashion of a historian, rather than a narrowly prescribed procedure, means that I have been able to use the data to address a range of historiographical debates of relevance to organization studies—namely, the early application of scientific management by Cadbury in 1913 (Rowlinson, 1988); the symbolism of the Cadbury centenary celebrations in 1931 in the company's corporate culture (Rowlinson & Hassard, 1993); the relationship between the corporate culture and the adoption of a multidivisional structure by Cadbury in 1969 (Rowlinson, 1995); the nostalgic historiography of Quaker firms (Rowlinson, 1998); and the heritage view of history presented by Cadbury World, the firm's visitor attraction that opened in 1990 (Rowlinson, 2002). I have also shared my data with other historians.

Validity and Reliability of Company Documentation

From a business historian's point of view, interviews are seen as supplementary to documentary research, because

> without extensive research in corporate records it is all too easy to accept one's informants' statements at face value or to mistake an external façade for an internal reality. Documentary research provides an excellent means to test the accuracy of different images and perceptions of the organization and to compare espoused and actual values. It may also furnish an alternative to the official version of the firm's history. (Dellheim, 1986, p. 20)

In contrast to the historian's confidence in documentary research, the view of organizational researchers seems to be that the problems of meaning and understanding in history are best overcome by qualitative, in-depth interviewing. This consigns "the analysis of documentary materials" to a supplementary role of "providing background information about an organization and those who belong to it" (Strati, 2000, p. 158). Even research that is noted in strategy and organizational studies for its use of historical documents mainly does so in order to supplement long semistructured interviews (e.g., Pettigrew, 1985, p. 40).

It may be the case, as organizational researchers allege, that "official publications such as brochures, annual reports, and press releases . . . typically reflect only what a team of executives and public relations people want to convey publicly" (Ott, 1989, p. 109). But the value of such publications as historical documents is that they can reveal what *past* executives wanted to be publicly conveyed, which may well be different to present executives. Commemorative company histories, for example, reveal much about the concerns of companies at the time they were commissioned (Rowlinson & Hassard, 1993, p. 306). Unpublished, private company documents, such as the minutes of meetings, are *not* composed, collected, and processed to establish subsequent social legitimation but to provide a record of decisions taken. As such, they are the outcome of a political process. The value of such archival materials is that they have not been collected, or concocted, for the benefit of the researcher, unlike stories and reconstructed memories elicited in interviews.

Historians do face the problem that the records of businesses that are no longer in existence are difficult to locate, and even the records of some companies that are still in existence may be very thin (Armstrong, 1991, p. 25). This tends to bias historical research toward companies such as Cadbury, where the importance attributed to the company's history results in a degree of reverence for historical documents that ensures their preservation. But I found little evidence to suggest that the documents collected by Cadbury had been continually or systematically edited in the light of current concerns for the company's public image. The biggest fear for historical researchers is that masses of documents are likely to be unsystematically discarded by companies. Historical documents may be discarded, but it is difficult for them to be systematically doctored. If a mass of documents has been preserved, as at Cadbury, then one of the most difficult tasks for the historical researcher is selecting documents from the sheer volume available.

History and Organizational Memory

Organizational studies tend to conflate history and memory, as in Weick's (1995) wry contention that every manager is a historian, and "any decision maker is only as good as his or her memory" (pp. 184–185). Lowenthal (1985, pp. 200–214), a historian concerned with representations of heritage, has described a distinction between history and memory that can be extended to distinguish between organizational history and organizational memory. Lowenthal maintains that memory—and by extension we can also say organizational memory—is *not* a repository of knowledge about past events. Instead, it consists of recollections of past events that express organization members' feelings about those events. Insofar as these feelings summarize organization members' sense of "past experience" (Weick, 1995, p. 111), they cannot be gainsaid, which means that there is necessarily a tension between memory and history, since history consists of a dialogue in which the past is continually, and deliberately, reinterpreted. Through an interpretation of documentary sources, a historian can contradict the past that organization members remember, which may be discomfiting.

Academic business historians may be wary of accepting a commission to write the history of a company in case it is seen as "a form of inferior journalistic hack-work" (Coleman, 1987, p. 145), and companies are advised that "book reviewers and the general reader are inherently skeptical about the objectivity and balance in 'management-sanctioned' corporate histories" (Campion, 1987, p. 31). Despite conceding that "corporate sponsorship usually means the loss of a critical stance," business historians still maintain that "good history is good business" (Ryant, 1988, p. 563), that it can help managers by "getting things, events and facts into shared memory" (Tedlow, 1986, p. 82) and "encourage investor interest and, not insignificantly, spark employee pride" (Campion, 1987). Hence, the proclamations of independence and objectivity on the part of business historians who do accept a commission to write a company history can be questioned. But even without doubting the integrity of business historians, it can be argued that the process of commissioning a company history favors a particular kind of historian writing a distinctive type of history (Rowlinson, 2000; Rowlinson & Procter, 1999).

My view is that, if companies are wary of letting historians rummage around in their archives, it is not because they know what is in the archives but because they *do not know* what is in them. Companies are right to be fearful of what documents a historian might find in the archives and how a reinterpretation of history might undermine their organizational memory and adversely affect their public image. Once found, a historical document becomes part of the historian's data. Even if the original document is destroyed, the knowledge of its existence resides with the historian and may become public knowledge if published. A problem for companies is that their preference for commissioning uncritical historians to write their histories has often produced unreliable as well as dull tomes that remain unread. But letting critical researchers comb their archives for contentious events with relevance for contemporary historiographical debates has the potential to be damaging for companies.

PERIODIZATION AND WRITING STRATEGIES

I now turn to the problem of periodization that confronts a historical researcher if chronology is to be used as a framework for analyzing and presenting historical data. Periodization involves the identification of suitable places to start and stop, as well as significant turning points in a narrative. It is barely noticed in qualitative organizational research, but the various procedures used for analyzing data, such as coding interviews or categorizing stories, represent alternatives to a chronological ordering of events. For example, a small sample of the volumes of Cadbury board minutes could be coded according to various criteria, such as the terminology used. Instead, I consulted all volumes of the board minutes from 1899 through to 1940, as well as from 1966 up to 1969, when Cadbury merged with Schweppes, taking note of any interesting items. I store the record cards on which I recorded the data in chronological order. The stored historical data could be said to constitute a chronicle, a chronologically ordered sequence of events (White, 1987, pp. 16–20). To construct a narrative, I needed to identify themes and connections between the events recorded. The procedure that I used resembled coding for interviews, in that I read through the record cards, marking the cards pertaining to a particular theme, such as the application of scientific management, and listing them. Not the least of the difficulties in this task was identifying connections between the records from various sources, such as the board minutes and the *Bournville Works Magazine*, in order to reconstruct events. The more the data are processed and interpreted, the less the final narrative will appear to be a mere chronicle, a purely chronological, day-by-day, year-by-year, ordering of data.

Periodization in the history of a company can come in various forms. The approach I used for Cadbury entailed identifying the origins of a series of institutions that developed in relation to the management of labor (Rowlinson, 1987; summarized in Rowlinson & Hassard, 1993, pp. 310–314). My periodization emerged from examining the data for Cadbury rather than external events in wider society, such as wars or changes in government. In other words, I did not assume that periods such as pre– or post–World War I would necessarily correspond to periodization within Cadbury. This meant that I collected a lot of data on the company from before and after the period I decided to write about in order to identify the period itself. My focus on the period 1879 to 1919 starts with the move to a purpose-built factory at Bournville in 1879; followed by the founding of the Bournville Village Trust in 1900 and the building of a "model village," the development of welfare for employees, the introduction of sophisticated personnel management techniques, and the formalization of a rigid sexual division of labor during the 1900s; the introduction of significant elements of scientific management from 1913; and, finally, the implementation of a Works Council plan in 1918. By 1919, the major labor management institutions associated with Cadbury were in place. As a result of my theoretical orientation, I traced the sources of ideas for each of these institutions to the then-contemporary social movements rather than the inspiration of individual members of the Cadbury family.

My approach to periodization, which could be called an institutional approach, can be contrasted with that of Charles Dellheim, who has studied Cadbury from a corporate culture perspective. Dellheim's (1987) account of the Cadbury corporate culture is bounded by symbolic events: "The period explored . . . begins in 1861, when George [1839–1922] and Richard [1835–1899] Cadbury took over the family business. It ends in 1931, when capitalist and worker celebrated the firm's values at its centenary. A historical approach to company cultures begins with the guiding beliefs of the founders" (p. 14). Dellheim attributes the development of the Cadbury corporate culture to the religious beliefs of the Cadbury family, namely their membership of the Religious Society of Friends (the Quakers).

Periodizing events through the use of company documentation tends to obscure the everyday experience of organizational participants that is constituted by regularities that are not recorded because they are taken for granted. Dellheim (1986) concedes that

> the historian who examines a firm exclusively from the viewpoint of founder-owners or managers runs the risk of naively assuming that the official view they put forth is accurate. Hence, it is also necessary to study company cultures from the perspective of workers. . . . The major obstacle to understanding workers' attitudes is the relative scarcity of source materials. (p. 14)

But the methodological problem of studying everyday life through company documentation does not merely arise from the hierarchical privileging of senior management records in the preservation of documents. Even if they are preserved, the minutes of workers' representatives' meetings, no less than board minutes, generally fail to record the stories from everyday life that can be interpreted to reveal the meanings that workers and board members attach to their experiences. I could find little in the way of personal correspondence, diaries, or unofficial newsletters, which might be more revealing, among the official company documents in the Cadbury collection.

Periodization emphasizes the singularity of historical events. My periodization of Cadbury, for example, stresses the firm's singularity in its adoption of scientific management ahead of most other British companies (Rowlinson, 1988). According to Dellheim (1987, p. 14), Cadbury "was not a typical British firm," although it is representative of the Quakers in business. By contrast, the focus on everyday experience in organizational ethnography is usually predicated on demonstrating typicality rather than singularity. The more singular and significant a company is deemed to be for business history, the less usefully typical it becomes for an organizational ethnography of everyday life.

The emphasis on periodization of events and singularity, as opposed to everyday life and typicality, has implications for the writing strategy in business history. As Czarniawska (1999) observes, organizational ethnographers are able to present findings for an organization that "may not exist, and yet everything that is said about it may be true . . . that is, it may be credible in the light of other texts" concerning similar organizations. In an effort to preserve anonymity for informants, and as a result of the stylization that suggests that findings can be generalized, the texts of organizational ethnographers tend toward "fictionalization" (p. 38). Revealing the unique periodization of an organization through narrative history derived from company documentation would undermine this fictionalized typicality.

However, the fictionalization that is permitted in organization studies would be anathema to historians. Business historians take for granted that the organizations they write about have actually existed in history and that their interpretations refer to the documentary traces of past events that can be verified through extensive footnotes citing sources. Verification becomes increasingly important if the interpretation of an organization's past emphasizes its singularity rather than typicality. Footnotes are part of the rhetoric of history (Hexter, 1998). In contrast to organizational studies, historians frequently relegate actual debate with other historians to the footnotes. But, more important, for my argument here, it is in the footnotes that the nature and interpretation of the evidence is laid out. If nonhistorians, including organizational researchers, read historical writing without reference to the footnotes, then they will miss the implicit debate about sources. The discourse of history can be described as debate by footnote. Each historian marshals her evidence to support an argument, hoping to bury her opponent under a barrage of footnotes citing superior sources.

CONCLUSION

Qualitative researchers using company documentation face a choice of whether to research and write in the genre of business history or organizational studies. Business history requires an extensive trawl through a mass of documentation, whereas in organizational studies, an intensive analysis of a limited selection of documents is likely to be acceptable (e.g., Forster, 1994). In organizational studies, an account of the research methodology is required, whereas such an account would be unusual in business history. Reflection on the nature of history itself is likely to be indulged in organizational studies, as in the emerging field of organizational history (Carroll, 2002). But such reflection, no matter how well informed, is rarely required in business history. In organizational studies, periodization tends to be subordinated to theory and macrohistorical generalizations. In business history periodization is a perennial problem as the data are chronologically ordered, which means that turning points and end points tend to be identified from the data themselves rather than imposed from prior theoretical postures.

Paradoxically, the scientistic pretensions of organization studies facilitate fictionalization through a demonstration of the typicality of everyday life presented in qualitative research. In business history, conscious fictionalization would not even be considered as a writing strategy. The implicit commitment to verisimilitude through verification makes writing in business history immensely satisfying as it can reinforce a naive sense of realism. Unfortunately, the different criteria for assessing truth claims have meant that organizational researchers and business historians have hitherto had little appreciation of each other's genres.

FURTHER READING

Scholarly historical research of the highest quality with numerous footnotes citing company documents can be found in the long-established journals *Business History* (UK) and *Business History Review* (United States). In recent years journals such as *Enterprise and Society* and *Journal of Industrial History* have encouraged more explicitly theoretically oriented articles but still with extensive footnotes citing company documents. Chandler's (1962) *Strategy and Structure* remains by far the most influential book in strategy and organizational studies, written by a business historian and based on company documents. Pettigrew's (1985) *Awakening Giant*, along with Whipp and Clark's (1986) *Innovation and the Auto Industry*, are outstanding examples of strategy and organizational researchers who have used extensive collections of company documents. Evans's (2001) *In Defence of History* provides an accessible introduction to the outlook of contemporary English-speaking practicing historians.

Theoretical writing by historians and philosophers of history is to be found in the journal *History and Theory*. The best theoretical articles from that journal over many years, dealing with issues such as the status of narrative (which is receiving increasing attention in organizational studies), have been put together by Fay, Pomper, and Vann (1998) in their edited collection *History and Theory*.

REFERENCES

Armstrong, J. (1991). An introduction to archival research in business history. *Business History*, *33*(1), 7–34.

Callinicos, A. (1989). *Making history*. Cambridge: Polity.

Callinicos, A. (1995). *Theories and narratives: Reflections on the philosophy of history*. Cambridge: Polity.

Campion, F. D. (1987). How to handle the corporate history. *Public Relations Journal*, *43*, 31–32.

Carroll, C. E. (2002). Introduction: The strategic use of the past and the future in organizational change. *Journal of Organizational Change Management*, *15*(6), 556–562.

Chandler, A. D. (1962) *Strategy and structure: Chapters in the history of the industrial enterprise*. Cambridge, MA: MIT Press.

Clark, P., & Rowlinson, M. (in press). The treatment of history in organization studies: Toward an "historic turn"? *Business History*.

Coleman, D. (1987). The uses and abuses of business history. *Business History*, *29*(2), 141–156.

Czarniawska, B. (1999) *Writing management: Organization theory as a literary genre*. Oxford: Oxford University Press.

Dellheim, C. (1986). Business in time: The historian and corporate culture. *Public Historian*, *8*(2), 9–22.

Dellheim, C. (1987). The creation of a company culture: Cadburys, 1861–1931. *American Historical Review*, *92*(1): 13–43.

Denzin, N. K., & Lincoln, Y. S. (2000). Strategies of inquiry. In N. K. Denzin & Y. S. Lincoln (Eds.), *Handbook of qualitative research* (2nd ed., pp. 367–378). London: Sage.

Evans, R. J. (1997). *In defence of history*. London: Granta.

Fay, B. (1998). Introduction. In B. Fay, P. Pomper, & R. T. Vann (Eds.), *History and theory: Contemporary readings*. Malden MA: Blackwell.

Fay, B., Pomper, P., & Vann, R. T. (Eds.). (1998). *History and theory: Contemporary readings*. Malden, MA: Blackwell.

Forster, N. (1994). The analysis of company documentation. In C. Cassell & G. Symon (Eds.), *Qualitative methods in organizational research* (pp. 147–166). London: Sage.

Hexter, J. H. (1998). The rhetoric of history. In B. Fay, P. Pomper, & R. T. Vann (Eds.), *History and theory: Contemporary readings*. Malden MA: Blackwell.

Johnson, B., & Christensen. L. (2003). *Educational research* (2nd ed.). Boston: Allyn & Bacon.

Johnson, B., & Christensen. L. (2005). Lectures: Historical research. Retrieved from http://www.southalabama.edu/coe/bset/johnson/dr_johnson/index2.htm.

Lowenthal, D. (1985). *The past is a foreign country*. Cambridge: Cambridge University Press.

Martin, J. (2002). *Organizational culture: Mapping the terrain*. London: Sage.

Orbell, J. (1987) *A guide to tracing the history of a business*. Aldershot, UK: Gower.

Ott, J. S. (1989) *The organizational culture perspective*. Pacific Grove, CA: Brooks/Cole.

Pettigrew, A. M. (1985) *The awakening giant: Continuity and change in imperial chemical industries*. Oxford: Blackwell.

Richmond, L., & Turton, A. (1997). *Directory of corporate archives: A guide to British businesses which maintain archive facilities* (4th ed.). London: Business Archives Council.

Rowlinson, M. (1987). *Cadburys' new factory system, 1879–1919*. Unpublished doctoral dissertation, Aston University, Birmingham.

Rowlinson, M. (1988). The early application of scientific management by Cadbury. *Business History*, 30(4), 377–395.

Rowlinson, M. (1995). Strategy, structure and culture: Cadbury, divisionalization and merger in the 1960s. *Journal of Management Studies*, 32(2), 121–140.

Rowlinson, M. (1998, Autumn). Quaker employers' review essay. *Historical Studies in Industrial Relations*, 6, 163–198.

Rowlinson, M. (2000). Review of N. Ferguson, *The world's banker: The history of the House of Rothschild*. *Human Relations*, 53(4), 573–586.

Rowlinson, M. (2001). Business history and organization theory. *Journal of Industrial History*, 4(1), 1–23.

Rowlinson, M. (2002). Public history review essay: Cadbury World. *Labour History Review*, 67(1), 101–119.

Rowlinson, M., & Hassard, J. (1993). The invention of corporate culture: A history of the histories of Cadbury. *Human Relations*, 46, 299–326.

Rowlinson, M., & Procter, S. (1999). Organizational culture and business history. *Organization Studies*, 20(3), 369–396.

Ryant, C. (1988). Oral history and business history. *Journal of American History*, 75(2), 560–66.

Silverman, D. (2000). *Doing qualitative research: A practical handbook*. London: Sage.

Smith, C., Child, J., & Rowlinson, M. (1990). *Reshaping work: The Cadbury experience*. Cambridge: Cambridge University Press.

Strati, A. (2000). *Theory and method in organization studies: Paradigms and choices*. London: Sage.

Tedlow, R. S. (1986, January–February). Why history matters to managers. *Harvard Business Review*, 81–88.

Tosh, J. (1991). *The pursuit of history* (2nd ed.). Harlow: Longman.

Turner, B. A. (1988). Connoisseurship in the study of organizational cultures. In A. Bryman (Ed.), *Doing research in organizations* (pp. 108–122). London: Routledge.

Van Maanen, J. (1988). *Tales of the field: On writing ethnography*. Chicago: University of Chicago Press.

Weick, K. (1995). *Sensemaking in organizations*. London: Sage.

Whipp, R., & Clark, P. (1986). *Innovation and the auto industry*. London: Pinter.

White, H. (1987). *The content of the form: Narrative discourse and historical representation*. Baltimore, MD: Johns Hopkins University Press.

White, H. (1995). Response to Arthur Marwick. *Journal of Contemporary History*, 30, 233–246.

Whittington, R., & Mayer, M. (2000). *The European corporation: Strategy, structure, and social science*. Oxford: Oxford University Press.

PART FOUR

Mixed Methods Research

Mixed Methods Research: Developments, Debates, and Dilemmas

John W. Creswell, *University of Nebraska–Lincoln*
J. David Creswell, *University of California–Los Angeles*

Calls have been made for social and human science researchers to expand their research methodologies beyond traditional quantitative approaches (Hoshmand, 1989; Ponterotto & Grieger, 1999; Johnson & Onwuegbuzie, 2004; Morrow & Smith, 2000; Gergen, 2001; Hanson, Creswell, Plano Clark, & Petska, 2005. As qualitative approaches find increased acceptance within the social sciences, it is likely that empirically oriented investigators will increasingly look for ways to expand and diversify their methods for tackling research problems. One specific approach—mixed methods research—holds potential to have wide application for conducting research in organizations. In fact, some scholars indicate that it represents the next evolutionary trend (the "third methodological movement," according to Tashakkori & Teddlie [2003, p. 45]) following the emergence of first quantitative and then qualitative approaches. Within 5 years, we predict, most social science research studies will involve the collection and analysis of both qualitative and quantitative data (Creswell, 2004). Mixed methods will reside as a research design much the way investigators view randomized control trials or ethnographies.

The momentum for mixed methods research has evolved through nine books largely devoted to this methodology since 1979 (Cook & Reichardt, 1979; Bryman, 1989; Brewer & Hunter, 1989; Reichardt & Rallis, 1994; Greene & Caracelli, 1997; Newman & Benz, 1998; Tashakkori & Teddlie, 1998; Bamberger, 2000; Creswell, 2003b). A recent 10th book, the *Handbook on Mixed Methods Research in the Behavioral and Social Sciences* (Tashakkori & Teddlie, 2003), provides 26 chapters on topics ranging from the philosophical foundations to methods and applications. In addition, several authors have published syntheses in select fields, such as evaluation (Datta, 1994; Greene, Caracelli, & Graham, 1989), in higher education studies (Creswell, Goodchild, & Turner, 1996), in counseling psychology (Hanson et al., 2005), and in family medicine (Creswell, Fetters, & Ivankova, 2004). Also, throughout the last 30 years, writers have discussed the philosophical and methodological issues in mixed methods research (e.g., Caracelli & Greene, 1993; Morgan, 1998; Morse, 1991) and applications across the social and human sciences, such as medicine (Creswell et al., 2004), management, sociology, and nursing (Tashakkori & Teddlie, 2003). Funding agencies, such as the National Institutes of Health (NIH), have established guidelines for combined quantitative and qualitative research (NIH, 1999), and private foundations have held recent workshops on mixed methods approaches (Creswell, 2003a).

Despite this outpouring of writings, many researchers are unfamiliar with mixed methods as a distinct methodological design. Perhaps this problem is due to the lack of communication among disciplines, such as evaluation, sociology, and medicine. More likely, scholars have yet to establish a consensus, even among mixed methods writers (Johnson & Onwuegbuzie, 2004) on fundamental topics such as a definition of this design, the types of research procedures used within it, the philosophical foundation for mixed methods inquiry, and the challenges in using this approach. In light of these needs, the intent of this discussion is to introduce researchers to mixed methods research, the types of designs that they might consider using when conducting research in organizations, and the critical philosophical and methodological issues in conducting this form of inquiry.

A DEFINITION

Mixed methods research is a research design or methodology for collecting, analyzing, and mixing both quantitative and qualitative data in a single study or series of studies in order to better understand research problems (Creswell, 2003b). This definition, evolving from a more general version of it in 1989 by Greene, Caracelli, and Graham, requires close inspection to understand the nature of mixed methods inquiries.

Consider the name of this design: mixed methods. This name seldom appears in the literature, and a review of many methodological discussions and published studies shows a wide range of terms used by authors. It has been called multitrait/multimethod research (Campbell & Fiske, 1959), integrating or interrelating qualitative and quantitative approaches (Fielding & Fielding, 1986; Steckler, McLeroy, Goodman, Bird, & McCormick, 1992), methodological triangulation (Morse, 1991), multimethod designs (Miles & Huberman, 1994), mixed methodology approaches (Tashakkori & Teddlie, 1998), or combined quantitative and qualitative research (Creswell, 1994). More recently, with the publication of the *Handbook* (Tashakkori & Teddlie, 2003), the term *mixed methods* has been frequently employed, and perhaps this name will be more consistently employed by inquirers.

The name aside, the definition calls attention to an investigation in which the researcher collects both qualitative and quantitative data. Qualitative data consist of collecting open-ended information without predetermined response categories, such as in unstructured observations; whereas quantitative data consist of close-ended information in which the researcher sets in advance the response possibilities, such as an instrument with responses from strongly disagree to strong agree. This further requires some understanding of what constitutes both forms of data: a dichotomy that is not always clear. Some designs naturally collect both forms of data, such as ethnography, which has a long tradition of gathering quantitative survey data and qualitative participant observation data (LeCompte & Schensul, 1999). Other designs, such as content analysis, involve both forms of data as well, when researchers transform qualitative data into quantitative scores, or a survey that incorporates both close-ended questions as well as open-ended options at the end of the instrument.

Another aspect of the definition is that researchers analyze both the quantitative and qualitative data. Each type of data involves its own distinct analysis approaches. Qualitative researchers analyze text or image data (e.g., transcriptions, field notes from observations, journals, pictures), while quantitative researchers analyze numeric data. In qualitative research, one finds some numeric data analyzed (e.g., when ethnographers or case study writers present a descriptive table of demographic information, or in quantitative research when text data are converted into frequencies), but overall, the two forms of data analyzed are distinct. So also are the procedures for analysis that range from statistical tests (descriptive, inferential) and effect size checks in quantitative research as compared with thematic development of qualitative research that begins by coding text segments, building themes or categories from the codes, and interrelating the themes, such as that found in grounded theory or the chronology of a narrative study. Although some writers have minimized the differences in analytic procedures (e.g., Punch, 1998, discusses how the process used in deriving qualitative themes bears close resemblance to item clustering in factor analysis), the distinctions, on balance, are more different than similar.

Another aspect of the definition—*mixing*—requires further comment. The inclusion of this term into the definition is a recent development (Creswell, 2003), suggesting that some form of mixing or interrelating the data provides better insight into research problems than collecting only quantitative or qualitative data or collecting both forms but not forging a connection between them. The advantage of collecting both forms results in quantitative data yielding generalizable trends and qualitative data providing in-depth voices and experiences of individuals within specific settings or contexts (Greene & Caracelli, 1997). To capture both trends and in-depth perspectives provides more information than either quantitative or qualitative alone can offer. To combine the two forms of data seems to enhance the utility of each.

This utility can be seen in two procedures for mixing. First, researchers can *integrate* or converge the quantitative and qualitative data by collecting both forms of data and then combine, integrate, or compare the two data sets. This integration requires some thought because it involves merging numeric data with text data. A typical procedure is to integrate the two forms of data in a discussion section of a research article by first stating a statistical finding and then illustrating the finding with a qualitative quote. Integration can also occur when researchers first analyze the qualitative data for codes, and then convert or transform the codes into numbers (e.g., 15 individuals talked about the code "safety"). Investigators then input these numbers into a statistical program for descriptive or inferential analysis.

A second approach to mixing involves *connecting* the quantitative and qualitative data collection and analysis. For example, the first phase of a project yields statistical results that investigators can then follow up with in-depth qualitative interviews with outliers, or with a normative subsample. In this example, the researcher can interpret and expand on the quantitative data analysis by following up with qualitative data collection. The mixing involves connecting the quantitative data analysis phase with the qualitative data collection phase.

The definition also suggests that mixed methods studies can be single investigations or multiple investigations within a program of study. The focus of mixed methods writers to date has been on the single investigation (e.g., Creswell et al., 2003); however, mixed methods designs may be implemented across studies, an approach typically taken within large, multiyear-funded projects. This approach is not new to most social scientists, given that they have long engaged in programmatic, multimethod approaches to understanding phenomena (Campbell & Fiske, 1959). As one example, some recent approaches have focused on collecting multiple forms of qualitative data (e.g., interviews and observations) or on quantitative data collection (e.g., experimental data and survey data) in a series of studies (Morse, 2003). Whether investigators prefer using mixed methods designs in a single study or in a program of research, these approaches can greatly strengthen the validity and insight into the research question beyond what a single design can provide (Morse, 2003).

Whether the mixed methods component is either a single investigation or more than one, a challenge in conducting mixed methods research is that social scientists will need to develop methodological skills in both quantitative and qualitative data collection and analysis, skills that are not always possessed by the lone researcher. Thus, initial mixed methods investigations can profit from teams of individuals with expertise in both qualitative and quantitative research (Hanson et al., 2005). Moreover, this design requires demanding resources over a sustained time. Thus, it comes as no surprise that large, funded, multiyear federal projects are easier to conduct in a mixed methods format than small inquiries by single investigators. The lone researcher needs, at a minimum, basic skills of quantitative and qualitative data collection and analysis and the resources to conduct this design. These skills involve collecting experimental, correlational, or survey quantitative data as well as conducting focus groups and interviews, observing, and gathering documents for qualitative data. Analysis involves descriptive and inferential analysis quantitatively, and thematic development qualitatively.

MIXED METHODS DESIGNS

With a basic understanding of the definition of mixed methods research, our attention can now turn to procedures for conducting this form of inquiry. Writers have identified the types of mixed methods designs and a classification of them, building on a basic typology in the field of evaluation (Greene et al., 1989). They reviewed 57 evaluation studies, developed a classification system for them based on the purpose of the design, and then analyzed the studies in terms of design characteristics. Their classification yielded four types: (1) quantitative and qualitative data could be combined to: use results from one method to elaborate on results from the other method (complementarity); (2) use results from one method to help develop or inform the other method (development); (3) recast results or methods from one method to questions or results from the other method (initiation); and (4) extend the breadth or range of inquiry by using different methods for different inquiry components (expansion) (Greene et al., 1989). Although many classifications have appeared since 1989 (see a review of these in Creswell et al., 2003), our discussion will focus on four primary designs typically found within the social science and human science literature.

Figures 18.1 and 18.2 illustrate these four designs (Creswell et al., 2003). The first two designs represent two-phase designs where quantitative and qualitative data are collected in sequence. The first is a *sequential explanatory design* that involves a quantitative data collection phase followed by a second phase of qualitative

Explanatory Mixed Methods Design

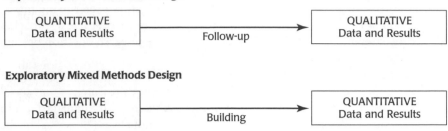

Exploratory Mixed Methods Design

Figure 18.1 Two Types of Sequential Designs

data collection. Uses of this design are to follow up on quantitative results from experiments, surveys, or correlational studies by probing the results in more depth through qualitative data such as focus groups, individual interviews, or observations. A similar design is the *sequential exploratory design* in which qualitative data collection is followed up with a second phase of quantitative data collection. This design is typically used to develop quantitative instruments when the variables are not known or to explore preliminary qualitative findings from a small group of people with a randomized sample from a larger population.

The second two designs collect quantitative and qualitative data in parallel at the same time in an investigation. The *triangulation design* collects both quantitative and qualitative data simultaneously so that the investigator can converge the data to make comparisons between detailed contextualized qualitative data and the more normative quantitative data. This design is used when researchers seek to compare the particular with the general or to validate quantitative data with qualitative data.

The final mixed methods design is the *nested design.* It is a slight variation on the triangulation design in which the quantitative and qualitative data are both collected at the same time, but less emphasis is given to one, and the quantitative research question/hypotheses addresses different constructs than the qualitative research question. A classic example of this design would be procedures in which the investigator's overall goal is to conduct a randomized control experimental

Triangulation Mixed Methods Design

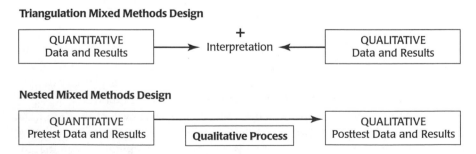

Nested Mixed Methods Design

Figure 18.2 Two Types of Concurrent Designs

trial to understand the impact of an intervention on outcomes, but at the same time, the researcher also seeks to understand the process that participants undergo during the study. In this design, the quantitative portion addresses outcomes, whereas the qualitative portion assesses process.

From these types of designs, it is clear that researchers make decisions about their procedures. Two types of procedural decisions owe much to Morgan (1998), who clarified that designs are driven by two decisions. Implementation decisions indicate whether the data will be collected in sequence (i.e., sequentially) or whether they will be gathered at the same or nearly the same time in the study (i.e., in parallel or concurrently). Unquestionably, the collection in sequence through two or more phases involves more time, and researchers may turn to the more efficient process of collecting data at the same time. This may explain why the triangulation design is the most popular in counseling psychology (Hanson et al., 2005) and is often used as a first choice in family medicine (Creswell et al., 2004). On the other hand, presenting a mixed methods study in sequential phases removes the awkward procedure of reconciling potentially conflicting quantitative and qualitative data (numbers and text data) in the triangulation design, and the use of phases provides a cleaner exposition than integrating the data in a written report. The author can present the first phase as a separate section followed by the second phase—this logic is easy to follow and understand within the complex data collection and analysis found in mixed methods inquiry.

Such complexity has led to the use of visual diagrams for the designs, visuals useful in proposals for funding and in presentations to graduate committees and conference participants. A notation system has been developed by Morse (1991). As shown in Figure 18.3, this system uses arrows to identify sequence and a "+" to identify concurrent data collection. The shorthand labels of "quan" and "qual" are used as well as capital letters for priority (i.e., QUAN) or lesser priority (i.e., quan). Beyond these notations, researchers can organize their visual diagram to include not only the general procedures but also the more detailed data collection steps, the "products" or "deliverables" to funding agencies, as well as a time line as shown in Figure 18.3. With increasing frequency, notational systems are developing to make the visuals more useful to explain the complex processes of mixed methods research, something called for by federal agencies (NIH, 1999).

PHILOSOPHICAL DEBATES IN MIXED METHODS RESEARCH

At a broader, more foundational level, procedures chosen by researchers relate to larger philosophical choices (Creswell, 2003b). These assumptions may be called knowledge claims, epistemologies, paradigms, or worldviews. Popular worldview stances are postpositivism, constructivism or interpretivism, and advocacy/participatory/critical perspectives (see, e.g., Lincoln & Guba, 1994). These philosophical assumptions inform aspects of inquiry such as what constitutes knowl-

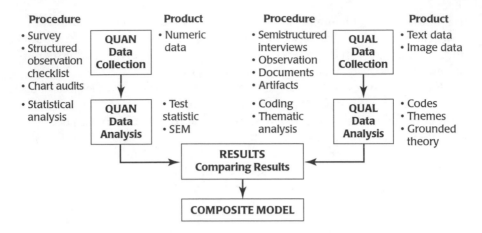

Figure 18.3 Concurrent Triangulation Design Visual Model

edge (ontology), how knowledge is known (epistemology), the values brought to the inquiry (axiology), the language used (rhetorical approach), and the process of the investigation (methodology) (Creswell, 2003b). The logic of inquiry flows from broad philosophical assumptions to specific questions, and then onto the methods used to answer the questions. Given the importance of these assumptions in the overall design, what philosophical assumptions form the foundation for conducting mixed methods research?

For more than 20 years, mixed methods writers have debated this question (see the "paradigm debate" by Reichardt & Rallis, 1994), and different answers have surfaced (Tashakkori & Teddlie, 2003, provide detailed discussions of the stances). The debate has led to stances that question the viability of mixed methods inquiries, to the use of a single worldview and the use of multiple worldviews.

One stance is that the postpositivist and interpretivist perspectives are not compatible, and hence researchers cannot conduct mixed methods research. Quantitative and qualitative approaches originate out of different worldviews (Lincoln & Guba, 1985; also see the "incompatibility thesis" from Smith & Heshusius, 1986). A corollary to this stance is that the paradigm or worldview must fit the methods (called the *paradigm-fit issue*). If certain methods "went" with certain worldviews (collect qualitative data using an interpretivist paradigm or collect quantitative data with a postpositivist paradigm), then mixed methods research is untenable. Both the incompatibility issue and the paradigm-method fit contributed, perhaps, to the slow development of consensus about the philosophical underpinning for mixed methods research.

Another stance has been the search for the "best" paradigm to fit mixed methods research. Two philosophical foundations have emerged: pragmatism and advocacy/emancipatory perspectives. Tashakkori and Teddlie (2003) cite 13 authors who embrace pragmatism as the philosophical foundation for mixed methods research. Pragmatism is a wide-ranging philosophical stance with roots in Peirce,

Dewey, and James and, more recently, with writers such as Rorty and West (Biesta & Burbules, 2003; Cherryholmes, 1992). From these authors, mixed methods researchers have drawn several ideas to serve as a philosophical basis for their research. Pragmatism advances multiple pluralistic approaches to knowing, using "what works" (highlighting the Deweyan consequences of inquiry as all important), a focus on the research questions as important with all types of methods to follow to answer the questions, and a rejection of a forced choice between postpositivsm and constructivism (Biesta & Burbules, 2003; Tashakkori & Teddlie, 2003). An alternative "best" paradigm is the advocacy/emancipatory framework. Mertens (2003) advocates for an emancipatory worldview for mixed methods research and creatively links this worldview to the stages in the process of research (e.g., searching the literature, writing research questions, and collecting data).

A final stance holds that rather than search for the "best" paradigm, one should employ multiple worldviews in mixed methods research. Greene and Caracelli (1997) advance a "dialectical" perspective in which researchers use these multiple worldviews, and these worldviews need to be made explicit and honored during the inquiry. In a slight refinement in this stance, Creswell (2003b) also argues for multiple worldviews but suggests that the worldview inform the questions asked and the methods or procedures of mixed methods inquiry. For example, in a design in which the researcher integrates both quantitative and qualitative data, pragmatism might represent the worldview that leads a researcher to this design because both forms of data are useful to address the problem. Alternatively, in a design in which the investigator begins with a survey and then follows up with several smaller qualitative interviews, the design seems to stem from more of a postpositivist perspective. Thus, although different stances on the worldview underpinning mixed methods research exist, many writers today advocate for pragmatism as the one best approach or the use of many worldviews that are each honored and explicitly conveyed.

Related to philosophical assumptions are the standards of rigor that should apply to mixed methods research. One benchmark in quantitative research has been that the research must be valid. Validity relates to the scores from instruments as well as the overall research design wherein the investigator minimizes the threats to internal and external validity (Creswell, 2003b). In qualitative research, the standards relate more to the accuracy of the findings as seen by the researchers, the participants in the study, or the readers of the report (Creswell & Miller, 2000). Interestingly, both quantitative and qualitative researchers have used many terms for types of validity (see the list of 40 terms in Tashakkori & Teddlie, 1998). For mixed methods research, the question arises as to whether separate forms of validity need to follow in the designs (one set for quantitative and one set for qualitative), whether different types of mixed methods designs introduce their own validity types, or whether an umbrella validity form exists for all mixed methods research. For example, within a sequential design, are there issues of validity that emerge about the design based on the selection of participants from a quantitative analysis (e.g., selection bias as a form of internal validity threat) that precedes the qualitative interviewing phase? Alternatively, is there one form of validity that transcends the entire design in a triangulation approach that involves the simultaneous collection of both quantitative and qualitative data? Would the name of this validity be "consequential validity" (Biesta & Burbules, 2003), to honor pragmatism as the philosophical foundation and using John Dewey's terms of attending to the consequences of the research as all-important? Currently, these questions remain unresolved as mixed methods writers debate the role of validity. Moving this debate forward requires identifying the types of mixed methods designs and then advancing the types of validity that best lodge within each type.

CURRENT DIRECTIONS IN MIXED METHODS RESEARCH

Mixed methods designs provide an important and useful contribution to extant methodologies in the social science, although many questions and debates remain about whether and when to implement such designs. Mixed methods research does have an important role in theory generation and development, case study research, explanation of findings, convergent evidence, and explanations of outliers. How social science fields such as management and human resource development interpret and use mixed methods research needs further understanding. How mixed methods research can be streamlined for the busy social scientists needs further analysis. With the roots of organizational research in quantitative approaches, the understanding of validity concerns merits closer inspection. Because triangulation seems to be a popular design type in the social sciences, we need more information about converging numeric and text data, how to display and report such analyses, and how computer software programs can aid in this analysis. With long-term lines of investigation called for by private foundations and public funding agencies, we need a better understanding of the designs available to multiple-phase studies.

Despite these issues, writers have made inroads about basic definitions of mixed methods research, the type of designs, and the philosophical foundations for this form of inquiry. Mixed methods research holds potential for conducting research in organizations by incorporating the value of quantitative and qualitative data, and with preparation for this design and a knowledge of the basic models, we anticipate that more projects in the future will be cast in this mode of inquiry. Although issues still loom large, the conversation has now shifted beyond quantitative methodologies or qualitative approaches to how our complex problems can best be addressed by mixing methodologies in our inquiries.

REFERENCES

Bamberger, M. (Ed.). (2000). *Integrating quantitative and qualitative research in development projects.* Washington, D.C.: World Bank.

Biesta, G. J. J., & Burbules, N. C. (2003). *Pragmatism and educational research.* Lanham, MD: Rowman & Littlefield.

Brewer, J., & Hunter, A. (1989). *Multimethod research: A synthesis of styles.* Newbury Park, CA: Sage.

Bryman, A. (1988). *Quantity and quality in social science research.* London: Routledge.

Campbell, D., & Fiske, D. (1959). Convergent and discriminant validation by the multi-trait–multimethod matrix. *Psychological Bulletin, 56,* 81–105.

Caracelli, V. J., & Greene, J. C. (1993). Data analysis strategies for mixed method evaluation designs. *Educational Evaluation and Policy Analysis, 15*(2), 195–207.

Cherryholmes, C. H. (1992). Notes on pragmatism and scientific realism. *Educational Researcher, 14,* 14–17.

Cook, T. D., & Reichardt, C. S. (Eds.). (1979). *Qualitative and quantitative methods in evaluation research.* Beverly Hills, CA: Sage.

Creswell, J. W. (1994). *Research design: Qualitative and quantitative approaches.* Thousand Oaks, CA: Sage.

Creswell, J. W. (2003a, December 5). *Mixed methods research: A workshop.* Presentation at the Robert Wood Johnson Foundation Faculty Scholars Program, Houston, TX.

Creswell, J. W. (2003b). *Research design: Qualitative, quantitative, and mixed methods approaches* (2nd ed.) Thousand Oaks, CA: Sage.

Creswell, J. W. (2004, January 29–31). *Mixed methods designs: Lengthening in the path of qualitative research.* Contributed research paper to The Fifth International Interdisciplinary Conference, Advances in Qualitative Methods, Edmonton, Alberta, Canada.

Creswell, J. W., Fetter, M. D., & Ivankova, N. V. (2004). Designing a mixed methods study in primary care. *Annals of Family Medicine, 2*(1), 7–12.

Creswell, J. W., Goodchild, L., & Turner, P. (1996). Integrated qualitative and quantitative research: Epistemology, history, and designs. In J. Smart (Ed.), *Higher education: Handbook of theory and research,* Vol. XI. New York: Agathon.

Creswell, J. W., & Miller, D. L. (2000). Determining validity in qualitative inquiry. *Theory into Practice, 39*(3), 124–130.

Datta, L. (1994). Paradigm wars: A basis for peaceful coexistence and beyond. In J. C. Greene & V. J. Caracelli (Eds.)(1997). *Advances in mixed-method evaluation: The challenges and benefits of integrating diverse paradigms.* New Directions for Evaluation, No. 74. San Francisco: Jossey-Bass.

Fielding, N. G., & Fielding, J. L. (1986). *Linking data.* Beverly Hills, CA: Sage.

Gergen, K. J. (2001). Psychological sciences in a postmodern context. *American Psychologist, 56,* 803–813.

Greene, J. C., & Caracelli, V. J. (Eds.)(1997). *Advances in mixed-method evaluation: The challenges and benefits of integrating diverse paradigms.* New Directions for Evaluation, No. 74. San Francisco: Jossey-Bass.

Greene, J. C., Caracelli, V. J., & Graham, W. F. (1989). Toward a conceptual framework for mixed method evaluation designs. *Educational Evaluation and Policy Analysis, 11*(3), 255–274.

Hanson, W. E., Creswell, J. W., Plano Clark, V. L., Petska, K. S., & Creswell, J. D. (2005). Mixed methods research designs in counseling psychology. *Journal of Counseling Psychology, 52*(2), 224–235.

Hoshmand, L. L. T. (1989). Alternate research paradigms: A review and teaching proposal. *Counseling Psychologist, 17,* 3–79.

Johnson, R. B., & Onwuegbuzie, A. J. (2004). Mixed methods research: A research paradigm whose time has come. *Educational Researcher, 33*(2), 14–26.

LeCompte, M. D., & Schensul, J. J. (1999). *Designing and conducting ethnographic research.* Ethnographer's Toolkit, No. 1. Walnut Creek, CA: AltaMira.

Lincoln, Y. S., & Guba, E. G. (1985). *Naturalistic inquiry.* Beverly Hills, CA: Sage.

Lincoln, Y. S., & Guba, E. G. (1994). Paradigmatic controversies, contradictions and emerging confluences. In N. K. Denzin & Y. S. Lincoln (Eds.), *Handbook of qualitative research* (2nd ed., pp. 163–188). Thousand Oaks, CA: Sage.

Mertens, D. M. (2003). Mixed methods and the politics of human research: The transformative-emancipatory perspective. In A. Tashakkori and C. Teddlie (Eds.), *Handbook of mixed methods in social and behavioral research* (pp. 135–164). Thousand Oaks, CA: Sage.

Miles, M. B., & Huberman, A. M. (1994). *Qualitative data analysis* (2nd ed.). Thousand Oaks, CA: Sage.

Morgan, D. L. (1998). Practical strategies for combining qualitative and qualitative methods: Application to health research. *Qualitative Health Research, 3,* 362–376.

Morrow, S. L., & Smith, M. L. (2000). Qualitative research for counseling psychology. In S. D. Brown & R. W. Lent (Eds.), *Handbook of counseling psychology* (3rd ed., pp. 199–230). New York: Wiley.

Morse, J. M. (1991). Approaches to qualitative quantitative methodological triangulation. *Nursing Research, 40*(1), 120–123.

Morse, J. M. (2003). Principles of mixed methods and multimethod research design. In A. Tashakkori & C. Teddlie (Eds.), *Handbook of mixed methods in social & behavioral research* (pp. 189–208). Thousand Oaks, CA: Sage.

National Institute of Health, Office of Behavioral and Social Science Research. (1999). *Qualitative methods in health research. Opportunities and considerations in application and review.* Washington, D.C.: Author.

Newman, I., & Benz, C. R. (1998). *Qualitative-quantitative research methodology: Exploring the interactive continuum.* Carbondale: Southern Illinois Press.

Ponterotto, J. G., & Grieger, I. (1999). Merging qualitative and quantitative perspectives in a research identity. In M. Kopala & L. Suzuki (Eds.), *Using qualitative methods in psychology* (pp. 49–62). Thousand Oaks, CA: Sage.

Punch, K. F. (1998). *Introduction to social research: Quantitative and qualitative approaches.* London: Sage.

Reichardt, C. S., & Rallis, S. E. (1994). The relationship between the qualitative and quantitative research traditions. In C. S. Reichardt & S. F. Rallis (Eds.), *The qualitative-quantitative debate: New perspectives* (pp. 5–11). New Directions for Program Evaluation, No. 61. San Francisco: Jossey-Bass.

Smith, J. K., & Heshusius, L. (1986). Closing down the conversation: The end of the quantitative-qualitative debate among educational researchers. *Educational Researcher, 15,* 4–12.

Steckler, A., McLeroy, K. R., Goodman, R. M., Bird, S. T., & McCormick, L. (1992). Toward integrating qualitative and quantitative methods: An introduction. *Health Education Quarterly, 19*(1), 1–8.

Tashakkori, A., & Teddlie, C. (1998). *Mixed methodology: Combining qualitative and quantitative approaches.* Thousand Oaks, CA: Sage.

Tashakkori A., & Teddlie, C. (2003). (Eds.). *Handbook on mixed methods in the behavioral & social sciences.* Thousand Oaks (CA): Sage.

Case Study Research Methods

Andrea D. Ellinger, *University of Illinois*
Karen E. Watkins, *University of Georgia*
Victoria J. Marsick, *Columbia University*

Case study research, one of the most prevalent forms of social science research, has been widely used in business, education, psychology, sociology, political science, social work, community planning, and economics (Dooley, 2002; Merriam, 1998; Yin, 2003). In particular, case studies are relevant when conducting research in organizations where the intent is to study systems, individuals, programs, and events. Although case studies are often qualitative, case study research can equally embrace the quantitative paradigm and be based on "any mix of quantitative and qualitative evidence" (Yin, 2003, p. 15).

WHAT IS A CASE STUDY?

The concept of a case study has been variously defined as a process, a unit of study, or an end product (Merriam, 1998). From a process perspective, Yin (2003) has defined a case study as "an empirical inquiry that investigates a contemporary phenomenon within its real-life context, especially when the boundaries between phenomenon and context are not clearly evident" (p. 13). Similarly, Scholz and Tietje (2002) define a case study as "an empirical inquiry that investigates a contemporary problem within its real-life context" (p. 9). Delimiting the object of study, the case, is "the single most defining characteristic of case study research" (Merriam, 1998, p. 27). Assessing the boundedness of the case is to consider how finite the data collection will be, whether there will be a limit to the number of interviews that can be conducted or number of observations that can occur. If there is no actual or theoretical end to some of these possibilities, the phenomenon is not bounded enough to be deemed a case (Merriam, 1998). Some scholars, however, argue that "cases are socially constructed and co-constructed between the researcher and the respondent. In this way, cases are not really defined or bounded until data collection—and even analysis—is finished" (Wells, Hirshberg, Lipton, & Oakes, 2002, p. 340).

As Yin (2003), Stake (1995), and others have articulated, in classic case study research, the case may be an individual, where the individual is the primary unit of analysis. Case study research may also be done on several individuals, or it can be an event or entity that is less well defined than a single individual. Other case study research has examined decisions, programs, an organization, an implementation process, organizational change, a country's economy, an industry, and policy (Yin, 2003).

Characteristics of Cases

The following are key characteristics of case study research:

- *Bounded.* A case study is a bounded study of an individual, a group of individuals, an organization, or multiple organizations. The phenomenon of interest is bounded through the choice of research problem and questions, which dictates the appropriate setting and/or sample from which to develop a rich understanding of that phenomenon. Theory and/or the research problem generally define(s) the boundaries of the study, though Wells et al. (2002) have argued that the nominal or constructivist perspectives suggest that the boundaries emerge during data collection.

- *Embedded.* Cases can be simple in terms of their bounded nature, but they are always embedded in larger systems; hence, the case is always a microcosm of a larger entity. As a result, a significant part of any case is a thorough description and bounding of the context. The context of a case may be a given organization, its industry, locale, or even a particular population of organizations.

- *Multivariate.* Case studies typically examine the interplay of multiple variables in order to provide as complete an understanding of an event or situation as possible.

- *Multimethod.* Case studies may illustrate a phenomenon, explore it in preparation for further study, accumulate instances of a phenomenon, or present contrasting or comparative examples of a phenomenon. Researchers use multiple methods (e.g., interviews, document analysis, participant observation, ethnographic observation, surveys, psychometric instruments, etc.) to collect data.

- *Multidisciplinary.* Case studies often call on multiple perspectives to thoroughly understand the phenomenon of interest. In organizational research, there is a strong tendency to draw on sociotechnical and sociocultural theories to explore an organization's dynamics. Case studies can be descriptive, historical, biographical, thematic explorations of a phenomenon, exploratory or explanatory, theory building or theory confirming, and so forth.

- *Multisite.* Case study research can be research of a single person or site, such as a division or an entire organization, or it can be multiple people or sites from which we make cross-case comparisons. Generally analysis begins with within-case analysis followed by cross-case analysis.

WHY AND WHEN CASE STUDY RESEARCH IS UNDERTAKEN

Case study research "comprises an all-encompassing method—covering the logic of design, data collection techniques, and specific approaches to data analysis" (Yin, 2003, p. 14). Having defined *case study* as an empirical inquiry that investigates a contemporary phenomenon in the context of its real life when the boundaries of the phenomenon and context are not as evident, Yin (2003) acknowledges that case study inquiry "copes with the technically distinctive situation in which there will be many more variables of interest than data points, and as one result relies on multiple sources of evidence, with data needing to converge in a triangulating fashion, and as another result benefits from the prior development of theoretical propositions to guide data collection and analysis" (pp. 13–14).

When Should Case Study Be Used as a Research Strategy?

Three conditions that are useful in determining whether case study should be used as a research strategy have been articulated by Yin (2003). The first condition relates to the type of research question that is being considered. Case study research is most appropriate when the researcher is interested in "how," "what," and "why" questions. The second and third conditions relate to the extent of control over behavioral events and the degree of focus on contemporary events. When the researcher is interested in contemporary events and does not have an ability to control or manipulate behavioral events, case study research is deemed an appropriate strategy.

Three types of case studies can be undertaken: explanatory case studies, exploratory case studies, and descriptive case studies (Yin, 2003). Case studies are particularly relevant when understanding of complex social phenomena is needed because "the case study method allows investigators to retain holistic and meaningful characteristics of real-life events" (p. 2). Additionally, case studies may be used in evaluation research to explain, to describe, to illustrate, to explore, or to be used as a meta-evaluation (Yin, 2003).

Case studies may be undertaken for a number of reasons. Case studies are very appropriate when the researcher is interested in process or seeks an in-depth understanding of a phenomenon because of its uniqueness. Stake (1994) identifies three motivations for studying cases: intrinsic case study, instrumental case study, and collective case study. According to him, an *intrinsic* case study is undertaken because the case itself is of interest. An *instrumental* case study is undertaken to gain insight into an issue. The case becomes secondary because it facilitates an understanding of something else. A *collective* case study is undertaken when a number of cases are selected jointly to provide insight on a phenomenon, population, or condition. A collective case study may result in enhanced understanding of the phenomenon or theorizing. Case studies can be descriptive, interpretative, or evaluative. Additionally, there are many types of qualitative case studies that can be undertaken: ethnographic, historical, psychological, or sociological.

Mixed Method Approaches to Case Study Research

Merriam (1988, 1998) argues that case study approaches are best suited to how and why questions, hence a qualitative approach. In fact, most educational case study research is single-paradigm, qualitative case study research. On the other hand, the case study clearly lends itself to mixed methodology by the very nature of the cases. In fact, Dube and Pare (2003) note that over 80% of studies in information systems are positivist case studies. Creswell (2003) acknowledges that a mixed approach involves collecting and analyzing both qualitative and quantitative data in a single study. By defining a case study as an approach whose purpose is to describe as accurately as possible the fullest, most complete description of the case, then it follows that the researcher wants to know not only how and why a phenomena occurs but also what it is, how much, how often, where it came from, and so on. In short, the very goal of capturing the complexity of the phenomena in its context requires, at a minimum, consulting multiple sources of data.

Using mixed methods in a case study requires considerable skill on the part of the researcher because it requires knowledge of both qualitative and quantitative research paradigms and often knowledge of how to work collaboratively as part of a research team. Case studies with multiple methods often involve research teams who study complex phenomenon in multiple sites and nested systems, such as schools, communities, or organization-level phenomena in many divisions and locations. Miles and Huberman (1994, p. 43) note that while one should not limit a study by a "'default' mode that sees qualitative data as the only way of proceeding," so, too, the lone researcher may not be able to manage multiple methods. Research teams, on the other hand, can fall into a trap if quantitative and qualitative researchers work separately and do not mine the advantages of mixed methods for one another.

Why Use Mixed Methods in Case Study Research?

Quantitative methods counteract the potential bias of individual judgment through more objective, systematic procedures, whereas qualitative methods contextualize findings and promote strategic comparison across cases (Firestone, 1987, in Miles & Huberman, 1994). Creswell (1994, 2003) notes that mixed methods permit triangulation and complementary, overlapping examination of a phenomena of interest, hence enhanced scope and breadth of understanding (simultaneous triangulation); or the methods may emerge developmentally, where one method prepares the way for the next (sequential triangulation). Some of the more common approaches to integrating mixed methods in case study research include the following:

- Both qualitative and quantitative methods can be used *simultaneously*, or concurrently, for different purposes with continuous, integrated, complementary data analysis. Data collection and analysis may be continuous, or fieldwork may be continuous with periodic use of quantitative methods in waves.

- An initial phase of exploratory qualitative study (using interviews, focus groups, or observation) is often undertaken to identify or fine tune focus, model, theory, or instruments. Insights can be used to locate a sample that is more representative, inclusive of variance or deviant cases, strategic, or theoretically driven or to modify the study's design or instrumentation for use in a subsequent quantitative phase of study.

- Surveys may be followed by fieldwork or interviews to deepen understanding, provide rich description, or test alternative explanations for a phenomenon. This qualitative phase can be followed by experiments or other quantitative designs.

Miles and Huberman (1994) point out that even cases that are not explicitly designed as quantitative in nature often include counts of one or another kind. It is helpful to know how many times a particular word or theme appears, how many respondents fall into different categories of responses, or how frequently an observed event reoccurs. Numbers alone do not tell the story of most case studies given that their purpose is insight, not coverage, that samples are not selected in ways that make findings generalizable, and that insights and perceptions may be theoretically important even if they are small in number. But content analysis counts, and conversions of qualitative data into "rough" rating scales or other descriptive statistics often helps tell the story of the case more effectively than words alone.

In Creswell's (1994) earlier work on combining qualitative and quantitative strategies, he elaborated on three specific designs: two-phase design, dominant–less dominant design, and mixed methodology design. In his two-phase design, the researcher conducts a qualitative phase and then a separate quantitative phase. In this design, each phase is separate. In the dominant–less dominant design, the researcher conducts a study with a dominant paradigm that also has a component that involves an alternative paradigm. For example, a quantitative study may be proposed in which a small component involves conducting qualitative interviews. In his third design, Creswell acknowledges that the mixed methodology design represents the highest degree of mixing paradigms, and the researcher would "mix aspects of the qualitative and quantitative paradigm at all or many methodological steps in the design" (p. 178). Creswell (2003) alludes to sequential, concurrent, and transformative procedures in mixed design approaches. In *sequential* procedures, the researcher "seeks to elaborate on or expand the findings of one method with another method" (p. 16). *Concurrent* procedures reflect the researcher's desire to collect both forms of quantitative and qualitative data at the same time. Using *transformative* procedures involves the use of a theoretical lens as an overarching perspective in a design that contains both quantitative and qualitative data. Within this lens, data collection could involve a sequential or concurrent approach.

Eisenhardt (1989, 2002) and Dooley (2002) argue for theory building from cases by combining case study, grounded theory, and mixed methods traditions. Qualitatively derived theory benefits from systematic examination using large samples and systematic methods for avoiding bias, getting information that would otherwise be overlooked, testing for generality, and verifying findings. Quantitative results can often be explained only with a holistic description of relationships and events over time. Using case study for theory building is highly iterative, often involves research teams, typically spreads the research out over a longer period of time, is characterized by multiple methods and cross-case analyses, and links the inductive logic of grounded theory for theory building with the logic of quantitative methods (if not the methods themselves) to test theories as they evolve. Its strength is in generating theory that is not idiosyncratic to one case, that "is likely to be testable with constructs that can be readily measured and hypotheses that can be proven false," and that is "empirically valid" (p. 547). However, theory-building cases are difficult to undertake by the neophyte researcher who has yet to master one set of methods, who may be proscribed from doing his or her research in teams, and who does not wish to extend the research period over many years. Eisenhardt also notes that theories built from case studies can be overly complex, narrow, and idiosyncratic.

Finally, Dube and Pare (2003) contrast constructivist and positivist case study research. Constructivist case studies, regardless of whether the data are qualitative or quantitative, focus on emergent hypotheses, on exploration of phenomena, on the meaning making of the interviewed. A positivist case study is explicitly positivist in its intent and the research design, whether drawing on qualitative or quantitative data, is driven from formal research hypotheses and explicit theoretical interests.

GENERAL COMPONENTS AND PROCESS OF CASE STUDY RESEARCH DESIGN

There are several important considerations in designing case study research. For Yin (2003), the research design "is *a logical plan for getting from here to there*, where *here* may be defined as the initial set of questions to be answered, and *there* is some set of conclusions (answers) about these questions" (p. 20). Yin contends that five design components for case study research are important: "a study's questions; its propositions, if any; its unit(s) of analysis; the logic linking the data to the propositions; and, the criteria for interpreting the findings" (p. 21). These five components, with some elaboration, provide a framework for carrying out case studies:

- Identifying the problem, purpose, and research questions
- Using the literature
- Selecting and bounding the case
- Designing the study
- Considering issues of validity and reliability in designing case study research
- Collecting the data
- Analyzing the data
- Integrating the study findings

- Interpreting findings and drawing conclusions
- Writing and reporting the findings

Identifying the Problem, Purpose, and Research Questions

It is not unusual for the case setting to drive initial interest in a study's problem, purpose, and research questions. A researcher is intrigued with a particular setting to which he or she has access and can see in that setting the outlines of problems and questions addressed by the literature and perhaps important to his or her practice. The first challenge the researcher faces is to get greater clarity on the research problem, which may be embedded or entwined with a problem of practice. The answers gained through research will not directly solve the problem of practice but will shed light on where the problem resides; where interventions are needed; the kind of action that will get desired results; or how to work with structure, culture, or other contextual factors in a setting that influence results. The purpose of the study captures what will be learned through the research that will help address the problem of practice and contribute to a larger body of knowledge in the field. Research questions define the scope of the study. What particular questions can be answered in this case study setting, given the problem and researcher's purpose?

Case study research is particularly relevant for addressing how, what, and why questions. Becoming clear about the nature of these will help the researcher focus on the kinds of information that he or she needs to collect in order to answer these questions. Yin (2003) notes that the study's propositions relate to identifying what the researcher will study to address the research questions. When the researcher is grounding the study in one or more theories, the theory directs attention to collecting relevant information about particular events, people, relationships, dynamics, or organizational considerations. In other words, "each proposition directs attention to something that should be examined within the scope of the study" (Yin, 2003, p. 22). Theory provides welcome guideposts in deciding what needs attention and what can be excluded in both data collection and analysis phases.

Using the Literature

Scholars disagree about when the relevant literature should be reviewed and how it should be incorporated into a study (Creswell, 1994, 1998, 2003; Merriam, 1998; Merriam & Simpson, 1995). The research design may dictate whether a literature review should be used to ground the hypotheses of the study, as in many quantitative designs; or whether the literature should not be carried out until after data are collected, as in a phenomenological study, in which the literature is used to add depth of understanding to the themes elicited by those interviewed about the phenomenon. The literature is used differently in case study research depending on the study's questions and research design.

However, in most case studies, the literature review should be used to establish the rationale for the research and questions to be asked. The literature review helps identify what is known about the context and focus of the study from research and, sometimes, from practice. Prior research, plus theory, helps the researcher find out what information he or she should make sure to gather because others have found it to be important. The literature review therefore shapes the design of the study.

Once the findings have been identified, the literature can help the researcher understand patterns in the data and therefore theorize about dynamics, relationships, and links in the data. Once conclusions have been drawn, the literature helps compare findings of the study to other studies and identify how this study builds the field's knowledge base by adding to, confirming, or contradicting prior findings. Because case studies are all about context, the literature review can point to studies in similar or different contexts to help the researcher understand the limits of the findings of this study. This helps the reader better understand how to use findings in a different setting.

Conceptual Framework

Yin (2003) notes that, in doing case study research, the researcher should link the data to propositions and establish the criteria for interpreting the study's findings. Miles and Huberman (1994) address this point in suggesting that researchers develop a conceptual framework for the study.

The conceptual framework grows out of the literature review and is made concrete by looking at theory in light of the emerging reality of the case. This framework is continually revisited and revised as the study progresses. Miles and Huberman (1994, p. 18) note that even if the researcher is proceeding in a highly inductive way, using theory to identify the "intellectual 'bins'" one expects to find in a study and then "getting clearer about their interrelationships lead you to a conceptual framework." That framework can be described in a narrative or through a graphic such as a flowchart or concept map; and it can be "rudimentary or elaborate, theory-driven or commonsensical, descriptive or causal."

The literature review provides the totality of the theoretical underpinnings of the study, but the conceptual framework is the "figure" dictated by particular people, places, and circumstances that stands out against this larger, theoretical "ground." It is also shaped by what the researcher knows, practically, about the setting of the study. Typically, a researcher's first "take" on a conceptual framework involves the overlap of multiple theories. As data are collected, a storyline emerges in the case that will help the researcher hone in on those particular aspects of these theories that are relevant to the story. Conversely, the story points to those places in the theory where the research will confirm, disconfirm, or add to theory by providing a contextualized understanding of how or why the particular stories in the case have unfolded. For example, a researcher with interests in organizational learning may start with one or more discipline-based accounts of how organizations learn. But the story of a particular set of people in a particular location of the organization over a particular issue and time frame will help the researcher understand how individuals, acting together, may learn in ways that become embedded in organizational practices, policy, structure, or processes. The story of that case will help to focus on illustrating and elaborating on how other organizations might learn.

Selecting and Bounding the Case

Identifying the unit of analysis is associated with "the fundamental problem of defining what the case is" (Yin, 2003, p. 22). In organizations and other settings such as multisite school studies, the study may include a nested set of cases within the same bounded system. The general guide that Yin offers in defining the unit of analysis (and therefore of the case) is related to the initial research questions that have been developed. The case should be bounded not only by the unit of analysis but also by the time period under study, the context, and whether or not the data will be retrospective, ongoing, or both.

The case may be selected because of intrinsic interest in, and access to, that setting or population or because one or more cases typify a larger problem or set of problems to be studied. If the latter, the researcher uses the theory behind the design and what is known about the range of available settings to make sampling choices. Eisenhardt (1989, 2002) recommends theoretical sampling as developed in grounded theory—that is, sampling for cases, or within cases, in order to best the lower and upper limits of a theory. This approach requires seeking cases that provide examples that confirm, disconfirm, or extend the context within which a particular phenomenon varies. Multiple case studies are richer than single case studies because they offer contrasts that help the researcher better understand why and how a phenomenon occurs in one way in one setting and a completely different way in another setting. One can choose cases because of some similarities, but multiple cases are almost always selected to provide variety across a spectrum of interest to the study. Cases can be biased toward "ideal" types or represent a mix of representative and extreme cases.

Sampling may need to be done within the selected case(s) as well. Researchers can seldom study every person, event, group, level, or time period within the case. Sampling within a case should be guided by the research questions and by the theory that underlies the initial conceptualization of the case. Because cases are supposed to shed light on complex relationships and dynamics within the bounded system, the researcher must sample the range of this complexity in a way that is appropriate to his or her research questions. The researcher will undoubtedly find more than he or she could have imagined when involved in fieldwork, so the sampling plan will be modified as the casework progresses. But the plan for the study should anticipate and include a range of expected situations, people, places, events, and time periods that are locations for the phenomena of interest that are indicated by the research questions.

Designing the Study

In addition to the differing intentions of the researcher for conducting case studies, there are also some variations in the design of case study research. A single case study approach is analogous to a single experiment (Yin, 2003) and may be the most appropriate design depending on the nature of the research question. Yin (2003) has articulated five rationales for selecting a single case study approach: critical case, extreme or unique case, representative or typical case, revelatory case, or longitudinal case. In selecting a critical case, typically the rationale revolves around testing a well-formulated theory for which there are a clear set of propositions, and the selection of a critical case enables the researcher to confirm, challenge, or extend theory (Yin, 2003). The critical case can represent a significant contribution to knowledge and theory building. Another appropriate use of a single case is when the case is unusual or rare, as in an extreme or unique case. When the researcher wants to capture the conditions of "an everyday or commonplace situation" (p. 43), a single representative case may be appropriate. The fourth rationale relates to the researcher's opportunity to observe a phenomenon that has been previously inaccessible to the researcher (Yin, 2003). Lastly, it may be appropriate to examine a single case at more than one point in time.

When a case study employs more than one case, a multiple case study approach is being undertaken. Yin (2003) suggests that multiple case studies are often considered more robust and compelling. However, conducting a multiple case study is time- and resource-intensive and may extend beyond the scope of a single researcher. In addition to single and multiple case studies, case studies may be holistic or embedded. *Holistic* case studies attempt to examine the global nature of the case, whereas *embedded* case studies involve more than one unit of analysis. A single and a multiple case study may be holistic or embedded.

If the researcher wants to build theory, this purpose must guide research design from the inception. Eisenhardt (1989, 2002) identifies distinctive steps in the process of building theory from case study research that should be kept in mind in defining the research question, selecting cases, crafting instruments and protocols, entering the field, analyzing data, shaping hypotheses, enfolding the literature, and reaching closure. Theory-building considerations are discussed throughout this chapter, but they will come to the fore in the study's design phase. These considerations may require that the researcher revisit the research questions and decisions about case selection

Because case study research is not as routinized as other strategies, the researcher needs to be prepared for the eventuality that the case inquiry may not always occur as planned. Yin (2003) suggests that researchers must be open to the possibilities of change but remain focused on the original purpose of the research. He likens the case study investigator to that of being a detective where the detective is collecting and recording information, but also making inferences about this information. To avoid the pitfalls of bias, Yin suggests that researchers must be open to the possibilities of contrary findings and prepared to consider alternative explanations of the data that is collected.

A significant aspect of the design involves the development of a case study protocol, which is more than a "questionnaire or instrument" (Yin, 2003, p. 67). The case study protocol contains both the instrument as well as the procedures to be followed in conducting the case study. The use of a protocol can help the researcher increase the reliability of case study research because it serves as an overall guideline for the inquiry and can ensure consistency in the conduct of a multiple case study. Yin advocates that the case study protocol should include the following components: an overview of the case study project (project objectives), field procedures, case study questions (the specific questions for collecting data), and a guide for the case study report (an outline, format for the presentation of data, bibliographic information) (p. 69).

Scholars acknowledge that the final preparation for data collection is the conduct of a pilot study. A pilot study is not a pretest, according to Yin (2003), but it enables the researcher to refine the overall approach to data collection as well as the relevant lines of questions to be addressed in the study. The intent of the pilot case study is to provide multiple insights to the researcher on the feasibility of the case study protocol, procedures for collecting data, and emergent findings.

ISSUES OF VALIDITY AND RELIABILITY IN DESIGNING CASE STUDY RESEARCH

Yin (2003) contends that case study researchers must be concerned about issues of validity and reliability when designing and conducting case study research and identifies "four tests that are relevant to case studies" (p. 34) and are common to all social science methods. Table 19.1 presents the four tests and tactics for maximizing these tests.

- *Construct validity.* Construct validity relates to the establishment of operational measures for the concepts being studied. Although Yin acknowledges that this first test can be problematic in case study research, articulating key constructs is an essential aspect of case study research. For example, he draws upon the notion of case studies that have previously examined the concept of change and consequences of change. To meet the requirements of construct validity, the researcher would need to articulate and select specific types of change to be studied relative to the objectives of the case study, as well as demonstrate that the measures of these changes reflect specific types of change that have been selected.
- *Internal validity.* Internal validity relates to establishing a causal relationship where specific conditions are shown to lead to other conditions. This issue is relevant to explanatory or causal case studies.

TABLE 19.1 Issues of Reliability and Validity

TESTS	CASE STUDY TACTICS	PHASE OF RESEARCH IN WHICH TACTIC OCCURS
Construct Validity		
Establishing correct operational measures for the concepts being studied	■ Use multiple sources of evidence	Data Collection
	■ Establish chain of evidence	Data Collection
	■ Have key informants review draft case study report	Composition
Internal Validity		
(for explanatory or causal studies only, and not for descriptive or exploratory studies): establishing a causal relationship, whereby certain conditions are shown to lead to other conditions, as distinguished from spurious relationships	■ Do pattern-matching	Data Analysis
	■ Do explanation-building	Data Analysis
	■ Address rival explanations	Data Analysis
	■ Use logic models	Data Analysis
External Validity		
Establishing the domain to which a study's findings can be generalized	■ Use theory in single-case studies	Research Design
	■ Use replication in multiple-case studies	Research Design
Reliability		
Demonstrating that the operations of a study can be repeated, with the same results	■ Use case study protocol	Data Collection
	■ Develop case study database	Data Collection

Source: Yin (2003).

■ *External validity.* External validity relates to establishing the domain for which a study's finding can be generalized. Can the findings from a case study be generalized beyond the case studied? This concept is often problematic to case study research, because, for example, the purpose of conducting a qualitative case study is not to generalize to other populations per se but to seek in-depth understanding of the case for which consumers of the case report may determine relevant applications to their own contexts. In contrast to survey research, which is intended to generalize to a larger universe, case studies rely on analytic generalization.

- *Reliability.* Reliability relates to demonstrating that the operations of the study can be repeated with the same results. The goal of reliability is to minimize the errors and biases in a study. According to Yin (2003), "the objective is to be sure that if a later investigator followed the same procedures as described by an earlier investigator and conducted the same case study all over again, the later investigator should arrive at the same findings and conclusions" (p. 37). The emphasis is on "doing the *same* case over again, not on 'replicating' the results of one case by doing another case study" (p. 37).

Yin notes tactics for each of these tests in Table 19.1 and suggests that the quality of the research design can be judged according to these tests. Some of these tactics are most relevant at the design stage, whereas others should be considered at the data collection and analyses phases of case study research.

Collecting the Data

Case study research enables the researcher to draw upon many approaches to data collection because "case study does not claim any particular methods for data collection" (Merriam, 1998, p. 28). Depending on the nature of the research questions and overall research design considerations associated with the case study, quantitative approaches to data collection may be used, such as surveys.

According to Yin (2003), data for case studies may come from many sources, but he identifies six important sources for data collection that are widely used: documentation, archival records, interviews, direct observation, participant observation, and physical artifacts. Qualitative case studies commonly employ interviews; in many studies, interviews represent the only form of data collection. In addition to interviews, observations and documents may also be sources of data for qualitative case studies (Merriam, 1998). Quantitative case studies rely heavily on questionnaires of key constructs, frequency counts of observed phenomena, or surveys (whether through interview or questionnaire) of critical respondents in a given case.

Three principles for data collection help researchers reap the benefits from these data collection sources: use multiple sources of evidence, create a case study database, and maintain a chain of evidence (Yin, 2003). These three principles are important in helping the researcher further establish construct validity and reliability of case study evidence. The use of multiple sources of evidence enables the researcher to address a broad range of issues within the case study as well as enables the researcher to triangulate the findings of the case study. Conclusions drawn may be more compelling from multiple sources of data as opposed to one source of data.

The second principle relates to organizing and documenting the data collected in case studies. Maintaining a database that documents case study notes, documents, narratives resulting from the case study research, and other pertinent information enables the researcher to connect answers to the evidence collected in the case study (Yin, 2003).

The final principle relates to increasing the reliability of the information in a case study so that conclusions drawn from the case can be traced backward.

Analyzing the Data

Data analysis in case studies proceeds much as data analysis does in either qualitative or quantitative research paradigms, depending on the dominant paradigm being used in the case study. In qualitative designs, it is emergent—that is, driven by each step of data collection and analysis. In quantitative designs, it is predefined, with data sorted by research question or hypothesis. However, in either approach, an overall plan is needed that lays out the sequencing of data collection methods and identifies ways phases of the design interact and shape one another. The plan lays out, by research question, how each kind of data will be analyzed and how the researcher expects to take advantage of differences in groupings of people, events, or circumstances in the case to look for patterns in the data.

Case study analysis can be overwhelming, initially to the neophyte because its purpose is to identify, sort through, and pattern relationships, dynamics, or other phenomena of interest within a bounded system. This means that the researcher must begin analysis in a reasonably open-ended way to develop, first, the descriptive account of important components of the case. Drawing on the constant comparative method, case study researchers enter into iterative cycles of data collection, analysis of some kind, and, in qualitative designs, use of insights from the analysis to guide the next steps of data collection. These cycles typically begin by drawing a broad circle within the bounded system that includes everything that the researcher can understand about the system being studied. However, as the analysis proceeds, the researcher aims for data reduction—that is, selection of data for inclusion in the study based on a growing understanding of the story to be told in the case and the theory that guides and is built by the findings of the study.

Analysis is guided by the story emerging from the data and by predefined conceptual frameworks that may grow and change over the lifetime of the study. A good rule of thumb for data analysis is to read and analyze the data for three sequential, somewhat overlapping purposes. First, read and code the data for a *descriptive purpose*—that is, the telling of the story or stories in the case(s) that best answer the research questions. At this point, the story is holistic and often chronological; it is an account that the people in the case could recognize as an accurate portrait of what they have said or done in these circumstances within the time period of the case study. Once the story is told, the researcher reads and codes the data a second time for an *analytic purpose,* pulling apart the story and case(s) in different ways to get underneath the story and shed light on the how, what, and why dynamics that drove the study's research questions. The final reading is done for *interpretive and explanatory* purposes—that is, to integrate knowledge and insights gained from different kinds of data and data sources in light of the conceptual framework and theoretical purposes of the study.

As data analysis proceeds, these three phases overlap and interact, but the relative emphasis shifts and the strategies used for analysis change. In the first phase, analysis seeks to capture complexity. The researcher does not want to rush to judgment before he or she understands the whole bounded system. When the case involves nested systems or multiple cases, the design might call for different subsystems or sites to be studied separately or concurrently. The researcher should keep in mind the logic of the relationships across subsystems or sites in regard to the purpose and research questions of the study. It might make sense to study all subsystems or sites in regard to a particular research question or subfocus of the analysis, or it may make sense to study one subsystem or case in depth before proceeding to the next subsystem or case. Often, the pattern used in one subsystem or site is refined and developed in one location and then used to guide analysis in the remaining subsystems or sites. Theory-building cases often begin with within-case analysis to understand the holistic dynamic within each case (or within each subsystem of a case), followed by iterative cycles of cross-case analysis.

Integrating the Study Findings

The power of case analysis is the ability to move from simple description to explanation of underlying dynamics that allows one to confirm, disconfirm, build, or expand theory that underlies the case. Drawing on Rein and Schön (1977), Miles and Huberman (1994, p. 91) call this an "analytic progression" that moves from "telling a first 'story' about a specified situation (what happened, and then what happened?), to constructing a 'map' (formalizing the elements of the story, locating key variables), to building a theory or model (how the variables are connected, how they influence each other)."

Miles and Huberman (1994, pp. 91–92) further note that, while words tell stories, displays of various kinds hold the key to both powerful analysis and powerful findings: "Valid analysis requires, and is driven by, displays that are focused enough to permit a viewing of a full data set in the same location, and are arranged systematically to answer the research questions at hand." They go on to explain that a full data set is not all of one's data, but rather, "condensed, distilled data . . . drawn from the full range of persons, events, and processes under study." Borrowing from quantitative analysis, Miles and Huberman note that data displays "(a) show the data and analysis in one place, (b) allow the analyst to see where further analyses are called for, (c) make it easier to compare different data sets, and (d) permit direct use of the results in a report, improving the credibility of conclusions drawn" (p. 92). Qualitative data analysis software supports rapid and effective use of data displays.

When subsystems of a case or multiple case sites are key to the study, the researcher must find ways to analyze findings and themes across cases. Cross-case analysis is challenging because of the uniqueness of the cases under study. A good design will seek some comparability of case components (although each case might represent a different point along a spectrum of foci of interest in the study). Cross-case analysis enhances the ability to generalize from the case and to deepen understanding and explanations for phenomena being studied. Cross-case analysis is especially facilitated by mixed methods designs.

Miles and Huberman (1994) suggest that cross-case analysis proceed from more exploratory, open-ended comparisons to more focused, theoretically guided comparisons. They recommend meta-matrices or "master charts assembling descriptive data from each of several cases in a standard format" for exploratory analysis. They suggest including all relevant data at first and then moving to partition and cluster the data in new ways to show contrasts among cases. Partitioning and clustering of data across cases allows for within-category sorting that enables further analyses—for example, observing variation over time, noting different clusters of categories within a primary cluster, and doing "if-then" tests to examine relationships in the data. New counts, patterns, and themes emerge from this in-depth analysis within category. Across-category clustering allows for further identification and analysis of differences and similarities that lead to more refined pattern development.

Scholz and Tietje (2002) propose a framework and strategies for knowledge integration that draws on work by experimental psychologist Egon Brunswik on perception that was subsequently adapted for social judgment theory. Their model identifies four types of knowledge integration: the lenses brought to a study by different disciplines, the understanding of different subsystems and their links in a case, the identification and comparison of multiple interest groups in a case, and the complementary of intuitive and analytic modes of thoughts.

Interpreting Findings and Drawing Conclusions

Analysis, by definition, involves using theory to guide interpretation of the findings. However, this step is taken differently depending on the following factors:

- Whether the conceptual framework for the case has been prestructured, in which case the researcher works from existing theory to code and analyze data, and uses existing data to interpret the findings—that is, discuss the meaning of the story vis-à-vis the theory that underlies the case as well as drawing out practical implications of the study for stakeholders of the case

- Whether the conceptual framework for the case was fairly clearly identified and little modified during data analysis, in which case, as in prestructured cases, meaning can be discussed without much additional theory building

- Whether the conceptual framework was fairly open-ended and significantly modified through iterative cycles of data analysis, in which case the researcher must often return to the literature, using different theories and lenses to explicate the case and understand how the study advances knowledge in the field and for stakeholders in the case

- Whether the case is a theory-building case, in which case, the conceptual framework, while identified, will be significantly modified through iterative cycles of data analysis and, as Eisenhardt (1989, p. 544) notes, through comparison of emergent theory with literature discussing both similar and conflicting findings. "The juxtaposition of conflicting results forces researchers into a more creative, framebreaking mode of thinking … [that results in] deeper insight … [and the] sharpening of the limits to generalizability of the focal research."

As findings are interpreted and conclusions are drawn from the research, the researcher must often go back to earlier work on the problem and purpose statements of the study to align different components of the study. Knowing what story he or she will tell, the researcher may go back to the literature review and cut out sections that have proved not to be important, elaborate on studies that are pertinent to findings, or add sources that emerged as important through the analysis.

Writing and Reporting the Findings

Once the analysis is completed, the researcher must decide how to report findings, interpretation, and conclusions and recommendations. The researcher must decide how to lay out the descriptive story in the data, and then report on the analyses and how they helped to understand and/or shape the theory behind the study. This is where the researcher mines the findings by showcasing the way in which they not only tell a story but also add to one's understanding of the field, whether that understanding is focused primarily on description or shaped more toward explanation and theory building.

The format of the report will be driven by the story told by the case(s). When multiple cases are reported, each case may be reported separately, and then cross-case analyses presented followed by interpretation in light of the literature. The narrative of the case is supported by vignettes (e.g., of people, places, activities, time periods, or events). The patterns and relationships developed through the analyses structure the storyline. Case studies typically integrate data across sources, but it may be necessary to report findings by data source, especially in mixed methods studies. When data are reported by source, it is not unusual to include an integrative discussion across source by case prior to moving to analyses across cases or across subsystems within a case.

Because cases are, by nature, contextual, they should include rich, thick description and verbatim accounts, actual quotes, of people in the case. Data displays are essential to uncovering the underlying dynamics of the story in such a way that the reader can quickly grasp essential features of the case as they relate to an explanation or theory being built from the data.

CONCLUSION

Case study research has often been criticized as "being a weak sibling among social science methods" (Yin, 2003, p. xiii), despite its extensive use. It has been considered less rigorous and systematic than other forms of research. Another concern about case study research has related to the inability of researchers' to achieve scientific generalization. Lastly, case study research is often deemed to be a time- and resource-intensive form of inquiry.

The intent of this chapter has been to address these criticisms by further establishing case study research as a robust research strategy that can powerfully address how, what, and why questions and illuminate these questions as embedded in their unique contexts. By presenting a systematic approach for conducting case study research drawn from such scholars as Yin (2003), Dooley (2002), Merriam (1998), and Stake (1995), among others, this chapter has integrated the use of mixed method approaches that further strengthen case study research as a rigorous research strategy and theory-building tool. We offer the sources in Table 19.2 for researchers and practitioners interested in pursuing additional readings on the subject of case study research and conclude by illustrating three examples of case study research that have employed mixed method approaches.

Table 19.2   Key Case Study Research References

Creswell, J. W. (2003). *Research design: Qualitative, quantitative and mixed methods approaches* (2nd ed.). Thousand Oaks, CA: Sage Publications.

Merriam, S. B. (1998). *Qualitative research and case study applications in education*. San Francisco, CA: Jossey-Bass Publishers.

Ragin, C. C. & Becker, H. S. (Eds.) (1992). *What is a case? Exploring the foundations of social inquiry.* Cambridge, United Kingdom: Cambridge University Press.

Robson, C. (2002). *Real world research* (2nd ed.). Oxford, United Kingdom: Blackwell Publishing.

Scholtz, R. W. & Tietje, O. (2002). *Embedded case study methods: Integrating quantitative and qualitative knowledge.* Thousand Oaks, CA: Sage Publications.

Yin, R. K. (2004) (Ed). *The case study anthology.* Thousand Oaks, CA: Sage Publications.

Yin, R. K. (2003). *Case study research: Design and methods* (Applied Social Research Methods Series, 5, 3rd ed.). Thousand Oaks, CA: Sage Publications.

EXAMPLES OF MIXED METHODS
CASE STUDY RESEARCH

The following three examples of mixed methods cases illustrate the reasoning behind research design decisions (e.g., whether quantitative and qualitative methods should be used sequentially or concurrently and for what purposes).

The Vienna Change Management Case Study:
Dominant-Dominant Simultaneous/Concurrent
Design: QUANT and QUAL

Scharitzer and Korunka (2000) used a single case study approach to examine the impact of several change interventions within a municipal service unit responsible for the area's public housing system for a city located in the western part of Austria. The change interventions included a comprehensive organizational restructuring process, the development of a new customer-centered orientation, autonomous budget responsibility, team leadership, an incentive system, and a general quality orientation. The study combined qualitative and quantitative data collection methods to obtain insights from two key stakeholder groups: employees and customers. Measurements were taken from both sets of stakeholders at three points in time: $t1$ at least 1 month before the organizational change, $t2$ shortly after the move to the new customer service centers, and $t3$ 1 year after the organizational change (about 11 months after $t2$).

Customer satisfaction was measured through interviews with representative samples of customers at three different points in time. Interviews with 182 customers were conducted before the organizational changes, and a questionnaire was mailed to randomly selected addresses to establish baseline values. Random samples of the customers who visited the service centers after opening enabled the researchers to interview 370 at $t2$ and 350 customers at $t3$. Customer satisfaction was measured by a means of a multidimensional scale. Customers were also asked to rate the importance of service quality criteria according to what an ideal service organization should be like.

The sample of employees consisted of all staff members from two customer service centers scheduled to be opened during the research period ($N = 104$). Subjective stress, perceived strain, emotional state, and job satisfaction were measured with existing instruments at all three time intervals. Perceived job characteristics were measured at $t1$ and $t3$. Information about the characteristics of the change management strategy was derived from interviews with the project manager. An interview guide was then developed. Participation and quality of training were evaluated by employees at two points in time through a questionnaire. The training itself was observed continuously. In addition to the surveys, interviews were conducted with the project manager, representatives of the staff council, and employees.

This study combined exploratory interviews with focused, validated questionnaires designed to elicit information about a specific construct. Through these multiple measures, the researchers obtained a complex, rich portrait of the impact of the change interventions over time on two groups of stakeholders. Not surprisingly, customers responded more favorably to these changes toward a more customer service orientation than did employees. With this rigorous time series study using strong quantitative measures of critical impact variables, we get a portrait of the movement from unstable to stable results from this change effort.

The CPA Case Study: Dominant–Less Dominant Simultaneous/Concurrent Design: QUANT and QUAL

Watkins and Cervero (2000) looked at the nature of the learning and development opportunities afforded an individual employed in a registered CPA firm and in a comprehensive business services firm. This study was initially commissioned in order to provide expert testimony to the state board. Watkins and Cervero asked, What is the role of the organizational setting on the learning and developmental experiences of certified professional accountants?

Three sources of data were used in this research project. First was a sample of the new accountant's work history from September 1, 1997, to February 28, 1998, at the CPA firm and a sample of his work history for the same time period one year later at the financial services firm. Time and billing reports, subdivided by categories of activities, were provided by both organizations. Second, a survey was developed based on prior research and on theories of workplace learning sampling 31 possible formal, informal, and incidental learning opportunities that could be available at each organization. Then, three principal parties to this case were surveyed to identify what learning opportunities were available and, among those learning opportunities, which the new accountant had actually participated in. The three individuals were the new accountant, his supervising accountant, and one of the owners of the firm. Finally, each individual was interviewed to identify examples and illustrations of the learning opportunities available in each organization as well as their role in supporting or participating in that learning.

The study concluded that the apprentice/coaching model of the profession and these organizations and the other activities of the senior staff, all licensed CPAs, at both firms more than met the state board standard of supervision of directing and inspecting the performance of the prospective CPA. Therefore, there was no material difference in the learning and developmental opportunities that were available at both organizations. Use of both qualitative and quantitative data enabled a rigorous and thorough examination of this phenomenon and therefore the highly credible and confident results required by expert testimony.

The Large-Scale Cascaded Training Innovation
Case Study: Dominant–Less Dominant
Sequential Design: qual to QUANT

Watkins, Ellinger, and Valentine (1999) examined the effectiveness of a large-scale organizational innovation, a cascaded training delivery strategy, at a Fortune 10 automotive manufacturer. An organization-wide effort to revamp engineering practices was under way at this corporation. The mission of the engineering group at this automotive manufacturer was to fundamentally change the way in which vehicles were designed and manufactured by imparting technical knowledge about robust engineering principles and procedures to an engineering community consisting of 19,000 engineers. Given the magnitude of the training task, the design institute of this organization implemented an innovation that involved using technical managers as instructors in a top-down cascaded training process.

The Concerns-Based Adoption Model (Hall & Hord, 1984) was selected as the theoretical framework to guide this study. This model outlines the developmental processes that individuals experience as a new innovation is implemented. Two diagnostic dimensions, concern and extent of use, associated with the way individuals change as they become more familiar with the innovation, were incorporated into the design of the study.

A survey design was selected as the overall approach to data collection and drew upon the relevant dimensions of the Concerns-Based Adoption Model. However, findings from a previously conducted qualitative study that was part of this research process were used to inform the survey development process. In the earlier qualitative phase of this overall study, a random sample of five employees who had experienced the manager-as-instructor approach were interviewed along with five managers who had participated in this process as instructors. Semistructured interviews were conducted with these 10 participants. Based on the analysis of the interview transcripts, six themes emerged that provided useful insights about this innovation from the perspectives of those who had served in an instructional capacity and those who experienced the subsequent delivery of this training. One theme that emerged, managerial role fit, reflected the managers' sense of fit with the role of serving as an instructor. This theme, coupled with a review of the extant literature on managerial roles, resulted in the creation of a scale that examined this aspect of the innovation. Based on the qualitative study, Watkins et al. were able to refine the questionnaire and capture language that was more reflective of the intended respondents.

In this case, using the emergent findings from the qualitative study to inform the survey development process in the dominant quantitative aspect of this project enhanced the rigor of the survey design that was implemented and enabled the researchers to have a more thorough understanding of this large-scale change process from the perspectives of those who had experienced it. The findings from the qualitative study that preceded the quantitative study served to corroborate the findings of the full survey implementation.

REFERENCES

Creswell, J. W. (1994). *Research design: Qualitative and quantitative approaches.* Thousand Oaks, CA: Sage.

Creswell, J. W. (1998). *Qualitative inquiry and research design: Choosing among five traditions.* Thousand Oaks, CA: Sage.

Creswell, J. W. (2003). *Research design: Qualitative, quantitative and mixed methods approaches* (2nd ed.). Thousand Oaks, CA: Sage.

Dooley, L. M. (2002). Case study research and theory building. *Advances in Developing Human Resources, 4*(3), 335–354.

Dube, L., & Pare, G. (2003). Rigor in IS positivist case research. *MIS Quarterly, 27*(4), 597–634.

Eisenhardt, K. M. (1989). Building theories from case study research. *The Academy of Management Review, 14*(4), 532–550.

Eisenhardt, K. M. (2002). Building theories from case study research. In A. M. Huberman & M. B. Miles (Eds.), *The qualitative researcher's companion* (pp. 5–35). Thousand Oaks, CA: Sage.

Hall, G., & Hord, S. (1984). Change in schools: Facilitating the process. Albany, NY: SUNY Press.

Merriam, S. B. (1988). *Case study research in education: A qualitative approach.* San Francisco: Jossey-Bass.

Merriam, S. B. (1998). *Qualitative research and case study applications in education.* San Francisco: Jossey-Bass.

Merriam, S. B., & Simpson, E. L. (1995). *A guide to research for educators and trainers of adults* (2nd ed.). Malabar, FL: Krieger.

Miles, M. B., & Huberman, A. M. (1994). *Qualitative data analysis* (2nd ed.). Thousand Oaks, CA: Sage.

Ragin, C. C., & Becker, H. S. (Eds.). (1992). *What is a case? Exploring the foundations of social inquiry.* Cambridge: Cambridge University Press.

Rein, M., & Schön, D. (1977). Problem setting in policy research. In C. Weiss (Ed.), *Using social policy research in public policy-making* (pp. 235–251). Lexington, MA: Heath.

Scharitzer, D., & Korunka, C. (2000). New public management: Evaluating the success of total quality management and change management interventions in public services from the employees and customers' perspectives. *Total Quality Management, 11*(7), S941–S954.

Scholz, R. W., & Tietje, O. (2002). *Embedded case study methods: Integrating quantitative and qualitative knowledge.* Thousand Oaks, CA: Sage.

Stake, R. E. (1994). Case studies. In N. K. Denzin & Y. S. Lincoln (Eds.), *Handbook of qualitative research* (pp. 236–247). Thousand Oaks, CA: Sage.

Stake, R. E. (1995). *The art of case study research.* Thousand Oaks, CA: Sage.

Watkins, K., & Cervero, R. (2000). Organizations as contexts for learning: A case study in certified public accountancy. *Journal of Workplace Learning, 12*(5), 187–194.

Watkins, K. E., Ellinger, A. D., & Valentine, T. (1999). Understanding support for innovation in a large scale change effort: The manager-as-instructor approach. *Human Resource Development Quarterly, 10*(1), 63–78.

Wells, A. S., Hirshberg, D., Lipton, M., & Oakes, J. (2002). Bounding the case within its context: A constructivist approach to studying detracking reform. In A. M. Huberman & M. B. Miles (Eds.), *The qualitative researcher's companion* (pp. 331–348). Thousand Oaks, CA: Sage.

Yin, R. K. (2003). *Case study research: Design and methods* (3rd ed.). Applied Social Research Methods Series, No. 5. Thousand Oaks, CA: Sage.

Theory Development
Research Methods

Richard J. Torraco, *University of Nebraska*

CHAPTER OUTLINE

Theory plays an important role in science and in professional disciplines. The purpose of this chapter is to describe the methods used to develop theories. It will demonstrate the relationship between the theories itself, the product of research, and the theory development research method used to develop it. Richer, more powerful theories are produced when researchers better understand the relationship between the theory and theory development research methods.

Formal and informal theories regularly come to our assistance, whether helping us solve everyday problems or providing explanations for the complex situations we encounter in organizations. A theory simply explains what a phenomenon is and how it works. A theory explains the phenomenon by identifying its main ideas, or *concepts,* and by stating the relationships these concepts have to each other. Concepts and their interrelationships are the elements of theory that are common to all research methods for theory development.

Theory development is important for establishing the theories and conceptual models needed to support organizational research and practice. Expanding the knowledge base with better theory is discussed in the research literature as an important contribution to advancing the impact and influence of emerging disciplines such as human resource development (HRD). This belief is shared widely in HRD (Holton, 2002; Ruona & Roth, 2000; Swanson, 2000) and has been an important foundation for the scholarly advancement of related disciplines such as management (Van de Ven, 1989), industrial-organizational psychology (Campbell, 1990), sociology (Cohen, 1989), adult learning (Marsick & Watkins, 1990; Revans, 1982), and psychology (Jensen, 1999).

THE PROCESS OF THEORY DEVELOPMENT RESEARCH

Theory development can be considered as a research *process* for creating theory. Theory development research has also been referred to as *theory construction, theory building,* and *theorizing.* Theory researchers approach their creative work from different paradigmatic perspectives, using their own preferred strategies and methods for developing new theoretical knowledge. Theory development methodologies vary in the paradigms or worldviews they represent. While alternative methodologies for theory research are available, researchers tend to pursue their work in ways that reflect their deep-seated values and assumptions about what constitutes knowledge (epistemology), the essence of being or existence (ontology), what constitutes value (axiology), and other basic philosophical beliefs. The researcher's personal intention and choice in these matters notwithstanding, some theory research methods are better suited for the particular purposes of theorizing than others. This chapter discusses alternative theory development research methods available to researchers.

Methodologies for developing theory in applied disciplines from the 1960s and 1970s have typically taken quantitative approaches to knowledge creation. Seminal sources for this approach to developing theory include Blalock (1969),

Dubin (1978), Freese (1980), Kaplan (1964), Kerlinger (1973), Reynolds (1971), and Stinchcombe (1968). However, many scholars report that these approaches to theory research are too standardized and formalized to reflect their theory development experiences (Van de Ven, 1989; Weick, 1989). Van de Ven (1989) observed over a decade ago that advancements in the process of theory development were needed to address the gap between researchers' espoused theory development methods and the methods that they actually used, and to provide more valid and practical ways to build good theory. Subsequently, new approaches to theory research have been developed that build on older, more traditional approaches. These include works by Cohen (1989), Eisenhardt (1989), Gioia and Pitre (1990), Lewis and Grimes (1999), Lynham (2002b), Moustakas (1994), and Strauss and Corbin (1998).

Combining traditional theory development methodologies with recent work in this area, the literature now contains a variety of descriptions of the process of theory research from quantitative, qualitative, and mixed methods perspectives. More than 20 substantive descriptions of the process of theory development research exist (see Torraco, 2004). These diverse approaches to theory research show the different ways in which a theory can be developed. Each theory development approach is based on different values, assumptions about what constitutes knowledge, strengths, limitations, and indications for use.

Theorists can choose to take more prescriptive approaches to theory building such as following Dubin's methodology or using the guidelines for grounded research. Alternatively, one's theory development may take its own unique path, since theory researchers, like other researchers, can employ a mixed combination of methods, including trial-and-error thinking, "disciplined imagination," or other approaches to conceptualizing their theories and models. Those new to theory research may find the prescriptive guidance of a particular theory development research method instructive and essential. Theorists seem to rely heavily on theory development research methodologies that provide explicit methodological guidance for working through the phases and procedures for developing theory. Explicit methodological guidance is particularly useful to scholars who are new to theory research, and the literature offers many examples of their use in theory development research.

OVERVIEW OF THE CHAPTER

The remainder of this chapter is divided into three parts. The first part discusses accepted theory development research methods according to three paradigm-related categories: quantitative, qualitative, and mixed method approaches to theory research. This first part attempts to make clear how each research method offers different methodological guidance for aspects of theory development. Selected research methods as applied to theory development are discussed. At the end of the chapter, these methods are summarized in Table 20.2 and referred to throughout the discussion.

In addition to these specific theory development methods, theories can be developed using research approaches that are novel mixtures of methods and unique to the individual theorist. Researchers innovate and take advantage of insights and techniques for theorizing that allow the rich, robust explanations for the phenomenon being modeled by the theory. As discussed by Weick (1989, 1995), experience theory scholars develop their own unique innovations to build theory as they gain mastery in the phenomena that interest them (the objects of their theorizing) and with theory building. Each of these unique approaches to theory development represents an innovation that can inspire other researchers. Indeed, published accounts exist of unique mixed method approaches to theorizing that are described explicitly enough to provide guidance to others about how theory is conceptualized and fully developed. In addition, theory journals occasionally offer special issues that provide valuable research and resources for theory researchers.

Regardless of the theory development research method that guides the research process, certain guidelines for good theory development research exist and are expected to be met by all theory development endeavors. These guidelines for theory building are discussed in the final section of the chapter.

RESEARCH METHODS USED IN THEORY DEVELOPMENT

This section discusses research methods used in theory development according to three paradigm-related categories: quantitative, qualitative, and mixed methods research.

Quantitative Approaches to Theory Development

Quantitative research methods for theory building include Dubin's (1978) methodology for theory research, meta-analytic theory development, theory development from quantitative case studies (Yin, 1994), and other quantitative approaches to theory building. (See Torraco, 2004, for a listing of works on positivistic theory building before and after 1980.)

Dubin's Theory Development Methodology

Dubin's (1978) methodology for theory building follows the quantitative research tradition and takes a hypothetico-deductive approach to knowledge creation. This method is based on the assumptions that knowledge is created to explain, predict, and control the phenomenon of interest; that new knowledge (theory) should serve technical/utilitarian interests for interrelating means and ends; and that the discovery of generalizable laws and explanations of human and organizational phenomena is possible and desirable.

Dubin's methodology provides a specific, eight-phase process for theory development research. (See Dubin, 1978, or Lynham, 2002a, for a discussion of Dubin's theory-building methodology.) An advantage of Dubin's methodology is that the theory-building purpose of each phase of the methodology is clearly specified and interrelated to other phases. The first five elements of Dubin's approach specify the methods for the initial construction and development of the theory. The last three elements represent the process of taking the theory into real-world contexts to conduct research for empirical verification. Thus, the methodology is comprehensive in providing for the initial development of theory and for the research to empirically verify the theory. Dubin's methodology is commonly used by those who adopt a *theory-then-research* strategy for theory building.

Hertzberg's (1966) two-factor theory of work motivation offers an elegant and straightforward example of Dubin's theory-building methodology. The system modeled by Herzberg's theory consists of individuals interacting in work situations in which *extrinsic factors* and *intrinsic factors* serve as motivators of individuals who react with *satisfaction* or *dissatisfaction* to these factors. In Dubin's terms, the "units of the theory" (or its conceptual building blocks) are *extrinsic factors, intrinsic factors, satisfaction,* and *dissatisfaction.* It is the relationships among these elements that constitute Herzberg's theory of work motivation. The key relationships ("laws of interaction") specified by the theory that explain work motivation are (1) there is an inverse relationship between the levels of an individual's dissatisfaction and the perceived adequacy of the extrinsic factors of a work situation, and (2) there is a positive relationship between the individual's satisfaction and the perceived adequacy of the intrinsic factors of a work situation. Herzberg's theory also shows how the *boundaries, system states, propositions,* and empirical components of Dubin's methodology are used in theory-building research. (See Dubin, 1976, for a complete discussion of Herzberg's two-factor theory as an example of this methodology.)

Meta-Analytic Research for Theory Development

Meta-analysis uses formal statistical techniques to sum up a body of separate, but similar, empirical studies. The purpose of meta-analysis is to synthesize and organize existing empirical findings on a topic into a coherent pattern. The meta-analytic approach seeks general conclusions across multiple studies as the basis for theory building. Yang (2002) describes a five-step process for meta-analytic theory building that leads to confirmation or disconfirmation of existing theory and/or the search for alternative theory. Theory is not always fully confirmed using meta-analysis, a finding that implies the need for the refinement or modification of existing theory based on these studies. On the other hand, disconfirmation of theory indicates the need for further theory building in the search for alternative theory.

Meta-analytic theory building offers several distinctive features to those seeking to build theory or refine existing theory. Meta-analytic findings provide powerful prescriptions for new theoretical understandings that are scientifically derived from bodies of existing studies. They also offer the scope and depth necessary for substantive advances in theoretical understanding because these findings are based on aggregated knowledge across studies of known quality. This capacity to integrate and synthesize empirical studies has yielded valuable contributions to theory about work groups and teams. A disadvantage of using meta-analysis for theory building is that theorists must use what is provided by existing studies; they cannot include new variables or reconfigure the factors examined in the original studies. Nonetheless, meta-analysis makes a distinctive contribution to theory building—its unique ability to cumulate existing empirical findings and to offer integrated results that can be used to develop or refine theoretical knowledge. This is particularly valuable for theorists seeking to resolve problems created by new developments in organizations that are inadequately explained by existing theory, a situation commonly found in applied disciplines when extensive research may already exist on these organizational phenomena. Meta-analysis can help theorists identify new directions for theorizing at the outset of theory building in a way that charts the proper course to fruitful areas of new knowledge.

An example of the use of meta-analysis for theory development is the work of Brewer and Shapard (2004), who reviewed a large body of studies on employee burnout and its etiology. They conducted a meta-analysis of 34 empirical studies of employee turnover and found a negative correlation between emotional exhaustion (a component of burnout) and the age of employees (i.e., older employees experience less burnout than younger employees). They also found a small negative correlation between years of experience in the field and emotional exhaustion (i.e., employees who have worked in a job or field for longer periods of time experience less burnout than employees who have worked in that type of job or field for shorter periods of time). These results raise serious questions about existing explanations of employee burnout and turnover (e.g., long-term employment leads to burnout and subsequent job change). The authors recommend additional theoretical and empirical studies of the relationship between burnout and key etiological factors such as age and years of experience. By aggregating and integrating findings across multiple empirical studies, meta-analysis identifies fruitful areas for new theoretical study by emphasizing specific concepts and relationships in existing theories that need further research.

Qualitative Approaches to Theory Development

Qualitative research methods for theory development include grounded theory research, phenomenology, and social-constructionist research.

Grounded Theory Research

Unlike quantitative methods for theory building, grounded theory research follows an inductive approach to generating or discovering theory. Theory evolves during grounded research through continuous interplay between analysis and data collection. Throughout the research process, theory is provisionally verified through a rigorous process of continuous matching of theory against data. Thus, grounded theory is distinctive in its approach to theory building because of its singular commitment to allow new theoretical understandings to emerge from the data. Theoretical conceptualizations derived in this way are intended to be closely connected to evidence through the continuous analysis and comparison of data and emergent theory (Strauss & Corbin, 1998). Rigorous matching of data with theory is pursued for verification of the resulting hypotheses *throughout the theory-building process*. In this way, grounded theory strives for *authenticity*— a faithfulness to the data that closely reflects the meanings and understandings of those involved in the phenomenon being modeled by the theory.

The use of grounded research for theory building is indicated when the type of theoretical knowledge sought cannot be compared to preexisting conceptions (i.e., for phenomena studied for the first time). Theory development using this approach is particularly well suited to generating new theoretical understandings and tentative hypotheses about the phenomenon of interest. Grounded research lends itself especially well to showing the relationship between the theory-building research process and the theory produced through this process.

The theory developed by Jones (1999) through grounded research to better understand the process of structuring a community-based curriculum for rural schools provides an exemplary illustration of the use of Strauss and Corbin's (1998) methodology to generate new theory. According to Strauss and Corbin, analysis of qualitative data for theory building involves the use of open coding, axial coding, and selective coding. *Open coding* allows the theorist to begin generating thematic categories from qualitative data. *Axial coding* refines the categories through "reassembling the data that were fractured during open coding" and systematically linking and integrating categories and subcategories into more robust classifications of data. However, Strauss and Corbin maintain that it is not until *selective coding* that "the major categories are finally integrated to form a larger theoretical scheme that the research findings take the form of *theory*" (italics in original). Jones's work allows the reader to follow the use of these data analysis procedures through a well-documented inductive theory-building process. The work traces the development of the theory with clear descriptions of how foundational concepts, empirical data, and theoretical logic were used to develop and refine the emergent theory.

Phenomenological Research for Theory Development

Moustakas (1994) offers guidelines for using phenomenology as a method for theory development. The goal of phenomenological research is to determine what an experience means to the individuals who have had it and be able to provide a comprehensive description of the experience (Moustakas, 1994). Phenomenological description, particularly of novel or unique experiences, enables a rich understanding of the phenomenon and can be used for theoretical explanation. Unlike other research methods, phenomenology searches for meanings and essences of experiences rather than explanations or measurements. It focuses on the wholeness of experience rather than on its objects or parts. Moustakas discusses methods of analyzing phenomenological data and using phenomenological processes and concepts (i.e., epoche, phenomenological reduction, imaginative variation, and synthesis of composite textual and structural descriptions) to create new knowledge and theory. Myers's (2000) phenomenological study provides a clear and well-developed example of how theory is developed using phenomenological methods. Using Moustakas's general guidelines for phenomenological research, Myers developed a model of management consultation used by employee assistance program (EAP) professionals in higher education that shows how these professionals serve their institutions.

Social Constructionist Research for Theory Development

Theory building for the social-constructionist is not undertaken to uncover a theoretical *truth* or *reality* but to model an understanding of the sense that people make of the social world in their everyday lives. Social-constructionist theory building is concerned with seeking explanations about how social experience is created and given meaning. The distinguishing features of social-constructionist theory building are its emphasis on the specific, the local, and the particular as means to more closely represent the lived experience of those studied. Kenneth Gergen, a leading scholar of social-constructionist thinking, has discussed the assumptions of contemporary organization science, refuted many of the tenets of positivistic inquiry, and argued for "organization science as social construction" (Gergen & Thatchenkery, 2004). Social-constructionist theory attempts to extrapolate these insights to seek transferability of ideas toward a redefinition of existing theoretical frameworks.

Unlike other approaches to theory development, social-constructionist research seeks increased powers of perception and understanding as an end in itself, whether it is rooted in interpretive, explanatory, or emancipatory objectives. In aiming for understanding and reconstruction of reality, the social-constructionist researcher remains visible and self-declared during the process of research and theory building, so that it is clear when the researcher's own voice is represented and when the voices of others are put forward. Thus, social-constructionist theory seeks to present authentic meaning through carefully crafted narratives of how people make sense of the social world in their everyday lives. Turnbull (1999) describes the potential richness of social-constructivist theory building to explain the influence of emotional labor on middle managers.

Mixed Methods Approaches to Theory Research

Mixed methods or multiparadigmatic approaches to theory development are distinct from pure quantitative and qualitative positivistic approaches. *Multiparadigm* means bridging across opposing paradigms (i.e., qualitative and quantitative) through synthesis to create new richer understandings of phenomena than may be possible from a single paradigmatic perspective. Multiparadigmatic approaches to theory development include case study research (Eisenhardt, 1995), the use of paradox for theory building (Poole & Van de Ven, 1989; Lewis, 2000), and theory building from multiple paradigms through *metatriangulation* (Lewis & Grimes, 1999).

Theory Development from Case Study Research

Case study research focuses on understanding the dynamics present within single settings. Although case study research and theory building from case study research are both based on the study of phenomena present within case settings, these research activities represent distinct contributions to new knowledge. *Case study research* takes advantage of the rich context for empirical observation provided by case settings to study a selected phenomenon using qualitative or quantitative methods without offering formal theoretical interpretations of the study. On the other hand, *theory building from case study research* generates explicit theoretical statements that explain the dynamics of phenomena occurring within case settings. An advantage of using case study research for theory building is that it does not rely on previous literature or prior empirical evidence. Thus, this methodology is particularly appropriate when little is known about a phenomenon, current perspectives seem inadequate because they have little empirical substantiation, or they conflict with each other or common sense (Eisenhardt, 1995). Another unique feature of this approach to theory building is that case study research is a methodology that is consistent with positivistic, naturalistic, or both paradigmatic approaches to the discovery of new knowledge. This feature allows case studies to be used for multiparadigm research, and it allows theorists to preserve opposing paradigmatic perspectives while developing richer, more diverse theory for complex phenomena.

Markus's (1983) study of resistance to the introduction and implementation of management information systems offers a good example of developing theory from a case study. This study compared and evaluated three basic theories of the causes of resistance to new technology: (1) resistance intrinsic to human agents, (2) resistance due to external factors (i.e., poor technical or environmental design), and (3) resistance based on interaction theory (i.e., resistance because of interaction between characteristics related to people and characteristics related to the system). The study used data from a case study to demonstrate the superiority of interaction theory to guide the implementation of management information systems.

Another good example of theory building from case study research is Margolis and Hansen's (2002) work, in which the authors develop a theory of organizational identity using a qualitative case study. The case provided a unique opportunity to study organizational identity during a pivotal period of crisis and decision making for a low-fare airline that had recently experienced an airline crash involving multiple fatalities and that was now in the process of working through a merger with another airline. The merger with the parent of another small airline was specifically targeted as the best vehicle for transforming the organization's image that had been damaged because of the intense and unrelenting negative media exposure since the fatal accident. Following an inductive and emergent process, the qualitative case study provided an opportunity to uncover insiders' perceptions of organizational identity within the context of a merger experience. The authors laid a theoretical framework and conducted three phases of interviews: during the premerger period, after the company's name change but before the merger was official, and after the merger. Theoretical validity (authenticity) was supported by using multiple and different sources and methods for data collection and analysis. The authors provide a full account of the procedures that they used to build their theory, allowing readers to follow the theory-building process from the research problem (sustaining organizational identity during traumatic change) to the theoretical outcome (a model of organizational identity).

Using Paradox for Theory Development

Paradox is a real or apparent contradiction between equally well-based assumptions or conclusions. In the same way that positivistic and naturalistic research paradigms are seen as contradictory or opposing worldviews, there are paradoxical (and paradigmatic) challenges to developing theories of human and organizational phenomena. Poole and Van de Ven (1989) took the first steps to resolve the contradictions between apparently opposing views by proposing four generic ways in which two opposing theses (or paradigms), A and B, might be related. They propose that we can keep opposing paradigms, A and B, separate and appreciate their contrasts. We can situate A and B at two different locations or levels in the social world (e.g., micro- and macrolevels, respectively). We can separate A and B temporally in the same location. Or we can find some new perspective that eliminates the opposition between A and B and thus advance a new conception of the relationship between the paradoxical elements that resolves the opposition between them. Described schematically, the four relations correspond to opposition, spatial separation, temporal separation, and synthesis. Poole and Van de Ven (1989) state, "These four states represent a logically exhaustive set of relationships opposing terms can take in the social world" (p. 565).

Multiparadigm means bridging across opposing paradigms (i.e., positivistic and naturalistic) through synthesis to create new and richer understandings. *Metaparadigmatic* is theory building that transcends paradigms (Lewis & Grimes, 1999). Van de Ven and Poole (1988) propose a multiparadigmatic approach to theory building that is also *metaparadigmatic*. They clarify the conceptual challenges posed by multiparadigm theory building by analyzing three paradoxical requirements of a theory of organizational change. For example, they examined the apparent paradox of *internal sources of change: external sources of change* and showed how accounting for the role of time helps resolve this paradox using Tushman and Romanelli's (1985) theory of punctuated equilibrium. To further advance the development of theory on organizational change, Van de Ven and Poole (1988) built a theoretical base that bridges paradigms and creates new understanding of this phenomenon that is not possible from either a positivistic or naturalistic paradigm alone. They propose the following key relationships as the basis of such a theory:

> Organizational change can be understood to arise from two basic sources: (a) Tensions that emerge over time between personnel action and structural forms which are created by and constrain purposive action at each level of organizational analysis, and (b) forces of conflict, coercion, and disruption at one level of organization, and forces of consensus, unity, and integration at another level—forces that are prerequisites and reciprocals of each other. (p. 57)

Van de Ven and Poole's work is an example of how opposing or contradictory assumptions and worldviews can be resolved to create a richer understanding of complex phenomena such as organizational change that is not possible from either a positivistic or naturalistic paradigm alone. Lewis (2000) elaborates on the use of paradox in theoretical research and helps researchers move beyond using paradox as a label by outlining strategies for identifying and representing paradox in research.

Theory Development through Metatriangulation

Gioia and Pitre (1990) take a multiparadigm perspective on theory building. Lewis and Grimes (1999) build on Gioia and Pitre's case for multiparadigm theory building by arguing for an approach to theory building from multiple paradigms through *metatriangulation*. Whereas multiparadigm theory building bridges opposing paradigms (i.e., positivistic and naturalistic), metaparadigmatic theory building moves beyond paradigms to create a novel understanding of the phenomenon. To distinguish multiparadigm research from the use of *metatriangulation* for theory-building research, Lewis and Grimes (1999) observe that multiparadigm research involves using paradigmatic lenses (X and Y) to collect and analyze data and cultivate their diverse representations of organizational phenomena. In metaparadigm theory building, theorists strive to juxtapose and link conflicting paradigm insights (X and Y) within a novel understanding (Z). Lewis and Grimes (1999) state, "Metaparadigm denotes a higher level of abstraction, from which 'accommodation' does *not* imply unification or synthesis but, instead, the ability to comprehend paradigmatic differences, similarities, and interrelationships. . . . Metatheorizing techniques help theorists explore patterns that span conflicting understandings" (p. 675). The authors describe a metatriangulation theory-building process and illustrate it with an example of the application of metatriangulation to their study of advanced manufacturing technology.

THEORY RESEARCH: ELABORATIONS AND INNOVATIONS

It is difficult to know how closely theorists follow the prescriptions for building theory offered by particular theory development research methods. In some published accounts of theory building, the author states explicitly that the theory was developed using a particular theory-building method such as grounded theory or Dubin's methodology. On the other hand, rather than following established prescriptions for theory building, many works that offer new theories describe a process of theoretical research that is unique to the theorist and the subject matter. Such research typically describes the methods and conceptual logic of the theory-building process by discussing existing literature and theory related to the topic, how data were collected and analyzed from various sources and then used, along with how foundational concepts and existing theory were integrated and synthesized to develop a new theory. Thus, it is likely that many of the accepted theories that we use result from improvisation by the theorist. Published accounts exist of unique approaches to theorizing that are described explicitly enough to provide guidance to others about how theory is conceptualized and developed. In addition, theory journals such as the *Academy of Management Review* occasionally offer special issues that provide valuable research and resources for theorists. This section discusses the most influential and relevant of these works for organizational theorists.

Publication of the Special Forum on Theory Building (*Academy of Management Review*, 1989) was important for the development of theory and theory-building expertise. It provided a collection of important works on evaluative criteria for theory (Bacharach, 1989; Van de Ven, 1989; Whetten, 1989) and some important innovations in theory development (Eisenhardt, 1989; Poole & Van de Ven, 1989; Weick, 1989). For example, Weick (1989) discusses theory building as a process of disciplined imagination. Weick's work bridges the boundaries between quantitative and qualitative theory development research methods. Like the other work discussed in this section, it represents an innovation or elaboration on traditional theory-building methods. Weick proposes that the quality of theory produced varies according to the accuracy and detail present in the problem statement that triggers theory development, the number of and independence among the conjectures that attempt to solve the problem, and the number and diversity of selection criteria used to test the conjectures. Weick uses the term *thought trials* to refer to the mental experimentation that theorists use to create theory; naturalistic theorists attempt to make these thought trials explicit.

A special forum of the *Administrative Science Quarterly* offers additional definition and structure to the challenge of theory research. This journal's Notice to

Contributors states, "If manuscripts contain no theory, their value is suspect." In response to queries from potential authors about what theory is and what is not, *Administrative Science Quarterly* reviewed important components of manuscripts that should not be considered theory (Sutton & Staw, 1995), elements of theorizing that should be emphasized by authors (Weick, 1995), and a rejoinder and synthesis (DiMaggio, 1995).

Typologies are a popular component of theoretical research because they provide a parsimonious framework for describing complex organizational and behavioral phenomena. Taking the position that typologies are frequently misunderstood and underutilized, Doty and Glick (1994) elaborate on the meaning and value of typologies and have developed a general approach for modeling typological theories.

Organizational phenomena of interest to research include many complex, multilevel constructs. Examples of important multilevel constructs include organizational restructuring learning and learning synergy at multiple levels (individual, group, and organizational learning), job design, strategy, and innovation. The Special Topic Forum on Multilevel Theory Building (*Academy of Management Review*, 1999) provided new perspectives on the development of multilevel theory and theory building. Among the important contributions in this special issue is the work of Morgeson and Hofmann (1999). They propose that multilevel theory requires consideration of both the structure and function of constructs since each dimension of the construct provides a different perspective on the construct's utility for multilevel theory. For example, a multilevel theory of work design theory requires the analysis of both the structure and function of work design constructs (Torraco, 2005).

The *Academy of Management Review* also published, in 1999, a Special Topic Forum on Evaluation, Reflections, and New Directions for theory development. This journal issue includes Lewis and Grimes's (1999) treatise that argues for an approach to theory building from multiple paradigms through metatriangulation. In addition, this issue presents an article by Langley (1999) discussing alternative strategies for theorizing from process data. Pentland (1999) considers building process theories from narratives.

Finally, an issue of *Advances in Developing Human Resource* provides an in-depth discussion of five theory-building research methods that are frequently used in applied disciplines (Lynham, 2002b). This special issue explains and illustrates the use of the theory-building research methods of Dubin (1978), grounded theory, meta-analytic theory building, the social-constructionist approach, and theory building from case study research. In addition, Lynham presents a General Method for Theory Building Research in Applied Disciplines that provides an overarching theory development construct and language for theory researchers. Given the wide variety of specific methodological approaches to the development of theory, Lynham's General Method calls upon multiple methods to address the various theory research components of conceptual development, operationalization, confirmation or disconfirmation, application, and continuous refinement and development. This approach also illustrates the theory and practice linkage—deductive to inductive and inductive to deductive strategies. Specific quantitative and qualitative research strategies covered in earlier chapters can be used for theory development research within one or more of the theory research components of conceptual development, operationalization, confirmation or disconfirmation, application, and continuous refinement and development.

REQUIREMENTS FOR EXCELLENCE IN THEORETICAL RESEARCH

Producing good theory requires familiarity with criteria for sound theory and theory-building research methods. In addition, the development of high-quality, provocative theories (i.e., theories that substantially alter the way we think about the world) seem to grow out of significant experience and study of both the phenomenon being modeled by the theory and refinement of one's approach to theory building. The capability for producing excellent theory rests on key characteristics of the theorist and of his or her work. Regardless of the theory-building research method that guides the research process, certain standards of good theory-building research are expected of all theory-building endeavors. These expectations can be represented as guidelines for developing good theory. These guidelines apply to the theorist, to the research process (i.e., the theorist's theory-building research method), and to the product (i.e., the theory itself). The following key characteristics are central to excellence in theory building:

- The theorist should have substantial knowledge about the two major domains for theory building.
- The theory should be based on the clear specification of the problem or need for theory building.
- The research should demonstrate explicitly the logic and theoretical reasoning used by the theorist to link the research problem with the theoretical outcome (e.g., the theory or model).
- The work should propose and discuss research propositions, questions, or hypotheses for further theoretical and empirical study of the phenomenon modeled by the theory.

Each of these important characteristics is discussed next.

Knowledge Domains for Theory Building

Good theory takes time and hard work to develop. Producing good theory is the result of intensive study of the phenomenon or topic of the theory, intense thought and conceptualizing by the theorist about the phenomenon and how it might work, and, usually, multiple attempts at crafting a theoretical model or framework that contains all of the necessary elements of the theory and that appears to offer a defensible explanation of the phenomenon. Often during the process of theory building, some bad theory or theory found to have key deficiencies is developed, from which the theorist learns and improves her or his theory building. Ultimately, however, good theorists develop theories that can potentially change the way we think about phenomena.

A necessary competency for theory-building research is knowledge of the elements of theory and of the process of developing new theoretical knowledge (i.e., knowledge of theory-building research methods). The main purpose of this chapter is to make explicit what is currently known about theory-building research methods. As discussed earlier, all theorists need some baseline level of knowledge about the basic processes for developing new theoretical knowledge. Nonetheless, in the course of maturing as theoretical researchers, each theorist refines his or her own unique approach to theory building. Knowledge of theory-building research, as a major component of the knowledge domain for theory building, is shown on the left side of Table 20.1.

The problems in today's organizations most in need of theory are quite complex yet poorly understood. It is for these problems that we benefit most from having theory that offers a clear, theoretical explanation of the basic issues and conflicts that underlie the problem. However, knowledge of such complex organizational phenomena does not likely reside in a single source. In a complex world, different perspectives on such problems make different sorts of information about them available. Discussing the type of knowledge production needed to address complex organizational problems, Van de Ven and Johnson (in press) propose a strategy of *intellectual arbitrage*—exploiting the different perspectives of theory and practice to produce knowledge about such problems. A research strategy based on intellectual arbitrage exploits the differing perspectives that scholars from different disciplines and practitioners from different functional experiences bring forth to address problems that are too complex to be captured by any one investigator or perspective. Such knowledge is produced through acquiring a deep conceptual understanding of the phenomenon or topic of the theory and through practical knowledge of the phenomenon (knowledge from experience). This major component of the knowledge domain for theory building is shown on the right side of Table 20.1.

The main premise of Van de Ven and Johnson's work is that knowledge for theory and practice, and knowledge about complex organizational phenomena, is produced through arbitrage, a dialectical method of inquiry where understanding and synthesis of a complex problem evolves from the confrontation of knowledge of science and knowledge from experience (practical knowledge). These components of knowledge of the phenomenon become, according to these authors, the objects of divergent thesis and antitheses as a new theory about the complex phenomenon takes shape. Presumably, a more comprehensive, powerful

TABLE 20.1 Knowledge Domains for Theory Building

THEORY BUILDING METHODOLOGY	VALUES AND ASSUMPTIONS	STRENGTHS AND INDICATIONS FOR USE	LIMITATIONS
Quantitative Dubin's Theory-Development Methodology	■ Knowledge is created for the purpose(s) of explanation, prediction, and/or control of the phenomena of interest. ■ New knowledge (theory) should serve technical/utilitarian interests for interrelating means and ends. ■ The discovery of generalizable laws and explanations of human and organizational phenomena is possible and desirable.	■ Dubin's methodology can be used for hypothetico-deductive knowledge creation. ■ Dubin's methodology offers a specific, multi-phased process for theory building. Each phase of theory building is clearly specified and interrelated to other phases. ■ The methodology is comprehensive in providing for the initial development of theory, and for the research to empirically verify the theory.	■ Dubin's methodology cannot be used for inductive knowledge creation. ■ This methodology has been criticized as linear, sequential, and unable to adequately represent the fluidity and emergent nature of many social and organizational phenomena.
Meta-Analytic Research for Theory Building	■ Cumulative and synthesizing the findings of separate, but similar, studies of an issue produces worthwhile new knowledge. ■ Rigorous research design and statistical analysis allow the researcher to remain impartial and detached from the outcomes of the research.	■ Meta-analysis is capable of integrating and synthesizing existing empirical studies of a phenomenon as the basis for theory building. ■ Meta-analysis can help theorists to identify fruitful areas of new knowledge at the outset of theory building, and can offer guidance for concept selection and research design. ■ Meta-analysis provides aggregate assessments of the relationships between explanatory factors and outcomes, thus revealing patterns of causal relationships. In this way meta-analysis offers a unique evaluation of the efficacy of competing theories.	■ Meta-analytic theory building cannot be used for inductive knowledge creation. ■ Meta-analytic approaches cannot be used for topics on which there are few studies.

Qualitative Grounded Theory-Research	■ Theory grounded in the interplay of data collection and theoretical analysis yields valuable social science knowledge. ■ Grounded theory rejects both strict determinism and nondeterminism—actors possess the means of controlling their destinies by their responses to conditions.	■ Grounded theory is of particular value for generating new insights and tentative hypotheses, regardless of existing theoretical explanations of a phenomenon. ■ Grounded theory's commitment to closeness of fit between theory and data yields theory with strong descriptive and explanatory power.	■ Grounded theory should not be used when breadth and generalizability of theoretical explanations are sought.
Phenomenological Research for Theory Development	■ Phenomenology seeks understanding of the meanings and essences of experience rather than explanation or measurement. ■ Phenomenology emphasizes the wholeness of experience rather than its objects or parts.	■ Phenomenological theory building creates new understandings of what experiences mean to individuals who have had them. Since phenomenology enables comprehensive description and understanding, particularly of novel or unique experiences, it can be used for theoretical explanation.	■ The phenomenological researcher must be completely open, receptive, and naïve in hearing research participants describe their experiences. Phenomenology relies on intuition, imagination, and openness for obtaining a picture of the dynamics of the experience. It should not be used to create knowledge for universal structures, standardization, or generalization.
Social Constructivist Research for Theory Development	■ Knowledge is created through understanding and explanation of how social experience is created and given meaning. ■ The complexity of lived experience and the variability of social relations mitigate against attempts to claim causality or generalizability in social constructionist theory.	■ Social constructionist theory building can model and enhance our understanding of how people intersubjectively create, understand, and reproduce social situations. ■ By emphasizing the specific, the local, and the particular, social constructionist theory building more closely represents the lived experience of those studied.	■ The use of social constructionist theory building is limited to the declared purpose of the research—seeking understanding of the sense that people make of the social world in their everyday lives.

TABLE 20.1 Knowledge Domains for Theory Building, *continued*

THEORY BUILDING METHODOLOGY	VALUES AND ASSUMPTIONS	STRENGTHS AND INDICATIONS FOR USE	LIMITATIONS
Mixed Method Theory Development from Case Study Research	▪ Since this methodology is consistent with positivism, naturalistic or both paradigmatic approaches to the discovery of new knowledge, it can reflect the values and assumptions of both paradigms.	▪ Theory building from case study research is of particualr value when a focus on single settings is the optimum context for theory building. ▪ Since it does not rely on previous literature or prior empirical evidence, this methodology is particularly appropriate in situations when little is known about a phenomenon, when current theory seems inadequate, or when present perspectives conflict with each other or common sense.	▪ This methodology has been criticized for producing theory that is rich in detail, but overly complex and lacking a coherent, integrated perspective on the phenomenon.
Using Paradox for Theory Development	▪ As a multiparadigm approach to theory building, the use of paradox reflects the values and assumptions of both positivistic and naturalistic paradigms.	▪ Using paradox for theory building bridges paradigms and allows opposing or contradictory assumptions and worldviews to be resolved. The use of paradox for theory building creates richer understandings of complex phenomena that are not possible from either a positivistic or naturalistic paradigm alone.	▪ Since paradox can be used for theory building to explain complex and ambiguous phenomena, its use necessarily involves describing conflicting demands, opposing perspectives, and/or seemingly illogical findings.
Theory Development through Metatriangulation	▪ As a multiparadigm approach to theory building, metatriangulation reflects the values and assumptions of both positivistic and naturalistic paradigms.	▪ Metaparadigm theory building justaposes and links conflicting paradigm insights (X and Y) within a novel understanding (Z). Metaparadigm theory building allows the comprehension of paradigmatic differences, similarities, and interrelationships.	▪ Since metaparadigm theory building strives to move beyond opposing perspectives to create new understanding of a phenomenon, researchers confront the challenges of meta-theory building (i.e., attempting to resolve conflicting understandings).

explanation of the phenomenon results when both components of knowledge of the phenomenon to be modeled by the theory (conceptual knowledge and practical knowledge) are involved in Van de Ven and Johnson's research strategy of intellectual arbitrage. Even without Van de Ven and Johnson's argument, there is no substitute for broad and deep understanding of the theorist of the phenomenon or topic to be modeled by the theory. Good theory cannot be generated without significant insight into the phenomenon.

In short, good theory requires the researcher to have knowledge in two major domains for theory development:

- knowledge of the elements of theory and of the process of developing new theoretical knowledge (i.e., knowledge of theory building) and
- deep conceptual understanding and practical knowledge (knowledge from experience) of the phenomenon or topic to be modeled by the theory.

"Problem" or "Need" as Catalyst for Theory Building

When modeling a fundamentally new phenomenon with theory for the first time, the theorist can take advantage of a wide open landscape for the development of theory. Because the phenomenon is relatively new (e.g., a new form of work design enabled by virtual audio-video technology), no prior theory exists to aid in its understanding. Fundamentally, new phenomena represent exciting and fruitful opportunity for theorizing. Many new, unexplained forces have destabilized organizations, industries, and the global economy. Virtual work and the virtual work environment are not well understood and represent new problems that are ripe for theoretical explanation. Theory is needed to help scholars and practitioners better understand these phenomena and, ultimately, to provide the new knowledge to enable fulfilling and productive work environments.

However, for an area or phenomenon for which related theory already exists, *identifying the problem or need for additional theory building is an important component of theory-building research*. The problem or need for theory building about a phenomenon or area that has been previously studied is based on identifying deficiencies, omissions, and inadequacies in existing theoretical knowledge about the phenomenon. The notion of *need* requires elaboration. *Need* is defined here as a condition or situation in which something is required or wanted. When applied to a piece of theoretical research, the notion of *need* is not synonymous with the purpose of the work. The notion of *need* retains a key element that is, a priori, external to the interests and purposes of the individual researcher. The *problem* or *need* for theory building on a phenomenon or area that has been previously studied is based on identifying deficiencies, omissions, and inadequacies in existing theoretical knowledge about the phenomenon. Readers of articles addressing this type of theory expect to see a comprehensive review of literature related to the topic of theory building, on which the problem or need to be addressed by additional theory should be based.

Connections between the Research Problem and the Theoretical Outcome

The research should demonstrate explicitly the logic and theoretical reasoning used by the theorist to link the research problem with the theoretical outcome (e.g., the theory or model). Features of particular theory-building research methods discussed earlier in the chapter lend themselves to productive theorizing depending on the nature of the phenomenon and the particular research purpose of the work. The selection and use of theory-building research methods depends, in part, on the nature of the phenomenon and the problem or need to be addressed by theory-building research.

Research that presents the theory-building process and the theory offers a holistic view of theory-building research. Such research provides a means for tracing the author's theory-building strategies as they give rise to a theoretical product. Showing the connections between the research problem and outcome allows the reader to appreciate the conceptual challenges the theorist encounters during the development of the theory, and then, to see how the challenges are resolved and reflected in the theory itself. On the other hand, presenting a theory or model without a description of the origin of its component constructs, their interrelationships, and the conceptual reasoning used to build the theory or model is akin to presenting the results and conclusions of an empirical study without discussing data collection and analysis. As with other types of research, readers of new theory expect to see how the logic and conceptual reasoning of the research process was used to develop the proposed theory.

The connections between the research problem and the theoretical product should be described clearly in theory-building research. As noted in the section of this chapter on theory building with qualitative case studies, Margolis and Hansen (2002) provide a full account of their process of using a qualitative case study to develop a theory of organizational identity. This discussion allows the reader to follow the connection between the research problem (sustaining organizational identity during traumatic change) and the theoretical outcome (a model of organizational identity). Other works also present explicit accounts of the relationship between the theory-building research process and its product (e.g., Dubin's [1976] discussion of how Herzberg's two-factor theory of work motivation follows Dubin's methodology for theory building).

Propositions and Questions for Further Research

Finally, the theory should propose and discuss research propositions, questions, or hypotheses for further theoretical and empirical study of the phenomenon modeled by the theory. *The statement of research propositions, questions, or hypotheses is necessary, not optional, for any theory that has not been tested or for theoretical research on topics that have not been studied exhaustively.* As Weick (1995) maintains, most of what is proffered as theory is "interim theory—an

**TABLE 20.2   Summary of Selected Research Methods
for Theory Development**

KNOWLEDGE OF THEORY BUILDING RESEARCH	KNOWLEDGE OF PHENOMENON TO BE MODELED BY THE THEORY
■ Knowledge of the elements of theory and of theory building methods.	■ Deep conceptual understanding of phenomenon/topic of the theory.
■ Knowledge and refinement of one's own unique approach to theory building.	■ Practical knowledge of phenomenon (knowledge from experience).

approximation of theory" (p. 494). As theorists work through the research process, theory is initially conceptualized through a review of related literature, through hunches and thought trials of the theorist, the use of foundational concepts, existing theory, the development of new concepts and new conceptual relationships, and, finally, if the emerging theoretical systems is based on the other "requirements" discussed here, a theoretical framework or model that reflects synthesis of the aforementioned components into a potentially powerful explanation of the phenomenon. However, regardless of the quality of the proposed theory, the work should offer research propositions, questions, or hypotheses for further study of the phenomenon for any theory that has not been tested or for theoretical research on topics for which study is not complete. Authors who do not offer this imply that their work is the final statement on the topic. Few, if any, great contributions to science occur in a single installment; good theory is cumulative.

REFERENCES

Bacharach, S. B. (1989). Organizational theories: Some criteria for evaluation. *Academy of Management Review, 14*(4), 496–515.

Blalock, H. M. (1969). *Theory construction.* Englewood Cliffs, NJ: Prentice Hall.

Brewer, E. W., & Shapard, L. (2004). Employee burnout: A meta-analysis of the relationship between age or years of experience. *Human Resource Development Review, 3*(2), 102–123.

Campbell, J. P. (1990). The role of theory in industrial and organizational psychology. In M. D. Dunnette & L. M. Hough (Eds.), *Handbook of industrial-organizational psychology* (Vol. 2, pp. 39–73). Palo Alto, CA: Consulting Psychologists Press.

Chamber, A. T. (1988). *Theory in the social sciences.* Reading, MA: Addison-Wesley.

Cohen, B. P. (1989). A theory and its analysis. In B. P. Cohen (Ed.), *Developing sociological knowledge: Theory and method* (2nd ed., pp. 199–225) Chicago: Nelson-Hall.

DiMaggio, P. J. (1995). Comments on "What Theory Is Not." *Administrative Science Quarterly, 40,* 391–397.

Doty, D. H., & Glick, W. H. (1994). Typologies as a unique form of theory building: Toward improved understanding and modeling. *Academy of Management Review, 19*(2), 230–251.

Dubin, R. (1976). Theory building in applied areas. In M. D. Dunnette (Ed.), *Handbook of industrial and organizational psychology* (pp. 17–39). Chicago: Rand McNally.

Dubin, R. (1978). *Theory building* (rev. ed.). New York: Free Press.

Eisenhardt, K. M. (1995). Building theories from case study research. In G. P. Huber & A. H. Van de Ven (Eds.), *Longitudinal field research methods: Studying processes of organizational change* (pp. 65–90). Thousand Oaks, CA: Sage.

Freese, L. (1980). Formal theorizing. *Annual Review of Sociology, 6*, 187–212.

Gergen, K. J., & Thatchenkery, T. J. (2004). Organization science as social construction: Postmodern potentials. *Journal of Applied Behavioral Science, 40*(2), 228–229.

Gioia, D. A., & Pitre, E. (1990). Multiparadigm perspectives on theory building. *Academy of Management Review, 15*(4), 584–602.

Herzberg, F. (1966). *Work and the nature of man.* Cleveland, OH: World.

Holton, E. F. (2002). The mandate for theory in human resource development. *Human Resource Development Review, 1*(1), 3–8.

Jensen, P. S. (1999). Links among theory, research, and practice: Cornerstones of clinical scientific progress. *Journal of Clinical Child Psychology, 28*(4), 553–557.

Jones, J. E. (1999). *The process of structuring a community-based curriculum in a rural school setting: A grounded theory study.* Unpublished doctoral dissertation, University of Nebraska–Lincoln.

Kaplan, A. (1964). *The conduct of inquiry.* San Francisco: Chandler.

Kerlinger, F. N. (1973). *Foundations of behavioral research* (2nd ed.). New York: Holt, Rinehart & Winston.

Langley, A. (1999). Strategies for theorizing from process data. *Academy of Management Review, 24*(4), 691–710.

Lewis, M. W. (2000). Exploring paradox: Toward a more comprehensive guide. *Academy of Management Review, 25*(4), 760–776.

Lewis, M. W., & Grimes, A. J. (1999). Metatriangulation: Building theory from multiple paradigms. *Academy of Management Review, 24*(4), 672–690.

Lynham, S. A. (2000). Theory building in the human resource development profession. *Human Resource Development Quarterly, 11*(2), 159–178.

Lynham, S. A. (Ed.). (2002a). Quantitative research and theory building: Dubin's method. *Advances in Developing Human Resources, 4*(3), 242–276.

Lynham, S. A. (Ed.). (2002b). Theory building in applied disciplines. *Advances in Developing Human Resources, 4*(3).

Margolis, S. L., & Hansen, C. D. (2002). A model for organizational identity: Exploring the path to sustainability during change. *Human Resource Development Review, 1*(3), 277–303.

Markus, M. L. (1983). Power, politics, and MIS implementation. *Communications of the ACM, 26*(6), 430–444.

Marsick, V. J., & Watkins, K. (1990). *Informal and incidental learning in the workplace.* London: Routledge.

Morgeson, F. P., & Hofmann, D. A. (1999). The structure and function of collective constructs: Implications for multilevel research and theory development. *Academy of Management Review, 24*(2), 249–265.

Moustakis, C. (1994). *Phenomenological research methods.* Thousand Oaks, CA: Sage.

Myers, N. F. (2000). *The experience of providing management consultation to supervisors and administrators for employee assistance program directors in higher education.* Unpublished doctoral dissertation, University of Nebraska–Lincoln.

Pentland, B. T. (1999). Building process theory with narrative: From description to explanation. *Academy of Management Review, 24*(4), 711–724.

Poole, M. S., & Van de Ven, A. H. (1989). Using paradox to build management and organizational theories. *Academy of Management Review, 14*(4), 562–578.

Revans, R. W. (1982). *The origins and growth of action learning.* Bickly, UK: Chartwell-Bratt; and Lund, Sweden: Studenlitteratur.

Reynolds, P. D. (1971). *A primer in theory construction.* Indianapolis: Bobbs-Merrill.

Ruona, W. E. A., & Roth, G. (Eds.). (2000). Philosophical foundations of human resource development practice. In *Advances in developing human resources.* San Francisco: Berrett-Kohler.

Stinchcombe, A. (1968). *Constructing social theories.* New York: Harcourt, Brace & World.

Strauss, A., & Corbin, J. (1998). *Basics of qualitative research: Techniques and procedures for developing grounded theory.* Thousand Oaks, CA: Sage.

Sutton, R. I., & Staw, B. M. (1995). What theory is not. *Administrative Science Quarterly, 40*(3), 371–384.

Swanson, R. A. (2000). Theory and other irrelevant matters. *Human Resource Development International, 3*(3), 273–277.

Torraco, R. J. (2002). Research methods for theory building in applied disciplines: A comparative analysis. In S. A. Lynham (Ed.), Theory building in applied disciplines. *Advances in Developing Human Resources, 4*(3), 355–376.

Torraco, R. J. (2004). Challenges and choices for theoretical research in human resource development. *Human Resource Development Quarterly, 15*(2), 171–188.

Torraco, R. J. (2005). Work design theory: A review and critique with implications for human resource development. *Human Resource Development Quarterly, 16*(2).

Turnbull, S. (1999). Emotional labour in corporate change programmes—The effects of organizational feeling rules on middle managers. *Human Resource Development International, 2*(2), 125–146.

Tushman, M. L., & Romanelli, E. (1985). Organization evolution: A metamorphosis model of convergence and reorientation. In B. Staw & L. Cummings (Eds.), *Research in organizational behavior* (pp. 171–222). Greenwich, CT: JAI.

Van de Ven, A. H. (1989). Nothing is quite so practical as a good theory. *Academy of Management Review, 14*(4), 486–489.

Van de Ven, A. H., & Johnson, P. E. (in press). Knowledge for theory and practice. *Academy of Management Review* (AMR Ms. #03-0169.1).

Van de Ven, A. H., & Poole, M. S. (1988). Paradoxical requirements of a theory of organizational change. In R. E. Quinn & K. S. Cameron (Eds.), *Paradox and transformation: Toward a theory of change in organization and management* (pp. 19–63). Cambridge, MA: Ballinger.

Weick, K. E. (1989). Theory construction as disciplined imagination. *Academy of Management Review, 14*(4), 516–531.

Weick, K. E. (1995). What theory is not, theorizing is. *Administrative Science Quarterly, 40*(3), 385–390.

Whetten, D. A. (1989). What constitutes a theoretical contribution? *Academy of Management Review, 14*(4), 490–495.

Yang, B. (2002). Meta-analysis research and theory building. In S. A. Lynham (Ed.), Theory building in applied disciplines. *Advances in Developing Human Resources, 4*(3), 296–316.

Yin, R. (1994). *Case study research.* Beverly Hills, CA: Sage.

Action Research Methods

Lyle Yorks, *Columbia University*

CHAPTER OUTLINE

This chapter provides an introduction to action research (AR) as an approach to conducting research in organizations. Kurt Lewin (1946) is generally acknowledged to have coined the term *action research* (Greenwood & Levin, 1998; Susman & Evered, 1978). It is important to acknowledge at the outset, however, that the family tree of action research has many roots and branches (Dickens & Watkins, 1999; Reason & Bradbury, 2001). Influenced by National Training Laboratories in the United States, the sociotechnical system studies conducted by the Tavistock Institute in the United Kingdom, Scandinavian work reform movements, and liberationist educators in the Southern Hemisphere, the intellectual roots and foundations of AR are diverse, even while sharing a broader sense of identity that often brings them together (Elden & Chisholm, 1993; Greenwood & Levin, 1998, Reason, 1994). A novice action researcher should be aware of the diverse limbs of this family tree. (Four excellent sources for developing an awareness of the diversity of the AR family tree, along with the epistemic issues involved, are Reason & Bradbury, 2001; Greenwood & Levin, 1998; Dickens & Watkins, 1999; and Peters & Robinson, 1984.)

WHAT IS ACTION RESEARCH?

Lewin introduced the term *action research* as a label for a way of conducting social science that linked the generation of theory to changing a social system through action. For Lewin, action research was a means for dealing with social problems through a process of both changing and generating knowledge about the system.

Core Values Underlying the Practice of Action Research

In a sense, AR epitomizes the idea of "theory to practice and practice to theory," linking the two in a reciprocal relationship in the knowledge creation process. "Nothing is as practical as a good theory," and "The best way to understand something is to try to change it": these two famous statements credited to Kurt Lewin reflect the core epistemic assumptions of action research. Greenwood and Levin (1998) summarize the essence of these assumptions when they write, "In AR, we believe that the way to 'prove' a theory is to show how it provides in-depth and thorough understanding of social structures, understanding gained through planned attempts to invoke change in particular directions" (p. 19). Action researchers would agree in general terms with Heron and Reason (1987) when they argue that "practical knowing as expressed in effective action is in an important sense primary to theoretically expressed propositional knowledge presupposing a conceptual grasp of principles and standards of practice, presentational elegance, and experiential grounding in the situation within which the action occurs" (p. 281).

One of the common misconceptions of AR is that it is *solely* a qualitative research strategy. Although qualitative methods are prominent in the AR literature, action researchers often use the full range of research techniques, including various forms of quantitative methods as well as a wide range of qualitative methods. Mixed methods are often judged to be appropriate. The selection of research methods is a function of the presenting problem and the situation. The only caveat is that "the reason for deploying them has been agreed on by the AR collaborators and . . . they are used in a way that does not oppress the participants" (Greenwood & Levin, 1998, p. 7). All of the methods described in this book are potentially useful in AR.

How Action Research Is Conceptualized and Defined

Although often presented as a form of problem solving, AR is also a form of scholarship (Greenwood & Levin, 1998; McNiff & Whitehead, 2000; Schön, 1995). Going beyond the notion that theory can simply inform practice, action researchers argue that "theory can and should be generated through practice" (Brydon-Miller, Greenwood, & Maguire, 2003, p. 15).

Greenwood and Levin (1998) go on to distinguish between AR and "applied research," explicitly rejecting the separation between thought and action underlying the pure-applied distinction. Their position is a derivative of pragmatism, consistent with Dewey's belief "that thinking and action are just two names for a single process—the process of making our way as best we can in a world shot through with contingency" (Menand, 2001, p. 360). As abstract as this argument is, it goes to a fundamental justification of AR: that complex and highly unstructured problems can only be addressed through engagement with processes of inquiry that take place in the world of uncertainty. By definition, action research privileges action and values theory to the extent that it effectively informs action. The purpose of action research is to produce reliable and useful knowledge that is validated through action, what McNiff and Whitehead (2000) describe as "a form of practical theorizing in action" (p. 3).

French and Bell (1995) offer a basic definition of AR's purpose as "research on action with the goal of making that action more effective while simultaneously building a body of scientific knowledge" (p. 137). One of the most widely quoted definitions of AR is Rapoport's (1970): "Action research aims to contribute both to the practical concerns of people in an immediate problematic situation and to the goals of social science by joint collaboration with a mutually acceptable ethical framework" (p. 499). Watkins and Brooks (1994) offer a process oriented definition as "an iterative cyclic process of intervening, collecting data on the effectiveness of the intervention, reflecting on the results, and designing new interventions" (p. 100). Greenwood and Levin provide a comprehensive definition that captures the practical and scholarly dimensions of AR as well as its underlying values:

> Social research carried out by a team encompassing a professional action researcher and members of an organization or community seeking to

improve their situation. AR promotes broad participation in the research process and supports action leading to a more just or satisfying situation for the stakeholders. Together the professional researcher and the stakeholders define the problems to be examined, cogenerate relevant knowledge about them, learn and execute social research techniques, take actions, and interpret the results of actions based on what they have learned. (p. 4)

This definition is consistent with the core beliefs of HRD that

organizations are human-made entities that rely on human expertise to establish and achieve their goals. . . .

Human expertise is developed and maximized through HRD processes and should be done for the mutual long-and/or short-term benefits of the sponsoring organization and the individuals involved. . . .

HRD professionals are advocates of individual/group, work process, and organizational integrity. (Swanson & Holton, 2001, p. 10)

A purpose of contemporary AR in organizations is "making change and learning a self-generating and self-maintaining process in the systems in which the AR researchers work" (Elden & Chisholm, 1993, p. 125) while both solving problems and contributing to general theory. By extension, AR should be a core component of scholarship related to research in organizations, especially if one holds a systems perspective on practice in organizations.

Tensions Inherent in Action Research

Inherent in the definitions of AR is the tension between making a contribution to solving the problems confronting an organization and following the widely accepted criteria of the larger social science community for acceptable empirical research. Studying systems as they react to experimental interventions in real-world settings while *also* seeking to reinforce commitment to democratic decision-making values (Dickens & Watkins, 1999) further complicates matters.

Early on, Deutsch (1968) acknowledged this tension: "Considerable experience with action research, however, has indicated that the goals of action and the goals of research may often be incompatible. The danger that confronts the research worker in such situations is the possibility that his research design or methodology will be sacrificed to the achievement of the social action objective" (p. 466). Another well-known pioneer of classical AR offered the same observation, noting that "there is a degree of inherent incompatibility between action and research" (Seashore, 1976, p. 103). For Seashore, this incompatibility was not absolute but required of the researcher a heightened "awareness of design properties, types of scientific contribution, and varieties of valid and useful data" (p. 117) in making choices to optimize both the scientific and problem-solving outcomes of an action research project.

THE GENERAL METHOD OF PRACTICING ACTION RESEARCH

AR is an orientation to inquiry, not a specific methodology. One implication of this position is that there is no dogma or orthodox way of conducting an AR project. However, this doesn't mean anything goes. There is a general method or approach to this kind of inquiry. Within this general method, specific methodologies (quantitative and/or qualitative) that allow researchers to effectively pursue their research questions within the context of their setting should be utilized. The research process has to be explicit about its epistemic assumptions and contain agreed-upon procedures that will provide for self-correcting awareness. Specifically, to be considered research, AR has to generate learning that represents new knowledge and meaning or provide support for theoretical perspectives that have been tested against alternative explanations. Reflexivity in the research process should challenge preferred or expected outcomes.

Building on the ideas advanced by Elden (1981), six critical steps are basic to any action research project. These steps broadly fall under two categories: (1) initiating and organizing the project and (2) implementing the project:

Initiating and Organizing the Project
- Defining the problem and research questions
- Defining roles and relationships among those actively engaged in the AR process and entering the system
- Deciding on how the problem will be studied and choosing methods that will provide the data necessary for answering the research questions

Implementing the Project
- Gathering and interpreting the data through an appropriate analysis process (both in the early stages of the project for diagnostic and base line purposes, and at critical phases throughout an AR project for evaluation of findings and theory building)
- Identifying appropriate and meaningful actions
- Deciding on how the findings should be disseminated and used (who are the primary intended learners from the research?)

In any research undertaking, these steps and required decisions have to be made in a way that produces alignment within the project. However, the situational and iterative nature of AR adds complexity and nonlinearity to the decision-making process. For example, in traditional basic research, applied research, and AR, the anticipated learners and primary stakeholders who ultimately validate the research are significantly different (Elden, 1981). In traditional basic research, the primary audience is the academic community composed of other researchers and scholars. Problems are derived either from theory, usually in the form of hypotheses, or from dilemmas or gaps in formal knowledge. Research design and methodology are constructed to produce answers that will be found as credible by the peer community of researchers. Applied research typically has a primary sponsor or client with acceptable outcomes contributing toward the development a final product or service. In action research, the primary audience is often diverse, including scholars, practitioners in the system, and other stakeholders. Each group may have a different set of criteria that must be satisfied if the end result is to be credible actionable knowledge and producing a system with an increased capacity for learning.

The overarching design principle is that AR efforts need to be explicitly defined as sociotechnical processes. The social dimension of AR involves the creation of a set of relationships in which the goal is the creation of a set of circumstances that are consistent with reflexive team learning processes. The technical aspect involves the methodological practices adopted for answering the inquiry question(s). In practice the two dimensions are opposite sides of a single process, which suggests a dual role for the experienced action researcher. The first is bringing appropriate research skills to the process (the technical dimension); the second is providing learning facilitation skills (the social dimension). Of the two, the facilitation skills are core. As with any research project, depending on the methods that are required to address the question, the action research team may need to bring in colleagues to help with various methodological issues.

Action research has been used to initiate and learn about the emergence and dynamics of interorganizational networks in projects of national workplace reform (Engelstad & Gustavsen; Eriksson & Hauger, 1996; Gustavsen, 1998), performance improvement in corporate systems (Ayas, 2003; Ledford & Mohrman, 1993), and production of social knowledge and improvement of community life through a collaboration between a university and a large public school system (Ledford & Mohrman, 1993). Two case examples follow that illustrate the general method. The first example of AR presented is chosen because as a participant in the project, I am intimately familiar with how the process unfolded. The project involved a focus on changing behavior within a large, complex bureaucratic system. Project goals were directed toward enhancing the capacity of the system and had explicit research objectives. Finally, the cast of stakeholders in the research was highly diverse, adding to the complexity of the project. The second case, conducted by Karen Ayas and senior leaders and project managers at Fokker Aircraft, took place in the private, for-profit sector and was directed toward both learning and performance. Both cases were academically rigorous and involved complexity in terms of the presenting practical problems facing the organization, and both illustrate the decisions made in the overall general method.

The VA Stress and Aggression Project

The following is a robust example of an action research project in the U.S. Department of Veteran Affairs (VA). With funding from both the VA and the

National Science Foundation, the VA Stress and Aggression project involved a diverse cross section of inquirers, including a range of practitioners (health care providers, administrators, union officials, and rank-and-file employees including custodians and groundskeepers) and a group of academic researchers with different disciplinary specialties and epistemic assumptions. The project had multiple objectives, which included reducing levels of stress and aggression among VA employees, developing the capacity of individuals and work teams to learn how to address the dysfunctional issues that produce stress and aggression, and learning more about the dynamics of carrying out this kind of research.

Overview of the Project

As is many times the case in action research, the early stages of organizing and designing the project were highly emergent, characterized by an iterative and interactive process of *defining the problem and research questions, defining necessary roles, and deciding on how the problem should be studied and selecting methods* for carrying out the study. The project began in 1998 with internal conversations among midlevel VA managers about the problem of workplace aggression. These early conversations among practitioners led first to the identification of two psychologists prominent in the literature on aggression in organizations, and then to an agreement to gather data while creating an instrument for measuring stress and aggression. The two psychologists were excited by the possibility of both developing a valid research instrument for measuring stress and aggression and having access to organization-wide data that would permit testing certain theoretical principles.

Subsequent conversations among practitioners in the VA raised the question of whether doing a study on the causes of stress and aggression and producing a report would really change anything in the organization. One of the practitioners brought the project to the attention of academics associated with a university-based center for human resource management research that brought two additional foci to the project. The first was the development of quantitative models that could be used to develop a business case for reducing stress and aggression in the organization, and the second was the adoption of a practice-grounded action research model to the process. This shift subsequently resulted in additional networking by the participants, which led to inviting an academic specializing in adult and organizational learning to join the project. These goals became formalized within a National Science Foundation grant proposal and with the addition of the learning coach concept to the project design, which now included the establishment of 11 action teams located in self-selected sites within the VA and composed of employees from the local site, along with 16 comparison sites that allowed data gathering but did not engage in active interventions beyond the survey. The research questions focusing the project were as follows:

- What are the sources of workplace stress and aggression in the VA (the original presenting problem)?

- How does workplace stress and aggression affect the quality and cost of services within the VA (the business case for working on stress and aggression)?

- How does workplace stress and aggression affect the satisfaction veterans hold about the services they receive (also part of the business case)?

- What actions and practices reduce stress and aggression and improve individual satisfaction (part of the business case and also demonstrating change)?

- What is the role of collaboration and learning in identifying, implementing, and sustaining effective actions (demonstrating and sustaining change)?

Reflecting their commitment to mixed methods inquiry that strives toward realizing the governing values of "Model II" organizational learning systems (Argyris & Schön, 1996), project team members referred to their action research approach as "data-driven collaborative action inquiry." The project team now consisted of 4 academics from different disciplines and 11 VA practitioners from different functions within the VA. This diversity was a strength and a challenge for the team. Coming with diverse skills and frames of reference, project team members had to learn how to blend their talents with one another in collaboratively working on the project. Learning about processes for effectively doing this was one of the project goals, reflected in the fifth research question listed earlier. With funding through the National Science Foundation grant and various sources within the VA, a 3-year project was initiated in 2000. Following an orientation and training meeting, the site action teams embarked on working collaboratively with the project team on *gathering and interpreting initial data,* as well as *identifying appropriate and meaningful actions.* Survey data were collected to help focus actions and provide a baseline for future posttest comparisons.

Important events over the course of the 3 years included (1) training learning coaches nominated by each site to facilitate learning in the action teams; (2) collaboration between the project team and the action teams in the final design and administration of a stress and aggression survey at the sites; (3) collaboration between the project team and the action teams in the analysis and sense making of the survey data; (4) action teams reporting back the survey results from their sites to employees; (5) action teams developing interventions based on site specific data; (6) the creation of qualitative "context maps" and facilitated discussions between project team members and each action team for the purpose of learning from the experience; (7) collaboration between the project team and action teams in the design and implementation of a second survey toward the conclusion of the 3-year cycle; (8) collaboration between the project team and action teams in the design of a final assessment and sense-making meeting.

Summary of Results

Dissemination of the results and theoretical implications from the project have been and will continue to be reported elsewhere (Harmon et al., 2003; Kowalski, Harmon, Yorks, & Kowalski, 2003). The following paragraphs provide a summary of results in order to provide context for the reader. We begin by quoting from the report on the project to the National Science Foundation (Harmon, 2004):

> Results show that pilot (experimental) sites demonstrated significantly more improvement than comparison ("control") facilities over the course of the project. For example:
> - There were significant reductions in stress and in all forms of aggression in pilot sites but not in comparison sites
> - Eight out of 9 behaviors related to occupational work compensation claims were significantly reduced at the pilot sites, whereas none were significantly reduced at the comparison sites.
> - Six out of 9 behaviors related to equal opportunity claims were significantly reduced at the pilot sites, whereas only 2 out of 9 were significantly reduced at the comparison sites.
> - Employee satisfaction increased substantially more in pilot sites than in comparison sites
>   . . . Differences across local action teams in the impacts of their change efforts were related to variation in both site factors and the uptake of collaborative action inquiry processes by the teams (Kowalski et al., 2003). Not surprisingly, positive impacts on facility-wide outcomes varied according to the project's scope/scale relative to the size of each facility. Impacts tended to be greater at the smaller sites (e.g., 33–260 employees) in which the team and their programs reached virtually the entire facility (i.e., a relatively large-scale intervention), and tended to be smaller at the larger sites (e.g., 630–2797 employees) in which the communications and interventions of the action teams were of proportionately smaller scale. (pp. 2–4)

Detailed analysis of the data and presentation of the various actions taken by sites can easily be the subject of a number of papers. A brief example can be provided by the case of the Houston National Cemetery, a small site whose workforce is largely involved in physical work (i.e., preparing and maintaining grave sites and the grounds). At the beginning of the project in 2000, the cemetery had a workforce separated by occupation, race, and gender, as documented in interviews and reflected in one of the highest rates of EEO complaints and grievances in the National Cemetery Service. Productivity measures were declining, as were employee satisfaction measures in the VA survey data. The site had high levels of aggression and stress (measured by the project team's stress and aggression survey). Some employees viewed the site director as an "autocrat," and he had recently received an anonymous death threat.

The site action team consisted of a union shop steward, workers, and white-collar administrative employees, along with an employee from human resources who was trained as a learning coach and functioned as a full member of the team. Members of the action team fed back survey data to all site employees, inviting comments on reasons for reported perceptions, meaning of data, and possible interventions or action steps. The action team created a "rover," someone who would mingle throughout the workplace on a regular basis to take the "pulse of things" and identify emergent disputes between employees. This latter activity was integrated with an action team–initiated dispute resolution process that was supported by training from an American Federation of Government Employees union national officer. Inquiry practices learned through the project were employed for discussing disputes and crafting informal resolutions. Additionally, employees now serve on committees that the director relies on for employee input. All these actions became grist for reflection and learning about the social dynamics of the site. In the words of one worker on the action team, "I came to realize that until I changed my own behavior, I could not influence anyone else."

Data for the Houston site show that in 2003, there was a statistically significant 16% decrease in self-reported stress and a statistically significant 31% decrease in total reported acts of aggression. In addition, productivity (burials per worker) increased by 9%, while workload increased by 9%, representing an 18% positive change. There are no outstanding EEO complaints or grievances, with none having been filed in the past 2 years. Perhaps most significant, a blue-collar member of the action team recently visited a VA hospital experiencing significant employee relations issues and stress and aggression issues as part of a group of project team members invited to the hospital to share their experience in the project. This worker presented on the cemetery's experience to both blue-collar and medical staff at the hospital.

Each of the 11 sites is a unique story. It is not specific interventions that were the most significant lessons learned, but rather each site engaging in a process of inquiry, asking members of the project team for additional "cuts" of the data and using the data to point toward problem areas with an increased capacity for seeing patterns and diagnosing analogous situations. A revelation to members of the project team was the extent to which action team members had engaged this role. In the words of one member of the project team, echoing a widely held sentiment among the team, "When the action teams started reporting interventions, the project team viewed some as superficial. Then we visited the sites and saw the context and targeted complexity of the intervention."

It is also important to note that some sites were more effective than others. One hospital pilot site dropped out of the study due to labor–management issues. In addition, one benefits site had such limited participation in project activities that its results were omitted from most analyses. The latter has since reconstituted its action team. We are still learning about how legacy issues around power and control, as well as other contextual factors, influenced the local action teams in their inquiries. This aspect of the inquiry process continues.

The Fokker Aircraft Project

Innovation requires both creative capacity for new ideas and the managerial skills to transform these ideas into practice (Van de Ven, Angle, & Poole, 1989). Putting innovative ideas into practice involves change and threatens established ways of doing things, requiring that people give up the known and tried and define the change process as an opportunity for learning and adaptation. In a competitive business environment, optimizing this opportunity is critical for strategic success.

The aircraft industry provides a fertile field for learning more about the challenges of managing technological innovation projects. As Ayas (2003) notes, (1) its products are among the most complex in industry, with new product development involving hundreds of people in diverse specializations who must work cohesively in developing a new aircraft; (2) aircraft development projects are of long duration (several years), involving the transfer of knowledge across temporal stages within projects; and (3) the large number of parallel projects means that transfer across projects is an important form of organizational learning and knowledge management.

The opportunity for conducting an action research project within Fokker presented itself when the overlap between the major research question that interested Ayas and the problem definition at Fokker Aircraft Corporation (FAC) became evident. Those responsible for new product development were aware of problems caused by a lack of learning and communication within and across projects, and the researcher was interested in extending and applying concepts in organizational learning to the management of innovation projects. The major research question that guided the project was "How can technological innovation projects be managed and designed for maximum effectiveness of learning?" (Ayas, 2003, p. 20). In addressing this question, the project focused on (1) how the learning process could be defined in the context of the organization, (2) the role of learning in an innovation project, (3) the implications for project management, (4) the contextual requirements for increasing the effectiveness of learning in innovation projects, and (5) how innovation projects might be designed so that these requirements are met. This case provides a variation of the action research process, consisting of a sequence of phases, with each phase involving all six of the critical decisions. Whereas in the VA project the initial data gathering for diagnostic purposes involved a quantitative survey feedback methodology, the Fokker Aircraft project began with Ayas creating a conceptual framework from the literature that provided a rationale for exploring alternatives approaches to design and management of innovation projects. Engagement with the organization then began with her collaborating with practitioners in conducting a series of extensive case studies that enabled a broader overview of the product development process and the variety of problems confronted during the innovation process.

Overview of the Project and Results

An initial 6-month field study consisting of conducting case studies of multiple new product development projects was agreed to by management. The agreed-upon deliverable for these case studies was an action plan consisting of a set of guidelines for effective innovation management and mechanisms that could facilitate learning within projects and increase the capacity for innovation in new projects. Contingent on approval of the delivered action plan, the project would be extended another 2 years allowing for testing of the proposals.

Working on the principle that "participatory action research is a type of scientific inquiry that presumes research occurs with and for people" (Ayas, 2003, p. 22), Ayas strove to create conditions of collaboration with the people involved to create knowledge that would meet their needs. Participants from the field sites were involved with gathering and analyzing data. The major cycles of the project were, first, initially addressing the research questions conceptually, drawing on convergent findings from the existing empirical and theoretical literature. This phase produced a conceptual model of learning while innovating, including identification of possible contextual factors and the conceptual model that was created from the initial framework for carrying out the 6-month field study. This involved a case study approach to eight ongoing projects at various stages of the project life cycle. Two recently terminated projects were also studied, along with any available documentation of other projects. Completion of the field studies fortuitously corresponded with a change program in the engineering organization. The Agile Competitive Engineering Program (ACE) was a major restructuring proposal to "ensure that Fokker—now a member of the European Aeronautic Defense and Space Company (DASA) family—would assume a lead company role in the regional aircraft market" (p. 24). The ACE-P4 project was charged with further developing the organization of the product development (P) sector for achievement of target performance levels defined by ACE. Ayas was assigned to the ACE-P4 team as an active participant tracking the changes and, along with a small group of dedicated project members from the company, worked toward the best possible solution.

An additional year of action research was dedicated to the implementation of the new design that evolved from the combined learning from the previous steps. Based on both the case studies and the implementation experience, a revised framework for project management and a design for learning were developed to answer the research question and provide a comprehensive framework for increasing the ability of the project organization to continually improve its performance with each new innovation project. A pilot study was conducted to "test the effectiveness of the revised framework in terms of its contribution to improving project performance and building learning capacity" (p. 26).

Subsequent to the pilot study the new model was fully implemented with more than satisfactory results, being sustained until the withdrawal of DASA and the closing down of FAC. Additionally, the action research approach was effective in addressing the research question, producing new knowledge about processes of innovation and learning, knowledge about an alternative approach to project management and design, and insights about the complexity of attention necessary for effective management of innovation.

Guiding Principles for Action Research

Action research is situational, and project designs are emergent reflecting the presenting problem and the desired outcomes in terms of learning and theorizing. Designs are products of collaboration between researchers and those involved with the problem. Roles are negotiated and renegotiated. As with the case of VA Stress and Aggression Project, they often evolve, perhaps beginning with more of an expert model and then, with the realization that studying the problem will not promote change, adopting an action research approach (see also the case the University of Pennsylvania and the Philadelphia Public Schools; Ledford & Mohrman, 1993). As with the Fokker case, AR projects often evolve in phases, with the success of one phase providing the basis for moving onto a subsequent, more extensive phase.

In the VA Stress and Aggression project, there were three different sets of academics, organizational psychologists, a management researcher, and an adult learning researcher. Each was interested in contributing to their respective fields. In addition, there were an equally diverse group of practitioners from the VA who wanted to produce results that would be compelling for managers in the system. The metatheme that held the group together through many inevitable conflicts rooted in their different professional meaning schemes was a common commitment to creating a better workplace for employees and clients of the system. Fokker was also a complex initiative involving academics, engineers, and project managers, each with their own rationale for participating in the AR project. This complexity requires that action researchers have strong group facilitation skills for creating the kind of collaborative social space within which methodological issues can be constructively discussed and resolved.

Creating Collaborative Social Space

While AR is often described as a cyclical process of diagnosing, planning, acting, evaluating, and learning, this cyclical process takes place within a collaborative social space that has to be created. Greenwood and Levin (1998) refer to this space as communication arenas that "create room for learning processes resulting in meanings that participants trust" (p. 117). These arenas are similar to what Susman and Evered (1978) term a "client system infrastructure" (p. 588). This kind of space is akin to what Fisher and Torbert (1995) call a "liberating structure" that they describe as "turn[ing] tensions, dilemmas, and gaps . . . into occasions for learning and improved competence" (p. 7). Establishing such conditions is not easy: Society and organizations place large barriers in the way of processes of learning (Fisher & Torbert, 1995).

This kind of space contains both a structural and a process dimension. AR teams can be defined as organizational learning mechanisms (OLMs) (Popper & Lipshitz, 1998) providing the structural and procedural arrangements that allow for the systematic collection and analysis of data, and the dissemination and use of the resulting learning. Echoing the findings of Kasl, Marsick, and Dechant (1997) on the importance of team learning conditions, Popper and Lipshitz argue that OLMs such as AR teams must share certain organizational learning values. These values include transparency (exposing one's thoughts and actions to others in order to receive feedback); inquiry (persisting in a line of inquiry until a satisfactory understanding is achieved); integrity (giving and receiving full and accurate feedback with defending oneself and others); issue orientation (focusing on the relevance of information to the issues, regardless of social standing or rank of the source); and accountability (assuming responsibility both for learning and for implementing the lessons learned). By agreeing to explicit norms that operationalize these values, an AR team can provide itself with a framework for reflexivity on its processes and provide a foundation for validity testing of its findings.

Establishing this kind of space requires developing the conversation among the actors into one characterized by active listening, use of inquiry skills, and dialogue to surface and test assumptions. Among the issues that can be expected to emerge are (1) tensions over control, (2) tensions around timing and action, (3) tensions around role boundaries, and (4) questions about the validity of data and knowledge. Underlying these tensions are often more fundamental issues of purpose and visions of what would constitute a successful project, diverse motivations for participating, and the confrontation between deeply held worldviews about what constitutes meaningful knowledge, how it can be generated, and what will be required for having it taken seriously by various audiences both within the organization and broader publics. One practitioner in the VA project commented that early on she felt that her work "has to be viewed as practical. I felt I was being contaminated by theorists. Initially I tried to keep each role contained." Organizations value action while academics value careful planning and control, issues that go to the heart of the tension between action and conventional research.

In fostering this collaborative space, the action research professional needs to function as a learning facilitator, looking for opportunities that will allow participants to experience the value of learning practices. These practices, often derided by executives, have to be used judicially, timed to surface concerns that are inhibiting the group from moving forward. The practices are only accepted through the experience of having a particular practice help the group's progress.

Participants in the VA project learned how collaborative space is fragile, subject to disruption by strong personalities and situational forces. But when regression occurs, corrections can be made more quickly when the group has established habits of reflective practices. It is also the arena where generative learning takes place. Although she doesn't describe her work in terms of creating collaborative social space within Fokker, Ayas (2003) illustrates the need for creating reflective space in terms of continually testing "the emerging picture of reality," comparing "the responses of many project managers and members, and confront[ing] them with one another's construction of reality" (pp. 22–23).

Defining the Problem and Research Questions

Problem definition is the first technical task of an AR team. The process of establishing collaborative space begins as the group organizes itself around the inquiry problem and the research questions it seeks to answer. Action research projects typically begin when an individual, or a group of people, problematize some aspect of their practice or organization's performance and seek out others who also find the problem compelling and have either expertise or resources that can be brought to bear in solving it. Like the VA project, this may begin as a networking process. As the group of potential co-inquirers drawn from inside and outside the organization are identified and approached, the emerging group has to clarify the problem. Kasl et al. (1997) identify *framing* and *reframing* as important team learning processes. The iterative nature of AR means that reframing may occur at various points in the research process (and consequently creating dilemmas of maintaining the integrity of previously gathered data).

The starting point is a conversation around a series of questions that help the group shape the problem and the research questions:

- *What is the problem in practice that we are seeking to improve?* Because different people often perceive the problem differently, it is often helpful to have various members state the problem as they see it, explain their rationale for how they are framing it, and identify any assumptions that they are making about the problems. One method for doing this is in a reflection and dialogue format, with each person taking a few minutes to write down his or her answers to this question, and then going around in turn, with everyone's answers being posted. Discussion is withheld until everyone has been heard. The problem is reframed as necessary.

- *What inquiry questions must be answered for addressing the problem as stated?* This step links the research process to the problem. Look for commonalities and differences in the various questions. It is also useful to keep in mind scope and feasibility at this point. One of the challenges that repeatedly confronted the project team in the VA was dealing with the complexity and scope of the project. Although funding for travel and meetings existed, all of the members had significant regular job responsibilities. Only a couple of VA people were essentially dedicated full-time on the project. During a symposium at the 2000 Academy of Management Meeting, Michael Beer, a discussant, asked a question that become a continuing point of reference for the project team: "Are you prepared to feed the 'elephant'?"

■ *What do we know about the problem, and what do we not know?* Addressing this question begins the diagnostic process. One way of systematically answering this question is to use the metaphor of "the learning window" (Stewart, 1997). The learning window is an example of a tool for testing ideas and assertions (see Table 21.1 for an example).

To meet the test of "what we know," the data or evidence on which a claim is based needs to be explicitly stated with consensual agreement about its interpretation. Otherwise, a claim is "what we think we know" and needs to be either tested further or accepted as an attribution. Through this process, the conversation often surfaces additional unknowns that are brought into the team's awareness. As the VA project went through various iterations of actions and analysis, content shifted through the cells of the window, and new statements and assertions were added. Cumulatively, the window's evolution becomes a record of the project's development. The metaphor of the window also has proven to have considerable credibility as a learning practice with practitioners. Questions such as "Do we know that or think we know that?" and "What are the data for that claim?" were commonly asked. Whether or not the explicit tool is used, asking the questions is important.

■ *What is there about the problem and questions that interests me?* The point was made earlier that each person has his or her own reasons for participating in the research. For example, in the VA project, the interests of the participants, while complementary, were also somewhat divergent. The initiator of the project had a very practical concern: "I was repeating what I have done for 16 years. The disciplinary process does not address the

TABLE 21.1   The Learning Window

WHAT I KNOW AND WHY I KNOW IT What data do I have to support my belief? Do others interpret the data as I do?	WHAT I THINK I KNOW AND WHAT I NEED TO DISCOVER IN ORDER TO KNOW IT
WHAT I KNOW I DO NOT KNOW	I MUST BE OPEN TO WHAT I DO NOT EXPECT

Source: Based on Stewart (1997).

underlying causes of problems." Another of the practitioners was attracted to the project because she had "grown frustrated with seeing so many change efforts fail and with the differences between the espoused and actual values in practice." The university researchers wanted to "engage the organization for data for testing existing theories of workplace aggression and to validate new instruments and develop effective interventions." Being explicit about these varied interests was important for designing the project. For example, gathering baseline data and having matched sites for purposes of quasi-experimental design were important for meeting the university researchers' objectives. Avoiding an expert model and involving action teams at the local level were important for achieving the practitioners' objective.

- *What concerns do you have?* This corollary question is also useful. In the case of the VA project, there were issues of publishing rights, how shared authorship was going to be handled, and at what point might the research cross over to consulting. Gaining clarity around these issues from the beginning was important. All members of the project agree that surfacing issues of concern, rather than smoothing them over during the early stages of the project, was important for resolving difficult issues down the road.

Designing the Action Research Project

Having framed the problem and research questions, the issue becomes planning the project. In planning the project, three issues have to be addressed: (1) designing actions relevant for addressing the research problem and questions, (2) systematically capturing data on the experience, and (3) interpreting or making valid sense out of the data. This last step may involve reframing the problem and questions, designing additional actions, or answering the question in terms of both implications for practice and theory. These issues must be addressed within the context of the setting, and they involve decisions about the timing of cycles of action and sense making.

Designing Actions Relevant for Addressing the Research Problem and Questions

AR research takes place in the crucible of the *theory–practice* relationship. The process of identifying actions that might be taken in order to answer the question can be facilitated by asking questions such as the following:

- *What is it about the problem and questions that we are trying to learn?* AR problems typically are rooted in a need for a deeper understanding of a situation in order improve it or advance a broader vision (McNiff & Whitehead, 2000, p. 206). An important test of the relevance of any proposed actions is being explicit about what one expects to learn by taking them.

- *What do we think we know that we want to test?* Most AR researchers come to a project with some predetermined ideas about what they expect they will find. I have found it is important to capture and document these expectations, as they are biases that represent potential validity threats. It is important to design actions with the expectation that one will find the unexpected and structure them as experiments with clarity of how they may test underlying assumptions held by members of the AR team.

- *What theories are relevant in terms of addressing the problem, and what form would suggested actions look like in the local setting?* Although AR is often thought of as a process of producing theory from action, it is also reasonable to draw on existing theory to suggest possible actions as ways of testing general theory in practice. To paraphrase Greenwood and Levin (1998, p. 124), general theory must apply to particular cases; AR develops particular cases, testing the validity of general laws.

- *What actions are suggested by our existing diagnostic data, and why?* Baseline data gathered during the early stages of the AR project helps target actions, particularly when trying to impact system performance problems.

The answers to these and similar questions are going to vary from project to project. One of the roles of the professional action researcher is to facilitate this kind of conversation around these questions as the AR team engages in the design process. Again, it is important to remember the cyclical nature of the process. Ayas (2003) describes how at Fokker she

> acted as a facilitator to define the next set of interventions, finding the appropriate sequence of actions and responses, and gradually moving to deeper levels of understanding. This was an ongoing, evolving process of learning where new knowledge was created as more information was revealed about the situation, thereby validating or reformulating concepts developed as the research went on. (p. 28)

Systemically Collecting Data

It is important to think through what data are relevant. The obvious question is, What data do we need to collect for answering the AR question? However, a number of more specific considerations should be part of the decision process around data gathering.

- How can we capture data on the experience of taking action in a way that is transparent and can be shared with others (both in and outside the project) for interpretation?

Questionnaires and interviews along with observation and field notes are standard possibilities for data gathering. Tape or video recordings of meetings are other possibilities. In AR, researchers strive not to demonstrate changes in relationships among measures (although that is useful) but to show how changes have taken place in a situation. McNiff and Whitehead (2000) express this point nicely when they write, "You need to turn the data into evidence as an ongoing process. You need to show how an earlier scenario transforms into a later one" (p. 208). Unlike experimental and cross-sectional research efforts, the assumption in AR is that the inquiry process involves changes in the researchers as well as in others. The researchers are part of the situation being studied. As McNiff and Whitehead (p. 209) note, this kind of research does not take place in a cause and effect relationship, where the researcher says, "These changes are happening because I did such and such." Action researchers need to show that certain changes took place as they changed practices and their relationship to the setting. Data gathering needs to focus on documenting what was done and how key elements of the settings changed as a result. The latter may include both performance matrixes and the perceptions people in the setting have regarding their relationships to one another.

Interpreting or Making Valid Meaning from the Action

The specifics of analysis will, of course, vary depending on the project and the kind of data gathered during the process. Possibilities include a mix of statistical and qualitative data analysis strategies. Demonstrating how certain changes occurred as certain actions were taken involves linking the story of key events to various markers of change.

One way of structuring this analysis is to have members of the AR team write down the critical events that have occurred during some period of time during a project on sticky notes and then place them on a time line set up on the wall. Once all the notes are on the time line, the group works its way through the time line, with each person sharing his or her reflections on the event. This process was done at two points during the VA project under the theme of "harvesting the learning." Drawing theoretical implications from this kind of storyline involves a dialogic, inductive process of collective reflection and testing alternative possibilities against the story. The overall logic of the learning window should be a guiding principle throughout the process of developing and interpreting the storyline and converting it into a theoretical model.

Members of the VA project constructed a model of how the action teams engaged in the interpretative, sense-making process (Figure 21.1). With some variation it applies to the project team as well. It provides a good overview of the analysis and interpretation process in AR.

Throughout the analysis process, it is important to be aware of possible sources of validity threats. The goal is to produce theoretical interpretation and recommendations for future action that are well grounded and supportable. The validity practices advocated in the qualitative research literature are particularly useful in AR for addressing issues of epistemic validity (e.g., Kirk & Miller, 1986; Guba & Lincoln, 1981; Strauss & Corbin, 1990).

The principles of AR require that epistemic validity is a necessary but insufficient criterion for assessing AR. As previously discussed, participation and the

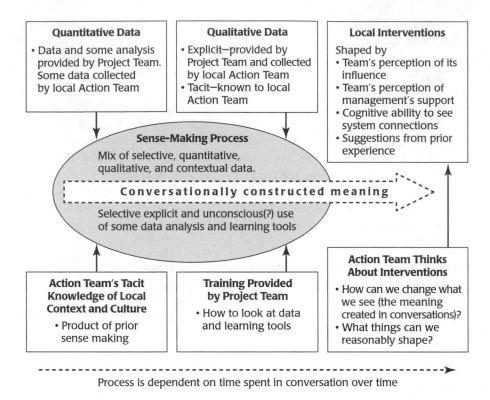

Figure 21.1 Action Team Data Sense-Making Process
Source: Kowalski et al. (2000).

building of learning capacity in the system are fundamental values of AR. Lincoln's (1990; see also Lincoln & Guba, 1986) development of the concept of authenticity as a standard of validity testing is particularly relevant for AR. She offers four authenticity criteria. The first is *fairness*—does the record demonstrate that the viewpoints of participants have been given evenhanded representation? Throughout the interpretation process, the professional action researcher needs to strive toward having the team demonstrate that all parties participated as co-inquirers and all voices in the system have been given space to be heard without being intimidated through power relationships.

The next three criteria explicitly relate to the learning dimension of AR and, by extension, its fit with HRD. The second criterion is *ontological authenticity*—the extent to which there is evidence that participants have gained increased awareness of the complexities of the issues surrounding the problem. The third criterion is *educative authenticity*—the existence of evidence that participants have gained increased appreciation for the sources of alternative positions around the problem. The final criterion is *catalytic authenticity*—establishing that participants in the AR and the system have a willingness to be involved in change. These criteria speak to a key marker of valid AR: that it has produced change in the participants and their context. The story of the Houston site in the VA alludes to these sources of authenticity, as do various examples that could be provided from the project team.

Other sources of validity threats in AR relate to maintaining the openness of the collaborative space. Defensive routines and groupthink are two phenomena in group dynamics that can inadvertently subvert the collaborative space and lead to distortion in the interpretation process. *Defensive routines* can be defined as thoughts and actions used to protect the usual ways of dealing with reality among the members of the group. Argyris (1985) argues that defensive routines are "powerful and omni-present with groups, emerging without being taught or encouraged. The most powerful ones emerge where the intentions are honorable—namely, to increase effectiveness" (p. 35). Janis (1982) defines *groupthink* as a tendency toward concurrence seeking. As a modification of Janis's (1972) definition somewhat, in AR, groupthink results in flawed interpretations "when the members' striving for unanimity overrides their motivation to realistically appraise alternative" explanations (p. 9). Groupthink and defensive routines result in what Elmes and Gemmill (1990) have more broadly identified as a condition of group mindlessness. Bringing in devil's advocates (Janis, 1982), embracing productive reasoning (using data that are accepted as valid by individuals with contradictory views; Argyris, 1985), while balancing advocacy with inquiry and illustration (Fisher & Torbert, 1995), are all ways of maintaining open and critically reflective inquiry and sustaining the collaborative space.

CONCLUSION

Action research is an orientation toward inquiry that centers on the conjunction of three elements: research, action, and participation. Action researchers seek to promote positive social and organizational change, while building a capacity for learning into the social setting and generating new knowledge. Within this broad value system are many roots and branches of AR practice. This chapter has been written from the perspective of pragmatist AR.

In practice, action researchers are often faced with dilemmas around ethics, goals, and initiatives that are created by the values and principles on which AR is based. Although all researchers can confront these kinds of dilemmas, because action researchers are actively engaged with the systems with which they are working, and their work typically is directed toward diverse audiences, these dilemmas are more frequently confronted in AR. Reflexivity on the part of the researchers on their decisions in addressing these dilemmas is critical.

Developing communications arenas, or collaborative space, is a core task of action researchers. This kind of space is fragile and can be created and maintained through the judicious use of various learning practices. AR teams function as organizational learning mechanisms. A wide range of social science research methods, both quantitative and qualitative, are available to the action researcher. Methods selection is a function of the research problem and questions. Action research does not center on a cause-and-effect relationship, where the researcher says, "These changes are happening because I did such and such." AR settings are complex and dynamic. Action researchers need to show that certain changes took place as they changed practices, documenting their relationship to the setting and how different relationships in the setting evolved. Data gathering needs to focus on documenting what was done and how key elements of the settings changed as a result. In addition to conventional validity-testing practices, action researchers should utilize authenticity criteria. They also need to pay attention to the possibility of groupthink and defensive routines distorting their interpretation of the experience.

REFERENCES

Argyris, C. (1985). *Strategy, change and defensive routines.* Boston: Pitman.

Argyris, C., & Schön, D. A. (1996). *Organization learning II: Theory, method, and practice.* Reading, MA: Addison-Wesley.

Ayas, K. (2003). Managing action and research for rigor and relevance: The case of Fokker Aircraft. *Human Resource Planning, 26*(2), 19–29.

Brydon-Miller, M., Greenwood, D., & Maguire, P. (2003). Why action research? *Action Research, 1,* 9–28.

Coghlan, D., & Brannick, T. (2001). *Doing action research in your own organization.* Thousand Oaks, CA: Sage.

Deutsch, M. (1968). Field theory in social psychology. In G. Lindzey & E. Aronson (Eds.), *The handbook of social psychology, Vol. 1* (2nd ed., pp. 412–487). Reading, MA: Addison-Wesley.

Dickens, L., & Watkins, K. (1999). Action research: Rethinking Lewin. *Management Learning, 30,* 127–140.

Elden, M. (1981). Sharing the research work: Participative research and its role demands. In P. Reason & J. Rowan (Eds.), *Human inquiry: A sourcebook of new paradigm research* (pp. 253–266). New York: Wiley.

Elden, M., & Chisholm, R. (1993). Emerging varieties of action research: Introduction to the special issue. *Human Relations, 46,* 121–141.

Elmes, M. B., & Gemmill, G. (1990). The psychodynamics of mindlessness and dissent in small groups. *Small Groups Research, 21,* 28–44.

Engelstad, P. H., & Gustavsen, B. Swedish network development for implementing national work reform strategy. *Human Relations, 46,* 219–248.

Eriksson, K., & Hauger, M. (1996). Workplace development and research: Two examples. In S. Toulmin & B. Gustavsen (Eds.), *Beyond theory: Changing organizations through participation* (pp. 31–40). Amsterdam: Benjamins.

Fisher, D., & Torbert, W. R. (1995). *Personal and organizational transformations: The true challenge of continual quality improvement.* London: McGraw-Hill.

French, W. L., & Bell, Jr., C. H. (1995). *Organizational development: Behavioral science inter-ventions for organizational improvement* (5th ed.). Englewood Cliffs, NJ: Prentice Hall.

Greenwood, D. J., & Levin, M. (1998). *Introduction to action research.* Thousand Oaks, CA: Sage.

Guba, E., & Lincoln, Y. (1981). *Effective evaluation.* San Francisco: Jossey-Bass.

Gustavsen, B. (1998). From experiments to network building: Trends in the use of research for reconstructing working life. *Human Relations, 51,* 431–448.

Harmon, J. (2004). *Report to NSF on VA Stress and Aggression Project* (Final Draft). VA Stress and Aggression Project.

Harmon, J., Scotti, D., Behson, S., Farias, G., Petzel, R., Neuman, J., & Keashly, L. (2004). Effects of high involvement work systems on employee satisfaction and service costs in the Veterans Health Administration. *Journal of Health Care Management, 48,* 393–406.

Heron, J., & Reason, P. (1997). A participatory inquiry paradigm. *Qualitative Inquiry, 3,* 274–294.

Janis, I. L. (1972). *Victims of groupthink.* Boston: Houghton Mifflin.

Janis, I. L. (1982). *Groupthink.* Boston: Houghton Mifflin.

Kasl, E., Marsick, V. J., & Dechant, K. (1997). Teams as learners: A research-based model of team learning. *Journal of Applied Behavioral Science, 33,* 227–246.

Kirk, J., & Miller, M. L. (1986). *Reliability and validity in qualitative research.* Sage University Paper Series on Qualitative Methods, Vol. 2. Beverly Hills, CA: Sage.

Kowalski, R., Harmon, J., Yorks, L., & Kowalski, D. (2003). Reducing workplace stress and aggression: An action research project at the U.S. Department of Veterans Affairs. *Human Resource Planning, 23*(2), 39–53.

Ledford, Jr., G. E., & Mohrman, S. A. (1993). Self-design for high-involvement: A large-scale organizational change. *Human Relations, 46,* 143–173.

Lewin, K. (1946). Action research and minority problems. *Journal of Social Issues, 2,* 34–36.

Lincoln, Y. (1990). The making of a constructivist: A remembrance of transformations past. In E. Guba (Ed.), *The paradigm dialog* (pp. 67–87). Newbury Park, CA: Sage.

Lincoln, Y., & Guba, E. (1986). But is it rigorous? Trustworthiness and authenticity in nat-uralistic evaluation. In D. Williams (Ed.), *Naturalistic evaluation* (pp. 73–84). New Directions for Program Evaluation, 30. San Francisco: Jossey-Bass.

McNiff, J., & Whitehead, J. (2000). *Action research in organizations.* New York: Routledge.

Menand, L. (2001). *The metaphysical club: The story of ideas in America.* New York: Farrar, Straus & Giroux.

Peters, M., & Robinson, V. (1984). The origins and status of action research. *Journal of Applied Behavioral Science, 20,* 113–124.

Popper, M., & Lipshitz, R. (1998). Organizational learning mechanisms: A structural and cultural approach to organizational learning. *Journal of Applied Behavioral Science, 34,* 78–98.

Rapoport, R. N. (1970). Three dilemmas in action research. *Human Relations, 23,* 488–513.

Reason, P. (1994). Three approaches to participatory inquiry. In N. K. Denzin & Y. S. Lincoln (Eds.), *Handbook of qualitative research* (pp. 324–339). Thousand Oaks, CA: Sage.

Reason, P. (2003). Pragmatist philosophy and action research. *Action Research, 1,* 103–123.

Reason, P., & Bradbury, H. (Eds.). (2001). *Handbook of action research: Participative inquiry and practice.* Thousand Oaks, CA: Sage.

Schön, D. (1995). Knowing-in-action: The new scholarship requires a new epistemology. *Change, 27*(6), 26–34.

Seashore, S. E. (1976). The design of action research. In A. W. Clark (Ed.), *Experimenting with organizational life* (pp. 103–117). New York: Plenum.

Stewart, T. A. (1997). *Intellectual capital: The new wealth of organizations.* Garden City, NY: Doubleday.

Strauss, A., & Corbin, J. (1990). *Basics of qualitative research: Grounded theory procedures and techniques.* Newbury Park, CA: Sage.

Susman, G., & Evered, R. (1978). As assessment of the scientific merit of action research. *Administrative Science Quarterly, 23*, 582–603.

Swanson, R. A., & Holton III, E. F. (2001). *Foundations of human resource development.* San Francisco: Berrett-Koehler.

Van de Ven, A. H., Angle, H. A., & Poole, M. S. (1989). *Research on the management of innovation: The Minnesota studies.* New York: Ballinger/Harper & Row.

Watkins, K., & Brooks, A. (1994). A framework for using action technologies. In A. Brooks & K. Watkins (Eds.), *The emerging power of action inquiry technologies* (p. 99ff.). New Directions for Adult and Continuing Education, 43. San Francisco: Jossey-Bass.

Research Resources

CHAPTERS

Using Journals and Databases in Research

Thomas J. Chermack and David L. Passmore,
The Pennsylvania State University

Using journal catalogs and databases as resources is critical to any research, no matter the form, circumstance, or method. Journal catalogs and databases are key tools commonly used to ground research studies in previous research, conduct literature reviews, develop theoretical frameworks, and provide general support for arguments, cases, and opinions. Databases can provide enough data to support multiple research studies, and the difficulties become knowing the most appropriate and meaningful questions to pose to the data.

The purpose of this chapter is to provide a clear and explicit description of how to use journal catalogs and databases as research resources. We will first review journal catalogs and their key uses, and provide a general process for using journal catalogs. Then we will do the same for databases.

JOURNAL CATALOGS

A source within the Penn State Library System suggests that "theoretically" 100% of all journals are cataloged in some form. However, there is no single catalog that contains all of them; rather, the catalogs attempt to arrange journals by subject. These catalogs, then, vary in how much of the subject area they actually provide access to, which can be anywhere from about 20% to 60% of "the literature" in that subject area. Thus, accessing the majority of the literature regarding a single subject area requires searches in multiple catalogs.

Most academic institutions have Internet interfaces with multiple large, electronic journal catalogs. These catalogs are, in essence, subscriptions to sometimes literally thousands of journals. Corporations and other institutions can purchase memberships and therefore access to any of these catalogs. The mode of accessing these catalogs is usually through an Internet page and search engine, the details of which will vary from institution to institution. The most important question is not how these catalogs are accessed but which catalogs are accessed. Put plainly, catalogs that deal explicitly with medical research are not likely to be helpful to scholars interested in organizational research as it has been outlined in this book. However, even the most seemingly appropriate journal catalogs can flood you with irrelevant information.

What Are Journal Catalogs?

Journal catalogs can generally be described as collections of written resources pertaining to certain areas of interest. There are journal catalogs that center around medical research, arts and humanities, history, and, of course, business. Journal catalogs are allocated by subject area, so they are a quick way to access large amounts of research, writing, and practical reports around general or specific topic areas. Given the size of most catalogs, searching them can be overwhelming until you become familiar with some of their features.

Key Uses for Journal Catalog Searches

The use of journals is critical to any form of research, but a few specific types of research papers feature the use of journals as a key research method.

Probably the most common of these are literature reviews and conceptual articles.

Literature Reviews

Literature reviews have their basis in journal catalog searches. Literature reviews aim to summarize the current body of literature related to some phenomenon, and the structure of literature review articles is driven by the content and the key themes that it reveals with a goal of providing a comprehensive summary. The literature review may constitute only one section of an article, or it can become the entire article. An example of the literature review as an entire article is found in Weinberger's (1998) often-cited article "Commonly Held Theories of Human Resource Development." In it, Weinberger provides a comprehensive list of the varying definitions of human resource development (HRD) as a discipline and explores common theories underlying the execution and delivery of HRD work. Descriptive research often begins with an extensive review of the literature related to a given phenomenon, while more advanced research studies involve a literature review component.

Conceptual Articles

Conceptual articles bring together multiple varying streams of content with a goal of providing some novel insight into the occurrence or understanding of some phenomenon. A classic example is Van de Ven and Poole's (1995) award-winning article "Explaining Development and Change in Organizations." Their article brought organization theory, development theory, and change process theory together in a summative and conceptual explanation of how, why, and under what conditions development and change works and fails in organizations. In this case, the focus of their article was on the theories in these domains and did not include organizational research that has been conducted within each of these domains.

A General Process for Using Journal Catalogs

So, how does one begin? This chapter will now turn to a general process of using journal catalogs as research resources. Such an approach should follow a series of steps: (1) choose the topic, (2) select the appropriate catalog, (3) perform keyword searches, (4) select relevant articles, (5) locate the articles, and (6) integrate your learning and writing.

Choosing the Topic: Begin with the Perceived Problem

Clear problems drive clear research projects. Weick (1989) and Van de Ven (2002) have provided lengthy descriptions about the importance of precise problem statements. For the purposes of journal catalog searches, it is not always possible to start out with a precise problem statement. Problems should be constantly revisited with an aim of increasing and refining the precision. Once the topic is selected, journal catalogs can be searched for relevant articles, and the problem statement should be formulated and refined throughout the research process.

Using the Van de Ven and Poole (1995) article as an example, we may note that the authors might have started with a simple task of attempting to describe development and change in organizations. This was a simple enough topic to begin with that yielded a precise problem statement later on.

Selecting the Appropriate Journal Catalog

Research in organizations will draw from catalogs that generally contain business-related journals, magazines, newspapers, and other publications. Catalogs usually contain some amount of both of two key types of materials: journals and periodicals. Journals are typically academic in content, meaning that they will contain scholarly and refereed articles. Periodicals will generally contain nonrefereed articles and include newspapers, magazines, and other nonacademic publications. The choice of journal catalog can be clarified by making this distinction between academic and nonacademic catalogs. Although all catalogs contain a range of materials in both the academic and nonacademic classifications, most search interfaces have a limiting function that allows the display of only refereed or only nonrefereed search results.

Common and extensive catalogs for organizational research include the following:

ABI/Inform. This is a business-oriented article database for subjects such as advertising, marketing, company information, industry trends, human resources, economic policy, health care, and consumer products and services.

Academic Search Premier. The world's largest academic multidisciplinary database, Academic Search Premier provides full text for nearly 4,600 scholarly publications, including full text for more than 3,500 peer-reviewed journals.

Business Source Premier. The Business Source Premier database includes both scholarly journals and periodicals from more than 3,000 business publications mainly for practitioners.

EconLit. International in scope, EconLit is an index to research in all aspects of economics from books, journals, and dissertations. This is an enhanced version of the *Journal of Economic Literature.*

ERIC (Educational Resources Information Center). The ERIC database is the world's largest source of education information, containing more than 1 million abstracts on education research and practice. ERIC covers two types of literature:

- Journals (in *Current Index to Journals in Education* [CIJE], 1969–)— scholarly, professional and practitioner journals
- Documents (in *Resources in Education* [RIE], 1966–)—nonjournal literature, such as full-text curriculum guides, theses, conference papers, standards, reports, and so forth; not peer reviewed

LexisNexis. LexisNexis provides access to a wide range of news, business, legal, and reference information, covering many news sources for 20 years. Court cases and statutes from all federal and state jurisdictions are included. Most resources can be searched in full text.

JSTOR. JSTOR presents electronic journals available through the Internet in the areas of ecology, economics, finance, history, mathematics, political science, and population studies.

WorldCAT. WorldCAT includes more than 38 million records for books, periodicals, magazines, and any other type of material cataloged by OCLC member libraries. The database includes records for material as early as the 11th century.

A proper search for organizational research would include all of these catalogs, as each contains unique journals and sources. Although there is some overlap, a comprehensive search must include all of these. Most universities have access to all of these catalogs electronically through a library home page and search engine. Businesses can purchase access to any of these.

Once you have selected a set of catalogs to search, the next step is to start searching them. Again referring to the Van de Ven and Poole (1995) article, we may assume that a simple choice of business catalogs was likely made, as opposed to medicine or biology catalogs.

For clarity, we have provided a few screen shots in Figures 22.1 and 22.2 of the search interface through the Pennsylvania State University's library system. Figure 22.1 displays the list of catalogs available for search. To use this, one would simply select the catalog of interest and then click "go there."

Performing Keyword Searches

The first part of performing keyword searches is to define the keywords themselves. The definition of keywords is generally driven by the topic and content, but a few tips can prove helpful. First, start with general terms and work toward narrowing your search. Second, using combinations of topic words, or words related to the topic, can be helpful in getting further sources. Third, conduct as comprehensive a search as you can. That is, use as many of the catalogs that you have access to as you can.

For example, Van de Ven and Poole (1995) may have begun with keyword searches for "organization theory," "development theory," and "change process theory." Depending on the results, these keyword searches might have been further specified as "organization and development theory," "development and change process theory," and other combinations. Again, based on results, keyword searches can be refined according to new discoveries made by assessing the search results.

Figure 22.2 shows a keyword search interface in the JSTOR Catalog. In this form, one types keywords into the blank fields and then uses the drop-down

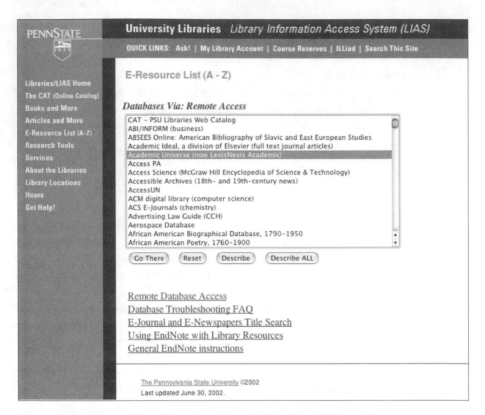

Figure 22.1   Journal Search Interface through Penn State's Library System

menu (currently displaying "citation and abstract") to select various fields to search. For example, one can select "author," "article title," "abstract," and other fields for the defined keywords. Other important features of this catalog include the check boxes that allow you to limit the search to scholarly and refereed articles, as well as full-text articles. In this example, we have typed in a keyword of "strategy" and selected "article title" as the search field. This indicates that the search will only return articles with the word *strategy* in the article title.

You must also be sure to select disciplines and related journals to search. Note that the "Business" box is checked. Figure 22.3 provides the results of this search.

Here you can see that the search yielded 602 refereed articles. You can also see the review options below each journal title. For example, you can access the abstract and the citation information, print the article, download it, and save this particular citation. Given the volume of resources that resulted from this search, specifying this search further would provide a more manageable number of results; however, a comprehensive search on "strategy" has begun.

JSTOR Advanced Search

Basic Search | Advanced Search | Expert Search | Search Help

All of these words:	strategy
The exact phrase:	
At least one of these words:	
None of these words:	

Search

NOTE: All content in all journals is searched by default. Narrow your search below.

Narrow Your Search To:

These Fields: ☐ Title ☐ Author ☐ Caption ☐ Abstract

These Types: ☐ Article ☐ Review ☐ Opinion piece ☐ Other items

These Dates: From: [ ] through: [ ] (specify dates as yyyy, yyyy/mm, or yyyy/mm/dd)

These Journal Title(s): [ ] (separate titles with semicolon)

Show All Titles in New Window
- OR -

These Discipline(s) and/or Journal(s):
- ⊞ ☐ African American Studies - 8 journals
- ⊞ ☐ African Studies - 16 journals
- ⊞ ☐ American Indian Studies - 2 journals
- ⊞ ☐ Anthropology - 19 journals
- ⊞ ☐ Aquatic Sciences - 2 journals
- ⊞ ☐ Archaeology - 14 journals
- ⊞ ☐ Architecture & Architectural History - 6 journals
- ⊞ ☐ Art & Art History - 19 journals
- ⊞ ☐ Asian Studies - 15 journals
- ⊞ ☐ Biological Sciences - 37 journals
- ⊞ ☐ Botany & Plant Sciences - 9 journals
- ⊞ ☑ Business - 58 journals

Figure 22.2 A Keyword Search in JSTOR

Your access to JSTOR is provided by
The Pennsylvania State University

Preview the new JSTOR Citation Search

EXIT JSTOR

strategy AND sn:(00014273 OR 00014826 OR 00018392 OR (Search) (Modify Your Search)

Basic Search | Advanced Search | Expert Search | Search Help

Show [25 ▾] results per page. (Display)   Results 1-25 of 44993 for « strategy in multiple journals » (0.36 seconds)

Sort by [Relevance ▾] (Sort)   Save All Citations on This Page | View Saved Citations
You have saved 0 citations

28% **The Seeking of Strategy Where it is Not: Towards a Theory of Strategy Absence: A Reply to Bauerschmidt**
Andrew C. Inkpen
Strategic Management Journal > Vol. 17, No. 8 (Oct., 1996), pp. 669-670
Stable URL: http://links.jstor.org/sici?sici=0143-2095%281996l0%2917%3A8%3C669%3ATSOSWI%3E2.0.CO%3B2-5
Citation/Abstract | Page of First Match | Print | Download | Save Citation

25% **Speaking of Strategy**
Alan Bauerschmidt
Strategic Management Journal > Vol. 17, No. 8 (Oct., 1996), pp. 665-667
Stable URL: http://links.jstor.org/sici?sici=0143-2095%281996l0%2917%3A8%3C665%3ASOS%3E2.0.CO%3B2-S
Citation/Abstract | Page of First Match | Print | Download | Save Citation

24% **An Empirical Analysis of Strategy Types**
Craig Galbraith; Dan Schendel
Strategic Management Journal > Vol. 4, No. 2 (Apr., 1983), pp. 153-173
Stable URL: http://links.jstor.org/sici?sici=0143-2095%281983O4%2F06%294%3A2%3C153%3AAEAOST%3E2.0.CO%3B2-B
Citation/Abstract | Page of First Match | Print | Download | Save Citation

24% **Operationalizing the Concept of Business-Level Strategy in Research**
Donald C. Hambrick
The Academy of Management Review > Vol. 5, No. 4 (Oct., 1980), pp. 567-575
Stable URL: http://links.jstor.org/sici?sici=0363-7425%281980l0%295%3A4%3C567%3AOTCOBS%3E2.0.CO%3B2-A
Citation/Abstract | Page of First Match | Print | Download | Save Citation

Figure 22.3 Search Results for Keyword "Strategy" in JSTOR

Select the Relevant Articles

Selecting the relevant articles is again driven by the content of what you are trying to summarize and the precision of your problem statement. The tools and ease of access provided by technology make this task much easier. For example, you can quickly review the abstracts from multiple articles online as in the search example provided in Figure 22.3. Remember that the keywords you use will determine the results; thus, refining, specifying, or making your keywords more general will provide different, fewer, or a greater number of resources, respectively. You must also consider the context and population for whom you are writing. For example, when writing for a practitioner audience, the sole use of scholarly articles is likely to cause some confusion. However, the sole use of practitioner articles misses an opportunity to expose practitioners to scholarly work. In applied fields such as business, education, public policy, and the like, it is imperative to include both scholarly and practitioner-oriented publications in any research-based literature search.

A general rule to err on the side of inclusion is appropriate for comprehensive literature review manuscripts. For conceptual papers, you will have to skim or read articles to ascertain their importance for the topic you are writing about and for the argument or synthesis you are trying to make.

Locate the Articles

Most articles are available electronically, which means they can be downloaded right from the search results page in Portable Document Format (PDF). Articles that are available for download are usually marked with a PDF icon. Articles that are not available for download (which are usually older articles that simply have not yet been archived) require a trip to the library armed with a pocket full of change for making copies.

Integrate Your Learning and Writing

By far the most difficult part of using journal catalogs as research resources is structuring the synthesis of all the reading that is usually required. A few notable tips might help you as you begin writing. First, an outline is a really effective way to begin structuring your thinking. Second, beginning with a clear problem statement helps you avoid many problems later on. Using sticky notes is another way to begin structuring your ideas. In particularly complex conceptual papers, a section entitled "Preview of the Argument" can be extremely helpful. Whatever the progression of your writing, the classic whole-part-whole method of structuring content has been proven to be extremely effective, yet it is often ignored. These are all tools that can be useful in structuring and synthesizing large amounts of data and ideas gleaned from literature searches.

- *Outlines.* In the beginning stages, the outline merely serves as a way to *start* writing. Soon, though, the outline becomes a valuable content-structuring tool. It should be revised and altered often until you have settled into a structure that allows you to effectively and efficiently present a valid and intelligent synthesis of the content.

- *Problem statement.* A clear heading of "Problem Statement" is sometimes an effective way to draw attention to and clarify the main problem that the research attempts to solve. This approach also allows you to be really clear about formulating a precise and effective problem statement; there should not be any confusion about the problem under investigation. This is also an appropriate heading under which to include your research questions.

- *Sticky notes.* Other writing tools include sticky notes. Described by Whetten (2002) as tools for structuring thinking in theory construction efforts, sticky notes can function similarly to outlines. By writing your key concepts, headings, or sections on these notes, you can shift them, move them, add them, and delete them easily. Particularly for those who think best with visual prompts, this method can be effective for bringing structure to ideas.

- *Whole-part-whole.* Swanson and Law (1993) provide a comprehensive review of the whole-part-whole learning model. Astoundingly intuitive but often overlooked, the whole-part-whole method of structuring content is a simple and effective way to structure your writing. The first whole provides an initial framework or mental scaffolding, dissecting and mastering the parts gets at the substantive detail, and the second whole integrates the parts for a holistic understanding of the phenomena. This model is an effective tool to integrate your learning and writing.

- *Preview of the argument.* The use of a section labeled "Preview of the Argument" can be very helpful in articles that are particularly difficult to structure. This heading is useful in conceptual papers that draw from numerous bodies of literature that readers from any single discipline might not be completely familiar with. Previewing the argument is an effective strategy that is linked to the whole-part-whole model. By providing a concrete description of what is coming up, you prepare readers for this complex content.

Although not a definitive list of tools for structuring your writing content, this brief description provides some helpful ways to begin thinking about structure as you write papers that involve the use of journal catalogs. Perhaps the most important tip of all is that you make time to write *every* day.

DATABASES

Advances in methodology, computer storage and technology, and data distribution and analysis systems allow more general use of common data sets collected by organizations or government agencies by many more researchers than previously possible. For example, the *National Longitudinal Surveys of Labor Market Experience* (NLS) (see www.bls.gov/nls/home.htm) are a set of surveys designed to gather information at multiple points in time on the labor market activities and other significant life events of several groups of men and women. The NLS effort is funded entirely by the U.S. federal government. NLS data contain thousands of variables measured longitudinally and cross-sectionally and are grouped into a number of databases that are available to the public through an Internet download.

Since the 1960s, NLS databases have served as an important tool for economic, social, and educational research and were used as the data sources for literally thousands of scientific studies (see www.nlsbibliography.org/). Many of the variables—such as measures of job satisfaction, locus of control, and working conditions—that are available for analysis in the NLS databases certainly are familiar to researchers in organizational development. Use of these databases could offer considerable cost savings and other advantages over collection of original data.

In the United States, census data, monthly populations surveys, special data collections (such as the NLS data), and administrative data are becoming more widely available for research and information gathering. Collecting and organizing such databases requires the allocation of resources, probably not available to individual researchers, to serve many research purposes. Researchers in organizational development can plumb these freely available databases for their own original research work.

Use of Databases

Researchers can use databases compiled for administrative uses or research activities to study new problems that possibly are secondary to the original purposes for the data collections. Secondary analysis involves use of existing data, collected for the purposes of a prior study, in order to pursue a research interest that is distinct from that of the original work (Hinds, Vogel, & Clarke-Steffen, 1997; Szabo & Strang, 1997). Recycling of such data can help answer new research questions that perhaps are completely orthogonal to the purposes of the original data collections. Secondary analyses of data might provide alternative perspectives—perspectives derived over nations or organizations—to questions pursued in local or single organizational settings by a researcher. Moreover, secondary analyses of available databases could fulfill a planning function by helping researchers hone the questions they will pose in subsequent research they are attempting to design.

Use of databases for research in organizations involves a trade-off between costs and control. On one hand, savings for conducting secondary analyses of existing databases include offloading the expense of collecting and organizing data to the original database compiler. On the other hand, users of databases usually forego any opportunity to influence how variables are defined, operationalized, and measured, how data are collected, and how collected data are screened, coded, and stored for future use.

Secondary analysis differs from systematic reviews of literature and meta-analyses of published research studies. Secondary analysis of existing data is meant to create new knowledge. Literature reviews and meta-analyses aim, instead, to compile and assess extant evidence relating to a common concern or area of practice.

Sources of Databases

Databases for secondary analysis in organizational research are available from a variety of sources. Databases could be obtained for secondary analysis from individual researchers or organizations. Far more common, however, is the use of databases available from public sources. Typically, these public databases are purged of any information that could allow individuals to be identified directly or indirectly.

An excellent resource for databases is the Inter-University Consortium for Political and Social Research (ICPSR) (www.icpsr.umich.edu/). ICPSR maintains and provides access to a vast archive of social science data for research and instruction, and offers training in quantitative methods to facilitate effective data use. To ensure that data resources are available to future generations of scholars, ICPSR preserves data, migrating them to new storage media as changes in technology warrant. In addition, ICPSR provides user support to assist researchers in identifying relevant data for analysis and in conducting their research projects.

Examples of public databases in the ICPSR archive that hold promise for research in organizational development include the following:

- *Current Population Survey* (www.bls.census.gov/cps/). The Current Population Survey (CPS) is a monthly survey of about 50,000 households conducted by the U.S. Bureau of the Census for the Bureau of Labor Statistics. The CPS is the primary source of information on the labor force characteristics of the U.S. population. The sample is selected to represent the civilian noninstitutional population of the United States. Respondents are interviewed to obtain information about the employment status of each member of the household 15 years of age and older. The sample provides estimates for the nation as a whole and serves as part of model-based estimates for individual states and other geographic areas. Estimates obtained from the CPS include employment, unemployment, earnings, hours of work, and other indicators. Estimates are available by a variety of demographic characteristics including age, sex, race, marital status, and educational attainment. These estimates also are available by occupation, industry, and class of worker. Supplemental questions to produce estimates on a variety of topics also are often added to the regular CPS questionnaire. Some examples of supplementary questions in recent surveys

include contingent workers and alternative employment (www.bls
.census.gov/cps/contwkr/sdata.htm), job tenure and occupational mobility
(www.bls.census.gov/cps/jobten/sdata.htm), and work schedules (www.bls
.census.gov/cps/worksch/sdata.htm).

- *Americans' Changing Lives: Waves I and II, 1986 and 1989* (webapp.icpsr
  .umich.edu/cocoon/ICPSR-STUDY/06438.xml). This study is part of a
  larger research program designed to investigate (1) the ways in which a
  wide range of activities and social relationships that people engage in are
  broadly "productive"; (2) how individuals adapt to acute life events and
  chronic stresses that threaten the maintenance of health, effective functioning, and productive activity; and (3) sociocultural variations in the
  nature, meaning, determinants, and consequences of productive activity
  and relationships. Focusing especially on differences between African
  Americans and white Americans in middle and late life, these data constitute both the first and second waves in a national longitudinal panel survey covering a wide range of sociological, psychological, mental, and
  physical health items. Among the topics covered are interpersonal relationships (spouse/partner, children, parents, friends), sources and levels of
  satisfaction, social interactions and leisure activities, traumatic life events
  (physical assault, serious illness, divorce, death of a loved one, financial or
  legal problems), perceptions of retirement, health behaviors (smoking,
  alcohol consumption, overweight, rest), and utilization of health care
  (doctor visits, hospitalization, nursing home institutionalization, bed
  days). Also included are measures of physical health and psychological
  well-being, and indices referring to cognitive functioning. Background
  information provided for individuals includes household composition,
  number of children and grandchildren, employment status, occupation
  and work history, income, family financial situation, religious beliefs and
  practices, ethnicity, race, education, sex, and region of residence.

- *National Longitudinal Surveys of Labor Market Experience* (www.bls.gov/
  nls/home.htm). The National Longitudinal Surveys provide data designed
  primarily to analyze sources of variation in labor market behavior and
  experience. The original groups consist of Older Men ages 45–59 in 1966,
  Mature Women ages 30–44 in 1967, Young Men ages 14–24 in 1966,
  Young Women ages 14–24 in 1968, and Youth ages 14–21 in 1979. The
  major topics that are covered in these surveys may be classified under the
  following headings: (1) labor market experience (including labor force
  participation, unemployment, job history, and job mobility); (2) socioeconomic and human capital (including education, training, health and
  physical condition, marital and family characteristics, military service, job
  attitudes, retirement plans, and occupational aspirations and expectations); and (3) environmental variables (size of labor force in local area,

unemployment rates for local area, and index of demand for female labor and for teenage male labor). In addition, special topics are covered for particular cohorts or study years.

- *National Organizations Survey* (www.soc.umn.edu/~knoke/pages/nos91tec .htm). This database is a representative sample of U.S. work organizations, with data from informants about human resources policies and practices. Employed respondents gave identification and location information about their employers and the employers of working spouses. Each employee interviewed in person was matched to his or her employer, and an informant from the work establishment (either the personnel director or the chief executive officer) was interviewed by telephone or by mail questionnaire. Industry data from published government sources were merged with these data. Topics covered include employer staffing procedures, interval job ladders, promotion chains, job training programs, employee benefits and incentives, and structural characteristics of organizations.

- *Reliability of Organizational Measures* (webapp.icpsr.umich.edu/cocoon/ ICPSR-STUDY/09469.xml). This project had several objectives: (1) to estimate the reliabilities of diverse organizational measures by studying organizations of various types and sizes to determine the impact of size and type on reliability, (2) to develop techniques that facilitate common measurement across all organizational types, (3) to determine the characteristics of respondents most likely to provide the modal or typical response for an organization, and (4) to demonstrate that high-quality samples of diverse organization types are technically feasible and affordable. Measures of age, size, external setting, internal structural differentiation, and organizational culture were obtained from 370 government, social service, and business organizations. The database contains information from at least five centrally located decision makers (executives, administrators, officers) of each organization sampled. Characteristics of the respondents were included, with major emphasis on experience with the organization as well as current position and standardized demographic data. The unit of analysis for the project was the organization.

- *Workplace Ethnography Project, 1944–2002* (www.sociology.ohio-state .edu/rdh/Workplace-Ethnography-Project.html). The Workplace Ethnography project generated content-coded data from the full population of book-length English-language organizational ethnographies. Drawn from Australia, Canada, China, Colombia, France, Great Britain, Hungary, India, Israel, Japan, Norway, the Philippines, Scotland, South Africa, Sweden, Taiwan, United States, and Zambia, these ethnographies provided deep descriptions on a wide range of topics, such as worker behavior, management behavior, coworker relations, labor process, conflict and resistance, citizenship behavior, emotional labor, and sexual harassment.

Coding of these characteristics yielded variables based on descriptions of work life in specific organizational settings. The study data were collected in mainly two periods: the early 1990s and the early 2000s. The study generated 204 ethnographic cases. The general scope of questions included organizational factors such as occupation, workplace organization, pay scheme, employment size, the situation of the company, the nature of company ownership, staff turnover, layoff frequency, how well the organization operated in terms of communications, recruitment and retention of personnel, and maintenance of equipment, as well as substantive facts concerning labor market opportunity and labor force composition. On the topic of management, questions addressed leadership, organization of production, sexual harassment, and control strategies. Community factors were assessed through questions regarding unemployment and whether the area was rural or urban. A series of questions addressed job satisfaction, pay, benefit package, job security, effort bargain, conflict with management/supervisors, training, worker strategies, conditions of consent/compliance, and nature of consent/compliance. The nature of work was queried through questions regarding autonomy, creativity, meaningful work, freedom of movement, comfort of work, injuries, employment status, and frequency of conflict with customers. Additional questions included size and nature of the focal group, group dynamics, conflict between the focal group and management, basis of alternative social groups at work, and whether work friendships carried over to the outside. Questions about methodology covered ethnographer's theoretical orientation, focus of ethnography, ethnographer's gender, data collection method, supplemental data used, main type of supplemental data used, and position of key informants in the study.

These six examples represent some of the public databases that might hold interest for researchers in organizational development. ICPSR provides a bibliography of data-related literature at www.icpsr.umich.edu/citations/index.html to help find publications that are linked back to the databases themselves. The ICPSR's social sciences variables database (http://webapp.icpsr.umich.edu/cocoon/SSVD/basicSrch) allows all ICPSR's databases to be searched across studies to find various databases that measure essentially the same variables. Each of these databases is available for downloading through the ICPSR Web site, although access to data often requires some affiliation or work through a university, college, or other organization that is an ICPSR member (a list of more than 500 members is available at www.icpsr.umich.edu/membership/ors.html). Researchers who are not affiliated with ICPSR member institutions pay a fee for access to the databases.

ICPSR supplies data files for use with statistical software, such as SAS or SPSS. For researchers who do not have access to commercial statistical analysis packages, ICPSR also makes available an online Data Analysis System to perform analyses over the Web without requiring analysts to download any data or to own any special statistical software (see www.icpsr.umich.edu/access/sda.html).

General Guidelines and Cautions for Using Databases

A public database assembled for one activity usually is not a perfect match for the research needs to which it might be applied in some other context. In addition, database processes and documentation often are complex and technical. Therefore, some care is necessary in selection and use of databases in organizational research to ensure validity of intended outcomes.

It should go without saying that researchers interested in using databases for secondary analyses should determine carefully whether databases of interest actually match their research problems. Yet, the use of databases is seductive. So much data, usually well prepared and easily accessible, are available that it is tempting—like the character, Procrustes, in ancient myth who adjusted his guests to their bed by either stretching them or chopping off their legs to fit—to mold the research problem to fit the database. Certainly, some practical accommodation between research needs and available data is required in most research, even research in which the data collection and organization is entirely under the researcher's control. Such an accommodation walks a fine line between credibility of outcomes and containment of costs. However, in no case should data drive the research.

What matters should an organizational researcher consider before using a database? Here are six guidelines and cautions for database users:

1. *Evaluate target population.* Is the target population for the database under consideration appropriate for research needs? The target population is the people, places, and objects to which the database information is intended to be generalized. Most research samples information from a population for cost considerations and infers population information from the sample. For instance, the target population for the Current Population Survey is the civilian noninstitutional population of the U.S. age 15 years and older. Tabulations from the CPS created from responses of people in 50,000 U.S. households are meant to represent this target population. Researchers need to consider whether the target population matches the targets for their research interests. Alternatively, researchers must accept some degree of mismatch, offset by reduced costs of data analyses, between the target population of a database and the target population of interest to the researchers.

2. *Study documentation.* There is no substitute for having an encyclopedic knowledge of a database. Again, databases are so easy to use that it is pos-

sible to become lulled into merely ripping data off the Internet or from a CD-ROM without a complete understanding of all concepts and measures in the database as well as any limitations embedded in the database. For instance, perhaps a database contains a variable "age." Is this age in integer years? In years with decimal months? Age at last birthday? Age rounded up to next birthday? The specific answers to these questions not only will dictate the precision with which researchers will use these data but also will help explain anomalies present in comparisons between outcomes from research with the database and from other studies. Review questionnaires and other data-recording devices. Determine similarities between measures of variables in database and other commonly held or applied definitions used in the field of practice. Examine the directions provided to data collectors or coders. Failure to understand the exact nature and form of information in a database is to beg equivocation about subsequent findings.

3. *Muck about the data.* Learn more about the database by running frequency distributions, descriptive statistics, and plots of distributions of individual variables of interest. Are data out of range or otherwise anomalous? For example, is there information from any 160-year-old people in the database? From people who held 12 jobs at once? Did someone earn $25,000 per hour in wages from their primary job (an actual data point for a retail trade worker in one of the NLS databases)? Are there scales of, say, job satisfaction that should produce scores between 0 and 40, although some scores are greater than 40? Also, cross-tabulate variables to reveal possible irregularities in data. For instance, are there respondents listed as "deceased" who provide responses to questionnaires after their dates of death? Have some people received income from wages and salaries while they were classified as unemployed?

4. *Examine work flow.* Processes that generated variables in databases frequently are conditional, complex, and confusing. For instance, a database might contain measures of job satisfaction *only* for employed respondents to a survey. As a result, the database might record a large amount of missing data because people not employed were skipped legitimately, not because they failed or refused to answer questions. Most databases differentiate by some sort of code between respondents who were not "in the universe" for a data element, such as a questionnaire response, from those who actually failed to provide data. However, researchers might find that careful scouring of the work flow of information collection for databases is necessary to uncover such fine discriminations between legitimate skips and missing data. The process of uncovering the details of responses often leads researchers back through questionnaires, documentation, and, if a database is really well documented, instructions to data collectors in the

form of flowcharts and directions. However, some databases have complex and potentially confusing skip patterns resulting in collection of data only if certain conditions are met and, as a consequence, require detailed examination to reveal legitimate responses.

5. *Take account of complex sampling.* Most public databases are produced as a result of complex sampling strategies. As an example, the NLS databases were intended to help understand problems with labor force participation, especially among economically disadvantaged groups. A sample of people according to their proportions in the population would produce too few economically disadvantaged sample members for analyses. Therefore, the NLS conducted an oversampling of economically disadvantaged people in NLS samples, which allows detailed tabulations to contain enough data from economically disadvantaged people to allow full analyses. However, simple tabulations of sample members would reveal too many economically disadvantaged people as an estimate of their proportion in the population. So, instead of estimating that the economically disadvantaged people is composed of, say, 12% of the population, the proportion in the population based on the sampling strategy might appear to be 24% erroneously NLS record in databases. For instance, each economically disadvantaged person's response might have a weight equal to one-third of other sample members' responses. In this way, the overall proportions of sample members are reconciled with the population proportions. For this reason, always use sampling weights when available in public databases. Fortunately, many Web interfaces to public databases take into account sampling weights transparently so that the user does not need to be concerned about such a technical issue.

6. *Keep an eye on quality.* Many public databases have a back-end research program to investigate the reliability and validity of measures applied. However, not all do. So, as a result, finding the reliability of variables such as sex or age might prove difficult. At times, analysis of components of indexes, such as individual item responses that comprise a scale of job satisfaction, are available for the researcher using public databases to compute reliabilities of measures. Another factor the database analyst should be aware of is using so few data points from the database that the resulting estimates contain more noise than information. For example, perhaps a table that lists respondents to a survey by sex, age, race, and occupation might contain table cells with very small counts. Most public databases will carry warnings about interpreting tabulations with low cell counts because the error in estimating population values from these low cell counts is large. However, such warnings do not stop the unwary analyst from creating and interpreting error-laden tables. Some databases will not produce tabulations with low cell counts due to privacy issues.

CONCLUSION

This chapter has described the utility of journal catalogs and databases for research in organizations. It has provided processes and descriptions of how to use these resources in organizational research. Some tips and tools for structuring writing content have been suggested as well as explicit instructions on how to access a specific list of journal catalogs and databases that are relevant to research commonly conducted in an organizational context.

REFERENCES

Hinds, P. S., Vogel, R. J., & Clarke-Steffen, L. (1997). The possibilities and pitfalls of doing a secondary analysis of a qualitative data set. *Qualitative Health Research, 7*(3), 408–424.

Swanson, R. A., & Law, B. (1993). Whole-part-whole learning model. *Performance Improvement Quarterly, 6*(1), 43–53.

Szabo, V., & Strang, V. R. (1997). Secondary analysis of qualitative data. *Advances in Nursing Science, 20*(2), 66–74.

Van de Ven, A. H. (2002). The buzzing, blooming, confusing world of organization and management theory. *Journal of Management Inquiry, 8*(2), 118–125.

Van de Ven, A. H., & Poole, M. S. (1995). Explaining development and change in organizations. *Academy of Management Review, 20*(3), 510–540.

Weick, K. E. (1989). Theory construction as disciplined imagination. *Academy of Management Review, 14*(4), 516–531.

Weinberger, L. A. (1998). Commonly held theories of human resource development. *Human Resource Development International, 1*(1), 75–93.

Whetten, D. A. (2002). Modelling as theorizing: A systematic methodology for theory development. In D. Partington (Ed.), *Essential skills for management research* (pp. 45–65). Thousand Oaks, CA: Sage.

Managing an Effective and Ethical Research Project

Miles T. Bryant, *University of Nebraska*

CHAPTER OUTLINE

This last chapter in the book directs your attention to several important considerations that accompany research in organizations in general and human resource development in particular. Several important questions organize this chapter. What makes you effective as a researcher? What makes your research effective? And what ethical practices should shape your work?

As in many social science disciplines, organizational researchers typically have the need to disseminate their work to a field of practice; otherwise their efforts will have little influence or impact. The voices of organizational researchers must be attentive to practice because applied disciplines have a strong tradition of informing and influencing practice.[1] Second, because most organizational researchers arrive at conclusions about human beings, there is a strong obligation for these researchers to be ethical in both method and conclusions. How one gathers information from human subjects must be in accordance with accepted ethical principles of research. What one reports may well have a significant impact on other human beings, and thus one is obligated to be responsible to those other people.

This chapter is divided into two sections, each discussing these two particular facets of organizational research—effectiveness and ethical behavior—that ultimately should guide the researcher. I should note that occasionally these two faces look darkly upon one another. A very catchy and well-received research finding may be based on erroneous data, thus falling short in ethical terms; conversely, a very cautious, reserved, and well-designed research report may not be welcomed with great applause by a community of practitioners seeking easy answers to intractable problems. Researchers need to be aware of both the qualities that yield effective research and the ethical conditions to which that work should conform. And while a comprehensive treatment of this topic is worthy of several books, this chapter will indicate some common themes for your consideration.

RESEARCH EFFECTIVENESS

There are many understandings of what makes research effective. At times there is the conviction that the simple completion of a research project means that it can be labeled effective. For example, the dissertation completed is certainly, to the doctoral researcher, an example of effective research. While I understand such a position, I am orienting this chapter to a higher standard of effectiveness. Measures of effectiveness that come to mind quickly are these: (1) research that has influenced and shaped the beliefs and behavior of others, (2) research that is accepted within a community of peers and is published in that community's major journals or in books widely read, and (3) research that benefits others in clear and compelling ways.[2] These would be possible definitions of effective research.

Bearing in mind such understandings about what makes effective research, you should also consider some critical factors. The first has to do with you as a researcher. In order to design, complete, and disseminate effective research, there are personal attributes that shape a person's capacity for effective research. A second factor is the nature of your research. To be labeled effective, your research has to have relevance and meaning to others. A third factor has to do with how your research is communicated to others. Your research must be shared. It would be difficult to label research as effective if no person knows of it other than the researcher.

BEING AN EFFECTIVE RESEARCHER

Unless the researcher is effective, the research is not likely to be effective. Research is hard work. Often in academic settings, research is lonely and done in isolation. It is what I have referred to as "solo scholarship" (Bryant, 2003). In teams or groups, research can be full of social pleasure. Some maintain that the most creative work is done in connection with groups or networks of individuals who provide creative ideas and acute critical thinking. For example, Collins (1998) completed a study in which he found that most highly significant new ideas were fully developed within some sort of movement or social group. Such monumentally creative people as Freud, Degas, Hegel, and Darwin all worked with colleagues in developing their seminal ideas (Gladwell, 2002). Hackman (1985) and Van de Ven and Johnson (2004) have proposed an engaged collaborative of academics and researchers as a way of bridging the theory–practice gap, thus making research more effective. Scholars who work in academic settings with doctoral students recommend support networks as a device to help improve completion rates (Rackham Graduate School, 2004; Bryant, 2003). It seems relatively clear that one mechanism to help make your work more effective is to make sure your work is seen by critical colleagues.

Still, even when supported by a social group, research is hard work demanding commitment, time, and persistence. There are a great many organizational researchers who conduct research but not as their primary responsibility in life. Few are the researchers who are only researchers. This reality leads to the variables that are associated with the person doing the research. A number of characteristics describe the effective researcher.

Active researchers must find ways to mute all of the many competing calls for one's attention. Work, family, more attractive projects, and personal needs can easily move one's research to a lower priority in the queue of life's obligations. The time-honored tactic to guard against such intrusions is to establish a work schedule and timetable and stick to both. Find a time of the day when you are likely to be at your best, and schedule research activities into that time period. Make sure that others in your life understand this routine and can respect it. Such a simple albeit strangely difficult strategy will cause those around you to adjust to your schedule. Some people may also suggest that you make sure you keep your body healthy as this will make for a healthy mind. All are excellent points. But such sage advice misses several critical elements of research effectiveness, for one's inclination to permit distractions may be a symptom of a larger issue: the degree to which the researcher is intellectually engaged with the research. Certain dispositions seem to accompany the researchers whose work becomes known and appreciated and therefore effective.

Passion, Curiosity, Skepticism, and Memory

Obviously a huge number of personal factors or dispositions can help make a person effective as a researcher. In the interest of parsimony, however, I am only going to speak to four of these: passion, curiosity, suspicion, and memory. Each is important, and there is ample evidence of their significance in the biographies of notable scholars. Each of these terms offers the possibility of multiple interpretations.

Passion
First, if you believe that your research has the potential to be of significance and consequence, then you will be less susceptible to intrusion and distraction. We can think of this as a passion for the object of the research. This passion or deep involvement in one's research is characteristic of almost all researchers who make significant contributions to their fields. Louis Pasteur would not have made his singular contributions to microbiology, immunology, virology, and bacteriology had he lacked a deep commitment to his work. You need not be compulsive to be an effective researcher, but you do need to have a commitment to your work. Lacking such a commitment, the research may languish and never be completed or may be done poorly. You can gauge your commitment to your research project if you welcome distractions or if you find them frustrating.

Curiosity
Second, it helps if one's research work is motivated by a desire to know. Sometimes, particularly in academic settings, the motivation to carry out a research project is externally determined—must write a dissertation or must publish or perish. The motivation to do research may result from some external pressure and not from the intrinsic value of the research work. If such is the case, it may be difficult to be truly engaged with the project. But a researcher will be less likely to be an effective researcher if the only object is to satisfy an external force.

To be curious means that the researcher pursues questions and quandaries to some resolution, searching deeply for information. Curiosity appears when there is a thirst to know as much as you can about a topic of study. Curiosity shows itself when you want to know about what others have discovered about the subject. It is a willingness to seek and to find. Curiosity extends not only to what some other person may have discovered but to how the person discovered that new knowledge. Curiosity manifests itself not only in understanding the findings reported by another but also in understanding how that scholar conducted the study. Curiosity means an inquiring frame of mind. It can exist comfortably with external pressure for it is the researcher who controls the level of curiosity.

Skepticism

In working as a professor who helps graduate students design research projects, I like to remind everyone that "perfection is for another place." That is, no research design is without flaws. Thus, another earmark of the effective researcher is an attitude of skepticism, of critical disbelief. This helpful character attribute of skepticism should apply equally to what others have done as well as to your own work.

Skepticism means that you want to be cautious about accepting at face value the conclusions that others have reached. If it is true, as Suppe (1977), Lincoln and Guba (1985), Campbell and Overman (1988), and many others have suggested, that knowledge is not absolute and is a construction of our minds, then obviously one needs to be cautious in accepting what others proclaim and what your own work proclaims. Psychologists use the term *calibration* to describe how certain an individual is that he or she is right. It is a useful concept in speaking of a researcher's skepticism. A researcher's level of certainty about the work of others should be guarded. Would you have arrived at the same conclusions if you had done another's study using their methodology? Do their conclusions seem compatible with what others have discovered? Do their conclusions test conventional wisdom or common sense? If their method were altered, would their results differ significantly? Skepticism about the research done by others has led to academic revolutions (i.e., new understandings or new paradigms) (Kuhn, 1962). Additionally, researchers' level of certainty about their own work should be guarded. This same critical eye should be directed toward your own work. What factors in your design were you unable to control? Would another person develop a different set of answers or conclusions?

By definition, research is an activity that eventually leads to a conclusion— supporting a claim about how things work, refuting a claim, or deciding the evidence is inconclusive. Each is a form of reporting a finding based on some evidentiary base. Skepticism comes into play when one questions whether the conclusion is valid, reasonable, and defensible. The more critical you are of your work and others, the more likely you are to *get it as right as you can*. And, the more likely it is that you will be an effective researcher.

Memory

You will be more effective as a researcher if you ascribe value to the work that has preceded you. This may seem a simple matter. But in truth, many researchers do not know well the history of their own scholarly domain. In more familiar terms, researchers refer to knowing one's field as "doing the literature review." This knowledge grounds the researcher in the field and locates the specific research effort within a scholarly community or tradition. Often, some critical gap in knowledge held by this community or research tradition will provide a reason for carrying out a study. Creswell (2003) refers to this gap as a *deficit* and suggests that the search for a deficit provides a compelling reason for combing the literature in the field of inquiry.

I like the term *memory* as a way of capturing that disposition in a researcher to know all she or he can about their research tradition. *Memory* is my shorthand expression for being truly knowledgeable about the scholarship that has gone before. The very concept of a research or scholarly community bespeaks a history. This history may be interpreted by different generations of scholars; it may be a history that contains sorry chapters as well as highly significant ones. To ignore the history of a research field under investigation is analogous to the totalitarian government's actions that either purposefully erase history or purposefully rewrite history. That is, the past is ignored or forgotten or distorted. When this happens, the result is usually neither effective nor pleasant. It is highly unlikely that an external audience will judge your research work as effective if it is completed with no utilization or acknowledgment of past work.

There is a more commonplace example of the importance of history to your work. You might view your work as that which opens new frontiers and knowledge. Yet, if others have done the same work and had it judged as highly effective, how can your research be very significant? You might make the claim that you wish to replicate the work of another in order to validate a prior claim. However, you can't replicate another's work if you are ignorant of that work. I wish to note that I am not speaking here of the formal literature review in a dissertation or research report. I am speaking of your knowledge of your intellectual tradition that should be the grounding for your research. It is also important to recognize this point for those who now believe that research should connect in meaningful ways to practice (e.g., Boyer, 1990). A study will probably be ineffective if it has little relevance for the practitioners who comprise the study's logical audience.

Memory, as manifested in your knowledge of your research tradition and in your ability to ground your study within that tradition, will help improve the probability that you will be an effective researcher.

Having defined the effective researcher with a high degree of seriousness, I need to recognize what Hackman (1985) wrote some years ago: "Most of us do our best work when it feels more like play than like toil" (p. 127). Sometimes an intellectual playfulness yields research that has unexpected value and achieves unexpected influence. If you enjoy doing your work and look forward to it, that feeling may be one of the best indicators that you are an effective researcher. This leads us to what it is that makes for effective research.

EFFECTIVE RESEARCH

I want to turn now to some of the aspects of effective research. I am going to continue to understand the phrase *effective research* as meaning that one's research has influenced and shaped the beliefs of others, that one's research is accepted within a community of scholars and practitioners, and that one's research benefits others or holds the promise to do so. I repeat this definition not to deny other definitions that focus more on the intrinsic value of an individual's work but to give some thought to the realities of academic research as typically practiced.

Universities are the great factories of social science research. They produce most of the research, and they train virtually all who do social science research. Within these institutions, a great deal of attention is given to what makes research effective. Courses in research methodology prepare future researchers. Many texts are written about how to carry out research. Scholars develop the knowledge base of their disciplines. Research methods are probed and studied. New approaches attract attention and often help shape academic reputations. All of these factors and more impact the conditions under which research is judged to be effective or not. Generally, the academic convention holds that external judgments about research are the one's to be most trusted. Respected academic journals rely on a peer review process; an academic publisher submits a manuscript to a list of external critics; a doctoral student satisfies a faculty committee. In discussing how these elements influence how research is judged to be effective or not, I want to limit my observations to the external forces that shape what is normally deemed as effective research.

First, however, I want to acknowledge that research may be imbued with intrinsic worth and uninfluenced by popular opinion. Sometimes researchers motivated by a passion for their focus produce such significant work that its effectiveness transcends the normal external judgments of a disciplinary community. Indeed, sometimes such research transcends disciplinary boundaries and helps shape new ideas in many fields. Research of this type can be understood broadly as the creating of new knowledge. Some of the world's great thinkers were, in fact, researchers according to this definition. Yet, it is common knowledge that those who set out to challenge the dominant belief structures of a field face detractors and ridicule. Pasteur was ridiculed; Newton struggled between his desire to promote his scientific theories and his distaste for public criticism; people laughed at Alfred Wegener's theory of continental drift and plate tectonics. Yet these individuals, like many of mankind's most creative thinkers, were driven to do their work in spite of external forces. This is one type of effective research.

For many organizational researchers, however, indifference to external forces and to the good opinion of other researchers is not common. I have said that effective research is deemed so by others. This does not negate the worth or value of a research project that languishes unnoticed. But, generally, research is judged effective when it meets with approval by others. What qualities of research lead to such approval? Three important aspects of a research project that influence that external judgment come quickly to mind: (1) the quality of the research design, (2) the quality of the writing, and (3) the dissemination and publication of the findings.

Quality of the Research Design

A good research design is one that provides a reader and fellow scholar with a clear view of what was done, why it was done, how it was done, what was found out, and what recommendations were made for needed future research. Given different methodological research traditions, the format in which such information is conveyed may vary widely. But for a research project to be judged effective, these parts of a design must be clearly found and clearly expressed. Most research textbooks and earlier chapters in this book provide you with guidance about the component pieces of research design. Think of these as road signs that guide your reader through your research project. Each signals a necessary direction. A clear objective or purpose and statement about why the research was important permit the reader to frame your work within her or his generalized knowledge about your topic. The match of your research method with your purpose and the clarity with which you present your procedures for gathering data are all-important. The presentation of data in a format that conveys relevant information helps your reader evaluate the quality of the factors that your research method has netted.

Think of a fisherman in a boat. The objective of purpose is to catch fish. The purpose is important for the fisherman's livelihood. His chosen method is to use a net. He casts a net. It may or may not catch fish. If he does catch fish, he can present these fish as proof of the strength of his purpose and method. A research design is analogous. You have a purpose; you cast a net; there is an outcome. How good is the outcome? How believable are the findings obtained? Would a different kind of *net* have resulted in different or better outcomes?

Another example helps capture the critical nature of the quality of the design. Einstein and Infeld (1938) write:

> In our endeavor to understand reality, we are somewhat like a man trying to understand the mechanism of a closed watch. He sees the face and the moving hands, even hears it ticking, but he has no way of opening the case. If he is ingenious, he may form some picture of a mechanism which could be responsible for all things he observes, but he may never be quite sure his picture is the only one which could explain his observations. He will never be able to compare his picture with the real mechanism and he cannot even imagine the possibility or the meaning of such a comparison. But, he certainly believes that, as his knowledge increases, his picture of reality will become simpler and simpler and will explain a wider and wider range of his sensuous impressions. (p. 33)

Most research in the social sciences, be it quantitative or qualitative, does face the challenge implicit in the words of Einstein and Infeld. There are three important lessons in these words. First, our design wants to move us (and our readers) closer to understanding reality. Second, the more we can explain, the more complete will be our picture of how things work. Finally, as our knowledge increases, our understanding of reality will become simpler. This last point reminds one of Occam's Razor (Heylighen, 2000), the principle that the simplest and most parsimonious explanation is normally the best explanation. Occam's Razor could serve as an additional measure of effective research. In terms of Einstein and Infeld's watch, how does the research design approach the problem of gathering data in order to interpret what is going on inside the *watch*? Does the resultant interpretation of the data offer a reasonable argument for what is going on in the *watch*? The clarity of research design is paramount and key to whether or not your work is judged to be effective.

Quality of the Writing

Obviously writing is an important medium in the reporting of research. To achieve the clarity called for here, one must be able to write well. There are internal contradictions in what it means to write well in an academic setting. On the one hand, one must follow the conventions of whatever style manual is accepted as the authoritative manual within one's discipline. In social science fields, the most prevalent style manual is that published by the American Psychological Association (APA, 2001). This manual is full of both requirements for how to structure a research report as well as tips for how to write effectively. On the other hand, academic writing is often stripped of any personal style or quality that might give it power. That is, *good writing* is not necessarily good academic writing. The poet may seek to write lines that accommodate many different interpretations. Figurative language is important to fiction. Academic writing needs to be literal and, other than where rhetorical purposes dictate, precise enough to permit only one interpretation.

Saddled with this expectation for writing, the researcher can still be alert to the conventions of good writing. To see how this can be so, examine the advice to be found in a famous little book by Strunk and White (1959) called *Elements of Style*. This book offers a treasure trove of advice on how to write effectively. It is worth immersing yourself in both a style manual and in a book like *Elements of Style*. What you will gain is a greater capacity to look carefully at how you write what you write.

The end message is that if your writing is clear and cogent and persuasive, your work will be perceived as more significant and more effective. It is not uncommon for the messenger to share equal importance with the message. If you would have your work judged effective by an external audience, you must write effectively.

Dissemination and Publication of the Findings

When, by the measures already discussed, an effective research report is completed, it still awaits an audience beyond the author. At this stage, a researcher's work is judged by others, and one of the clear signals that a person's research is effective is that the judgment is favorable. This favorable judgment may be seen in a progression of activities—for example, presentation of the work at a scholarly conference or perhaps a number of conferences. If the data from a research project are capable of yielding multiple presentations and papers, this will add to an increase in perceived effectiveness. Publishing the work in both professional and lay journals adds to the audience that comes into contact with the work. These are standard ways to bring research findings to a field. It is true that in some venues the standards for acceptance are low. It is also true that the more people learn about a research project and researcher, the more influential that work becomes. Using research as the basis for workshops or seminars for practitioners is another means of dissemination. Developing Web sites with information yet another.

I want to use another analogy to explain conceptually how the dissemination of research leads to a judgment of research effectiveness. In this discussion I want to move the dissemination of research beyond the narrow confines of academic reporting to a wider "community of discourse" (Piatanida & Garmen, 1999). That is, while research findings may appear in journals, competitive conferences, and dissertation abstracts of academia, there is a wider audience for research that is important. I believe this to be particularly true for organizational research, where practitioners are also consumers of research.

In a classic work, Rogers (1962) writes about what he labels the *diffusion of innovation*. What Rogers describes in this book is the process by which a new idea or new product is adopted in a specific population of people. He and other researchers who have explored the variables that undergird the successful dissemination and adoption of a new idea have created a model that has relevance for how one's research can become influential and widely known. The framework of that model gives you some clues as to the qualities your research might possess if it is to be judged effective.

Four elements in Rogers's model are relevant to the dissemination of research work within a wider community of researchers and practitioners: (1) the idea itself, (2) the communication, (3) the social system, and (4) time. Each of these can impact the spread of your research within your community of discourse.

First, does your research contribute something new to the knowledge surrounding your topic? Is your work a needed answer to a problem that has perplexed your field? Does it offer something useful in the way of a conceptual understanding or in the way of a tested intervention that works? In short, what utility does your research have for those in your field? When a critic asks you why anyone should care about your research, do you have a good answer?

Second, communicating your work to a social network can be significantly enhanced if you consider the ways in which new ideas are adopted. The act of communicating a new idea via a social network to individuals within that network is certainly desirable, and that is what traditional academic publishing practices mirror. But, within social networks, individuals speak to individuals, and that is where you have the power to shape the communication of your work. In particular, opinion leaders function within all networks. It is important to know those individuals and to ensure that your work is known to those individuals. This increases the probability that your work will become known within your community of discourse and will therefore be judged as more effective.

Third (and this point is tied directly to how your work is communicated), social systems have properties that will shape how your work is accepted or not. All academic disciplines have norms and traditions. Some journals or conferences are judged as superior to others; some communication efforts are deemed worthy, while others are not. Academics may frown on seeing their work or that of others written about in newspapers. Some feel that books that achieve public popularity must be flawed in serious ways. One needs to understand the social system within which one operates and be attentive to what that system expects. One also has to be practical. A researcher needs to think about how to improve access to the research. That is, reading long academic tomes may work for some readers but not for others. Thus, effective researchers are able to present their work in ways that do not distance an audience or impede understanding.

Time is the fourth factor. If effective research waits decades before it is noticed, can one think of it as effective? Or, put somewhat indelicately, posthumous recognition may gratify one's descendants but will probably not impress the author of the research. Clearly you want your research to become known within a reasonable amount of time. Rogers's model on the dissemination of new ideas suggests several salient factors that influence the rate at which a new idea spreads. Awareness, interest, and the opportunity to evaluate the new idea all influence that rate. All are achieved as you publish your work within that community of discourse. This suggests clearly that once the work is completed, one must be active in communicating the results through a variety of channels.

Summary

The discussion thus far has been designed to help you think through the factors that will cause your work to be judged as effective. If one final thought can embody all the suggestions offered here, it is this: When you complete your research, your work is not completed if you wish to have your work judged as effective. Providing that how you report your work is clear and significant, you must make an active and intentional effort to share that work with a community of discourse. Otherwise, your work is unlikely to meet the standards of effectiveness that I posed at the beginning of this section.

ETHICAL RESEARCH

Just as a number of factors help make a researcher and his or her research more effective, important ethical considerations have evolved over time that guide researcher behavior. You and your work may well be judged by your adherence to these ethical guidelines. As noted earlier, one encounters many, many issues of ethical behavior in carrying out social science research. Again, I will elect a certain degree of parsimony and discuss only those areas of ethical concern that appear to me to be particularly salient. Because most of our research needs to be approved by an external body that assesses the risk we may impose on our subjects, the standards guiding that external body have much to do with ethics. Honesty in how we recognize the work of others and in how we analyze and report our own findings is another area that raises ethical questions. These are two important ethical areas for a research in organizations.

Institutional Review Board

> The expression "basic ethical principles" refers to those general judgments that serve as a basic justification for the many particular ethical prescriptions and evaluations of human actions. Three basic principles, among those generally accepted in our cultural tradition, are particularly relevant to the ethics of research involving human subjects: the principles of respect of persons, beneficence and justice. (National Commission for the Protection of Human Subjects, 1979)

Most researchers operate within some organizational setting in which policies and procedures require the scholar to secure permission prior to conducting research involving human subjects. The agency granting permission, normally called an *institutional review board*, is charged with upholding research standards and principles established by the federal government. Do not be alarmed that the federal government is defining ethical research. It is. But many different groups of academics were enlisted to develop ethical standards for research.

In examining ethical research practices, it is useful to look at the justification for such review boards. In July 1974, the National Research Act was signed into law and created a commission charged with protecting the well-being of human and subjects. The main work of the commission was to establish basic ethical principles that should guide the work of those who gather data from human beings. This group wrestled with methodological issues that continually challenge social science researchers. One of the first had to do with the boundaries between practice and research. The Belmont Report (recommended reading and available online), which the commission produced, defined *practice* as *interventions* designed to enhance the well-being of an individual patient or client. The term *research* designated an activity designed to test a hypothesis and/or contribute to generalized knowledge. The Belmont Report went on to articulate a set of principles that should guide researchers. Those principles remain operative today and are respect for persons, beneficence, and justice.

Respect for persons means that individuals should be treated as (1) autonomous agents capable of making decisions and choices or (2) as persons with diminished autonomy in need of special protection. For the first category of subjects, respect means that these subjects must be allowed to enter into the research voluntarily and with adequate information on which to base their decisions to do so. For those in the second category, respect means extra precautions, even including the possibility that they will be excluded from activities that might produce harm. The degree of extra protection that is afforded persons with diminished autonomy requires balancing both the potential for harm and the potential for benefit.

The principle of beneficence has to do with the researcher's obligation to protect human subjects. The maxim "do no harm" applies. The determination of benefit applies both to the individual subject and to the larger society. Researchers are obligated to give thought to both. Assuming that there is the possibility of results that have some social benefit, what can be done to reduce risk to individuals? If that risk is too substantial, perhaps the social benefits are simply not worth the risk to individual well-being. This principle requires researchers to be candid and forthright in assessing risk and benefit.

The principle of justice requires that equality be operative in determining who will bear the burden of human subjects research. An illustration may make this clear. In the Nazi concentration camps, the burden of serving as medical research subjects fell entirely on the shoulders of those held as prisoners. In the United States, rural black men were the subjects for a large study of syphilis even though the disease transcended that population. Thus, the principle of justice requires that the burden of serving as a research subject be distributed equally. In the "death" camps for rural African Americans, the burden was distributed unequally. Obviously, a study of teenage drinking need not include drinking by elderly grandmothers. However, the use of a vulnerable segment population to the exclusion of other segments usually constitutes a violation of this ethical principle of justice.

These principles lead to a number of specific safeguards that a social science researcher using human subjects needs to follow. To respect autonomy, research subjects must be asked to consent to being part of a study. And they must be fully informed about what participation means, including what benefits and risks they might experience.

Institutional review boards are bureaucracies. Sometimes they are very difficult bureaucracies. However, the values that give rise to these institutional bureaucracies are significant and should guide the ethical behavior of researchers.

Plagiarism and Attribution

The following statement encapsulates the importance of honoring the contributions others have made to knowledge:

> Any intellectual enterprise—by an individual, a group of collaborators, or a profession—is a mosaic, the pieces of which are put together by many hands. Viewed from a distance, it should appear meaningful whole, but the long process of assemblage must not be discounted or misrepresented.

Anyone who is guilty of plagiarism not only harms those most directly affected but also diminishes the authority and credibility of all scholarship and all creative arts and therefore ultimately harms the interests of the broader society. (American Association of University Professors [AAUP:, 2001, p. 138)

Plagiarism is an ethical matter when one relies on the work of others. In conducting research, it is usually a matter of how to recognize the work of others rather than whether or not one should do so.

A common dictionary definition of *plagiarize* is to steal and use the ideas and writings of another as one's own. The AAUP (2001, p. 138) calls plagiarism "taking over the ideas, methods, or written words of another without acknowledgment and with the intention that they be credited as the work of the deceiver." The American Psychological Association's (2001) style manual states unequivocally that "an author does not present the work of another as if it were his or her own work." As defined in this way, one should not plagiarize. To do so is unethical and is tantamount to theft. That which is clearly the intellectual property of another should be acknowledged as belonging to that individual. I like the word *attribution* meaning to *assign as belonging to* another.

But, in today's world, the dilemma arises in defining exactly what it is that another owns. Can I own certain figures of speech because I take out a copyright on them? At what point does an idea become so common as to no longer need an attribution? We all know, for example, that *haste* normally *makes waste*, but do we need to delve into the past until we find out who actually first coined the idea and expressed it in this unique form? If I write a political speech in which I use the line "They should ask what they can do for their country," do I need to acknowledge that John Kennedy made this idea famous in his 1961 inaugural speech? It is not always clear what requires attribution and what does not. This is the focus of a recent article by Gladwell (2004). "Do words belong to the person who wrote them?" is the question he asks. And the answer is not always clear. As Gladwell notes in his article, words don't always belong to the person who wrote them. Gladwell struggles with the ethical precept because sometimes the words written can be used in new and creative ways. Sometimes we accept egregious borrowing of ideas and formats from others where we would deny permission to lift an exact sentence from another's work.

Still, norms can be applied. Plagiarism remains a prohibited activity for a researcher. We know that knowledge is constructed. As you carry out research, you are constructing your own understanding of knowledge. How you build that edifice should be clear to all. The elements of your ideas and borrowing from others should be traceable. Other scholars should be able to track what you did and how you pieced together your research findings. They should be able to see clearly any debts you owe to others so that they might look at those resources to determine whether your judgments were reasonable. This cannot be done if your work lacks attribution when attribution is required. Make sure that you make every effort to acknowledge the contributions that others make to your own work.

How Much to Read and What to Believe

Another ethical issue that surfaces frequently in regard to research reviews centers on how much one should know about an article or book before citing the research. One frequently encounters attributions that one author makes of another author. Should one, therefore, make sure to read the primary sources of all work cited? Is it right to quote the author if I have not read the work? Or may one accept what a fellow author reports to be true about a primary source? For example, I used the work of Everett Rogers earlier. Should you accept what I say about Rogers's work without checking it out first? Or is it alright for you to accept my description of Rogers's work as accurate and cite Rogers?

In this example, I do not use Rogers's writings to make claims about my own work, so your need to know exactly what Rogers wrote is less acute. But if I was reporting research that leads to a finding of importance, your need to know about that work might be highly important. Should you read the work or not? Should you accept what another says about that work or not? Is it enough to just read the abstract of a dissertation, or should you locate and read the full study?

Because the volume of research productivity is so great, it is sometimes impossible to read every piece of work that one might wish to acknowledge. This practical impediment means that one may elect to cite a piece of work based on what others have said about it. All you have to go on is the judgment of a fellow scholar, which may be wrong. For me the test is the quality of how the research work is reported. If I have a full description of what was done, why it was done, and how it was done, I may feel comfortable accepting the synopsis or review of the particular research without reading it. If all I have is a statement to the effect that *a research study done in a certain year reported these results,* I will be uncomfortable accepting such a review. Ethically it is a gray area as to how to act. One risk is that you may perpetuate bad research by acknowledging it.

Intellectual Honesty

A number of expected behaviors for researchers fall under this heading. For example, a researcher is expected to refrain from submitting the same article to more than one publishing source. To do so compromises the publisher should she or he accept the article, for a publisher expects some ownership rights to the article as a condition of publishing it. Researchers are also expected to avoid errors of commission and omission in dealing with data. That is, the scientific method relies on observations that can be verified. If data were constructed falsely (*cooked*, in some researcher parlance) or if significant data were omitted, a researcher would be guilty of falsifying results.

These are some of the ethical practices that guide scholarly inquiry. A sincere interest in seeking the truth and in acknowledging the contributions of others will go a long way in avoiding unethical behavior.

CONCLUSION

> The great international economic, technological, and geopolitical forces
> reshaping the world are hardly by-passing higher education.We will not
> only lead new developments in globalization and technology, we will be
> reshaped by them. (Kellogg Commission, 2000, p. 16)

In 1990, Ernest Boyer wrote a book called *Scholarship Reconsidered: Priorities of the Professoriate.* His book has had a wide influence in higher education and suggests to us that as the world changes, what those in higher education have understood to be effective research may be unacceptable in the future. Or, at the very least, definitions need to be broadened. Boyer opines that universities and colleges have lost their role as a critical social institution because they have become isolated from their larger communities. He proposes a four-part view of scholarship—discovery, integration, application, and teaching—intended to help *engage* the university with its wider social setting. With his notions of expanding intellectual climate, working across disciplines, integrating ideas from many fields, and applying scholarly work to the larger community, Boyer presaged the recent call for engaged scholarship made by Van de Ven and Johnson (2005). Roughly 15 years ago, Boyer introduced to the academic community the notion that higher education might have to change significantly as societal forces began demanding a different kind of university. These changes are well under way, as can be seen in examining the work of those who study globalization (Friedman, 1999; Schumpeter, 1976; Grove, 1999; Thurow, 1999; Gorbachev, 2003).

Thus, the discussion here has approached an understanding of effective research from a somewhat traditional viewpoint located within the academy. But I should be remiss in ignoring the many external forces that are reshaping traditional notions of effective research. Some of these forces are demanding that more access to research findings be expanded and that the pace of research activity be increased. The spread of electronic journals and of freely accessible electronic text material serves as an example of how changing times have impacted research activities. Universities in particular and society in general have developed many initiatives in the area of *technology transfer*—the term used to translate the scholarship of the academy into products with utility and commercial value. University faculty members are often pressured to carry out research for granting agencies, thus subordinating their own research agendas to those of external groups. To a large degree, the factors that label research as effective may well have to do with the utility of that research to a user of it, not to the intrinsic worth of the research within a scholarly discipline. The marketplace of ideas may become a more potent determiner of what is effective or ineffective. Should the power of external forces reshape how the academy defines effective research, many of the conventions and traditional practices discussed in this chapter will be altered.

Still, even in a new academy shaped by the forces of globalization, I think effective research will be that which is acknowledged by those in a field, is well designed and soundly carried out, and has the potential for having a beneficial impact on others. I also think that were one to assemble a room full of professors in the various fields of organizational studies, a much longer list of effective and ethical research practices than I have presented would be produced. It is worth asking colleagues for their definitions of both, and I encourage you to do so.

NOTES

1. Delineating a clear tie between research and practice has long been important in organizational research, and how best to create this link has long been debated. Anderson, Herriot, and Hodgkinson (2001), Rynes, Bartunek, and Daft (2001), Weick (2000), and Van de Ven (2002) are examples of scholars who have recently explored what is often called the *gap* between theory (read research) and practice. See also Lawler et al. (1985), who have explored research useful to both theory and practice.

2. In making these claims for what constitutes effectiveness, I am including the notion that one's research is noticed by both academic peers and practitioner peers. Research in organizations that is ignored by either of these two key players is unlikely to have a lasting presence.

REFERENCES

American Association of University Professors. (2001). *AAUP: Policy documents and reports* (9th ed). Washington, DC: Author.

American Psychological Association. (2001). *Publication manual of the American Psychological Association* (5th ed.). Washington, DC: Author.

Anderson, H., Herriot, P., & Hodgkinson, G. P. (2001). The practitioner–researcher divide in industrial work and organizational (IWO) psychology: Where are we now and where do we go from here? *Journal of Occupational Psychology, 74,* 391–411.

Boyer, E. L. (1990). *Scholarship reconsidered: Priorities of the professoriate.* New York: Carnegie Foundation for the Advancement of Teaching.

Bryant, M. T. (2003). *The portable dissertation advisor.* Thousand Oaks, CA: Corwin.

Campbell, D. T., & Overman, E. S. (Eds.). (1988). *Methodology and epistemology for the social sciences: Selected papers.* Chicago: University of Chicago Press.

Collins, R. (1998). *The sociology of philosophies: A global theory of intellectual change.* Cambridge, MA: Harvard University Press.

Creswell, J. (2003). *Research design: Qualitative, quantitative, and mixed method approaches* (2nd ed.). Thousand Oaks, CA: Sage.

Einstein, A., & Infeld, L. (1938). *The evolution of physics.* New York: Simon & Schuster.

Friedman, T. (1999). *The Lexus and the olive tree.* New York: Farrar, Straus & Giroux.

Gladwell, M. (2002, December 2). Groupthink: What does *Saturday Night Live* have in common with German philosophy? *New Yorker.*

Gladwell, M. (2004, November 22). Something borrowed: Should a charge of plagiarism ruin your life? *New Yorker,* pp. 40–48.

Gorbachev, M. (2003). *Facets of globalization: Challenges of modern development.* Moscow: Alpina.

Grove, A. (1999). *Only the paranoid survive: How to survive the crisis points that challenge every company.* New York: Doubleday.

Hackman, J. R. (1985). Doing research that makes a difference. In R. E. Lawler III, A. Mohrman Jr., S. Mohrman, T. Cummings, & Associates (Eds.), *Doing research that is useful for theory and practice.* San Francisco: Jossey-Bass.

Heylighen, F. (2000). Referencing pages in Principia Cybernetica Web. In F. Heylighen, C. Joslyn, & V. Turchin (Eds.), *Principia Cybernetica Web.* Brussels: Principia Cybernetica. Retrieved December 1, 2004, from http://pespmc1.vub.ac.be/REFERPCP.html.

Kellogg Commission. (2000). *Renewing the covenant: Learning, discovery and engagement in a new age and different world.* Washington, DC: National Association of State Universities and Land-grant Colleges.

Kuhn, T. (1962). *The structure of scientific revolutions.* Chicago: University of Chicago Press.

Lawler III, R. E., Mohrman, Jr., A., Mohrman, S., Cummings, T., and Associates. (1985). *Doing research that is useful for theory and practice.* San Francisco: Jossey-Bass.

Lincoln, Y. S., & Guba, E. G. (1985). *Naturalistic inquiry.* Beverly Hills, CA: Sage.

National Commission for the Protection of Human Subjects. (1979, April 18). *Belmont Report: Ethical principles and guidelines for the protection of human subjects of research.* Washington, DC: Department of Health, Education, and Welfare.

Piatanida, M., & Garmen, N. B. (1999). *The qualitative dissertation: A guide for students and faculty.* Thousand Oaks, CA: Corwin.

Rackham Graduate School. (2004). Retrieved December 2, 2004, from http://www.rackham.umich.edu/StudentInfo/listings/SupportGroups/workforyou.html.

Rogers, E. M. (1962). *Diffusion of innovation.* New York: Free Press.

Rynes, S. L., Bartunek, J. M., & Daft, R. L. (2001). Across the great divide: Knowledge creation and transfer between practitioners and academics. *Academy of Management Journal, 44*(2), 340–355.

Schumpeter, J. A. (1976). *Capitalism, socialism and democracy.* New York: Harper Torchbook.

Strunk, W., & White, E. B. (1959). *The elements of style.* New York: Macmillan.

Suppe, P. (1977). The structure of scientific theories (2nd ed). Urbana: University of Illinois Press.

Thurow, L. (1999). Building wealth: The new rules for individuals, companies, and nations in a knowledge-based economy. New York: HarperCollins.

Van de Van, A. H. (2002). 2001 presidential address: Strategic directions for the Academy of Management—This academy is for you! *Academy of Management Review, 27*(2), 171–184.

Van de Van, A. H., & Johnson, P. E. (2004). *Knowledge for theory and practice.* Unpublished manuscript, Carlson School of Management, Minneapolis.

Weick, K. (2000). Gapping the relevance bridge: Fashions meet fundamental in management research. *British Journal of Management, 12*(Special Issue): S71–S75.

Name Index

Tedlow, R.S., 305
Temple, B., 250
Tenkasi, A., 272
Tesch, R., 249
Tetrick, L.E., 172, 175
Thacker, J.W., 172
Thatchenkary, T., 21
Thatchenkey, T.J., 358
Thiemann, S., 54
Thomas, M.D., 98, 102
Thomas, S.J., 100, 104, 109
Thomason, N., 68
Thompsett, R.E., 88–89
Thompson, B., 57–69, 120, 130
Thompson, S., 107
Thompson, W., 58
Thurow, L., 434
Thurstrone, L.L., 192, 197
Tietje, O., 328, 343, 345
Tinsley, D.J., 185, 190, 192, 193, 197
Tinsley, H.E.A., 132, 185, 190, 192, 193, 197
Tolbert, A., 182
Tomaskovic-Devey, D., 107, 108
Torbert, W.R., 387–388, 395
Torraco, R.J., 7, 9, 271, 351–371
Tosh, J., 299
Tracey, J.B., 162, 167, 176
Tragou, H., 251
Traugott, M., 109
Triandis, H.C., 278
Trice, H., 274
Troye, S.V., 156
Trumbo, C.W., 108
Tryon, W.W., 58–59
Tucker, C., 107
Turnbull, S., 239, 358
Turner, B.A., 301
Turner, P., 316
Turner, V.W., 223

Turton, A., 301
Tushman, M.L., 361

Umbach, 108, 109
Usunier, J.C., 107

Vacha-Haase, T., 67–68
Valentine, T., 348
Van Alstine, J., 172
Van de Ven, A.H., 4, 7, 12, 352, 353, 359, 360–361, 362, 365, 369, 385, 403, 404, 405, 421, 434, 435
Van de Vijver, F.J.R., 107
Van Maanen, J., 299, 300, 302
Vandenberg, R.J., 107, 144, 152, 153, 171, 172
Vann, R.T., 309
Veiga, J.F., 109
Velicer, W.F., 169, 188
Venter, A., 122
Visser, R., 222
Vogel, R.J., 410

Waclawski, J., 101
Wall, T.D., 163
Wampold, B.E., 123
Warr, P.B., 163
Wassermann, W., 122
Watkins, K.E., 194, 327–348, 352, 376, 377, 378
Watson, C.J., 131
Weaver, A., 249
Wegener, D.T., 182
Weick, K.E., 223, 225, 226, 305, 353, 354, 362, 363, 370, 403, 435
Weinberger, L.A., 403
Weinzimmer, L.G., 118, 122
Weissbein, D.A., 202
Weitzman, E.A., 249, 250
Wells, A.S., 328, 329

Welsch, R.E., 122
West, S.G., 120, 145, 152, 155, 156
Whetten, D.A., 362, 409
Whipp, R., 309
White, E.B., 427
White, H., 299, 300, 306
Whitehead, J., 377, 391, 393
Whittington, R., 300
Wicker, L.R., 129, 132
Widaman, K.F., 169, 172, 189, 193
Wilensky, A., 274
Wilkinson, L., 67, 69
Williams, L.J., 143–158, 174
Williamson, J.B., 165
Willimack, D., 107
Wilson, E.O., 7, 18
Winer, B.J., 81
Wisenbaker, J.M., 129
Wolcott, H.F., 244, 245
Wolf, F.M., 206, 208, 209
Wright, J.D., 98
Wright, P.M., 174

Yang, B., 181–197, 201–216, 355
Yi, Y., 172
Yilmaz, M., 122
Yin, R.K., 328, 329, 330, 333, 334, 335, 336, 337–338, 340, 341, 345, 354
Yorks, L., 375–396
Yun, G.W., 108

Zedeck, S., 152
Zeller, R.A., 166
Zhang, S., 169
Zhang, Y., 109
Zuckerman, A., 58
Zuckerman, M., 58

Subject Index

About the Authors

Rose M. Baker is an instructor of statistical applications with Penn State Management Development, the Pennsylvania State University. Her research focus is the impact of training on organizational development, statistical applications within manufacturing, and project management. She is a certified project management professional with the Project Management Institute. She received the Penn State Lavanda Mueller Award for Outstanding Academic Achievement and the Paul W. Welliver Outstanding Graduate Student of the Year award, and she authored a Pennsylvania Educational Research Association Distinguished Research Paper.

Kenneth R. Bartlett is an associate professor of human resource development at the University of Minnesota. His research interests focus on attitude and performance changes that individuals and organizations experience as a result of HRD participation, with a particular focus on the relationship between training and organizational commitment. In addition, he has published on international HRD, the role of occupational certification in workforce entry and development, and HRD in the public sector. He currently serves on the board of the Academy of Human Resource Development.

Reid A. Bates is an associate professor of human resource and leadership at Louisiana State University. His research focuses on learning transfer in organizations, and he is currently active in a number of research partnerships in various parts of the world to study and improve learning transfer systems. Bates is widely published, is an award-winning educator, and is recipient of the 2001 Richard A. Swanson Distinguished Research Award. He is an active consultant with more than 15 years' experience working with organizations in the United States, Africa, and the Asia-Pacific region.

Allen W. Batteau leads the Institute for Information Technology and Culture at Wayne State University. A graduate of the University of Chicago in anthropology, he has published articles in the *American Anthropologist, American Ethnologist,*

Human Organization, and *Human Factors in Aerospace Safety*. He was formerly an American Anthropological Association Congressional Fellow, where he helped shape economic programs in the U.S. Senate. He is currently leading an interdisciplinary team studying coordination among first responders in multi-jurisdiction disaster management.

Miles T. Bryant is a professor of educational administration at the University of Nebraska–Lincoln. He serves as the chair of the Joint University of Nebraska–Lincoln and University of Nebraska–Omaha doctoral program in educational administration. He teaches courses in research methods for graduate students. His research has focused on rural education, educational administration, and educational policy. He recently authored a book intended for doctoral students in the social sciences. Bryant is active in the American Educational Research Association, serving as one of the officers of a special interest group.

Michael F. Burnett is the J. C. Floyd Professor and director of the School of Human Resource Education and Workforce Development at Louisiana State University. His teaching and research focus on statistics and research methods, including those focusing on organizational studies. His research has been published in numerous journals including the *Human Resource Development Quarterly*, the *Family and Consumer Sciences Research Journal*, the *International Journal of Training and Development*, the *Journal of Vocational Education Research*, the *Journal of Vocational and Technical Education*, and the *Journal of Agricultural Education*.

Jeni L. Burnette is pursuing her Ph.D. at Virginia Commonwealth University. She received her undergraduate degree from the University of North Carolina at Chapel Hill. Her research focuses on interpersonal and intragroup processes. In particular, she is interested in forgiveness in romantic relationships, exclusion from groups, and groupthink decision making on mountaineering expeditions.

Thomas J. Chermack is an assistant professor in the Department of Learning and Performance Systems at the Pennsylvania State University. Chermack is the author of several articles that have examined the theoretical base of scenario planning, and his current research examines the use of scenario planning as a tool for managing uncertainty. He has also worked as a consultant for companies such as Viacom, Inc., Key Investment, and Personnel Decisions International.

Pamela Crespin is an assistant professor of business and organizational anthropology at Wayne State University. Her research focuses on the globalizing processes and outcomes associated with work, workers, and work products. In 2004, she received her doctorate in anthropology from UCLA, where her honors included Fulbright, National Science Foundation, Javits, and UCLA Anthropol-

ogy and Chancellor Fellowships. In 1999–2000, Crespin served as the Enders
Chair in Canada–U.S. Relations at the University of Calgary. Prior to enrolling at
UCLA, she enjoyed a successful corporate career in marketing and advertising.

J. David Creswell is a Ph.D. candidate in social and health psychology at the University of California, Los Angeles. His research focuses on empirical investigations of self-regulation and stress processes, and how they, in turn, impact disease outcomes. Specifically, he is currently conducting investigations incorporating quantitative and qualitative methodologies to examine the stress-buffering effects of self-affirmation and mindfulness in early stage breast cancer populations and in HIV.

John W. Creswell is the Clifton Institute Professor of Educational Psychology in the graduate program of Quantitative and Qualitative Methods in Education, director of the Office of Qualitative and Mixed Methods Research at the University of Nebraska–Lincoln, and an adjunct professor of family medicine at the University of Michigan. He specializes in research methods and design, qualitative inquiry, and mixed methods research, and he has authored eight books and numerous chapters and journal articles. His most recent three books address quantitative and qualitative research design, qualitative inquiry, and educational research.

Andrea D. Ellinger is an assistant professor in the Department of Human Resource Education at the University of Illinois at Urbana-Champaign. Her research is on managerial/leadership roles, coaching, informal learning, and organizational learning and the learning organization concept. She received the Malcolm S. Knowles Dissertation of the Year Award in 1998 and the 2003 Richard A. Swanson Research Excellence Award. She was also awarded a Cyril O. Houle Fellowship funded by the Kellogg Foundation. She has served on the AHRD Board and the ASTD Research to Practice Committee.

Carol D. Hansen is an associate professor of human resource development at Georgia State University. She studies the cultural and cross-cultural frames that shape belief systems and about employee and organizational development. She has taught and conducted research with universities in Europe and Africa, and she was a Fulbright scholar to India. She also served as an HRD branch chief at the United States Department of State.

Timothy R. Hinkin is a professor of management at the School of Hotel Administration, Cornell University. His research focuses primarily on leadership, managing service quality, employee turnover, and research methods. He is coeditor of *Journal of Quality Assurance in Hospitality & Tourism* and a member of the editorial board of *Organization Research Methods*. He is author of *Cases in Hospitality:*

A Critical Incident Approach (2nd ed.) and has published numerous journal articles and book chapters. He is an active member of the Southern Management
Association and the Academy of Management.

Amy L. Hoover is an assistant professor in the Industrial Engineering Technology
Department at Central Washington University and teaches aviation. Her research
includes investigations of human error and human factors in aviation, including
cockpit task prioritization studies. She has numerous publications in the aviation
literature and actively promotes flight safety through public speaking engage-
ments on a regional and national level.

Elwood F. Holton III is the Jones S. Davis Distinguished Professor of Human
Resource, Leadership, and Organization Development in the School of Human
Resource Education at Louisiana State University, where he coordinates degree
programs in human resource and leadership development. His research focuses
on improving human systems and performance in organizations. He has been
elected to the International Adult and Continuing Education Hall of Fame, was
the founding editor of *Human Resource Development Review*, and is a past president of the Academy of Human Resource Development.

Yvonna S. Lincoln is Ruth Harrington Chair of Educational Leadership and Distinguished Professor of Higher Education at Texas A&M University. She is the
coauthor of *Naturalistic Inquiry* and *Fourth Generation Evaluation* and the coeditor of the first three editions of the *Handbook of Qualitative Research* (with Nor-
man Denzin). She is the coeditor of the journal *Qualitative Inquiry,* and her
research interests lie in qualitative research methods, organizational theory and
leadership preparation.

Victoria J. Marsick is the codirector of the J. M. Huber Institute for Learning in
Organizations and Professor of Adult & Organizational Learning, Department of
Organization and Leadership, Teachers College, Columbia University. Her
research is on informal and incidental learning at the individual, team, and organizational levels; action learning; and organizational learning assessment. She
received the AHRD Scholar of the Year Award in 1996 and has served on the
AHRD Board and the ASTD Research to Practice Committee, which she has also
chaired.

Christine Miller is a lecturer at Wayne State University. Her research interests
focus on transnational organizations, innovation, and organizational learning.
She is particularly interested in changes within organizations resulting from
globalization and the extensive infusions of technology. Miller serves as assistant
director for global initiatives in the Institute of Organizational and Industrial

Competitiveness (IOIC). She is a research associate in the Institute for Information Technology and Culture (IITC) and serves on the board of the National Association of Practicing Anthropologists (NAPA).

David L. Passmore is a professor of education and operations research at the Pennsylvania State University, where for more than 25 years he has held appointments as professor of adult education, professor of mineral engineering management, senior scientist in the Institute for Policy Research and Evaluation, university director of the Office for Research Compliance, and faculty fellow of the Center for Academic Computing. He also has served as visiting scholar in Maternal and Child Health at the Harvard School of Public Health and director of Economic Research at the National Technical Institute for the Deaf.

Michael Rowlinson is a professor of organization studies in the Centre for Business Management at Queen Mary, University of London. Prior to joining the center, he taught at the University of Nottingham, Royal Holloway, University of London, and London Metropolitan University. His research interests are in organization theory, critical management studies, and the emerging field of organizational history. Rowlinson's current research explores the relation between documentary corporate history and knowledge management, examining how companies use historical knowledge of the past in the present.

Darlene Russ-Eft is an assistant professor of adult education and higher education leadership at Oregon State University. Her research, books, and articles focus on evaluation, learning and development, and competency research. She was the former director of research at AchieveGlobal, Inc., and at Zenger-Miller. She is the current editor of the *Human Resource Development Quarterly*, and she received the 1996 Editor of the Year Award from Times Mirror and the Scholar of the Year of the Academy of Human Resource Development.

Wendy E. A. Ruona is an associate professor of human resource and organization development at the University of Georgia. She actively researches and publishes in foundations of HRD (philosophical, theoretical, and historical) and strategic HRD (see, e.g., her Web site at http://www.arches.uga.edu/~wruona/). She was awarded the Outstanding Assistant Professor Award by the University Council for Workforce and Human Resource Education in 2002 and the Richard A. Swanson Research Excellence Award in 2000. She is currently the editor in chief of *Advances in Developing Human Resources* and serves on the board of directors for the Academy of Human Resource Development.

Richard A. Swanson is a professor of human resource development at the University of Minnesota. His research has focused on organizational performance improvement, results assessment, and the strategic roles of human resource development. Swanson has authored many books and articles and his recent work has delved into theory development research. He received a Distinguished Alumni Award from the University of Illinois and has been inducted into both the International Adult and Continuing Education Hall of Fame and the Human Resource Development Scholar Hall of Fame.

Bruce Thompson is a professor and Distinguished Research Scholar, Department of Educational Psychology, and a professor of Library Sciences, Texas A&M University. He is a coeditor of the *American Educational Research Journal: Teaching, Learning, Human Development.* He is the author/editor of 10 books, 14 book chapters, 184 articles, 28 notes/editorials, and 12 book reviews. His contributions have been especially influential in spurring a greater emphasis on effect size reporting and interpretation, and promoting improved understanding of score reliability.

Richard J. Torraco is an associate professor in the Department of Educational Administration at the University of Nebraska–Lincoln, where he is a faculty member in the educational leadership and higher education program and serves as the coordinator of the graduate program in human resource development. He is editor of *Human Resource Development Review* and has served as editor of the *Academy of Human Resource Development Conference Proceedings.* Torraco has also served as the vice president for research for the Academy of Human Resource Development.

Andrew H. Van de Ven is the Vernon Heath Professor of Organizational Innovation and Change at the Carlson School of Management of the University of Minnesota. He directs the Minnesota Innovation Research Program, which has been tracking how innovations develop from concept to implementation in a wide variety of organizations. Van de Ven was the 2000–2001 president of the Academy of Management, and in 2002, he received the Distinguished Scholar Award from the Technology and Innovation Management Division of the Academy of Management.

Karen E. Watkins is the interim associate dean for research, technology, and external affairs for the College of Education and a professor of adult education at the University of Georgia. Her research is in the areas of human resource and organizational change and development, action science, action research, and organizational learning culture assessment. She received the AHRD Scholar of the Year Award in 1999 and served as president of the AHRD from 1994 to 1996. She was inducted into the International Adult and Continuing Education Hall of Fame in 2003.

Larry J. Williams is a professor of management at Virginia Commonwealth University (VCU). His main research interests involve the application of structural equation methods to various substantive and methodological concerns in organizational research. Williams has served as the founding editor of *Organizational Research Methods*, a journal sponsored by the Research Methods Division (RMD) of the Academy of Management. He also chaired the Research Methods Division of the Academy of Management and currently serves as the director of the Center for the Advancement of Research Methods and Analysis at VCU.

Baiyin Yang is an associate professor of human resource development and adult education at the University of Minnesota. His primary research focus has been on the development and validation of a holistic theory of knowledge and adult learning. His research interests include program planning and evaluation, adult and organizational learning, power and influence tactics, cross-cultural studies of learning and organizational behavior, and quantitative research methods. He is presently serving as the quantitative method editor of *Human Resource Development Quarterly* and is an editorial board member of *Adult Education Quarterly* and *Human Resource Development International*.

Lyle Yorks is an associate professor in the Department of Organization and Leadership, Teachers College, Columbia University, where he teaches courses in strategy development, human resource development, and research methods and is director of the AEGIS doctoral program in adult education. His current research interests center on action learning, collaborative inquiry, and organizational learning. He is currently associate editor of the *Human Resource Development Review*, a journal of the Academy of Human Resource Development.

About Berrett-Koehler Publishers

Berrett-Koehler is an independent publisher dedicated to an ambitious mission: Creating a World that Works for All.

We believe that to truly create a better world, action is needed at all levels—individual, organizational, and societal. At the individual level, our publications help people align their lives and work with their deepest values. At the organizational level, our publications promote progressive leadership and management practices, socially responsible approaches to business, and humane and effective organizations. At the societal level, our publications advance social and economic justice, shared prosperity, sustainable development, and new solutions to national and global issues.

We publish groundbreaking books focused on each of these levels. To further advance our commitment to positive change at the societal level, we have recently expanded our line of books in this area and are calling this expanded line "BK Currents."

A major theme of our publications is "Opening Up New Space." They challenge conventional thinking, introduce new points of view, and offer new alternatives for change. Their common quest is changing the underlying beliefs, mindsets, institutions, and structures that keep generating the same cycles of problems, no matter who our leaders are or what improvement programs we adopt.

We strive to practice what we preach—to operate our publishing company in line with the ideas in our books. At the core of our approach is *stewardship*, which we define as a deep sense of responsibility to administer the company for the benefit of all of our "stakeholder" groups: authors, customers, employees, investors, service providers, and the communities and environment around us. We seek to establish a partnering relationship with each stakeholder that is open, equitable, and collaborative.

We are gratified that thousands of readers, authors, and other friends of the company consider themselves to be part of the "BK Community." We hope that you, too, will join our community and connect with us through the ways described on our website at www.bkconnection.com.

Be Connected

Visit Our Website

Go to www.bkconnection.com to read exclusive previews and excerpts of new books, find detailed information on all Berrett-Koehler titles and authors, browse subject-area libraries of books, and get special discounts.

Subscribe to Our Free E-Newsletter

Be the first to hear about new publications, special discount offers, exclusive articles, news about bestsellers, and more! Get on the list for our free e-newsletter by going to www.bkconnection.com.

Participate in the Discussion

To see what others are saying about our books and post your own thoughts, check out our blogs at www.bkblogs.com.

Get Quantity Discounts

Berrett-Koehler books are available at quantity discounts for orders of ten or more copies. Please call us toll-free at (800) 929-2929 or email us at bkp.orders@aidcvt.com.

Host a Reading Group

For tips on how to form and carry on a book reading group in your workplace or community, see our website at www.bkconnection.com.

Join the BK Community

Thousands of readers of our books have become part of the "BK Community" by participating in events featuring our authors, reviewing draft manuscripts of forthcoming books, spreading the word about their favorite books, and supporting our publishing program in other ways. If you would like to join the BK Community, please contact us at bkcommunity@bkpub.com.